AF705783

Media Law in Cyprus

Media Law in Cyprus

Third Edition

Achilles C. Emilianides
Costas Stratilatis

This book was originally published as a monograph in the International Encyclopaedia of Laws/Media Law.

Founding Editor: Roger Blanpain
General Editor: Frank Hendrickx
Volume Editors: Peggy Valcke & Eva Lievens

Wolters Kluwer

Published by:
Kluwer Law International B.V.
PO Box 316
2400 AH Alphen aan den Rijn
The Netherlands
E-mail: lrs-sales@wolterskluwer.com
Website: www.wolterskluwer.com/en/solutions/kluwerlawinternational

Sold and distributed by:
Wolters Kluwer Legal & Regulatory U.S.
920 Links Avenue
Landisville, PA 17538
United States of America
E-mail: customer.service@wolterskluwer.com

DISCLAIMER: The material in this volume is in the nature of general comment only. It is not offered as advice on any particular matter and should not be taken as such. The editor and the contributing authors expressly disclaim all liability to any person with regard to anything done or omitted to be done, and with respect to the consequences of anything done or omitted to be done wholly or partly in reliance upon the whole or any part of the contents of this volume. No reader should act or refrain from acting on the basis of any matter contained in this volume without first obtaining professional advice regarding the particular facts and circumstances at issue. Any and all opinions expressed herein are those of the particular author and are not necessarily those of the editor or publisher of this volume.

ISBN 978-94-035-1608-0

e-Book: ISBN 978-94-035-1618-9
web-PDF: ISBN 978-94-035-1628-8

© 2024 Kluwer Law International BV, The Netherlands

All rights reserved. No part of this publication may be reproduced, stored in a retrieval system, or transmitted in any form or by any means, electronic, mechanical, photocopying, recording, or otherwise, without the prior written permission of the publisher.

Permission to use this content must be obtained from the copyright owner. More information can be found at: www.wolterskluwer.com/en/solutions/legal-regulatory/permissions-reprints-and-licensing

The Authors

Costas Stratilatis (1976) is a full-time associate professor at the University of Nicosia, where he teaches various courses in Public Law. Apart from Media Law, his research interests include Constitutional Law and Human Rights, Comparative Constitutional Theory, and Jurisprudence. He holds a PhD in Law and an LLM in Public Law & Political Sciences from the Law Department of the Aristotle University of Thessaloniki. He also holds an MSc in Political Theory from the London School of Economics and Political Science. Costas has collaborated as a researcher with the Institute of Constitutional Research of Athens and has also taught Philosophy & Methodology of Law at the Law Department of the Aristotle University of Thessaloniki. He has also been a visiting lecturer for the postgraduate programme of the Journalism Department of the Aristotle University. He is a practising advocate and has worked as a senior associate in the law firm Zepos & Yannopoulos (the Greek member of Lex Mundi).

Major publications in the field of Media Law include: Self-Regulation in the Context of Network Communication: Neoliberal Cyber-Anarchy or Democratic Cyber-Autonomy? in T. Papachristou et al.; Self-Regulation 99 (Sakkoulas, 2005, in Greek); Constituting the Right to Public Electronic Communication: Mass Communication, Freedom and Democracy in the Information Age (Sakkoulas, 2006, in Greek); Entrepreneurial Pluralism and Information Polyphony in Mass Communication Media in K. Zoras et al. (eds); Democracy and Mass Media 37 (Livanis, 2011, in Greek); 'Is the Internet Public Sphere in Need of Special Regulation?', Administrative Law Journal, vol. 1/2014, pp. 94–111 (in Greek); 'On the Distinction Between Statements of Fact and Value Judgments: A Comment on Petrenco v. Moldova', Annuaire International des Droits de l'Homme, vol. VIII, 2014, pp. 725–749, The Right of Journalists Not to Disclose Their Sources and the New Media. In T. Synodinou, P. Jougleux, C. Markou, T. Prastitou (eds), EU Internet Law-Regulation and Enforcement (Springer, 2017); S. Iordanidou and C. Stratilatis (eds), Versions of Liberty in Our Media Reality (Advanced Media Institute & Metamesonykties Ekdosis, 2018, in Greek).

The Authors

Achilles C. Emilianides is a professor and dean of the School of Law at the University of Nicosia and a practising advocate, and senior partner of the law firm A&E C. Emilianides, C. Katsaros and Associates LLC. He has been elected as a founding member and secretary-general of the Cyprus Academy of Sciences, Letters, and Arts, as an ordinary member of the European Academy of Sciences and Arts, and as a member of the UNESCO Conciliation and Good Offices Commission. He further represents the Cyprus Academy to ALLEA (All European Academies). He holds a PhD in Law and an LLM from the Aristotle University of Thessaloniki and an LLM from Leicester University. He is the consulting editor of the Cyprus Review and the chair of the Royal Commonwealth Society Cyprus Branch. He has extensive experience in media, having been a member of the board and an advocate of the free-to-air Cypriot *Mega Channel*, an advocate and secretary of the Board of Directors of premier pay Television (TV) channel *Lumiere TV (LTV)*, as well as Consulting Editor of the monthly magazine Sygxroni Apopsi. He is also a founding member and a member of the Board of Directors of Advanced Media Institute. His publications in the IEL series, published by Kluwer, are: *Religion and Law in Cyprus* (4th, 2024), *Constitutional Law in Cyprus* (3rd, 2024), *Family and Succession Law in Cyprus* (3rd, 2024), *Labour Law in Cyprus* (3rd, 2024), *Competition Law in Cyprus* (2021), *Tort Law in Cyprus* (2021), *Civil Procedure in Cyprus* (2020), *Media Law in Cyprus* (2nd, 2019), *Private International Law in Cyprus* (2015).

Table of Contents

The Authors 3

List of Abbreviations 13

Preface 17

General Introduction 19

§1. General Background of the Country 19
I. Political and Constitutional History 19
II. Form of Government 21
III. Geography and Population 23

§2. The Media Landscape 24
I. Print Media 24
II. TV Stations 27
III. Radio Stations 30
IV. The Press and Information Office and the Cyprus News Agency 31
V. Critical Observations 32

§3. Sources of Media Law 33
I. The Constitution 33
II. European Union Law 34
III. International Treaties 35
IV. The European Convention on Human Rights 37
V. Ordinary Legislation 38
VI. Administrative Regulations and Orders 39
VII. Jurisprudence 40
VIII. The Journalistic Ethics Code 41

Part I. Freedom of Speech 43

§1. The Scope and Contents of Freedom of Speech 43

§2. Limitations upon Freedom of Speech 46

§3. Freedom of Speech and Judicial Proceedings 50
I. Contempt 50

II. Interference with Judicial Proceedings by Publications in the Press 51
III. Freedom of the Press and Fair Trial 53
IV. The Press and Freedom of the Journalists 54

Part II. Regulation of Print Media 57

Chapter 1. The Journalists' Profession 57

§1. The Definition of Journalists in Law 145/1989 57

§2. The Union of Cyprus Journalists 59

Chapter 2. Journalists' Rights 61

§1. Role of Journalists as Watchdogs of Society 61

§2. Journalists' Independence 62
I. The Principle of Independence 62
II. The Publication and Circulation of Newspapers in the Republic 62

§3. Protection of Journalistic Sources 66

Chapter 3. Journalists' Liability 68

§1. Criminal Liability 68

§2. Civil Law Defamation 69
I. Constitutionality 69
II. Defamatory Publications 70
III. Defences 72
IV. Case-Law 76
V. Remedies 78
VI. Private International Law Aspects 80

§3. Protection of Privacy 81

Chapter 4. Right of Reply and to Rectification 84

Chapter 5. Access to Public Information 88

§1. Public Documents and Meetings 88

§2. Court Hearings and Documents 89

Chapter 6. Press Council, Press Authority and Self-Regulation 91

§1. The Press Council 91

§2. The Press Authority 93

§3. The Media Complaints Commission 94

§4. The Journalistic Ethics Code 95

Part III. Regulation of Audiovisual Media (Broadcasting) 99

Chapter 1. Public Service Broadcasting 99

§1. The Cyprus Broadcasting Corporation 99

§2. The Concept and Mission of Public Service Broadcasting 102
I. The Legislative Definition of Public Service Broadcasting 102
II. The Specification of the Public Service Mandate 103
III. The Economic Aspects of Public Service Broadcasting 105
IV. Emphasis on Cultural, Linguistic and Religious Diversity 105
V. The Supreme Court on the Role of the Cyprus Broadcasting Corporation 106

§3. The Organization of Public Service Broadcasting 110
I. The Organizational Aspects of the Cyprus Broadcasting Corporation 110
A. Legal Nature 110
B. Appointment and Term of Office of the Board of Directors 110
C. Competences of the Board of Directors and of the President 112
D. The General Director 113
E. Functions of the Cyprus Broadcasting Corporation 114
II. Supervision of the Cyprus Broadcasting Corporation 116
A. Supervision by the Cyprus Radio and Television Authority 116
B. Supervision and Possible Interventions by Governmental Authorities 117
C. Supervision by the Auditor General of the Republic 118
III. The Supreme Court on the Independence of the Cyprus Broadcasting Corporation 119

§4. The Financing of Public Service Broadcasting 121

Chapter 2. Private Broadcasting 123

§1. Different Categories of Private Broadcasters 123

§2. Licensing Requirements and Procedure 124
I. Licensing Requirements 124
A. Absolute Requirements 124
B. Criteria of Evaluation 126
C. Terms of Licence 127
D. Prohibition of Unauthorized Changes: The Logos Case 128
E. Licence Fees 129
F. Revocation of Licence 130
II. Licensing Procedure 130
A. The Plan of Radio Coverage 130
B. Determining the Number and the Type of Licences 131
C. Public Call by the Cyprus Radio and Television Authority 132
D. Evaluation of Applications 133

§3. The Transition to DTT 134

Chapter 3. Programme Standards 136

§1. Introduction 136

§2. Human Dignity 137

§3. Objectivity, Timeliness, and Precision of Information 138

§4. Pluralism and Diversity of Viewpoints 140

§5. Other Rules and Standards for News and Current Affairs Programmes 140

§6. Protection of minors 142
I. The Provisions of AVMS Directive 142
II. The Ranking System 143
A. Private TV and Radio Stations 143
B. Cyprus Broadcasting Corporation 144
C. The Supreme Court on the Ranking System 145
III. Violence, Indecency, and Other Provisions 146
A. Violence 146
B. Indecency 148
C. Participation and/or Presentation of Minors in/by Audiovisual Programmes 148

§7. Respect for Privacy 150

§8. Respect for Personality and for the Presumption of Innocence 154

§9. Right of Reply 157

§10. HIGH QUALITY, DECENCY IN LANGUAGE, AND THE SOCIAL MISSION OF BROADCASTERS 159

Chapter 4. Political Broadcasting 161

§1. FAIR REPRESENTATION IN ELECTION PERIODS 161
I. Introduction 161
II. Cyprus Broadcasting Corporation 161
A. Presidential Elections 161
B. Parliamentary Elections 163
C. The Supreme Court on Political Parties and Fair Representation 163
III. Private Radio and Television Stations 166

§2. POLITICAL ADVERTISING IN ELECTION PERIODS 168

§3. POLLS 170

§4. FAIR REPRESENTATION IN NON-ELECTION PERIODS 170
I. Cyprus Broadcasting Corporation 170
II. Private Radio and TV Stations 171

Chapter 5. Advertising Rules 173

§1. INTRODUCTION 173
I. Forms of Audiovisual Commercial Communication 173
II. Application of Certain Provisions of AVMS Directive to Radio Broadcasting 174
III. The Two Codes of Advertising 174
IV. The Supreme Court on Restrictions on Advertising 175

§2. RESTRICTIONS ON CONTENT AND ON FORM 176
I. Audiovisual Commercial Communications (Directive) 176
II. Television Advertising (Directive) 178
III. Codes of Advertising 180
A. Introduction 180
B. General Rules and Principles 180
C. General Requirements 181
D. Special Categories of Advertising 182
E. Protection of Minors 184
F. Separation of Certain Advertisements from Programmes for Minors 187

§3. TIME AND FREQUENCY RESTRICTIONS 187
I. General Time and Frequency Restrictions (Directive) 187
II. The '3.5 Minutes Requirement' of Article F.3 CA 189
III. Other Provisions on Advertising 190

§4. Sponsorship 191
I. Basic Requirements (Directive) 191
II. Part E, CA 192

§5. Product Placement 193

Chapter 6. Right to Information 196

§1. Access to Events of Major Importance 196
I. General Provisions (Article 14 of the Directive) 196
II. Specification of Criteria and Procedures 196
III. The List of Events of Major Importance 198
IV. The Special Right of the Cyprus Broadcasting Corporation (Section 17e CyBCL) 199

§2. Short News Reporting 200
I. The Transposition of Article 15 of the Directive into the Cypriot Media Law 200
II. The *Sky Österreich* Judgment of the CJEU 201

§3. Obligation to Transmit News and Current Affairs Programmes 202

Chapter 7. Access to Networks 204

§1. Must-Carry Rules 204
I. On Must-Carry and Universal Service Generally 204
II. Must-Carry Rules in Cyprus? 205

§2. Access Obligations of the DTT Network Providers 208
I. The Regulatory Status of DTT Network and Services Providers 208
II. Access and Other Relevant Obligations of Velister Ltd 208

Chapter 8. Standards and Interoperability 211

Part IV. Cross-Ownership Regulation 215

§1. Introduction 215

§2. Monomedia Ownership Requirements 216

§3. Crossmedia Ownership Requirements 216

§4. Transparency Obligations 216

Part V. Supervision: Media Regulator 219

Chapter 1. Organization 219

§1. The Cyprus Radio and Television Authority 219

§2. The Consultation Committee of Radio and Television 222

Chapter 2. Mission and Tasks of the CRTA 224

§1. The Mission of the CRTA 224

§2. The Jurisdiction of the Republic and of the CRTA 224

§3. The Tasks of the CRTA 226

Chapter 3. Sanctioning Powers and Procedure 228

§1. Sanctioning Powers of the CRTA 228
I. On AVMS Providers in the Private Broadcasting Sector 228
II. On Cyprus Broadcasting Corporation 230

§2. Procedure to Be Followed for the Imposition of Sanctions 231

§3. The Sigma Case before the European Court of Human Rights 234
I. The Judgment of the Supreme Court 234
II. The Judgment of the European Court of Human Rights 237

Selected Bibliography 243

Index 245

Table of Contents

List of Abbreviations

AKEL	Progressive Party of Working People
ANPP	Association of Newspapers and Periodical Publishers
API	Application Programme Interface
AVCC	Audiovisual Commercial Communication
AVMS	Audiovisual Media Services
AVMS Directive	Directive 2010/13/EU of the European Parliament and of the Council of 10 March 2010
BoD	Board of Directors
CA	Code of Advertising, Tele-Commerce Messages and Sponsorship Programmes (Annex IX to the RTSR)
CBA	Commonwealth Broadcasting Association
CIRCOM	European Association of Regional Television
CJE	Code of Journalistic Ethics for Electronic Media (Annex VIII to the RTSR)
CJEU	Court of Justice of the European Union
CLR	Cyprus Law Reports
CMCC	Cyprus Media Complaints Commission
CNA	Cyprus News Agency
COPEAM	Permanent Conference of the Mediterranean Audiovisual Operators
CPC	Commission for the Protection of Competition
CRTA	Cyprus Radio and Television Authority
CyBC	Cyprus Broadcasting Corporation (RIK)
CyBC-CA	Code of Advertising and Tele-Commerce Messages (Annex III to the CyBCR)
CyBC-CE	CyBC Code for Elections (Annex B to the CyBCRFT)
CyBC-CJE	CyBC Code of Journalistic Ethics (Annex I to the CyBCR)
CyBC-CNC	CyBC Code for the News Coverage of Political Parties (Annex A to the CyBCRFT)

List of Abbreviations

CyBCL	CyBC Law, Chapter (Cap.) 300A, as amended and currently in force
CyBCR	CyBC (Journalistic Ethics and Advertising Codes) Regulations of 2001 (93/2001)
CyBCRFT	CyBC (Fair Treatment of Political Parties) Regulations of 1985 (118/1986)
CYTA	Cyprus Telecommunications Authority
DISY	Democratic Rally
DTT	Digital Terrestrial Television
EBU	European Broadcasting Union
EC	European Community
ECC Directive	Directive (EU) 2018/1972 of the European Parliament and of the Council of 11 December 2018
ECHR	European Convention on Human Rights
ECtHR	European Court of Human Rights
EMIR	Radio and Television Stations (Events of Major Importance) Regulations of 2004 (451/2004)
EPG	Electronic Programme Guide
EU	European Union
IFJC	International Federation of Journalists Code of Ethics
JEC	Journalistic Ethics Code of Conduct
NAA	Normative Administrative Act
OEMM	Owners of Electronic Mass Media
OJ	Official Journal
PIO	Press and Information Office
PSB	Public Service Broadcasting
R/T	Radio and Television
RECL	Regulation of Electronic Communications Law 24(I)/2022
Reg.	Regulation
RTSL	Radio and Television Stations Law 7(I)/1998, as amended and currently in force
RTSR	Radio and Television Stations Regulations of 2000, as amended and currently in force (10/2000)
RTSRFT	Radio and Television Stations (Equal Treatment of Political Parties and of Candidates) Regulations of 2006, (193/2006) as amended and currently in force
TEC	Treaty Establishing the European Community
TEU	Treaty of the European Union
TFEU	Treaty on the Functioning of the European Union
TV	Television

UCJ	Union of Cyprus Journalists
UNGA	United Nations General Assembly
UNSC	United Nations Security Council
VoD	Video on Demand
VSPs	Video Sharing Platforms

List of Abbreviations

Preface

The General Introduction and Parts I and II were written by Dr Achilles Emilianides. Parts III, IV and V were written by Dr Costas Stratilatis. There was collaboration for the final text. This is the Third Edition of this Monograph; the First Edition was published in 2015 and the Second Edition in 2019.

Dr Costas Stratilatis wishes to express his thanks to Professor Mary Koutselini, former Member of the Cyprus Radio and Television Authority (CRTA) and to Mrs Constantia Michaelidou, Legal Counsel of the CRTA, for providing useful information about various issues regarding the regulation of Radio and Television (R/T) broadcasting. Dr Achilles C. Emilianides wishes to express his gratitude to the many individuals who have collaborated with him over the years and have helped him expand his views on media law, but particularly to Constantinos Emilianides, Giorgos Xinaris, Costas Katsaros, Sofia Iordanidou, Mary Koutselini, Michalis Kontos and Costas Stratilatis. He dedicates this book to the memory of his father Constantinos Emilianides.

General Introduction

§1. General Background of the Country

I. Political and Constitutional History

1. The constitutional history of the Republic of Cyprus is characterized by continuous attempts to overthrow, modify or replace the constitutional structure.[1] The Republic of Cyprus was established as an independent and sovereign republic on 16 August 1960, when its Constitution came into force and the British sovereignty over Cyprus, as a crown colony, ceased.[2] The establishment of the Republic was the outcome of the Zurich and London Agreements of February 1959, on which the fundamental provisions of the Constitution were based.[3] As a result, the constitutional structure of Cyprus was essentially decided without the participation of the people of Cyprus. Consequently, the people of Cyprus considered that the Constitution had been imposed on them.

2. The structure provided by the Zurich Agreement was considered as a compromise between the Greek demand for union with Greece and the Turkish demand for partition of the island. Further, the United Kingdom retained – and continues to retain – sovereignty over two 'Base Areas', one in Akrotiri and the other in Dhekelia, which cover 250 sq. km of the land area of the island of Cyprus. The Constitution is unique in its perplexity and in the multiplicity of safeguards that it provides for the principal numerical minority of the island, namely the Turkish community.[4] The principle of bi-communality permeates the whole constitutional structure, according, in many respects, an equal status to the Greek community, representing 82% of the population, and to the Turkish community, representing 18%. It has, therefore, been correctly argued that the constitutional rules embodied in the

1. *See*, in general, A. Emilianides, *Beyond the Constitution of Cyprus* (Sakkoulas 2006, in Greek); K. Chrysostomides, *The Republic of Cyprus: A Study in International Law* (Martinus Nijhoff 2000).
2. Cyprus Act, 1960, §1, Republic of Cyprus Order in Council 1960 S.I. 1960 No. 1368, *Cyprus: Presented to Parliament by the Secretary of State for the Colonies, the Secretary of State for Foreign Affairs and the Minister of Defence*, Cmnd. 1093, July 1960.
3. A. Emilianides, *The Secret Negotiations: The Establishment of the Republic of Cyprus* (Papazisis/CECL 2022, in Greek).
4. *See* A. Emilianides, *Constitutional Law in Cyprus* (2nd ed., Kluwer 2019); P. Polyviou, *The Problem of Cyprus: Constitutional and Political Aspects* (1974).

Constitution might as well have been conceived by a constitutionalist and a mathematician in a nightmarish dialogue.[5]

3. Not surprisingly, the Zurich Agreement failed to establish cooperation between the Greek and Turkish communities of the island[6] and proved to be unworkable in practice.[7] In 1963 there was an outbreak of violence in the island which led to a constitutional breakdown.[8] In 1964 a United Nations Peacekeeping Operation came to the island and has remained there ever since.[9] The United Nations Security Council (UNSC), with Resolution 186/1964, and the United Nations General Assembly (UNGA), on 18 December 1965, called upon all States to respect the sovereignty, unity, independence and territorial integrity of the Republic of Cyprus and to refrain from any intervention with it.[10] The Government of the Republic of Cyprus continued to be recognized by the international community as the only legitimate representative of the Republic.[11]

4. Inter-communal talks began with the aim of achieving a satisfactory solution to the 'Cyprus Problem'.[12] However, in July 1974 the Republic of Turkey, one of the 'guarantor powers' of the independence, sovereignty and territorial integrity of Cyprus, invaded the country with its armed forces and occupied the northern part of the island. Turkey alleged that its invasion had the purpose of restoring the constitutional order on the basis of the provisions of the Treaty of Guarantee following a coup against President Makarios[13] by the Greek military government (*junta*), which was then in power in Greece.[14] However, this allegation was not accepted by the international community.[15] Resolution 360/74 expressed the official contempt, on

5. A.S. De Smith, *The New Commonwealth and Its Constitutions* 282 (Stevens & Sons 1964).
6. *See* A. Emilianides, *The Parliamentary Co-existence of Greeks and Turks in Cyprus* (Epifaniou 2003, in Greek).
7. C. Tornaritis, *Peculiarities of the Constitution of Cyprus and Effect on the Normal Function of the State* (1980, in Greek); T.W. Adams, *The First Republic of Cyprus: Review of an Unworkable Constitution*, 19 Western Political Quarterly 475 (1966).
8. *See* S. Kyriakides, *Cyprus: Constitutionalism and Crisis Government* (University of Pennsylvania Press 1968); T. Ehrlich, *Cyprus 1958–1967: International Crises and the Role of Law* (Oxford University Press 1974).
9. A. Emilianides, *The United Nations Forces Function, Its International Conflicts and Civil Strifes,* in *Melanges Bridel* (Imprimeries Réunies): 147–168 (1968); G. Kaloudis & P. Lang, *Role of the UN in Cyprus from 1964 to 1979* (Peter Lang 1991).
10. SC Resolution 186/64. There followed twenty-eight Security Council Resolutions up to 1974, affirming SC Resolution 186/64.
11. *See* further C. Tornaritis, *The Legal Position of the Present Government of the Republic,* in C. Tornaritis, *Constitutional and Legal Problems in the Republic of Cyprus* 43–55 (1972).
12. *See* P. Polyviou, *Cyprus in Search of a Constitution: Constitutional Negotiations and Proposals* (1976).
13. *See* L. Loucaides, *The Legal Effect of the Coup of 15 July 1974* (2nd ed., 1976, in Greek); A. Loizou, *The Coup, the Usurpers and the Rule of Law in Cyprus: History, Problems and Struggle of Its People* 503–533 (G. Tenekides & N. Kranidiotis eds, Hestia 1981, in Greek).
14. For the Turkish position *see* Z. Necatigil, *The Cyprus Question and the Turkish Position in International Law* (2nd ed., Oxford University Press 1993).
15. *See* I. Brownlie, *The Prohibition of the Use of Armed Force for the Solution of International Differences with Particular Reference to the Affairs of the Republic of Cyprus*, in *International Law Conference on Cyprus* 198–213 (Cyprus Bar Council 1979); R. McDonald, *International Law and*

behalf of the UNSC, of the unilateral military force undertaken against the Republic of Cyprus, while Resolution 3212/74 of the UNGA demanded that all foreign armed forces leave at once from the Republic of Cyprus and that any foreign intervention with the Republic of Cyprus's affairs should cease immediately. The latter Resolution was endorsed by Resolution 365/74 of the UNSC.[16]

5. As a result of the Turkish invasion, the Greeks and other Christians of the region were displaced to the southern part of the island. The Turks of the southern part of the island were forced to move to the north. The area occupied by Turkey amounts to 36.4% of the territory of the Republic of Cyprus. It is the richest part of the island in natural and productive resources. The Turkish invasion resulted in grave human suffering and material economic loss. Its effects are still evident today, with more than one-quarter of the population of the island being displaced and more than 1,000 people being classified as '*missing persons*'. Forty-three thousand Turkish military troops, armed with the latest military weapons, continue to be based illegally on the island while settlers are being brought to Cyprus in an effort to change the demographic character of the island.[17]

6. The Turkish occupation in Cyprus continues to the present day; therefore, the Republic of Cyprus is prevented from exercising its powers over the occupied territory. Several attempts to achieve a solution to the Cyprus Problem have so far failed.[18] Cyprus became a full member of the European Union (EU) on 1 May 2004.[19] However, the application of the *acquis communautaire* in the occupied areas has been suspended until a solution to the Cyprus Problem is found. What is more, the *acquis* does not apply in the British Sovereign Base Areas. Prior to accession, the Republic of Cyprus was, from 1961 until 2004, a member of the non-aligned movement.

II. Form of Government

7. Cyprus' system of government is a presidential democracy. The main state organs provided for in the constitution are the President, the Council of Ministers,

---

the Conflict in Cyprus, 19 Canadian Yearbook of International Law 3 (1981); D. Constantopoulos, *The Turkish Invasion of Cyprus from the Aspect of International Law* (1978).

16. Similar Resolutions of the Security Council from 1974 until 2004 amount to eighty-seven.
17. *See* C. Tornaritis, *The Turkish Invasion of Cyprus and Legal Problems Arising Therefrom* (1975); L. Clerides, *Violations of Human Rights by Turkey During the Invasion in 1974 and Continuing Violations Today*, 17 Cyprus Law Review 2669 (1987) (in Greek); Cyprus Bar Association, *Turkey's Violations of Human Rights in Cyprus: Findings of the European Commission of Human Rights and Continuing Violations by Turkey* (1995). *See also* K. Chrysostomides, *The Republic of Cyprus: A Study in International Law* (Martinus Nijhoff 2000).
18. *See, inter alia*, A. Emilianides et al., *The Annan Plan: Five Critical Essays* (Ypsilon/Aigaion 2003, in Greek); C. Palley, *An International Relations Debacle* (Hart 2005); A. Syrigos, *The Annan Plan: The Legacies of the Past and the Prospects of the Future* (Patakis 2005, in Greek); A. Emilianides, M. Kontos & G. Kentas, *A Marked Deck: The Confidential Documents of the Negotiations between Christofias and Talat* (Power Publishing 2010, in Greek).
19. *See* S. Laulhé Shaelou, *The EU and Cyprus: Principles and Strategies of Full Integration* (Brill 2010).

the parliament, called the House of Representatives, the Supreme Constitutional Court and the Supreme Court. The President is the Head of State, representing the Republic in all its official functions. The President belongs to the Greek-Cypriot community and is elected for a five-year term directly, by universal suffrage and secret ballot. The President appoints and dismisses the members of the Council of Ministers and, in general, has vast executive powers. The Council of Ministers is composed of eleven Ministers who are chosen from outside the House of Representatives. The Council of Ministers exercises executive power alongside the President. The House of Representatives exercises the legislative power of the Republic. The representatives are elected for a term of five years in free, general and direct elections. The number of representatives is currently fifty-six. The judiciary is independent of the executive and the legislative organs, and it is a powerful factor both in legal and social life. The highest Cypriot courts are the Supreme Constitutional Court and the Supreme Court of Cyprus. Many of the Courts' decisions have been on the highest legal and political impact.[20]

8. In accordance with the principle of bi-communality, Cyprus is a unitary state, comprised of two communities, the Greek community and the Turkish community.[21] The principle of bi-communality permeates the constitutional structure as a whole, according, in many respects, an equal status to the Greek community, representing 82% of the population, and to the Turkish community, representing 18%.[22] It was, therefore, provided that a Greek-Cypriot President should be elected by members of the Greek community while a Turkish-Cypriot Vice President should be elected by members of the Turkish community. The President and the Vice President would retain broad powers of veto on decisions of the Council of Ministers concerning foreign affairs, defence and security, as well as with respect to the laws enacted by the House of Representatives. It was further provided that the Council of Ministers would comprise seven Greek-Cypriots appointed by the President of the Republic, and three Turkish-Cypriots appointed by the Vice President. The House of Representatives would consist of fifty Representatives. Once again, 70% of the members of the House of Representatives were to be elected separately by the members of the Greek community while 30% were to be elected separately by the members of the Turkish community. The Constitution also provided for two communal chambers: a Greek communal chamber and a Turkish communal chamber, which should have legislative power in educational, cultural, religious and other matters of a purely communal nature.

---

20. *See* Emilianides, *Constitutional Law in Cyprus* (2nd ed., Kluwer 2019); C. Kombos, *Cypriot Constitutional Law* (Nomiki Vivliothiki 2021, in Greek); A. Markides, *The Republic of Cyprus,* in Kortmann et al., *Constitutional Law of 10 EU Member States* (Kluwer 2006); A. Loizou, *The Constitution of Cyprus* (2001, in Greek).
21. C. Tornaritis, *The Constitution of Cyprus*, 6 International Relations 28 (1964); T. Tsatsos, *Observations on the Constitution of Cyprus* (A. Sakkoulas 1965, in Greek).
22. G. Papademetriou, *The Constitutional Problem of the Republic of Cyprus*, 39 Cyprus Law Tribune 850 (1991) (in Greek); N. Antonopoulos, *Les Tendances Constitutionelles des États Avant Accédé Récement à l' Independance: La Constitution de la République de Chypre*, 15 Revue Hellénique de Droit International 307 (1962).

9. In its essence the structure provided by the Constitution aimed at ensuring that each community would enjoy partial administrative autonomy, while the numerically smaller Turkish community would effectively participate in the exercise and functions of government in such a way as to avoid a de facto supremacy of the larger community. De Smith noted that the 1960 Constitution is a tragic and, occasionally, an almost ludicrous document, and he noted that it is possibly the most rigid, detailed and complicated Constitution in the world, weighed down by checks and balances, procedural and substantive safeguards, guarantees and prohibitions which set daunting obstacles to the people who are called to abide by it.[23]

10. As a result of the Cyprus Problem and of the abnormal constitutional situation prevailing in the island, constitutional provisions which refer to the Turkish-Cypriot community have not been in force for sixty years even though they are considered to be fundamental and, thus, not subject to modification. Thus, there is no Turkish Vice President, Ministers or Representatives. A doctrine of necessity has been accepted by the Supreme Court of Cyprus so that the House of Representatives may enact laws even contrary to those provisions of the constitution which are temporarily not in force because of the Cyprus Problem. This has resulted in a fundamental differentiation between the written form of the 1960 Constitution and the living Constitution, as applied in Cypriot case law and practice since 1964. No analysis of the constitutional order of Cyprus might be accurate without an understanding of the importance of the doctrine of necessity in the perseverance, interpretation and function of the Constitution.[24]

III. Geography and Population

11. Cyprus is the third largest Mediterranean island after the Italian islands of Sicily and Sardinia. Cyprus is situated in the Eastern Mediterranean, at a distance of 300 km from the north of Egypt, 90 km from the west of Syria, 60 km from the south of Turkey and 360 km from the north-west of Greece. It covers an area of 9,251 sq. km (3,572 sq. mi) and it has 648 km of coastline. The Republic of Cyprus is divided into six districts, namely Nicosia, Limassol, Famagusta, Larnaca, Paphos and Kyrenia. The capital of the Republic is the town of Nicosia. Cyprus also has two mountain ranges – the Pentadaktylos range, which runs along the entire northern coast, and the Troodos massif in the central and south-western parts of the island. Between the two ranges lies the fertile plain of Messaoria.

12. Since the Turkish invasion, providing precise figures with respect to the population of Cyprus has presented certain difficulties due to the abnormal situation

23. De Smith, *The New Commonwealth*, 296.
24. On the doctrine *see* A. Emilianides, C. Papastylianos & C. Stratilatis, *The Republic of Cyprus and the Doctrine of Necessity* (Sakkoulas 2016, in Greek), P. Polyviou, *The Case of Ibrahim, The Doctrine of Necessity and the Republic of Cyprus* (Chryssafinis and Polyviou 2015), C. Kombos, *The Doctrine of Necessity in Constitutional Law* (Sakkoulas 2015).

prevailing in the island. The Statistical Service of the Republic of Cyprus has estimated, however, that by the end of 2006, the population of Cyprus was 867,600, out of which 660,600 (76.1%) belonged to the Greek community while 88,900 (10.2%) belonged to the Turkish community. The remaining 118,100 (13.7%) were foreign residents, including, mainly, Greek and British citizens, as well as citizens of Russia, the Philippines, Sri Lanka, Romania, Bulgaria and other countries.[25] Out of the members of the Greek community, 2,700 (0.4%) were Armenians, 4,800 (0.6%) were Maronites, and 900 (0.1%) were Roman Catholics. According to the 2011 official census, the population of Cyprus was 840,407, out of which 667,398 (79.41%) were Cypriots, 106,270 (12.64%) were European citizens and 64,113 (7.62%) were third-country nationals (the majority being Asian or Russian nationals).[26] An official census was also carried out in 2021, but only preliminary results have so far been released; the population seems to have increased to 923,272. It should be noted that it is difficult to estimate with precision the actual number of Turkish-Cypriots residing in Cyprus. It is estimated that 57,000 Turkish-Cypriots have emigrated from Cyprus following the invasion of 1974. The number of settlers currently residing in Cyprus is not known. It is estimated, however, that more than 100,000 settlers from mainland Turkey are currently residing in the occupied areas. Illegal settlers are not included in any estimation of the current population of Cyprus.[27]

§2. The Media Landscape

I. Print Media

13. The origins of print media in Cyprus can be traced to the beginning of the British Rule of Cyprus in 1878. During the Turkish Rule of Cyprus (1571–1878) there were no technical means for printing and there were no journalists in Cyprus, whereas freedom of expression was limited and freedom of the press was virtually non-existent as a concept. Furthermore, the great majority of the population was illiterate. The first Cypriot moveable printing press was brought to Larnaca from Egypt in the summer of 1878 and the first Cypriot newspaper, entitled *Cyprus*, was published on 29 August 1878. The British authorities, however, demanded that the newspaper be published simultaneously in both Greek and English.[28] Within the next four years, there were six printing shops in Cyprus (three in Larnaca, two in Limassol and one in Nicosia) and a respective number of newspapers. During the same period, the Government Printing Office was organized and published the

25. Source: Statistical Service of the Republic of Cyprus.
26. The remaining 0.33% were unidentified. Source: Statistical Service of the Republic of Cyprus.
27. *See* Council of Europe, 2 May 2003, Doc. 9799, *Colonisation by Turkish Settlers of the Occupied Part of Cyprus* (Rapporteur Mr Laakso); L. Loucaides, *Expulsion of Settlers from Occupied Territories: The Case of Turkish Settlers*, in L. Loucaides, *Essays on the Developing Law of Human Rights* 108–138 (Martinus Nijhoff Publishers 1995); M. Stavrinos, *Settlements as a Crime in International Law* (Parga 2013, in Greek).
28. *See* A. Sofokleous, *Contribution to the History of the Cypriot Press*, vol. I (Intercollege Press 1995, in Greek).

Cyprus Gazette, which is the official gazette of Cyprus. Since 1878, more than 400 newspapers and periodicals have been published, mainly in Greek, and also in English, Turkish, Armenian and Russian, a comparatively large number that is due both to the interest of Cypriots to receive information and to the brief lifespan of most newspapers and periodicals.[29]

14. It could be argued that there has been a steady progress in print media in Cyprus. All newspapers have adopted modern printing techniques and computerization, and they have significantly developed the quality of their printing and layouts. Newspapers and periodicals have also significantly increased in size and employ a large number of journalists and other staff. There are currently five daily morning newspapers. These are *Phileleftheros*, *Politis*, *Alithia* and *Haravgi*, which are in the Greek language, and *Cyprus Mail*, which is in the English language. *Phileleftheros*, which is not party affiliated, has been in publication since 1955 and it has, by far, the largest circulation. Considered for many decades by the wider public as a newspaper that is nearly always supportive of the government, *Phileleftheros* has been mostly critical of the last cabinets and it is generally being considered as the most independent newspaper. Its online edition and website also enjoy the highest market penetration.[30] Its daily edition includes a separate sports newspaper entitled *Goal News*. *Phileleftheros* further publishes several periodicals and, until September 2017, the *Cyprus Weekly* newspaper, which was the most widely read English weekly newspaper.

15. The remaining newspapers have a relatively similar market penetration. *Politis*, founded in 1999, is the only daily newspaper that was published after 1976, a fact which proves the difficulty of newcomers to enter the market. *Politis* has enjoyed a steady readership since its launch, priding itself on several widely-discussed journalistic revelations. Its website is quite popular as well.[31] While non-party affiliated, it retains a close association with politicians representing a specific part of the ideological spectrum, namely those who supported the Annan Plan for the solution of the Cyprus Problem in 2004.[32] Some of its most prominent journalists became part of the team of journalists who were hired in order to support the previous right-wing President of the Republic, a fact which undermined the perception of *Politis* by part of the public as an independent newspaper.

---

29. A. Sofokleous, *The Cypriot Media of Mass Information* 29 (Nikokles 2008, in Greek); *id.*, *Contribution to the History of the Cypriot Press*, vols. I–IV (Intercollege Press 1995–2007, in Greek).
30. www.philenews.com.
31. www.politis.com.cy.
32. The Annan Plan was a comprehensive proposal for the solution of the Cyprus Problem which was submitted in separate simultaneous referenda in 2004. The Plan was rejected by the people of Cyprus as 75.83% of the members of the Greek Cypriot community voted against it, while 65% of the Turkish-Cypriot community voted in favour of it. *See supra* n. 18, as well as A. Emilianides, *Constitutional Study of Annan V*, in A. Varnava & H. Faustmann, *Reunifying Cyprus: The Annan Plan and Beyond* 95–106 (Tauris 2009), S. Papasavvas, *The Annan Plan: A Constructively Vague Constitutional Future for Cyprus* (Sakkoulas 2003, in Greek).

16. *Haravgi* is the official newspaper of Progressive Party of Working People (AKEL), the Cypriot Communist party. It has been published since 1956 and its readership consists of members and supporters of AKEL.[33] Whereas not an official newspaper of the governing right-wing party Democratic Rally (DISY), *Alithia* is affiliated with DISY and has almost always had unofficial representation in the party's cabinet when it was in power. *Alithia* was founded in 1952 as a weekly newspaper and has been a daily newspaper since 1982.[34] The only daily English newspaper, *Cyprus Mail*, has been published since 1945. It is an independent newspaper, enjoying a steady readership of not only English-speakers but also Greek-speakers.[35] In 2019 Cyprus Mail was bought by advocate Andreas Neocleous; this came only a few years after the latter's firm had been convicted for bribery of the former Deputy Attorney-General, a fact that led to criticism regarding the newspaper's independence.[36]

17. A number of weekly, fortnightly or monthly newspapers are also being published. The most important Sunday newspapers are the editions of *Simerini* and *Kathimerini*. *Simerini* was founded in 1976 and was initially supportive of DISY, the right-wing party. During the last two decades, it has distinguished itself from DISY and it considers itself independent, although it remains a right-wing newspaper. It was published as a daily newspaper until May 2017, when it decided to discontinue its daily edition and to remain as a Sunday newspaper only. *Simerini* is part of the wider *Dias Publishing Group* which publishes several periodicals and also controls one of the most significant private TV stations of the island. The website of the newspaper is considered to have the second largest market penetration after *Phileleftheros*.[37] *Kathimerini* is a more recent Sunday newspaper, which was founded in 1998 and which is the Cypriot branch of the Greek daily right-wing newspaper *Kathimerini*. The readership and impact of *Kathimerini* are steadily growing but remain relatively small. Kathimerini has never succeeded in becoming as influential in the Cypriot market as it has been in the respective Greek one. *Machi*, a right-wing newspaper, was founded in 1960 and, until recently, was a daily newspaper. However, financial problems have caused it to shut down. There are also a significant number of local or specialized newspapers, as well as newspapers published in English, Russian, Armenian or Arabic.[38]

18. Further to the above, there are also several weekly or monthly periodicals of specialized interests. Publications from *Phileleftheros*, the *Dias Group* and *Eidikes*

33. www.haravgi.com.cy.
34. www.alithia.com.cy.
35. www.cyprus-mail.com.
36. *See*, e.g., 'How to Wipe Away Digital History: Buy a Newspaper', Medium, 6 Mar. 2019, available in https://medium.com/mediapowermonitor/how-to-wipe-away-digital-history-buy-a-newspaper-f29edb44df79.
37. www.sigmalive.com.
38. The data of the PIO refer to twenty-seven weekly newspapers (a number that includes the official Gazette of the Republic of Cyprus), thirty-two newspapers published more occasionally, four weekly periodicals and sixty-eight periodicals published more occasionally.

Ekdoseis mostly dominate the market of periodicals, with most publications, however, focusing on lifestyle or specialized issues. The Turkish-Cypriot press is mainly published in the areas not under the control of the Republic of Cyprus and, accordingly, is not considered in this study. It is only observed that in the Turkish-occupied area, there are eight daily newspapers, representing one of the highest concentrations of newspaper titles per capita in the world.[39] In addition to the print media, which have their own online editions and web pages, it should be also noted that there is a growing number of web newspapers. These include the Greek daily *Reporter*,[40] the English daily *Financial Mirror*[41] and a continuously growing number of web news portals.

II. TV Stations

19. The state-owned Cyprus Broadcasting Corporation (CyBC) began broadcasting in 1957, twice a week for a total of four hours per week. There was a gradual increase in the number of days and total hours covered by the transmissions of the CyBC, and since December 1968 CyBC had been broadcasting a daily program, beginning at 17:00 and ending at midnight. CyBC was a pioneer in introducing local news programs, documentaries, series, etc. From 1982 colour transmissions, instead of black and white ones, were introduced and new technologies were adopted for filming and viewing programs. The role of CyBC in the social and cultural development of the island and in the information and entertainment of Cypriots has been of extreme importance.[42] CyBC had a monopoly over broadcasting operations until the early 1990s when licensing of private TV stations was started in the island. Despite competition from private TV stations and whereas CyBC no longer ranks as the leading TV station of the island, it has retained a relatively high number of viewers, being the fifth largest TV station in the island. In addition, CyBC has introduced new technologies and broadcasts its programs overseas through digital satellite to Cypriots living abroad and through the internet. It should be further noted that CyBC currently administers a Digital Terrestrial Television (DTT) platform, a fact that has advanced the quality of its signal.

20. A second CyBC channel was introduced in 1992 in order to cope with the emerging competition from private TV stations. However, its market penetration remains comparatively limited. Both CyBC channels are broadcasted daily on a twenty-four-hour basis. During the morning hours, the second channel of CyBC broadcasted Euronews. Furthermore, the Greek, state-owned TV channel (Euronews) is broadcasted directly in Cyprus through the CyBC terrestrial platform. It should be noted that the CyBC Law makes a brave attempt to accommodate the various minority interests by providing access to the media and ensuring

39. *See* M. Vassiliadou, *The Cypriot Media Landscape*, in *European Media Governance: National and Regional Dimensions* 203–204 (G. Terzis ed., University of Chicago Press 2007).
40. http://www.reporter.com.cy/.
41. http://www.financialmirror.com/.
42. A. Pavlides, *Cyprus Broadcasting Corporation*, in *Great Cypriot Encyclopedia* vol. 15, 247–249 (Filokypros 1996, in Greek); Sofokleous, *The Cypriot Media*, fn. 29 above, 65ff.

that all religious groups may enjoy a certain amount of broadcast time.[43] The state-owned CyBC is expected to promote issues concerning the three religious groups of the Republic (Maronites, Armenians, Roman/Latin Catholics), as well as the Turkish-Cypriot community. Section 19 of the CyBC Law, Cap. 300A (CyBCL), specifies that CyBC shall ensure the provision of public radio-television service with unbiased attention and respect to the interests and sensitivities of the Greek-Cypriot and Turkish-Cypriot communities, the religious groups and the various minorities in Cyprus.[44]

21. The first private television channel in Cyprus belonged to the Orthodox Church and it was named *Logos*. The Church received governmental permission to broadcast a private TV channel in 1992. *Logos* first aired on 26 April 1992 with live coverage of the Christian Easter celebrations from the St. John Cathedral in Nicosia. The purpose of the television channel was to promote and transmit Christian spirituality, Orthodox tradition, the Church's role and actions as well as its contribution to the struggle for the liberation of semi-occupied Cyprus, without, however, neglecting the need to provide accurate, objective and direct information to the public, as well as entertainment. Due to financial problems, the Church had decided to rent its governmental permission to broadcast to the Greek television channel *Mega* in exchange for monetary compensation (for the legal implications of this transaction *see* Part III, Chapter 2, §2 I *E*). The Cypriot television channel *Mega* was, in essence, a local branch of the Greek television channel *Mega*, mainly broadcasting serials, movies and other programmes also transmitted in Greece. Nevertheless, *Mega* also transmitted programmes of local interest, such as news bulletins and current affairs programmes, talk shows or Cypriot entertainment productions (mainly TV series). The Orthodox Church had retained, according to the agreement to rent its permission, the right to transmit certain religious or spiritual programmes through the channel and even participate, albeit in a limited manner, in the policy decisions of the channel with respect to the Cyprus Problem. Recently, the Archdiocese signed a new agreement in accordance with which the Orthodox Church became the dominant shareholder and administrator of the *Mega* channel; since then, local productions have further increased. However, financial problems in the Greek channel *Mega* led to the termination of both the name *Mega* and the transmission of the respective Greek programme. The channel was renamed to *TVOne* in 2017 and the licence was eventually rented out, by the Church, to a company led by right-wing businessman and former Minister Socratis Hasikos in 2018 who renamed it to *Omega*. *Omega* is currently the third or fourth-largest free-to-air private television channel in Cyprus and broadcasts seven days a week, twenty-four hours a day.

---

43. *See* D. Gomien, *Pluralism and Minority Access to Media*, in *The Strength of Diversity: Human Rights and Pluralist Democracy* 57 (A. Rosas & J. Helgesen eds, Martinus Nijhoff Publishers 1992).
44. A. Emilianides, *Law and Religion in Cyprus* (2nd ed., Kluwer 2014), Second Report Submitted by Cyprus, pursuant to Art. 25, para. 1 of the Framework Convention for the Protection of National Minorities, 27 Oct. 2006, paras 35, 48ff.

22. *Antenna TV* began transmitting on 28 June 1993 as the local branch of the Greek television channel *Antenna*, retransmitting serials, movies and other programmes also transmitted in Greece, and also transmitting programmes of local interest, such as news, talk shows or Cypriot productions. *Antenna* is one of the largest TV stations in the island, the other traditionally largest TV station being *Sigma TV*, which began transmitting on 3 April 1995. *Sigma* is owned by the *Dias group*, which also owns the *Simerini* newspaper, several periodicals and the *Radio Proto* radio station. *Sigma's* programme emphasizes Cypriot productions, news and talk shows, although it also collaborates with Greek TV stations in order to broadcast programmes which are also transmitted in Greece. Both TV channels broadcast continuously during the week. A new islandwide licensed TV channel, named *Alpha Cyprus*, has been transmitting since April 2016, initially as the local branch of the Greek *Alpha TV*. In April 2018, it was sold to the Papaellinas Group for EUR 7 million. *Alpha Cyprus* has succeeded in becoming one of the largest free-to-air private television channels in Cyprus and broadcasts seven days a week, twenty-four hours a day.

23. The four largest private TV stations and the state-owned CyBC are relatively close when it comes to number of viewers. Other private TV stations in the island have a significantly lower number of viewers and their importance is more limited. The chronologically fourth free-to-air private TV station to be granted a licence to transmit in the entire geographic area of Cyprus was *CNC Plus TV*, a television station initially affiliated with AKEL, the communist party of Cyprus, until it was sold to the Proteas group due to financial struggles. Other local TV stations which now transmit digitally to the entirety of Cyprus are *Extra TV*, *Capital TV* and *Vergina TV* which all broadcast from Limassol. The aforementioned TV channels mainly retransmit content from low-budget movies, or collaborate with Greek TV stations, in order to retransmit their programme in Cyprus. They also have low-budget domestic productions. A few local TV channels with limited market penetration can also be found in Limassol, Larnaca and Paphos.[45]

24. Pay TV has also been of importance in the development of the Cypriot media market. The first subscriber TV channel to broadcast was *Lumiere TV* (*LTV*), which remained the undisputed leader in Cypriot pay TV for twenty years. LTV began transmitting in June 1993 covering the entirety of Cyprus, and at its peak it had over 50,000 paying active subscribers. Its success was due to the transmission of high-quality programs, such as premier sports events, movies and series. In 1995 licence was granted to a second pay TV channel (*Alfa TV*), which was owned by Socratis Hasikos, a prominent politician and Minister of DISY, the then (and now) governing party. However, *Alfa TV* almost immediately decided to collaborate with *LTV* in consideration of a fee, thus offering *LTV* a second TV channel to broadcast its programmes. *LTV* channels were transmitted over the years both digitally (and analogically before the introduction of digital TV in Cyprus) and through various digital or broadband technology platforms, such as *Nova Cyprus*, *Cytavision*, *Primetel*,

45. For reference purposes only, it is observed that in the occupied areas there are approximately fifteen television channels.

Cablenet and *Athina Sat*. Various additional *LTV* channels had been introduced, such as LTV 2, LTV 3, LTV Sports 1, LTV Sports 2 and LTV Races. Financial difficulties, intense competition and price inflation, however, as well as problems arising from piracy, led *LTV* to a financial breakdown and a decision to sell its TV rights to *Cytavision* and cease operations.

25. The first digital satellite pay TV service to be introduced in Cyprus was *Nova Cyprus*. This was owned by *Multichoice Cyprus*, a subsidiary of *Multichoice Greece*, which also owned the leading digital satellite Greek pay TV service, Nova. *Nova Cyprus* was initially a partner with *LTV*. However, in July 2006, following a dispute, *LTV* and *Alfa TV* removed their services from *Nova*, and they terminated their agreement with Multichoice. Since the breakdown of their agreement with *LTV*, *Nova Cyprus* never managed to reclaim its importance in Cypriot pay TV services, mainly due to the fact that it suffered from piracy issues, as well as competition from the Greek *Nova* platform, to which many Cypriots were subscribers. *Nova Cyprus* transmits the main Greek Nova Cinema and Nova Sports channels, as well as a substantial number of foreign news, entertainment or sports TV channels. Another short-lived digital satellite pay TV service was *Athina Sat* which broadcasted from 2005 to 2008.

26. The major broadband pay TV service is owned by the state-owned Cyprus Telecommunications Authority (CYTA). In addition to its telephone and internet services, CYTA launched in 2004 *Cytavision* (initially branded as miVision), which acts as a platform for pay TV services. Exploiting its dominance in the Cypriot telecommunications market, *Cytavision* spent an inordinate amount of money, in order to acquire the rights of Cypriot football teams and stave off competition. In 2006 it began its collaboration with *LTV*, which resulted in CYTA gradually becoming the largest pay TV service in the island. *Cytavision* offers a wide range of TV channels and services to its subscribers. The main competitors of CYTA are *Primetel* and *Cablenet*, which are both private telecommunication enterprises which offer a wide array of pay TV services using broadband technology. There are also licensed TV stations which are transmitted through broadband TV services, such as *Greek Cinema*, *Smile TV* and *Village Cinema*.

III. Radio Stations

27. CyBC began transmitting its radio services in 1952, broadcasting a total of approximately forty-three hours in three languages, Greek, Turkish and English.[46] Gradually, additional radio programmes have been introduced, so the CyBC currently has four distinct programmes. The monopoly of CyBC lasted until the early 1990s. During the late 1980s groups of young journalists and technicians began broadcasting illegally from small and movable radio stations in Nicosia. Pioneer in this respect was *Radio Aftodiathesi*, which was controlled by displaced persons from Karpasia and which began transmissions on 15 November 1987. On 6 July

46. Before Independence as the Cyprus Broadcasting Service.

1989, the Municipalities of Nicosia and Limassol decided to welcome private radio stations for one day in the municipalities, so as to broadcast test programmes of sound and music. The success of this event led to the licensing of private radio stations in the island.[47]

28. The first private radio station was *Radio Super*, which began broadcasting on 23 July 1990. However, it shut down two years later due to financial difficulties. Recently, *Radio Super* re-started broadcasting, without, however, enjoying its initial success. The second and more lasting was *Radio Proto*, which is owned by the *Dias Group*, the owner of *Sigma TV* channel and *Simerini* newspaper. *Radio Proto* first broadcasted on 3 September 1990, and it has since remained one of the leading radio stations of the island. The official radio station of AKEL, the communist party of Cyprus, *Radio Astra*, first broadcasted on 14 April 1991, whereas the radio station of the Orthodox Church, called *Logos*, had been transmitting since 24 April 1992 for twenty-six years and focused on religious, spiritual and cultural programmes, Greek music, as well as talk shows. It has now been substituted by *Alithinos Logos*, which was until 2022 a local radio station named *St Demetrius*. Other islandwide radio stations are *Ant1*, *Athina*, *Politis*, *Diesi*, *Capital Radio*, *Radio Sfaira*, *Choice*, *Kanali Exi*, *Kanali 7*, *Mix*, *Dromos*, *NRJ Energy*, *Russian Wave*, *RFR Sport FM 95*, *Radio Paphos*, *107.4 Active*, *Radio Deejay*, *Supersport*, *Zenith*, *Kiss*, *Klik*, *Joy*, for a total of twenty-six islandwide private radio stations. There are also twenty-three local radio stations.[48]

IV. The Press and Information Office and the Cyprus News Agency

29. Following the end of World War II, the British colonial rule established the Public Information Office. The Cypriots considered that it mainly served as the propaganda of the British administration. The role of the office was upgraded after Independence, with the Government Spokesman acting as the political director of the Office, which was renamed the Press and Information Office (PIO). Since 1983 a public servant has been acting as the Director of the PIO. The stated mission of the PIO is to inform world opinion on the Cyprus problem and to promote Cyprus abroad. Its mission is also to inform Cypriots about the work of the government and publicize the statements and activities of the officials of the Republic of Cyprus. In addition, the PIO monitors the local and foreign media. The PIO is the central publishing agency for the Government and produces printed and audiovisual material in order to achieve its aims. The PIO is further responsible for the application of the press and cinema laws, the official certification of translations and the representation of Cyprus in Council of Europe committees on mass media. Through its website, it provides constant information to the public, which is updated on a daily basis.[49]

47. Sofokleous, *The Cypriot Media*, fn. 29 above, 59.
48. Source: PIO.
49. www.pio.gov.cy.

30. The Cyprus News Agency (CNA) was established on 16 February 1976 at the initiative of the then-Director General of the CyBC. A private news service had been previously functioning as the news agency of Cyprus from 1957 until 1967 when it closed down. Since 1989, the CNA has become a semi-governmental news organization, which, however, maintains editorial independence from the Government. It issues news bulletins in Greek, Turkish and English and cooperates with several established foreign news agencies. A landmark was the 1996 cooperation agreement with the Athens News Agency, which provided CNA with its first computerized editing system. The CNA is a member of major press organizations. It should be noted that there are also major foreign news agencies which are present in Cyprus. These include the Athens News Agency, the New York-based Associated Press, the London-based *Reuters*, *Agence France Presse*, the Italian *ANSA*, the Spanish *EFE*, the Russian *Itar-Tass* and the Chinese *Xinhua News Agency*.

V. Critical Observations

31. Despite the growing number of newspapers and periodicals, the Cypriot press market seems rather stagnated. With the major exception of *Politis*, no other successful daily newspapers have been published in the last forty-five years. Even a leading Greek newspaper, such as *Kathimerini*, has not succeeded in attracting the expected number of readership in the Cypriot press market. In recent years traditional outlets, such as *Simerini* and *Machi* were forced to shut down their daily editions due to financial constraints. The relatively small market causes additional difficulties for newcomers who want to invest in print media since the return profit of their investment would be marginal. Furthermore, the emerging internet news portals have not so far proved to be very influential, as they normally employ one to two members of staff and they restrict themselves to reproducing news from the major traditional news outlets, usually with some additional commentary.

32. Party affiliation of newspapers implies that many journalists should be members of the political party with which the newspaper is affiliated and that they do not have unfettered freedom in expressing their views or in objectively sharing information with the public. Besides, most newspapers function with minimum staff due to financial constraints and are heavily dependent on advertising for their survival. This implies that a journalist's freedom of expression is also restricted by the financial interests of the publisher and by the need to retain a working relationship with the main advertising outlets.[50] This was one of the main reasons why the Cypriot media had rarely criticized the banking system prior to its collapse in 2013, as the media are heavily dependent on banks for advertising. This is not, of course, a

50. *See Versions of Liberty in our Media Reality. The New Journalism and Its Challenges* (S. Iordanidou & C. Stratilatis eds Metamesonykties Publications 2018, in Greek).

Cypriot phenomenon but rather a global reality of modern journalism, which, however, becomes even more intense in the Cypriot small market.[51]

33. Financial constraints have also guided the evolution of the radio-television market. Limited income from advertising and other sources has led to dire financial problems for all TV and radio stations. The situation has been aggravated following the financial collapse in early 2013[52] when Cyprus agreed to a Eurogroup agreement for the recapitalization of the Cypriot banking sector by forcing the depositors in the two major Cypriot banks to bail in. A Memorandum of Understanding was signed with Troika[53] in order to loan the Cypriot economy. The agreement introduced a series of austerity measures in the island.[54] This led to significant budget cuts for the CyBC, whereas the financial situation of private TV and radio stations has deteriorated. The switch-over to the DTT, with the establishment of the digital platform for private broadcasters (*see* Part III, Chapter 2, §3 and Chapter 7, §2 below), has not met the expectations of private TV stations, as the consortium of the major Cypriot broadcasters, *Velister Ltd*, significantly overpaid the rights of acquiring the licence for the digital platform from the State, eventually bidding the amount of EUR 10 million, which is too high for a small market such as the Cypriot one. The unavoidable increase of access fees to the DTT implies that there is an insurmountable barrier to entry for newcomers who wish to emerge to the small Cypriot TV market. Thus, pluralism is being hindered. The breakdown of *LTV* and the emergence of semi-governmental CYTA as the main player in pay TV were also highly problematic, as they further restricted real competition in the island in pay TV rights.

§3. Sources of Media Law

I. The Constitution

34. The Constitution of Cyprus is a written and lengthy document, consisting of 199 Articles and three Annexes. Article 179, paragraph 1 of the Constitution provides that the Constitution shall be the supreme law of the Republic, while Article 179, paragraph 2 provides that no law or decision of the House of Representatives,

51. *See also* K. Kouros, *The Mass Media Law in the Republic of Cyprus: An Adumbration of the Evolutionary Formation of the Legal Framework of the Press Law from 19th Century Until Today* 77, 365–413 (Vivlioekdotiki 2008, in Greek) for a detailed analysis of the evolution of Cypriot Media Law and for helpful critical observations.
52. C. Ioannou & A. Emilianides, *How the Cypriot Crisis Came to Be: The Real Causes and Responsibility*, 12 Foreign Affairs: The Hellenic Edition 41 (2013) (in Greek).
53. The tripartite committee composed by the European Commission, the European Central Bank and the International Monetary Fund.
54. C. Ioannou & A. Emilianides, *Cyprus and EU following the Haircut of Deposits*, in *Cyprus in a New Era: Geostrategy, Economy, Foreign Policy* 124–153 (C. Ioannou, D. Sotiropoulos & A. Emilianides eds, Foreign Affairs Hellenic Edition and Hippasus 2014, in Greek); C. Ioannou & A. Emilianides, *The Haircut of Cypriot Deposits and the Protection of Fundamental Rights*, 2 Cyprus Human Rights Law Review 141 (2013).

or of any of the Communal Chambers, and no act or decision of any organ, authority or person in the Republic exercising executive power or any administrative function shall in any way be repugnant to, or inconsistent with, any of the provisions of the Constitution. The Constitution of Cyprus is the supreme law of the Republic and any ordinary laws, or international law instruments must not be inconsistent with the Constitution.

35. Following the Fifth Amendment of the Constitution with Law 127(I)/06, the supremacy is subject to the application of the new Article 1A, which provides for the application of mandatory provisions of EU or European Community (EC) law. Besides, the principle of supremacy, as enshrined in Article 179 of the Constitution, has to be read in conjunction with the doctrine of necessity. The main constitutional Articles relevant to Media Law are Article 19 safeguarding freedom of expression, Article 15 safeguarding the right to respect for private life, Article 17 safeguarding the respect for secrecy of one's correspondence, Article 25 which provides for the freedom to exercise trade and profession, Article 122 providing for the character of the CyBC as a Legal Person under Public Law, and Article 171 providing that the sound and vision broadcasting should be both for the Greek and Turkish communities.

II. European Union Law

36. The Court of Justice of the European Union (CJEU) has long considered that the Treaty of the European Union (TEU) is different from other treaties in that it has established a new legal order for the benefit of which the Member States have permanently limited their sovereign rights.[55] The CJEU has, therefore, considered that the supremacy and primacy of EU law extend even against the provisions of the national constitutions of the Member States of the EU.[56] Following the accession of the Republic of Cyprus to the EU, the Constitution was amended with the Fifth Constitutional Amendment of 2006, 127(I)/2006, which aimed at facilitating the exercise of the rights and obligations of the Republic of Cyprus as an EU Member State. The newly added paragraph 4 of Article 169 of the Constitution provides that the Republic may exercise any option and discretion provided for in the Treaty establishing the European Community (TEC) or the TEU and to any Treaties substituting or modifying them. Modified Article 179, paragraph 2 of the Constitution provides that no law or decision of the House of Representatives, or of any of the Communal Chambers, and no act or decision of any organ, authority or person in the Republic exercising executive power or any administrative function shall in any way be repugnant to, or inconsistent with, any obligation imposed upon the Republic as a result of its participation as a Member State of the EU.

37. Furthermore, the newly inserted Article 1A of the Constitution provides that no constitutional provision is considered to invalidate any laws, acts or measures

55. Case 26/62, *Van Gend en Loos* [1963] ECR I; Case 6/64, *Costav. ENEL* [1964] ECR 585.
56. Case 11/70, *Internationale Handelsgesellschaft* [1970] ECR 1125.

which are deemed necessary due to the obligations of the Republic of Cyprus as a Member State of the EU or may impede the legal effect and application of Regulations, Directives or other EU, or EC legal instruments of a binding nature in the Republic.[57] As a result, EU law now has an intra-constitutional effect, in the sense that it is considered to be an integral part of the Constitution, and no constitutional provision may invalidate any provision of a binding nature of EU law.

38. It should be noted that it is the Constitution itself which provides for the facilitation of EU law within the Cypriot legal order and its specific primacy. EU law is, therefore, accorded a constitutional status by the Constitution itself, in the sense that no other provision of the Constitution may be invoked so as to declare the provisions of EU law unconstitutional. Such effect is purely intra-constitutional as far as the Cypriot legal order is concerned. In addition to the EU's primary law, there are various Directives which are of direct interest to Cypriot Media Law. These include the Audiovisual Media Services Directive (AVMS Directive),[58] Directive (EU) 2018/1972 of the European Parliament and of the Council of 11 December 2018 (ECC Directive),[59] and the Radio Equipment Directive.[60]

III. International Treaties

39. Article 169, paragraph 1 of the Constitution provides that every international agreement with a foreign State or with any International Organization relating to commercial matters, economic cooperation (including payments and credit) and *modus vivendi*, shall be concluded under a decision of the Council of Ministers. Any other treaty, convention or international agreement shall be negotiated and signed under a decision of the Council of Ministers, in accordance with Article 169, paragraph §2, and it shall only be operative and binding on the Republic of Cyprus when approved by a law made by the House of Representatives whereupon it shall be concluded. The above are subject to the veto right of the President or the Vice

57. *See also* C. Lycourgos, *Cyprus Public Law as Affected by Accession to the European Union*, in C. Kombos, *Studies in European Public Law* 101ff. (Sakkoulas 2010), 101ff.; *id.*, *The Application of EU Law in Cyprus: Selected Aspects*, The Cyprus Yearbook of International Law 43 (2012); S. Laulhe Shaelou, *Back to Reality: The Implications of EU Membership in the Constitutional Legal Order of Cyprus*, in *Brave New World. Application of EU Law in the New Member States* 471–502 (A. Lazowski ed., TMC Asser Press 2010) C. Kombos, *The Impact of EU Law on Cypriot Public Law* (Sakkoulas 2015).
58. Directive 2010/13/EU of the European Parliament and of the Council of 10 Mar. 2010 on the coordination of certain provisions laid down by law, regulation or administrative action in Member States concerning the provision of AVMS, OJ L 95, 15 Apr. 2010, p. 1.
59. Directive (EU) 2018/1972 of the European Parliament and of the Council of 11 Dec. 2018 establishing the European Electronic Communications Code (Recast), OJ L 321, 17 Dec. 2018, p. 36; and Directive 2002/58/EC of the European Parliament and of the Council of 12 Jul. 2002 concerning the provisions of personal date and the protection of privacy in the electronic communications sector, OJ L 201, 31 Jul. 2002, p. 37, *See also* Regulation (EU) 2022/612 of the European Parliament and of the Council of 6 Apr. 2022, OJ L 115, 13 Apr. 2022, p. 1.
60. Directive 2014/53/EU of the European Parliament and of the Council of 16 Apr. 2014 on the harmonization of the laws of the Member States relating to the making available on the market of radio equipment and repealing Directive 1999/5/EC, OJ L 153, 22 May 2014, p. 62.

President of the Republic, provided for in Articles 50 and 57, paragraph §13 if the decision of the Council of Ministers relates to foreign affairs, defence or security. An international treaty, convention or agreement that has been concluded in accordance with the procedure described above shall have as from its publication in the Official Gazette of the Republic superior force to any municipal law, on condition that such a treaty, convention or agreement is also applied by the other party thereto, in accordance with Article 169, paragraph 3 of the Constitution.

40. In view of the above, the Constitution provides for a dualistic approach with respect to the relationship between national and international law. An international treaty, convention or agreement will therefore not become part of the Cypriot legal order unless and until it has been ratified by the Council of Ministers, approved by law by the House of Representatives and published in the Official Gazette of the Republic. It is only through publication in the Official Gazette that the international law instrument may be invoked before the Cypriot courts and be applied in the Cypriot legal order. Such international law instrument has superior force over any ordinary domestic legislation, not in the sense of an obligation to repeal any inconsistent domestic law, but in the sense of having superiority and precedence in its application. International law, once incorporated in the national legal order and published in the Official Gazette, is superior to any other municipal law, irrespective of whether such law is prior or subsequent to the international law instrument. An international law instrument may not be implicitly repealed through the enactment of conflicting subsequent municipal legislation.[61]

41. Hierarchically, international law instruments are therefore placed above any municipal legislation, with the exception of the Constitution. The Constitution, as the supreme law of the Republic, does not fall within the definition of municipal law of Article 169, paragraph 3 of the Constitution. Consequently, an international law instrument, either treaty, convention or agreement, is inferior to the Constitution, and the constitutional provisions prevail in case of any inconsistency between them and the provisions of the international law instrument.[62] It should be further noted that while an international law instrument has to be ratified and published in the Official Gazette in order to become part of the Cypriot legal order, its interpretation is governed by the principles and interpretation of international law, particularly those contained in the Vienna Convention on Treaties. The rules and principles of interpretation of ordinary statutes do not apply with respect to the interpretation of international law instruments.

42. Article 169, paragraph 3 of the Constitution introduces the condition of reciprocity, namely the condition that the international law instruments, either treaties, conventions or agreements, have to be applied also by the other party thereto, in

61. *Malachtou v. Armefti and Another* [1987] 1 CLR 207. *See also* C. Tornaritis, *The Introduction of International Law into the Legal System of Cyprus*, 3 Cyprus Law Tribune 460 (1990); *id.*, *The Treaty Making Power, Especially under the Law of the Republic of Cyprus* (Nicosia 1973).
62. *Malachtou v. Armefti and Another* [1987] 1 CLR 207; *Ship Owners Union and Another v. The Registrar of Trade Unions and Others* [1988] 3 CLR 457.

order to enjoy superior force over municipal legislation. It has been held, however, that the nature, objective and function of certain international treaties and conventions is such as to exclude the condition of reciprocity. These are multilateral conventions, the object of which is not to create any subjective or reciprocal rights for the contracting parties themselves, but rather to promote certain principles of law, moral and legal values, and which a contracting party signs and ratifies only for the realization of this objective. Examples of such international conventions are those which protect human rights or those whose aim is the improvement and formulation of common rules and the achievement of social justice. For an international law instrument to be applicable, it must be self-executing, in the sense that its provisions must be of such nature so that they may be applied by the organs of the State and be enforced by the Courts, or that they may create rights for the individuals, govern or affect directly relations of the internal life between the individuals, and the individuals and the State or the public authorities.[63]

IV. The European Convention on Human Rights

43. Part II of the Constitution of Cyprus which guarantees the fundamental rights and liberties is modelled on the European Convention on Human Rights (ECHR). However, the provisions of the ECHR have been extended and enlarged in some respects with a number of social and economic rights added in order to meet the basic requirements of a modern society.[64] Consequently, to the extent that it has been incorporated in constitutional provisions and to the degree that its provisions have not been altered during incorporation, the ECHR enjoys limited constitutional status.[65] It should be further observed that the Cypriot courts frequently invoke the case-law of the European Court of Human Rights (ECtHR), not only with respect to the interpretation of the ECHR but also with respect to the interpretation of the corresponding constitutional articles. Therefore, the courts will try, wherever possible, to interpret the relevant constitutional provisions in a manner which is consistent with the interpretation adopted by the ECtHR.[66] For this reason, references to the case-law of the ECtHR in this monograph, especially in Part I, shall be extended.

---

63. *Malachtou v. Armefti and Another* [1987] 1 CLR 207.
64. Acknowledged in several judgments of the Supreme Court of Cyprus, such as *Attorney – General v. Ibrahim* [1964] CLR 195, 225; *Attorney–General v. Afamis* 1 RSCC 121, 125–126. *See* further P. Evangelides, *The Republic of Cyprus and Its Constitution with Special Regard to Constitutional Rights* (Difo-Druck GmbH 1996); C. Tornaritis, *The Human Rights as Recognized and Protected by Law, with Special Reference to the Law of Cyprus* (1967); *id.*, *The Social and Economic Rights under the Law of the Republic of Cyprus*, in *Melanges Bridel* 533–556 (1968).
65. *See* A. Emilianides, *Beyond the Constitution of Cyprus* (Sakkoulas 2006, in Greek).
66. *See* further A. Loizou, *Cyprus and the European Convention on Human Rights* (Sakkoulas 2003, in Greek), C. Tornaritis, *The Operation of the European Convention for the Protection of Human Rights in the Republic of Cyprus*, 3 Cyprus Law Review 455 (1983); C. Clerides, *The Operation of the European Convention on Human Rights in the Civil Courts of Cyprus* 39–40 Cyprus Law Review 6029 (1992) (in Greek).

44. On 24 May 1961, the Republic of Cyprus became a member of the Council of Europe,[67] and on 16 December 1961, it acceded to the ECHR. The ECHR was ratified and incorporated into the internal legal order by the European Convention for the Protection of Human Rights (Ratification) Law 39/1962. The instrument of ratification was deposited with the Secretary of the Council of Europe on 6 October 1962. The International Covenant on Civil and Political Rights and the International Covenant on Economic, Social and Cultural Rights of 16 December 1966 were ratified by the Republic of Cyprus with Law 14/1969.[68] On the basis of Article 169, paragraph 3 of the Constitution, the ECHR and its Protocols, as well as the UN International Covenants, have superior force over any municipal law, either antecedent or subsequent to their ratification by Law. However, neither the ECHR nor the Covenants, are superior to the Constitution. Thus, the constitutional provisions shall prevail in case of any inconsistency between them and the provisions of the ECHR or the Covenants.[69] The most important provision of the ECHR relevant to Media Law is Article 10 safeguarding freedom of expression. Article 8 safeguarding the right to private and family life is also relevant.

V. Ordinary Legislation

45. Article 61 of the Constitution provides that the legislative power of the Republic shall be exercised by the House of Representatives in all matters except those expressly reserved to the Communal Chambers under this Constitution. Following the self-dissolution of the Greek Communal Chamber, and following the withdrawal of Turkish-Cypriots from all organs of the Republic after the events of 1963–1964, the whole of the legislative power of the Republic has been transferred to the House of Representatives. It has been held that the House of Representatives may exercise its legislative power not only in relation to general matters but also in relation to matters of a specific nature, such as loans, guarantees or similar legal obligations of the Government. Thus, the legislative power of the House includes the power to both enact general legislation which sets out rules of general application and legislation which concerns specific cases. The exercise of the legislative power of the House is, however, subject to the application of the principle of separation of powers, in the sense that the legislative power of the House of Representatives may not interfere with the powers of the executive or of the judiciary.[70] Laws directly relevant to Cypriot Media Law include the Radio and Television Stations

67. C. Tornaritis, *Council of Europe and the Republic of Cyprus* 42 (1978); A. Loizou, *Cyprus*, in R. Blackburn & J. Polakiewicz, *Fundamental Rights in Europe: The European Convention on Human Rights and Its Member States, 1950–2000* 219 (Oxford University Press 2001).

68. M. Triantafyllides, *A Comparison of the Provisions for Civil and Political Rights in the Cyprus Constitution with Relevant Internationally Adopted Provisions,* 6 Cyprus Law Tribune 3 (1967), 1 Cyprus Law Tribune 5 (1968); O. Ozgur, *Implementation of International Human Rights Norms in the Republic of Cyprus: Some Problem Areas*, in *10th Commonwealth Law Conference* 261–269 (1993).

69. T. Hadjanastassiou, *The European Convention on Human Rights Applicable in Cyprus*, 3 Cyprus Law Tribune 97 (1976).

70. A. Emilianides, *Constitutional Law in Cyprus* (2nd ed., Kluwer 2019).

Law 7(I)/1998, as amended and currently in force (RTSL), the Press Law 145/1989 and the Regulation of Electronic Communications Law 24(I)/2022 ('RECL').

46. It should be noted that the Laws of Cyprus in force immediately prior to Independence were compiled by then Attorney-General Criton Tornaritis and were published in six volumes in 1959, separated into 354 chapters (Caps).[71] These laws are referred to by their respective Cap. of the 1959 edition. Many of these Laws continue to be in force, sometimes with minor or no amendments, and they are referred to by their respective Cap of the 1959 edition. By virtue of Article 188 of the Constitution, the laws which were in force during the British rule of Cyprus remained in force to the extent that they were not subsequently repealed or modified by an act of the House of Representatives, and to the extent that they are not contrary to or inconsistent with the Constitution. Laws dating from the British Rule which remain in force, with amendments, and which are directly relevant to Cypriot Media Law, include the CyBCL, and the Civil Wrongs Law, Cap. 148; the latter legislation is of significance, because of its provisions on defamation.

VI. Administrative Regulations and Orders

47. When enacting primary legislation, the House of Representatives may authorize the various organs of the administration to issue administrative regulations or orders in the form of secondary legislation. Such administrative regulatory acts set rules of a legislative nature, which are general and impersonal, and which could apply to cases irrespective of whether they actually exist or may exist in the future.[72] The authority to enact regulatory acts is usually delegated by the House of Representatives to the Council of Ministers. However, the House of Representatives may delegate such power to any other administrative organ. If the primary legislation has not explicitly specified the administrative organ to which it has delegated the authority to issue administrative regulations, the Council of Ministers shall have the authority to make any order or regulation for the carrying into effect of the primary legislation, in accordance with Article 54(g) of the Constitution.[73]

48. The power of the administration to issue administrative regulations or orders is not autonomous; it is always dependent upon the primary legislation which should explicitly authorize the administration to enact secondary legislation in the form of administrative regulations. It is normal for the House of Representatives to determine the issues which ought to be regulated with administrative regulatory acts instead of primary legislation. The House of Representatives may well consider that it does not have sufficient time or expertise to regulate a specific issue or it might well consider that the administration is better equipped to regulate specific aspects in accordance with some general guidelines provided by the legislator. Indeed, it has

71. *The Statute Laws of Cyprus in force on 1 April 1959*, v. I–VI, London, 1959.
72. N. Charalambous, *Cypriot Administrative Law Textbook* (3rd ed., 2016, in Greek).
73. *Theodorides v. Central Bank of Cyprus* [1989] 3 CLR 1457; *Holy Archbishopric of Cyprus v. Republic* [1990] 3 CLR 1175 (in Greek).

been controversially held that in certain cases the House of Representatives has an obligation to authorize the administration to enact secondary legislation, rather than regulating the issues with primary legislation, so as to not violate the principle of separation of powers.[74]

49. It is often the case that the primary legislation provides certain guidelines or main rules, then authorizing the administration to regulate the matter in more detail. It should be noted that restriction of constitutional rights may normally occur only by legislation enacted by the House of Representatives and not by secondary legislation. The secondary legislation may, however, provide in more detail the manner in which the restrictions set by the primary law are to be applied.[75] Secondary legislation which is directly relevant to Cypriot Media Law includes the CyBC (Codes of Journalistic Ethics and of Advertising) Regulations 93/2001 (henceforth: 'CyBCR'), the CyBC (Fair Treatment of Political Parties) Regulations of 1985 (118/1986) (CyBCRFT), the Radio and Television Stations (Events of Major Importance) Regulations of 2004 (451/2004) (EMIR), the Radio and Television Stations Regulations of 2000, as amended and currently in force (10/2000) (RTSR), and the Radio and Television Stations (Equal Treatment of Political Parties and of Candidates) Regulations of 2006 (193/2006), as amended and currently in force (RTSRFT).

VII. Jurisprudence

50. The Cypriot legal system is a mixed legal system.[76] Thus, the principles of common law and equity apply in the Republic of Cyprus.[77] Previous judgments of the Supreme Constitutional Court and the Supreme Court are binding for lower courts. Thus, case-law is of great significance with regard to the interpretation of legal provisions.[78] The Supreme Constitutional Court and the Supreme Court itself may depart from their earlier decisions whenever they conclude that a previous decision is founded on an indisputably wrong principle of law, or on a principle leading to manifest injustice, or on a principle which cannot be reconciled to changed legal or social circumstances. It is thus noted that previous case-law is only binding so far as a subsequent law with different content has not been enacted. The legal rule which must be applied is the *ratio decidendi* or the legal principle on

74. E.g., *President of the Republic v. House of Representatives* [2015] 1 CLR 662 (in Greek).
75. *Spyrou v. The Republic* [1973] 3 CLR 627.
76. A. Emilianides, *The Republic of Cyprus: Everything Changes and Nothing Remains Still*, in *A Study of Mixed Legal Systems* (Farran et al. eds, Ashgate, 2014); S. Symeonides, *The Mixed Legal System of the Republic of Cyprus*, 78 Tulane Law Review 441 (2003); N. Hatzimichail, *Cyprus as a Mixed Legal System*, 3 Journal of Civil Law Studies 38 (2013).
77. L. Loucaides, *The Dependence of Cypriot Law from Common Law*, in *Topics of Cypriot Law* 36–77 (1982, in Greek); G. Pikis, *The English Common Law: The Rules of Equity and Their Application in Cyprus* (1981, in Greek).
78. C. Artemides, *The Principle of Commitment of Courts to Case-Law in English Common Law*, in *Aspects of Cypriot Law* vol. I, 219–231 (Asselia 1981, in Greek); S. Nikitas, *The Principle of Judicial Precedent in English Common Law*, in *Corpus de Jure Cyprii* vol. I, 119–133 (Legal Studies Council 1987, in Greek).

which the previous decision was founded. The *ratio* of the case is distinguishable from obiter dicta, which are statements on principles of law made in the course of a decision, but on which the decision does not depend. Having a substantially codified legal system, Cyprus applies common law principles where there is no Cypriot legislation in force and in so far as existing Cypriot legislation is not contradicted.[79]

51. With respect to constitutional and administrative law, however, the Supreme Court regularly cites judgments of continental law courts, such as the Greek *Symvoulio tis Epikrateias* and the French *Conseil d'État.*[80] It could, therefore, be argued that Cypriot constitutional justice forms an idiosyncratic osmosis between continental and common law.[81] Cypriot administrative law, in particular, is similar to Greek, French and German continental administrative law, and not to English administrative law. As a result, Greek and French authorities and jurisprudence have guided the evolution of Cypriot administrative law. It should also be noted that recourses against public authorities, including recourses against the CRTA, are administrative law recourses. With respect to human rights, the Supreme Court is regularly guided by the case-law of the ECtHR.

VIII. The Journalistic Ethics Code

52. The Union of Cyprus Journalists (UCJ) has adopted and incorporated in its Constitution the International Federation of Journalists Code of Ethics (IFJC). Adherence to it is considered compulsory for all its members.[82] In addition, the UCJ, the ANPP (Association of Newspapers and Periodical Publishers) and the Owners of Electronic Mass Media (OEMM) have approved a Journalistic Ethics Code of Conduct (JEC), which is binding for all media, print, electronic, semi-state or private, and their employees. The JEC was adopted on 21 May 1997, and it was amended in 2008 by the agreement of the founding organizations. On 18 October 2022, a new JEC entered into force, substituting the 1997 JEC.[83] A Cyprus Media Complaints Commission (CMCC) was also established by the three organizations and was entrusted with the task of overseeing the implementation of the JEC (*see* Part II, Chapter 6, §3). The CyBC acceded to the JEC and accepted the jurisdiction of the CMCC by the end of 1997. Andreas Mavrommatis, a former judge and former Permanent Secretary of the Ministry of Foreign Affairs was the drafter of the JEC and the first Chairman of the Commission. The JEC has been a major step towards

79. Symeonides, *The Mixed Legal System*, fn. 76 above, 441–455.
80. From 1960–1963, while the President of the Supreme Constitutional Court was the German Ernst Forsthoff, the Supreme Court regularly cited German jurisprudence with respect to constitutional law cases.
81. *See* S. Papasavvas, *La Justice Constitutionelle à Chypre* (Presses Universitaires d' Aix–Marseilles, 1998); *id., The Osmosis of Continental Public Law and Common Law in Cyprus*, 28 To Syntagma 693 (2002) (in Greek).
82. *See* Art. 29 of the Constitution of the UCJ, available at the official page of the Union http://www.esk.org.cy/.
83. 'New Code for Journalistic Ethics', CMCC, 18 Oct. 2022, available in https://cmcc.us.aldryn.io/el/news/νέος-κώδικας-δημοσιογραφικής-δεοντολογίας/.

self-regulation of the media, and, while not a legally binding instrument, it has been, as interpreted by the CMCC and as taken together with the IFJC, highly influential in the development of a culture of journalistic ethics in Cyprus. The contents of the JEC shall be presented in Part II, Chapter 6, §4 below.

Part I. Freedom of Speech

§1. The Scope and Contents of Freedom of Speech

53. Article 19 of the Constitution stipulates that every person has the right to freedom of speech and expression in any form. Such right includes freedom to hold opinions and to receive and impart information and ideas without interference by any public authority, regardless of frontiers.[84] The right to freedom of speech and expression is therefore paramount, having the attributes of a universal right.[85] The rights safeguarded by Article 19 of the Constitution are considered one of the cornerstones of democracy; it has been held that there can be no democracy without freedom of speech.[86] It has also been held that the safeguard of freedom of speech and expression is the hallmark of a humane and civilized society.[87]

54. Article 19 of the Constitution of Cyprus corresponds to Article 10 of the ECHR. Article 10 of the ECHR provides that everyone has the right to freedom of expression and that such right shall include freedom to hold opinions and to receive and impart information and ideas without interference by public authority, regardless of frontiers. The ECtHR has repeatedly held that the right to freedom of expression constitutes one of the essential foundations of a democratic, tolerant and pluralistic society and that it includes all forms of expression, such as paintings, books, films, statements in radio interviews and information pamphlets. Article 10 ECHR protects not only the substance of the ideas and information expressed but also the form in which they are conveyed.[88] It is not merely applicable to information or ideas

84. C. Tornaritis, *The State Law of the Republic of Cyprus* 148ff. (Cyprus Research Centre 1982, in Greek); A. Loizou, *Constitution of the Republic of Cyprus* 114ff. (2001, in Greek). *See* further P. Evangelides, *The Republic of Cyprus and Its Constitution, with Special Regard to the Constitutional Rights* (Difo-Druck GmbH 1996); L. Loucaides, *Freedom of Speech in the Republic of Cyprus*, 11 Cyprus and European Law Review 7 (2010) (in Greek); M. Papapetrou, *Freedom of Speech in Cypriot Society*, 11 Cyprus and European Law Review 16 (2010) (in Greek); Z. Nedjati, *Human Rights and Fundamental Freedoms* (1972), C. Paraskeva, *Cyprus Constitutional Law: Fundamental Freedoms* (Nomiki Vivliothiki 2015, in Greek).
85. *Republic v. Telegraphos Publishing Co Ltd* [1975] 3 CLR 394.
86. *Cyprus Sulphur and Copper Company Ltd v. Pararlama Ltd* [1990] 1 CLR 1051 (in Greek); *Hadjinicolaou v. Police* [1976] 2 CLR 63.
87. *Police v. Ekdotiki Eteria Inomeni Dimosiographiki Dias Ltd* [1982] 2 CLR 63.
88. *De Haes and Gijsels v. Belgium*, Judgment of 24 Feb. 1997, §48; Reports 1997-I; *Palomo Sanchez and Others v. Spain*, Judgment of 12 Sep. 2011, §53; Reports of Judgments and Decisions 2011.

regarded as inoffensive or indifferent but also to 'those that offend, shock or disturb the State or any sector of the population'.[89]

55. The ECtHR has consistently recognized that the public has a right to receive information of general or public interest.[90] This implies that careful scrutiny is called for when the measures taken by national authorities are capable of discouraging the participation of the press in the public debate in matters of legitimate public concern or hindering access to information.[91] It is thus not only direct but also indirect censorship, which purports to restrict preparatory acts of journalism, like the collection of information, which would call for close scrutiny.[92] The creation of forums for public debate, which is protected by Article 10 of the ECHR, is not limited to the media or professional journalists but further extends to non-governmental organizations and individuals which aim to inform public debate.[93]

56. It has been further considered that Article 10 ECHR implies a freedom to receive and have access to information,[94] although this right is not a general or absolute one.[95] The right to freedom to receive information prohibits a Government from restricting a person from receiving information that others wish or may be willing to impart to him.[96] The State has a positive obligation in matters of freedom of the press to eliminate barriers to the exercise of press functions where such barriers exist solely because of an information monopoly held by the state authorities. Although the press should not overstep certain boundaries in respect of the reputation and rights of others, its duty is to impart information and ideas on all matters of public interest, a role that is essential in a democratic society.[97] Journalistic freedom may cover even possible recourse to a degree of exaggeration or even provocation.[98]

57. The State has an obligation to refrain from unduly interfering with the freedom of expression of those who create or distribute works of literary or artistic

89. *See*, e.g., *Handyside v. the United Kingdom*, Judgment of 7 Dec. 1976, §49; Series A No. 24; *Feldek v. Slovakia*, Judgment of 12 Jul. 2001, §72; Reports of Judgments and Decisions 2001-VIII.
90. *See*, e.g., *Observer and Guardian v. the United Kingdom*, Judgment of 26 Nov. 1991, §59; Series A No. 216; *Thorgeirson v. Iceland*, Judgment of 25 Jun. 1992, §63; Series A No. 239.
91. *Bladet Tromsø and Stensaas v. Norway* [GC], Judgment of 20 May 1999, §64; Reports of Judgments and Decisions 1999-III; *Jersild v. Denmark* [GC], Judgment of 23 Sep. 1994, §35; Series A No. 298; *Timpul Info-Magazin and Anghel v. Moldova*, Judgment of 27 Nov. 2007, §31; hudoc.
92. *Dammann v. Suisse*, Judgment of 25 Apr. 2006, §52; hudoc; *Chauvy and Others v. France*, Judgment of 29 Sep. 2004, §66; Reports of Judgments and Decisions 2004-VI.
93. *Tarsasag a Szabadsagjogokert v. Hungary*, Judgment of 14 Apr. 2009, §27; hudoc; *Riolo v. Italie*, Judgment of 17 Jul. 2008, §63; hudoc.
94. *Sdružení Jihočeské Matky v. la République Tchèque*, Judgment of 10 Jul. 2006; hudoc; *Kenedi v. Hungary*, Judgment of 26 Aug. 2009, §§40–45; hudoc. *See* further L. Loucaides, *The Right to Information*, in *id.*, *Topics of Cypriot Law II* 143–156 (1988).
95. *Leander v. Sweden*, Judgment of 26 Mar. 1987, §§71–74; Series A No. 116.
96. *Loiseau v. France*, Judgment of 28 Nov. 2003; Reports of Judgments and Decisions 2003-XII (extracts); *Mustafa and Tarzibachi v. Sweden*, Judgment of 16 Mar. 2009, §41; hudoc.
97. *See*, e.g., *De Haes and Gijsels v. Belgium*, Judgment of 24 Feb. 1997, §37; Reports 1997-I.
98. *See*, e.g., *Prager and Oberschlick v. Austria*, Judgment of 26 Apr. 1995, §38; Series A No. 313; *Kulis v. Poland*, Judgment of 18 Mar. 2008, §38; hudoc.

nature and thus contribute to the exchange of ideas and opinions, as this is essential for a democratic society.[99] Freedom of expression also applies to civil servants. Accordingly, any limitations on such freedom on account of their status will be assessed by the ECtHR in order to determine whether a fair balance has been struck between the fundamental right of the individual to freedom of expression and the legitimate interest of a democratic State in ensuring that its civil service properly furthers its purposes.[100] Freedom of expression further applies to trade unions who seek to express their demands to their employers.[101]

58. The rights enshrined under Article 19 of the Constitution of Cyprus further extend to commercial speech.[102] In *Papakyriacou Ltd* the Appellant was convicted at first instance for advertising and promoting the sale of goods at a reduced price. The first instance court had concluded that the limitation to the freedom of expression was necessary for the protection of the rights of others, and in particular for safeguarding the rights of consumers. The Supreme Court reversed the conviction and held that the prohibition of advertisement did not protect the consumers in any way since the sale of goods at reduced prices was lawful. On the contrary, the prohibition of advertisement might prove to be detrimental to the interests of consumers, since they might not be promptly informed about the sale of goods at reduced prices. Furthermore, the prohibition of advertisement was not necessary for the protection of the rights of other sellers and competitors of the Appellant, since they only had a right to not be subject to unfair competition.[103]

59. No licence is required for the issue and publication of a newspaper, or for the exercise of freedom of expression.[104] However, Article 19, paragraph 5 of the Constitution authorizes the Republic to require, if it so deems appropriate, the licensing of sound and vision broadcasting or cinema enterprises, as there are limited resources for sound and vision broadcasting (*see* on this Part III, Chapter 2). This is permissible under Article 10 of the ECHR which provides that Member States may require the licensing of broadcasting, television or cinema enterprises. Clearly, any requirements concerning licensing should be reasonable and non-discriminatory. Another important provision with respect to freedom of the press is Article 19, paragraph 4 of the Constitution which provides that seizure of newspapers or other printed material is not allowed without the written permission of the Attorney General of the Republic. Such permission must be confirmed by the decision of a competent court within a period not exceeding seventy-two hours, failing which the seizure shall be lifted. In general, any restrictions to the freedom of the press should be interpreted as narrowly as possible.

---

99. *Karataş v. Turkey*, Judgment of 8 Jul. 1999, §49; Reports of Judgments and Decisions 1999-IV; *Alinak v. Turkey*, Judgment of 29 Mar. 2005, §42; hudoc.
100. *Vogt v. Germany* [GC], Judgment of 26 Sep. 1995, §43; Series A No. 323.
101. *Palomo Sanchez and Others v. Spain*, Judgment of 12 Sep. 2011, §56; Reports of Judgments and Decisions 2011.
102. *A. M. Papakyriacou Ltd v. Police* [1997] 2 CLR 397 (in Greek).
103. *Ibid.*
104. *Republic v. Telegraphos Publishing Co Ltd* [1975] 3 CLR 394.

§2. Limitations upon Freedom of Speech

60. The right to freedom of expression is not, however, an absolute one. In accordance with paragraph 3 of Article 19 of the Constitution, the exercise of the aforementioned rights may be subject to such formalities, conditions, restrictions or penalties as are prescribed by law and are necessary *only* in the interests of the security of the Republic or the constitutional order or the public safety or the public order or the public health or the public morals, or for the protection of the reputation or rights of others, or for preventing the disclosure of information received in confidence, or for maintaining the authority and impartiality of the judiciary. In addition, any such restriction should be considered to be necessary in a democratic society. The following main principles thus govern freedom of expression: (a) freedom is the rule and restriction is the exception; (b) restriction should be provided by law; (c) restriction should be necessary for a constitutionally prescribed legitimate aim; and (d) restriction should be proportional to the legitimate aim pursued within a democratic society.

61. For a norm to be regarded as a 'law' it should be formulated with sufficient precision so as to enable the citizen to foresee to a reasonable degree the consequences that a given action may entail in order to regulate his conduct. Foreseeability does not imply absolute certainty, as legislation by its nature needs to be interpreted and applied in light of the specific circumstances of each case. Persons who carry on a professional activity, such as publishing or journalism, should be expected to take special care in assessing the risk that their occupational activity entails.[105] The law should further indicate with sufficient clarity the scope of any discretion conferred on the competent authorities and the manner of exercise of such discretion.[106]

62. The Supreme Court has categorized the causes in respect of which freedom of expression may be limited into three sub-groups:[107] (a) the integrity of the State (this includes the grounds of state security, public safety, constitutional order and public order); (b) social harmony (this includes the grounds of public health, public morals, the protection of the reputation or rights of others[108] and the preservation of confidential information); and (c) justice (this includes the ground of authority and

105. *Lindon, Otchakovsky–Laurens and July v. France* [GC], Judgment of 22 Oct. 2007, §41; Reports of Judgments and Decisions 2007-IV; *Cantoni v. France*, Judgment of 15 Nov. 1996, §35; Reports of Judgments and Decisions 1996-V; *Delfi As v. Estonia*, Judgment of 10 Oct. 2013, §72; hudoc. *See also Sanoma Uitgevers BV v. the Netherlands* [GC], Judgment of 14 Sep. 2010, §81–100; hudoc.

106. *See* on this *Sunday Times v. the United Kingdom*, Judgment of 26 Apr. 1979, §§48–52; Series A No. 30; *Tolstoy Miloslavsky v. the United Kingdom*, Judgment of 13 Jul. 1995, §§37–44; Series A No. 316-B; *Rotaru v. Romania*, Judgment of 4 May 2000, §§53, 55–62; Reports of Judgments and Decisions 2000-V.

107. *Ibid.*

108. It was further stressed that the concept of 'rights of others' connotes rights which are legal rights, i.e., known to the law. It was thus held that the law acknowledges no right to any citizen for the enjoyment of the confidence of others. *See* on this *Police v. Ekdotiki Eteria Inomeni Dimosiographiki Dias Ltd* [1982] 2 CLR 63.

impartiality of the judiciary). In *Police v. Dias*, the Full Bench of the Supreme Court unanimously held that Article 19 enumerates exhaustively the causes in respect of which freedom of speech and expression may be limited.[109] Any other limitations of freedom of speech should be accordingly struck down as unconstitutional. It was further held that legislation which purports to limit fundamental rights is *ipso facto* of a temporary character. Therefore, even if the limitation was permissible at the time it was introduced by legislation in light of national or social realities prevailing at the time of enactment, it may still be declared unconstitutional if the grounds justifying its enactment have in the meantime disappeared. In order to declare whether a legislative measure was 'necessary' for the purposes of Article 19, paragraph 3 of the Constitution, there should be a serious, though not inevitable, risk that one or more of the causes defined therein will be imperilled.

63. In *Dias*, it was further held that the Constitution extends to both true and false statements.[110] The right of freedom of speech and expression is thus not qualified by the truth and accuracy of the content of the expression. However, whereas truth may be tolerated even where it appears to be damaging to, for example, state security, no such justification exists for suffering falsity in similar circumstances. Consequently, it was held that intolerance to false news or information, which is damaging to the causes for which freedom of speech and expression may be limited in accordance with the Constitution, is not intrinsically derogatory to the exercise of the right.

64. The issue at hand was the constitutionality of section 50, paragraph 1 of the Criminal Code, Cap. 154, which criminalized the publication of false news or information that may impair public order or the confidence of the public in the state or its organs. The Supreme Court drew a distinction between the institution of the State and the persons exercising state power. It was therefore held that, whereas it is legitimate under Article 19, paragraph 3 of the Constitution to limit freedom of expression, in order to sustain confidence in the institution of government, this would not be the case if the aim was to sustain confidence of the public in the holders of state offices. Any attempt to restrict criticism towards the holder of the institution would unduly limit freedom of expression. The holders of state offices, such as ministers, are, therefore, in their personal capacity, outside the notion of 'constitutional order' for the purposes of Article 19, paragraph 3 of the Constitution. With this clarification in mind, the Court unanimously held that the impugned legislation was constitutional, as it was necessary for the protection of State security and public order.

65. In previous rulings the Supreme Court held that section 51, paragraph 1 of the Criminal Code, Cap. 154, which criminalized publications and statements that encourage recourse to violence or promote feelings of ill will between different classes or communities or persons in the Republic, was constitutional.[111] It was held

109. *Police v. Ekdotiki Eteria Inomeni Dimosiographiki Dias Ltd* [1982] 2 CLR 63.
110. *Ibid.*
111. *Papadopoulos v. Republic* [1980] 2 CLR 10; *HjiNicolaou v. Police* [1976] 2 CLR 63.

that the restriction was necessary in the interests of the constitutional order and the public order, of the security of the Republic and of the rights of others. Taking into account the defences provided in section 51, paragraph 1 of Cap. 154, which expressly excluded from its ambit statements made in good faith to show that the Government had been misled or mistaken or had erred in its policies or legislation, the restriction to the freedom of expression was held to be in accordance with the principle of proportionality. Hate speech is generally considered a legitimate restriction of freedom of speech since the protection or reputation of others is a ground for restricting freedom of speech.[112] There are several legislative provisions which restrict and/or punish hate speech. If any offence has been committed against a group of persons due to bias against their race, colour, national or ethnic descent, religious or other beliefs, sexual orientation or gender identity, a Court may consider such a bias as an aggravating factor during the sentencing and imposition of any penalty. The Supreme Court has generally defined hate speech within the context also of the Council Framework Decision 2008/913/JHA,[113] as any speech publicly inciting to violence or hatred directed against a group of persons or a member of such a group defined by reference to race, colour, religion, descent or national or ethnic origin.[114]

66. In assessing whether the interference was necessary in a democratic society the Supreme Court should assess: whether the interference corresponded to a pressing social need; whether it was proportionate to the legitimate aim pursued; and whether the reasons given by the authorities to justify it are relevant and sufficient.[115] The potential impact of the medium of expression is an important factor in determining whether the interference is proportionate; the audiovisual media have a more immediate and powerful effect than the print media, and this is a factor to be taken into account when assessing the proportionality of the interference.[116] The nature and severity of the penalty or fine imposed are also factors to be taken into account when assessing the proportionality of the interference.[117] The sanction

112. *Lenis v. Greece*, Judgment of 31 Aug. 2023; hudoc.
113. Of 28 Nov. 2008 on combating certain forms and expressions of racism and xenophobia by means of criminal law, as enacted in Cyprus by Law 134(I)/2011.
114. *Police v. AA*, Crim. App. 4/21, Judgment of 1.7.2021 (in Greek).
115. *See*, e.g., *Sunday Times v. the United Kingdom*, Judgment of 26 Apr. 1979, §62; Series A No. 30; *Lehideux and Isorni v. France* [GC], Judgment of 23 Sep. 1998, §51; Reports 1998-VII. *See also Freedom of Expression of Journalists and Cartoonists. Protection and Restrictions of the Right under Greek and Cypriot Law* (S. Aktypis, P. Jougleux, T.E. Synodinou eds, Sakkoulas, 2016, in Greek).
116. *Jersild v. Denmark* [GC], Judgment of 23 Sep. 1994, §31; Series A No. 298; *Murphy v. Ireland*, Judgment of 10 Jul. 2003, §69; Reports of Judgments and Decisions 2003-IX (extracts); *TV Vest AS & Rogaland Pensjonistparti v. Norway*, Judgment of 11 Dec. 2008, §60; Reports of Judgments and Decisions 2008.
117. *Ceylan v.Turkey* [GC], Judgment of 8 Jul. 1999, §37; Reports of Judgments and Decisions 1999-IV; *Tammer v. Estonia*, Judgment of 6 Feb. 2001, §69; Reports of Judgments and Decisions 2001-I; *Perna v. Italy* [GC], Judgment of 6 May 2003, §39; Reports of Judgments and Decisions 2003-V; *Radio Twist AS v. Slovakia*, Judgment of 19 Dec. 2006, §53; Reports of Judgments and Decisions 2006-XV.

should not be such as to have a chilling effect on the exercise of journalistic freedom of expression.[118] However, a criminal measure as a response to defamation is not considered *by itself* as disproportionate to the aim pursued.[119]

67. It is considered that restrictions are more difficult to justify in the area of political speech or debate or in matters of public interest, where freedom of expression is of paramount importance.[120] It has been further held that the limits of acceptable criticism are wider as regards a politician, rather than with regard to a private individual, because it is considered that the former knowingly makes himself available to close scrutiny by journalists and the public at large, and he/she should consequently display a greater degree of tolerance, especially when they make public statements that are themselves susceptible to criticism.[121] A possible failure of a public figure to observe laws and regulations aimed at safeguarding important public interests, even in the private sphere, may constitute a matter of legitimate public interest.[122] The right of the public to be informed may thus, in certain circumstances, even extend to aspects of the private life of public figures insofar as the legitimate expectations of such persons to enjoy some protection of their private life are not hindered.[123] Private individuals may also lay themselves to close scrutiny once they participate in the arena of public debate.[124]

68. In order to assess the justification of an impugned statement, the Supreme Court, adopting the jurisprudence of the ECtHR, has drawn a distinction between statement of facts and value judgments. While the existence of facts can be demonstrated, the requirement to prove the truth of a value judgment is impossible to

---

118. *Cumpana and Mazare v. Romania* [GC], Judgment of 17 Dec. 2004, §114; Reports of Judgments and Decisions 2004-XI; *Mahmudov and Agazade v. Azerbaijan*, Judgment of 18 Dec. 2008, §49; hudoc; *Kaperzynski v. Poland*, Judgment of 3 Jul. 2012, §70; hudoc.
119. *Radio France and Others v. France*, Judgment of 30 Mar. 2004, §40; Reports of Judgments and Decisions 2004-II; *Rumyana Ivanova v. Bulgaria*, Judgment of 14 Feb. 2008, §68; hudoc.
120. *Alithia Publishing Company Ltd v. Aloneftis* [2002] 1 CLR 1863 (in Greek). *See* further *Brasilier v. France*, Judgment of 11 Apr. 2006, §41; hudoc; *Surek v. Turkey* [GC], Judgment of 8 Jul. 1999, §61; Reports of Judgments and Decisions 1999-IV; *Wingrove v. the United Kingdom*, Judgment of 25 Nov. 1996, §58; *United Communist Party of Turkey and others v. Turkey*, Judgment of 30 Jan. 1998, §45; Reports 1998-I.
121. *Drousiotis v. Papadopoulos* [2012] 1 CLR 102 (in Greek); *Themistokleous v. Koulias* [2012] 1 CLR 76 (in Greek). *See* further *Lingens v. Austria*, Judgment of 8 Jul. 1986, §42; Series A No. 113; *Vides Aizsardzības Klubs v. Lettonie*, Judgment of 27 May 2004, §40; hudoc; *Brasilier v. France*, Judgment of 11 Apr. 2006, §41; hudoc; *Scharsach and News VerlagsgessellschaftmbH v. Austria*, Judgment of 13 Nov. 2003, §30; Reports of Judgments and Decisions 2003-XI.
122. *Fressoz and Roire v. France* [GC], Judgment of 21 Jan. 1999, §50; Reports of Judgments and Decisions 1999-I; *Tønsbergs Blad A.S. and Haukom v. Norway*, Judgment of 1 Mar. 2007, §87; hudoc.
123. *Editions Plon v. France*, Judgment of 18 May 2004, §53; Reports of Judgments and Decisions 2004-IV; *Von Hannover v. Germany*, Judgment of 24 Jun. 2004, §64; Reports of Judgments and Decisions 2004-VI; *Standard Verlags GmbH v. Austria (No. 2)*, Judgment of 4 Jun. 2009, §48.
124. *See* on this *Nilsen and Johnsen v. Norway*, Judgment of 25 Nov. 1999; Reports of Judgments and Decisions 1999-VIII. With respect to companies *see Fayed v. the United Kingdom*, Judgment of 21 Sep. 1994, §75; Series A No. 294-B; *Steel and Morris v. the United Kingdom*, Judgment of 15 May 2005, §94; Reports of Judgments and Decisions 2005-II, *Markt Intern Verlag GmbH and Klaus Beermann v. Germany*, Judgment of 20 Nov. 1989, §§33–38; Series A No. 165, *Timpul Info-Magazin and Anghel v. Moldova*, Judgment of 27 Nov. 2007, §34; hudoc.

fulfil since value judgments are not susceptible to proof.[125] Where allegations are made about the conduct of a third party, it may sometimes be difficult to distinguish between statements of fact and value judgments. In any event, even where a statement amounts to a value judgment, there must exist a sufficient factual basis to support it,[126] consisting of generally known facts, basic verification or independent research.[127] In this respect, it has been held that requiring an individual to prove the truth of her statements, while depriving her of the opportunity to adduce evidence in order to support such statements, and thereby show that the statements constituted a fair comment, would amount to a disproportionate interference with his/her freedom of expression.[128]

§3. Freedom of Speech and Judicial Proceedings

I. Contempt

69. Article 162 of the Constitution provides that the Supreme Court shall have jurisdiction to impose a punishment for any contempt of itself. Any other court of the Republic shall have the power to commit any person disobeying a judgment or order of such court to prison, until such person complies with such judgment or order, in any event for a period not exceeding twelve months. The power of imposing punishment for contempt has always been regarded as an inherent power of the courts, a power which is founded upon immemorial usage. The notion of contempt is further expanded in section 44 of the Courts of Justice Law 14/60, where, *inter alia*, acts of disrespect, obstruction or disturbance of any judicial proceedings, including publications which are capable of prejudicing the fair trial of such proceedings, are penalized, and wrongdoers are held liable to imprisonment up to six months.[129]

70. The case of *Kyprianou* is of particular importance in this respect. Michalakis Kyprianou, an advocate and a former member of the House of Representatives, was defending two persons who were accused of murder before the Assize

125. *See*, e.g., *Lingens v. Austria*, Judgment of 8 Jul. 1986, §46; Series A No. 113; *Oberschlick v. Austria*, Judgment of 23 May 1991, §63; Series A No. 204.

126. *Pedersen and Baadsgaard v. Denmark* [GC], Judgment of 17 Dec. 2004, §76; Reports of Judgments and Decisions 2004-XI; *Lindon, Otchakovsky–Laurens and July v. France* [GC], Judgment of 22 Oct. 2007, §55; Reports of Judgments and Decisions 2007-IV; cf. *De Haes and Gijsels v. Belgium*, Judgment of 24 Feb. 1997, §§42, 47–48; Reports 1997-I.

127. *See* on this *Novaya Gazeta and Borodyanskiy v. Russia*, Judgment of 28 Mar. 2013, §§40–41; hudoc.

128. *Jerusalem v. Austria*, Judgment of 27 May 2001; Reports of Judgments and Decisions 2001-II; *Colombani and Others v. France*, Judgment of 25 Jun. 2002; Reports of Judgments and Decisions 2002-V.

129. A. Emilianides, *Reflections on the Law of Contempt in Light of Recent Cypriot Jurisprudence*, 2 Cyprus Human Rights Law Review 221 (2012); S. Stavrinides, *Contempt of Court in Cyprus*, 2 Cyprus Law Tribune 167 (1991) (in Greek).

Court of Limassol. Kyprianou was conducting the cross-examination of a prosecution witness, when the Court interrupted his questioning, holding that his cross-examination went beyond the extent it could go at that particular stage of the main trial. In response, Kyprianou declared that he stopped his cross-examination, and he asked for leave to withdraw from the case, on the basis that the Court seemed to consider that he was not doing his job properly in defending the accused. His request was denied. At that point, Kyprianou protested that the Court prevented him from conducting his cross-examination in an efficient manner. Kyprianou alleged that, while he was cross-examining the witness, the three members of the Court were talking to each other and they were sending '*ravasakia*' to each other.[130] The Assize Court considered that the words spoken by Kyprianou, and particularly the manner in which they were spoken, constituted contempt in the face of the Court. Eventually, the Assize Court, by majority, sentenced Kyprianou to five days imprisonment.

71. Kyprianou filed an appeal with the Supreme Court. However, his appeal was rejected, since it was considered that the power of courts to punish contempt is connected with their normal function, and the aim of such power is the protection of judicial institutions, which is essential in order to safeguard a fair trial. Kyprianou eventually lodged an application with the ECtHR against the Republic of Cyprus, alleging violations of Article 6 and Article 10 of the ECHR in relation to his conviction and imprisonment for contempt in the face of the court. In addition to finding a violation under Article 6 of the ECHR, the ECtHR held that, albeit discourteous, the applicant's comments were aimed at, and limited to, the manner in which the judges were trying the case, in particular concerning the cross-examination of a witness he was carrying out in the course of defending his client against a charge of murder. Accordingly, the ECtHR considered that the penalty imposed was disproportionately severe on the applicant and that it was capable of having a 'chilling effect' on the performance of lawyers of their duties as defence counsels. The ECtHR's finding of procedural unfairness in the summary proceedings for contempt served to compound that lack of proportionality. Thus, it was held that the Assize Court failed to strike the right balance between the need to protect the authority of the judiciary and the need to protect the applicant's right to freedom of expression.[131]

II. Interference with Judicial Proceedings by Publications in the Press

72. In *Cosmos Press* the appellants were convicted at first instance for interfering with judicial proceedings contrary to section 122, paragraph 6 of the Criminal Code, Cap. 154.[132] The appellants had published in the newspaper *Kypros* a news

---

130. '*Ravasakia*' is a Greek word, which can define either a short and secret letter, or a love letter, or even a short written message with unpleasant results.
131. App. No. 73797/01, *Kyprianou v. Cyprus*, Judgment of 15 Dec. 2005. *See* A. Emilianides, *Contempt in the Face of the Court and the Right to a Fair Trial,* 13 European Journal of Crime, Criminal Law and Criminal Justice 401 (2005).
132. *Cosmos Press Ltd v. Police* [1985] 2 CLR 73.

item which was considered as being calculated to obstruct or influence the proceedings in a criminal case pending before the District Court of Nicosia. The Supreme Court held that the legislative restriction of the freedom of expression was constitutional since its aim was to maintain the authority and impartiality of the judiciary. However, the Court noted that any restriction on the right of expression must be applied in each particular case in a manner as favourable as possible to the freedom of the press.

73. In light of the above, it was held that it was not safe in this particular case to hold beyond any reasonable doubt that the news item, in relation to which the appellants were convicted, was calculated or was likely to obstruct or influence the proceedings in the District Court. It was therefore accepted that exceptions to the freedom of the press must be narrowly construed, as the media have a task of publishing information and ideas concerning cases that come before the Courts, and the public also has a right to receive them. For a criminal offence to take place it has to be proved beyond reasonable doubt that the article in question was intended or calculated to prejudice the judicial proceedings.[133]

74. The issue was considered in more detail by the Full Bench of the Supreme Court in *Akkelidou*.[134] The appellant was the Minister of Health of the Republic of Cyprus and an ex officio Chair of the Antinarcotic Council of Cyprus. In her capacity as Chair of the Antinarcotic Council, the appellant had sent a letter to a judge of the District Court with respect to a pending criminal case regarding a drug user. The letter was accompanied by a report showing the progress of the accused in drug rehabilitation, expressing the view that the potential imprisonment of the accused might negate the progress achieved. The first instance court held that the appellant should be convicted for interfering with the judicial process, considering that her, otherwise laudable motive, did not change the fact that her actions were against the law.

75. The majority of the Supreme Court reversed the conviction and held that, whereas it was not permissible for the Minister to send the letter, this act did not amount to a criminal offence, since there was no substantial risk that the course of justice in the proceedings in question would be prejudiced. The communication of the letter simply informed the court about facts, and it would have otherwise been admissible evidence if it had been produced in the proper procedural manner. In justifying its conclusion, and drawing an analogy, the majority of the Supreme Court held that professional judges, contrary to laymen who act as juries, are not influenced by anything said in the media. Consequently, the mere fact that the media covers pending judicial proceedings and that the judges may read or watch this publication does not suffice to hinder the judicial process.[135]

---

133. *See* L. Loucaides, *Freedom of the Press and the Administration of Justice*, in *id.*, *Topics on Cypriot Law* 105–110 (1982, in Greek); A. Kapardis, *Freedom of the Press, Crime Reporting by Newspapers and Criminal Justice*, 1 Cyprus Law Review 1204 (1983).
134. *Akkelidou v. Police* [2005] 2 CLR 249 (in Greek).
135. *Ibid.* Reference to *Att-Gen v. BBC* [1981] AC 303.

III. Freedom of the Press and Fair Trial

76. A related question that might indirectly prejudice freedom of the press was considered by the Full Bench of the Supreme Court of Cyprus in *Fantis.*[136] Before the initiation of the criminal proceedings against him, the accused complained that his right to a fair trial had been violated because negative publications, which were detrimental to his case, had been circulated in the press. If it was accepted that publications might influence the continuation of judicial proceedings, this might cause journalists and the media to be more reluctant to publish anything about pending judicial proceedings, having the effect that journalists would impose on themselves a kind of self-censorship. The majority of the Supreme Court held that, whereas the media sometimes present pending judicial proceedings in a manner which is not permissible, they are not actors in the judicial proceedings, and a trial should not come to an end simply because there has been some form of 'trial by media'. The crucial consideration was that a different approach would negate the judicial process. In subsequent cases, it was clarified that the right to a free trial safeguards the carrying out of a trial and not its abolition due to negative publications in the press.[137]

77. A different question was considered by the Supreme Court in *Constantinides.*[138] The appellant, editor-in-chief of a daily newspaper, filed a libel action against a competitive newspaper regarding an article published by one of its columnists. His action was, however, dismissed, hence he filed an appeal. Before his appeal was heard by the Supreme Court, he wrote five articles in his newspaper attacking the impartiality of the judges who tried the case at first instance and accusing them of dishonesty, also casting doubt on the integrity of the justice system as a whole. The Supreme Court held that the appellant had sought to vindicate himself by a trial through the press and that a litigant, however, cannot seek the intervention of the Court while at the same time questioning its impartiality. The Supreme Court noted that the public and the press have a right to criticize judicial action and act as 'the watchdogs of judicial standards'. Thus, rigorous criticism will not constitute contempt, if it was made bona fide in the interests of the public. However, in this case the appellant was not exercising freedom of the press so as to criticize judicial action, but he was expressing a personal grievance. This behaviour was held to amount to abuse of process, and accordingly, the appeal was stayed until the appellant was restored by appropriate action, i.e., an apology, the authority of the Court to do justice in the case.

78. The subsequent *Efstathiou* case concerned an appeal of the Attorney General of the Republic of Cyprus against a highly publicized first instance judgment of the Assize Court, which acquitted ten policemen from charges of beating two Cypriot students. The verdict of acquittal led to reactions and protests across Cyprus, with the Attorney General of the Republic himself harshly criticizing the first

136. *Police v. Fantis* [1994] 2 CLR 160 (in Greek).

137. *Republic v. Ford* [1995] 2 CLR 232 (in Greek); *Attorney-General v. Sidereniou and others* [2008] 2 CLR 319 (in Greek); *Attorney-General v. Efstathiou* [2009] 2 CLR 501 (in Greek).

138. *Constantinides v. Vima and Others* [1983] 1 CLR 348.

instance Court, expressing his disappointment and partial distrust for the justice system, and declaring that the acquittal amounted to an endorsement of state terrorism. The Full Bench of the Supreme Court held that the statements of the Attorney General questioned the foundations of the justice system and were inappropriate for an institution of such importance as the Attorney General. However, in light of the statement of the Attorney General before the Supreme Court that he does not question the integrity or impartiality of the judges of the Assize Court, and that he has the utmost respect for the justice system, the Court found that there was no need to stay the appeals like in *Constantinides*.[139]

79. The general approach of the Supreme Court that publications in the press may not prejudice the trial to such a degree as to abolish it is a reasonable one. A different conclusion might enable the media to, either negligently or deliberately, abolish pending trials by publishing reports and articles which are adverse to the interests of the parties of the trial. This would indirectly hinder freedom of the press, while at the same time, it would enable the press to unduly influence the outcome of pending judicial proceedings by effectively abolishing them. The above notwithstanding, it is submitted that the press should exercise reasonable self-constraint so as to not undermine the right to a fair trial, which is as important a part of a democratic society as freedom of expression itself.[140]

IV. The Press and Freedom of the Journalists

80. The Supreme Court of Cyprus has adopted the principles of the jurisprudence of the ECtHR in assessing the freedom of the press and the limits of journalistic freedom. It has therefore been held that scrutiny of the factual basis that a journalist relies upon is not inconsistent with Article 19 of the Constitution. Even with respect to press coverage of matters of serious public concern and of political figures, the exercise of the freedom of the press carries with it duties and responsibilities, which are of significance when there is harm to the reputation of individuals, insofar as failing to fulfil such duties might undermine the 'rights of others'.[141] Freedom of the press is therefore subject to the proviso that the journalists are acting in good faith in order to provide reliable and accurate information in accordance with the ethics of journalism.[142] The Supreme Court will not substitute its own views for those of the press as to what technique of reporting should be adopted, as methods of objective and balanced reporting may vary considerably; it

139. *Attorney-General v. Efstathiou* [2009] 2 CLR 501 (in Greek).

140. K. Ebeku, *Revisiting the Acquittal of 10 Policemen: Issues of Judicial Independence, Trial by Media and Fair Trial in Cyprus*, 18 European Journal of Crime, Criminal Law and Criminal Justice 1 (2010).

141. *See*, e.g., *Pfeifer v. Austria*, Judgment of 15 Nov. 2007; hudoc; *Flux v. Moldova*, Judgment of 29 Jul. 2008, §26; hudoc; *Von Hannover v. Germany*, Judgment of 24 Sept. 2004; Reports of Judgments and Decisions 2004-VI.

142. *Constantinou and another v. Karamesini* [2011] 1 CLR 715 (in Greek), *Ekdoseis Arktinos Ltd v. Papaefstathiou* [2007] 1 CLR 856 (in Greek). *See* further *Bladet Tromsø and Stensaas v. Norway* [GC], Judgment of 20 May 1999, §65; Reports of Judgments and Decisions 1999-III; *Radio France*

may, however, assess whether the research done by the journalist before the publication of an untrue statement of fact was in good faith and whether it complied with the ordinary journalistic obligation to verify factual allegations.[143]

81. Recent case-law would suggest that the aim is to balance freedom of the press with an emerging right to the reputation of the parties affected.[144] The more serious the allegation is, the more solid the factual basis should be,[145] since the press may be required to provide a sufficient factual basis for their assertions.[146] The obligation of the press to verify factual statements that are defamatory of private individuals may not be dispensed, unless there are special grounds which depend on the nature and degree of the defamation in question and on the extent to which the press could reasonably regard its sources as reliable with respect to the allegations.[147] Whether the effort to verify the statements was sufficient will be assessed on the basis of the situation as presented to the applicant at the material time, rather than with the benefit of hindsight.[148]

82. With respect to news reporting based on interviews, a wider degree of protection is afforded to journalists. The punishment of a journalist for assisting in the dissemination of statements made by another person in an interview would seriously diminish the contribution of the press to the debate of matters of public interest, and it should not be envisaged unless there are compelling reasons for doing so.[149] The subject-matter of trials and court proceedings may also be reported and commented on by the media and the public has a right to receive such information.[150] Different

---

and Others v. France, Judgment of 30 Mar. 2004, §37; Reports of Judgments and Decisions 2004-II; *Colombani and Others v. France*, Judgment of 25 Jun. 2002, §65; Reports of Judgments and Decisions 2002-V; *Stoll v. Switzerland* [GC], Judgment of 10 Dec. 2007; Reports of Judgments and Decisions 2007-V.

143. *Krone Verlag GmbH v. Austria*, Judgment of 19 Jun. 2012, §§46–47; hudoc; *Novaya Gazeta and Borodyanskiy v. Russia*, Judgment of 28 Mar. 2013, §37; hudoc.
144. *Mavros v. Papapetrou,* Civil App. 59/2012, Judgment of 29 May 2018 (in Greek), *Constantinou and another v. Karamesini* [2011] 1 CLR 715, *Themistokleous v. Koulias* [2012] 1 CLR 76 (in Greek). This was the position advocated by former Cypriot Judge of the Court L. Loucaides, *Freedom of Expression and the Right to Respect Private Life*, 6 Cyprus and European Law Review 449 (2008).
145. *Rumyana Ivanova v. Bulgaria*, Judgment of 14 Feb. 2008, §64; hudoc; *Pedersen and Baadsgaard v. Denmark* [GC], Judgment of 17 Dec. 2004, §78; Reports of Judgments and Decisions 2004-XI.
146. *Lesnik v. Slovakia*, Judgment of 11 Mar. 2003, §57; Reports of Judgments and Decisions 2003-IV; *Cumpana and Mazare v. Romania* [GC], Judgment of 17 Dec. 2004, §101; Reports of Judgments and Decisions 2004-XI.
147. *McVicar v. the United Kingdom*, Judgment of 7 Aug. 2002, §84; Reports of Judgments and Decisions 2002-III; *Pedersen and Baadsgaard v. Denmark* [GC], Judgment of 17 Dec. 2004, §78; Reports of Judgments and Decisions 2004-XI; *Aleksey Ovchinnikov v. Russia*, Judgment of 16 Dec. 2010, §42; hudoc.
148. *Bladet Tromsø and Stensaas v. Norway* [GC], Judgment of 20 May 1999, §66; Reports of Judgments and Decisions 1999-III; *Flux v. Moldova*, Judgment of 29 Jul. 2008, §26; hudoc.
149. *Jersild v. Denmark* [GC], Judgment of 23 Sep. 1994, §35; Series A No. 298; *Kulis v. Poland*, Judgment of 18 Mar. 2008, §38; hudoc.
150. *Springer AG v. Germany* [GC], Judgment of 7 Feb. 2012, §80; hudoc; *News Verlags GmbH & Co. KG v. Austria*, Judgment of 11 Apr. 2000, §56; Reports of Judgments and Decisions 2000-I; *Campos Dâmaso v. Portugal*, Judgment of 24 Apr. 2008, §31; hudoc.

standards, however, apply with respect to press reports concentrating on sensational and lurid news which aim to titillate and entertain rather than to inform, and which refer to aspects of a person's strictly private life.[151] In such cases, freedom of expression is interpreted more narrowly, and it does not enjoy the full spectrum of protection afforded to freedom of the press.[152]

151. *Hachette Filipacchi Associés v. France,* Judgment of 14 Jun. 2007; hudoc; *MGN Limited v. the United Kingdom*, Judgment of 18 Apr. 2011; hudoc.

152. *Société Prisma Presse v. France*, Judgment of 1 Jul. 2003; hudoc; *Leempoel & S.A. ED. Ciné Revue v. Belgique*, Judgment of 9 Nov. 2006; hudoc. *See Mosley v. the United Kingdom*, Judgment of 15 Sep. 2011, §114; hudoc.

Part II. Regulation of Print Media

Chapter 1. The Journalists' Profession

§1. The Definition of Journalists in Law 145/1989

83. Section 2 of the Press Law 145/89 defines a 'Cypriot journalist' as a citizen of the Republic, or of an EU Member State, or an alien who has a main and regular occupation, in exchange for a fee, in a newspaper, or in several newspapers, published in the Republic, and who provides exclusively mental work as a director, editor-in-chief, editor, columnist, commenter, reviewer, cartoonist, satirist, caricaturist, photojournalist or corrector, dealing with the collection, editing or correcting of journalistic material. The term also includes newspaper correspondents who are situated in the Republic or abroad, as well as persons who are employed under the same conditions in a news agency which functions in the Republic, or who are employed in the editing of news content for the radio-television broadcasting bulletins of the CyBC. It further includes those servants of the PIO who exercise journalistic work.

84. A 'foreign journalist' is further defined in section 2 of Law 145/89 as an alien (i.e., a person who is not a citizen of Cyprus or of another EU Member State) professional journalist who represents a foreign news agency, radio or TV station in the Republic, or the correspondent or temporary representative of such an organization who has been accredited in the Republic. In order to become accredited as a foreign correspondent in Cyprus, a letter has to be submitted to the Foreign Press Registry of the PIO from the news organization in which the journalist is working, confirming his/her employment in Cyprus as a correspondent of that organization. A press card issued by the relevant authorities of the country of origin and some proof of previous journalistic work are also required. A Foreign Correspondent press card is normally issued within ten days from submission of the necessary documents. The Foreign Press Registry of the PIO is established by section 6 of Law 145/89, which provides that all foreign journalists who exercise their profession in the Republic should be therein registered, with the exception of those who visit the Republic for special purposes and for a period not exceeding one month. The application for registration should be submitted within a month from the entry of the foreign journalist in the Republic.

85. The definition of the term 'newspaper' is also of significance. Section 2 of Law 145/89 defines a newspaper as any printed form which aims to inform the public, which is published daily or in longer regular intervals of up to a month maximum, and which contains material of general political and social interest, in particular, news, reviews, studies, articles or readings on issues of public concern, as well as classifieds and advertisements. Unless otherwise defined in the Law, the term newspaper also includes periodicals. These are defined as printed forms which are published in regular intervals, at least once every four months, and whose content may not be described as that of a newspaper.

86. The above definitions give rise to certain observations. To begin with, the differentiation between a 'Cypriot journalist' and a 'foreign journalist' is a curious one. An alien is treated as a Cypriot journalist if he/she is occupied in a newspaper or periodical published in the Republic, even if such newspaper or periodical is published in a language other than the official languages of the Republic, and even if it is owned by non-Cypriots. A person is further considered a Cypriot journalist if he/she works as a journalist in a news agency (even a foreign one) which functions in the Republic. However, he/she is treated as a foreigner if he/she is occupied in the Republic for a foreign news agency (although he could be well considered as a Cypriot journalist in accordance with the definition of the Law) or radio or TV station. Why is such a distinction necessary or reasonable? If alien journalists are being treated in the same way as Cypriot journalists for the purposes of foreign newspapers and periodicals or the Cypriot news agency, why should they be treated in a different manner if they are employed in foreign news agencies or foreign radio or TV stations? Clearly, the distinction is not required for immigration purposes, as a work permit would be required for both aliens who work as journalists for the Cypriot news agency and those who work as journalists for a foreign news agency. In any event, if the purpose is to introduce a discretionary power of the PIO to choose which foreign correspondents to accredit, then it should be considered whether such an obligation is in accordance with Articles 19 and 25 of the Constitution, which safeguard freedom of the press and freedom to exercise a trade or profession respectively.[153]

87. It should further be observed that the definition of a journalist is a wide one, including not only persons who collect and edit news material but also those who correct such news material and cartoonists or caricaturists. It excludes, however, persons who are merely the owners or publishers of a newspaper. A journalist should have journalism as his main employment and should be employed regularly in the newspaper or journal. The requirement for regularity should be construed widely so as not to unnecessarily exclude part-time employees who do not have another main employment but cannot find regular employment due to limited availability of jobs. However, whereas Law 145/89 includes in the definition of journalists those who are employed in the state-owned CyBC, it excludes the numerous journalists working in

153. K. Kouros, *The Mass Media Law in the Republic of Cyprus*, fn. 51 above, 266 (Vivlioekdotiki 2008) argues that the provision is unconstitutional.

private television and radio stations.[154] It is understandable that in 1989 there were no private radio and TV stations. However, twenty-five years have passed since the Law was adopted, and yet this provision has not been amended in order to cover journalists working in the private radio-television broadcasting sector, despite the fact that the Law itself has since been amended. This is highly problematic. Equally problematic is the exclusion from the definition of all journalists working in electronic news-sites, as the legal definition of a 'journalist' refers only to journalists who are employed in the traditional printed media.

88. Similarly problematic is also the fact that journalists who are citizens of the Republic or of EU Member States, and who are employed for a foreign radio or TV station in the Republic as correspondents, do not fall under the definition of a journalist. This is so because the definition of 'foreign journalists' includes only aliens who are employed for such foreign radio or TV stations who are accredited in the Republic, and it does not include journalists who are Cypriots or EU citizens. The inclusion of public servants who are employed in the PIO as journalists has also been criticized, as it has been argued that journalists should belong to the private sector so as to avoid direct control of the press by state organs. Another argument to the same effect was that journalists who are employed in the public sector would have a conflict of interest in revealing to the public the arbitrary acts of their political supervisors. Whereas this might be true, it is also true that journalists working in the private sector often face similar conflicts of interest with respect to acts of their employers or major advertisers or sponsors of the media they are employed in. Furthermore, it could be argued that journalists employed in the semi-public CyBC, or in newspapers owned by political parties, might well face similar problems. In view of the wide definition of the term, which includes persons who do not exercise journalistic work *sensu stricto*, the inclusion of journalists employed in the PIO does not seem so problematic.

§2. The Union of Cyprus Journalists

89. The UCJ was established in 1960 and has currently more than 500 members who are employed in newspapers, periodicals, R/T station, or in news agencies. Its main objectives are to negotiate collective agreements of the terms of employment and working conditions of its members; to regulate the relations with media owners; to defend freedom of the press and to ensure the independence of journalists and their freedom of expression; and to raise the quality standard of journalism by continuous training and respect for the JEC. The UCJ is a registered trade union and elects its own leadership, an administrative council composed of nine members and chaired by a President who is directly elected by the regular members of the UCJ. In accordance with Article 3 of the Constitution of the UCJ, membership is open to any person, regardless of race, sex, nationality, citizenship or religion, if he/she exercises his/her main profession, from which he/she earns the main income for his/

154. N. Charalambous, *The Freedom to Access the Files of the Administration*, 1 Cyprus Law Tribune 36 (1992) (in Greek).

her livelihood in the employment of a newspaper or of a magazine published regularly in Cyprus, in a news agency registered in Cyprus, a radio or television station of a professional standard which operates in Cyprus, or if he/she works abroad as a correspondent for a Cypriot medium. Journalists who are employed in internet media have also been admitted as members of the UCJ.

90. Members may be employed in editing, proof-reading or managing journalistic material as professional journalists; or in capturing and recording events with photographs or cinematographic images as professional photographers or cameramen, covering the daily and current news, reports and the flow of information. News photographers and cameramen should have at least one year's experience. Members should further be holders of at least a school leaving certificate, not be at the age of retirement, and not have been sentenced to imprisonment for an offence of a dishonourable nature which renders them unfit for membership. They should also abide by the Constitution of the UCJ, by its JEC and by the provisions of the collective agreements which are concluded by the UCJ. A member should be either a citizen of the Republic or an expatriate, or a non-Cypriot if in the last case he/she holds a permit which authorizes him/her to work in Cyprus, and if he/she has been in continuous and full employment with Cypriot media.

91. UCJ members are further classified as Provisional, Regular, Associate or Honorary, in accordance with Article 5 of the Constitution of the UCJ. Members who satisfy the requirements of Article 3 are admitted as provisional members. The latter do not have the right to vote or to be elected, but they are entitled to obtain the UCJ press card. They enjoy the same benefits, as well as have the same obligations, as regular members. In addition to the general requirements, regular members should be: (a) holders of a diploma from a university-level school of journalism who have been employed in the media for at least six months; or (b) diploma holders of another university school or school of journalism (not at a university level) who have been fully employed in the media for at least one year; or (c) holders of a school leaving certificate of secondary education who have been fully employed in the media for at least two full years. Regular members have the right to vote and to be elected to the Administrative Council of the UCJ. Associate members do not have the right to vote or to be elected. They are mainly self-employed as journalists or as news photographers. Honorary membership is open to those who have particularly distinguished themselves for their intellectual, cultural, social or political activity, and for their contribution to society and to the country.

92. It is further provided that professional press correspondents, whether Cypriot or foreign, working with non-Cypriot mass media, who are based and reside in Cyprus, may register with the UCJ as members of an autonomous Foreign Correspondents' Sector associated with the UCJ (Article 24 of the Constitution of the UCJ). These members shall not have the right to vote and to be elected to the various organs of the UCJ, but they shall elect their own Committee, which will take care of issues concerning the foreign correspondents in Cyprus and the journalistic profession, and which shall cooperate in this respect with the Administrative Council of the UCJ.

Chapter 2. Journalists' Rights

§1. Role of Journalists as Watchdogs of Society

93. The Supreme Court has repeatedly made reference to the role of journalists as the watchdogs of society and of the courts themselves,[155] holding that freedom of the press is a blessing in any civilized community and, hence a right which should not be unduly curtailed.[156] Such emphasis on freedom of the press is closely connected with the contribution of the latter to the development of free debate in matters of public interest. It has thus been held that the press, by tradition, is considered as the fourth power in a State; one which acts as a guardian of the public interest against government arbitrariness.[157] In *Drousiotis* the Court held that a free, brave, courageous, but also responsible, journalism may alleviate several problems of a modern society.[158] The role of the press as a public watchdog in a democratic society is more important with respect to political persons and public figures insofar as these knowingly enter the public arena as politicians, major corporations or businessmen, as persons who engage in public debate, etc. Such public status doctrine does not extend to persons who are not public figures. Thus, in *Karamesini* it was held that the mere fact that the plaintiff had presented a widely discussed musical composition does not imply that she is a public figure.[159]

94. The following passage from *Hadjidemetriou* is relevant:[160]

> The press is a very important element in modern society. It renders an important service to the public. The press is rightly considered as the defender of freedom of opinion in the whole spectrum of life-political, economic, social, philosophic and literary. The press is often referred to as the fourth power of State. The true freedom of the press, however, implies equal freedom for all. The press has a great responsibility towards its readers and the public at large. True freedom, however, is the one that not only does not overlook but safeguards the freedom of others. The right to freedom of citizens and sections of the public must be justly balanced so that the right of the one is not exercised at the expense of the right of the other. A healthy equilibrium must be maintained between competing rights to freedom of expression.

95. In several judgments the Supreme Court has further adopted certain principles which should be respected by press functionaries. It has thus been held that responsible journalism necessitates the corroboration of the facts of a case or the presentation of the published material in such a way as to serve the public interest, with reference being made only to facts which have been corroborated and not to

155. *Onoufriou and Another v. K.K. Sygxrones Kourses Ltd* [2006] 1 CLR 742 (in Greek).
156. *Papadopoulos v. Kirix Publishing Co Ltd and others* [1963] 2 CLR 290; *Hadjinicolaou v. Police* [1976] 2 CLR 63; *Drousiotis v. Papadopoulos* [2012] 1 CLR 102 (in Greek).
157. *Makrides and another v. Minister of Interior* [1981] 3 CLR 321.
158. *Drousiotis v. Papadopoulos* [2012] 1 CLR 102 (in Greek).
159. *Constantinou and another v. Karamesini* [2011] 1 CLR 715 (in Greek).
160. *Hadjidemetriou v. Telegraphos Publishing Company Ltd and another* [1983] 2 CLR 268.

facts which have not been corroborated and which were not necessary for the publication.[161] Furthermore, it has been held that the press should follow the rule *audi alteram partem*, even if the presentation of all views might be considered as disappointing or disturbing for some members of the public. The right to receive complete and objective information as well as free dissemination of ideas and of opposing positions should not be restricted due to the misguided aim of protecting the audience from reading or listening to the 'wrong' views.[162] Whereas a journalist should in principle contact the affected person before the publication, this principle might be waived in the appropriate case, if on the basis of the facts of the case it is clear that there was no need to act in this way.[163] Moreover, it has been held that the use of media in order to deal with personal issues of the owner or of the editors of the media is contrary to the established principles of serious, honest and objective journalism.[164]

§2. Journalists' Independence

I. The Principle of Independence

96. The JEC (*see* General Introduction, §3 VII above and Chapter 6, §4 in this Part below) was a major step towards self-regulation and towards the independence of journalists. Indeed, the JEC specifically states that the CMCC has the duty to defend the independence of journalists. However, journalists have the obligation to defend their independence, not allowing any interference with their work. Interference in the work of journalists and intimidation, or attempted intimidation, or improper influencing of journalists through (public) statements, or in any other way, is impermissible. It could well be argued that the requirement that the independence of journalists should be safeguarded derives directly from the constitutional protection of freedom of the press. However, undeniably, as is the case with other professions, the true independence of journalists is seriously undermined by their economic dependency on their employers, especially in times of financial crisis. Since 2009, when the financial crisis started in Cyprus, many journalists have been unable to find employment, or they have been fired and remain unemployed or they have voluntarily received significant pay-cuts in order to retain their jobs. Independence becomes a rather empty word if the journalist is unable to sustain himself and his/her family in case he/she does not follow the directions of his/her employer.

II. The Publication and Circulation of Newspapers in the Republic

97. Section 9 of the Press Law 145/89 provides that no previous permit of any authority is required for the publication of a newspaper or of a periodical in the

161. *Phileleftheros Public Company Ltd and another v. Christodoulou* [2007] 1 CLR 856 (in Greek).
162. *Dias Publishing House Public Ltd and another v. Yennari* [2011] 1 CLR 1952 (in Greek).
163. *Eliades v. Venizelou and others* [2009] 1 CLR 960 (in Greek).
164. *Newspaper Apokalypsis of Paphos and others v. Koniotis* [2004] 1 CLR 1847 (in Greek).

Republic by a citizen of the Republic, or by citizens of another EU Member State, or by a legal person which is administered or controlled by citizens of the Republic or by citizens of another EU Member State. It is nevertheless required that, prior to the publication of the newspaper or periodical, an affidavit should be submitted to the Minister of Interior. The affidavit should be signed by the owner of the newspaper or periodical, and it should contain certain data relevant to the newspaper or periodical, such as its name, address, place of publication, ownership, language and frequency of publication.[165] In case the ownership of the newspaper or periodical changes, the new owner has to submit a new affidavit. A person who violates the provisions of section 9 of Law 145/89 is subject to a fine of up to approximately EUR 850.

98. In case the owner of the newspaper is a legal person, the owner of the newspaper shall declare, by virtue of section 11 of Law 145/89, at least three days prior to the commencement of publication, a natural person as the one who shall have the legal responsibility for the newspaper. The person responsible by law should be one of the members of the Board of Directors (BoD) of the legal person. The person responsible by law is subject to any criminal offences under the Press Law or under any other law, irrespective of any concurrent responsibility of the owner of the newspaper. He/she is not, however, presumed to have legal responsibility for the publications in cases of defamation, as the liability of a person for torts should be proved, and accordingly it should be proved, in defamation cases, that he/she approved or encouraged the publications.[166] If an owner fails to declare the person responsible by law, he/she is subject to a fine of up to approximately EUR 425, while the criminal court may order that he/she should make the declaration within ten days. In case he/she still fails to do so, the Minister of Interior may prohibit the publication of the newspaper until the declaration is made.

99. If the newspaper is to be published by an alien section 10 of Law 145/89 provides that a permit should be granted by the Minister of Interior consulting with the Minister of Foreign Affairs. The Minister of Interior may impose terms for the publication of the newspaper; terms which will take into account the security of the Republic; constitutional and public order; public safety and public morals; as well as that the international relations of the Republic are not hindered. A permit may be revoked if any of the terms imposed is violated. It is further provided that any person who violates section 10 of Law 145/89 commits a criminal offence and is liable to imprisonment of up to a year and/or a fine of up to approximately EUR 2,550, while in this case, all copies of the newspaper are subject to seizure.

100. It is submitted that section 10 of Law 145/89 is unconstitutional. It has been held that under Article 19 of the Constitution, no licence is required for the issue and publication of a newspaper, contrary to what is the case with respect to sound

165. By virtue of s. 41 of Law 145/89 the affidavit is considered to be a declaration signed before a court; something that might accordingly lead to prosecution for perjury, in case that the affiant knowingly made false statements.
166. *Kosmos Press Ltd v. Aristidou* [1996] 1 CLR 414 (in Greek).

and vision broadcasting and cinema enterprises, where the Constitution expressly provides that the Republic is not prevented from requiring their licensing.[167] Furthermore, the fundamental rights and liberties provided in Part II of the Constitution are in principle safeguarded for all persons, irrespective of their citizenship.[168] Article 19 of the Constitution does not differentiate with respect to the exercise of freedom of the press between citizens of the Republic and aliens. It is submitted that if there are lawful grounds for restriction of the publication of a newspaper, these cannot be examined in the form of preventive censorship, by requiring a permit for the publication of such newspaper.

101. Following the submission of the affidavit provided for in section 9 of Law 145/89 and the payment of the official fees,[169] the Minister of Interior issues a receipt. The receipt is accepted by the courts as a proof of the content of the affidavit, by virtue of section 12 of Law 145/89. Moreover, the owner of the newspaper for which the affidavit has been filed shall acquire ownership of the title of the newspaper in accordance with section 15 of Law 145/89. The right of ownership of the title of the newspaper shall be extinguished, if the newspaper has not been published for more than a year subsequent to the submission of the affidavit or if the newspaper suspends its publication for more than a year.

102. The above provisions imply that the Minister of Interior should undertake some preliminary examination in order to ascertain that the owner of the newspaper has completed the required data in the affidavit and that the title of the newspaper is available for use. Section 15 of Law 145/89 expressly provides that if the title of the newspaper so resembles an already registered one as to be likely to cause confusion, it may not be used. It is further provided that the publication of a newspaper which bears the title of an existing political party without the written permission of the leader or of the lawful representative of such party is prohibited, as it might mislead the public in considering that the newspaper is an official representative of the political party.

103. It has been held that the affidavit should not be considered a preventive measure, because the administrative authority with which it is deposited has almost no discretion at all to refuse the receipt in question, as the relevant provisions have to be interpreted strictly.[170] In *Telegraphos* the Supreme Court clarified that the Minister of Interior should not be expected to become simply a rubber stamp and disregard the violation of the rights of others, as would be the case if he did not

167. *Republic v. Telegraphos Publishing Co Ltd* [1975] 3 CLR 394; *Kosmos Press Ltd v. Republic* [1971] 3 CLR 387. *See also* C. Tornaritis, *The State Law of the Republic of Cyprus* 151 (Cyprus Research Centre, 1982, in Greek).
168. *Municipal Council of Aghios Dometios v. Christoforou and Others* [1994] 3 CLR 434 (in Greek).
169. These amount to approximately EUR 50 for Cypriot citizens and citizens of Member States of the EU, and to approximately EUR 170 for aliens. There seem to be no reasonable grounds for the aforementioned differentiation in the official fees.
170. *Kosmos Press Ltd v. Republic* [1971] 3 CLR 387; *Makrides and another v. Minister of Interior* [1981] 3 CLR 321. The cases referred to the pre-existing Press Law, Cap. 79. However, the pre-existing law contained identical provisions to the current Press Law on this issue. It was further

examine whether the title of the newspaper violates the proprietary rights of another person and was likely to cause confusion.[171] Thus, such limited discretionary powers granted to the Minister of Interior were held to be in accordance with Article 19 of the Constitution, as they were necessary in order to protect the rights of the proprietor of the title of a newspaper. In *Kosmos Press Ltd* it was further held that a person has no vested right in the title of a newspaper by merely filing an incomplete application.[172]

104. Circulation of newspapers is free by virtue of section 16 of Law 145/89. All copies of a newspaper published in the Republic should compulsorily carry on the top of their page the name and address of the owner; the person legally responsible; and the place of publication of the newspaper, in accordance with section 13 of Law 145/89; while any person who violates this provision is subject to a fine of up to approximately EUR 170 and in case of a second violation of up to approximately EUR 850.[173] The owner of the newspaper should further submit to the Minister a copy of the newspaper within three days from publication by virtue of section 14 of Law 145/89. Failure to do so might result in a fine of up to approximately EUR 170. The circulation of newspapers might be carried out by the publisher himself, or through press agencies and sub-agencies, kiosk owners and newspaper sellers.

105. Press agencies and sub-agencies should receive a licence from the Minister of Interior. By virtue of section 18 of Law 145/89, such licence may be granted only to citizens of the Republic or to citizens of EU Member States or to legal persons who are governed and controlled by citizens of the Republic or by citizens of EU Member States. The press agencies and sub-agencies are required, by virtue of section 20 of Law 145/89, to distribute and sell all newspapers on the same terms, irrespective of the political or other views of the newspaper. They are also required to dispose of such newspapers without discrimination and favouritism. Special terms might, however, be concluded for the distribution and sale of afternoon newspapers or of other newspapers or of periodicals which are published irregularly, if the usual terms seem unprofitable for the press agencies and sub-agencies. The press agencies may distribute the newspapers to the sub-agencies or directly to the kiosk owners and newspaper sellers, whereas the press sub-agencies are required to distribute and sell both the newspapers which are received by the press agencies and the newspapers which are received directly by the publishers.

---

held that the provision in accordance to which the owner of the newspaper had to grant a bond as security for the payment of potential damages for defamation to third persons was not inconsistent with Art. 19 of the Constitution, as it was necessary for the protection of the reputation or the rights of third parties. The current Press Law 145/89 has correctly abolished the requirement for a bond to be granted.

171. *Republic v. Telegraphos Publishing Co Ltd* [1975] 3 CLR 394.

172. *Kosmos Press Ltd v. Republic* [1971] 3 CLR 387.

173. It should be noted that all Cypriot newspapers seem to violate this provision, as they do not carry the relevant details at the top of all their pages.

106. Kiosk owners are further required to sell newspapers distributed to them by both the press agencies and sub-agencies and by the publishers (section 21 of Law 145/89). They are further required to not discriminate between the newspapers and to not enable the reading of newspapers by persons who have not bought them. Other newspaper sellers have the same obligations as kiosk owners; they are further allowed to pronounce publicly in public spaces and streets the title, price, headlines and contributors of a newspaper (section 22 of Law 145/89); they may not, however, pronounce publicly obscene titles or profanity against third persons. Kiosk owners or newspaper sellers who violate their obligations are subject to a fine of no more than approximately EUR 340. Any person who obstructs the free circulation of newspapers is liable to a fine of up to approximately EUR 8,500.

§3. Protection of Journalistic Sources

107. The JEC provides that journalists have a moral obligation to observe professional privilege regarding the source of information obtained confidentially. In any case, a journalist is not required to reveal the source of his/her information. The aforementioned obligation and privilege are moral, not legal. It has been properly argued, however, that there is a constitutional right deriving from Article 19 of the Constitution which safeguards the right of the journalist not to disclose his sources, and that exceptions should occur only if the constitutional requirements are met.[174] Section 8, paragraph 1 of the Press Law 145/89 introduced a legal immunity, providing that any journalist, either Cypriot or non-Cypriot, has the right: to not disclose the sources of the information he/she publishes; to refuse to give testimony; and to not be prosecuted due to such refusal. Accordingly, the protection of journalistic sources is also legally safeguarded. However, section 8, paragraph 2 of Law 145/89 introduces a limited exception to the protection of journalistic sources. It is thereby stipulated that any journalist who published information related to a criminal offence may be forced by the court dealing with this criminal offence, or by the coroner, to reveal his source, if the court or the coroner deems that the following requirements are met:

(a) that the information is relevant to the criminal offence;
(b) that the information cannot otherwise be secured; and
(c) there are superior and imperative grounds of public interest which necessitate the revelation of the source of the information.

108. It is suggested that, whereas the ambit of the exception to the protection of journalist sources should in principle be a narrow one, the wording 'information related to a criminal offence' might be potentially interpreted by the courts in a very wide manner. It is our view that the court should not force the journalist to reveal his/her sources, if the criminal offence in question is the publication of the information itself, e.g., by a public servant. Otherwise, the State might institute criminal

174. L. Loucaides, *The Journalist's Privilege*, in *id.*, *Topics on Cypriot Law* 111–127 (1982, in Greek). *See also Makrides and another v. Minister of Interior* [1981] 3 CLR 321.

offences against a public servant who is allegedly the source of the journalist, and it may subsequently request the court to order the journalist to reveal his/her source, in order to determine whether the public servant has committed the criminal offence of providing the journalist with sensitive information.[175] It is argued that the information published by the journalist should itself be related to a criminal offence, content-wise. Whether the publication of the information might lead to a criminal offence by the informant is not a ground for forcing a journalist to reveal his sources.

109. The protection of journalistic sources is a vital prerequisite of journalistic freedom and of freedom of the press.[176] The ECtHR has considered various cases where journalists were compelled to provide information on their sources, or the State authorities obtained access to journalistic information by circumventing such privilege. It has thus been held that a disclosure order requiring a journalist to reveal the identity of one of his sources who provided him with the information on an anonymous basis, and the fine imposed upon the journalist for having refused to reveal his source, amounted to an interference with the applicant's rights under Article 10 of the ECHR.[177] Orders seeking to disclose sources may have a negative effect not only on the particular source whose identity may be revealed but also on other potential sources who might become unwilling to provide information to journalists. This might undermine the ability of the press to provide accurate and reliable information, having an overall chilling effect on the freedom of the press and on the right of citizens to information.[178] Any order to reveal a journalistic source should be issued by a judicial organ only if there is an overriding public interest. It has further been held that searches of journalists' homes and workplaces seeking to identify the sources that provided journalists with confidential information will amount to an interference with their freedom of expression rights unless there are relevant and sufficient grounds justifying such interference.[179]

175. *See*, e.g., *Secretary of State for Defence and Another v. Guardian Newspapers Ltd* (1984) 1 AllER 453, where the informant was jailed. A more liberal approach in *Attorney-General v. Lundin* (1982) 75 CrAppR 90.

176. *See also* C. Stratilatis, *The Journalist Privilege as a Fundamental Right and the ECtHR Case-Law* in *Freedom of Expression of Journalists and Cartoonists. Protection and Restrictions of the Right under Greek and Cypriot Law* 35–68 (S. Aktypis, P. Jougleux & T.E. Synodinou eds, Sakkoulas, 2016, in Greek), *id.*, *The Right of Journalists Not to Disclose Their Sources and the New Media* in, *EU Internet Law* 339–365 (T.E. Synodinou, P. Jougleux, C. Markou & T. Prastitou eds, Springer, 2016).

177. *Goodwin v. the United Kingdom*, Judgment of 27 Mar. 1996; Reports 1996-II; *Voskuil v. the Netherlands*, Judgment of 22 Nov. 2007; hudoc; *Financial Times Ltd and Others v. the United Kingdom*, Judgment of 15 Dec. 2009; hudoc.

178. *Voskuil v. the Netherlands*, Judgment of 22 Nov. 2007, §65; hudoc.

179. *Nagla v. Latvia*, Judgment of 16 Oct. 2013; hudoc; *Roemen and Schmit v. Luxembourg*, Judgment of 25 Feb. 2003; Reports of Judgments and Decisions 2003-IV; *Ernst et autres v. Belgique*, Judgment of 15 Jul. 2003; hudoc; *Tillack v. Belgium*, Judgment of 27 Nov. 2007; hudoc.

Chapter 3. Journalists' Liability

§1. Criminal Liability

110. Defamation constituted a criminal offence in accordance with sections 194–202 of the Criminal Code, Cap. 154. However, criminal libel, as well as sections 46A–49 and 51 of the Criminal Code, which criminalized certain acts relevant to the exercise of freedom of speech in certain circumstances, were abolished with Law 84(I)/2003, which expressed modern approaches towards the de-criminalization of freedom of speech-related offences. Since 2003, the law of defamation exists solely in the field of private law, and no criminal charges may be brought against journalists or media outlets for defamation. It should be noted, however, that even now some controversial criminal provisions, namely those of sections 50 and 50A of Cap. 154, still remain in force. Section 50 of Cap. 154 criminalizes the publication of false news or information which may impair public order or the confidence of the public in the state or its organs,[180] whereas section 50A of Cap. 154 criminalizes the publication of confidential information relating to works or places used by the armed forces of the Republic.

111. The offence of circulation of blasphemous publications is provided for in section 142 of Cap. 154.[181] It is provided that any person who publishes a book or pamphlet or any article or letter in a newspaper or periodical which any class of persons considers as a public insult to their religion, with the intent to vilify such religion or to shock or to insult believers to such religion, is guilty of a misdemeanour. The good protected by this provision is public order, as well as the religious feelings of believers, which may be offended by the publication. The publication should have an element of vilification, ridicule or irreverence that would be likely to infuriate others. The court must be satisfied that the offender has intended to vilify such religion or shock or insult believers to such religion. The offence applies to all religions. A prosecution for the offence of circulation of such defamatory publication may not be commenced except by, or with the consent of, the Attorney General of the Republic of Cyprus.[182]

112. Another outdated piece of criminal legislation which remains in force refers to the Publication of Obscene Subjects Law 35/1963 which criminalizes the publication of obscene subjects. More specifically, a publication is declared obscene if

180. This provision has been declared as constitutional in *Police v. Ekdotiki Eteria Inomeni Dimosiographiki Dias Ltd* [1982] 2 CLR 63.

181. A. Emilianides, *Religion in the Criminal Law in Cyprus*, in *Religion and Criminal Law* 35–40 (M. Kottiranta & N. Doe eds, Peeters 2013).

182. *See* further A. Emilianides, *Can God Be Offended? The Common Law Offence of Blasphemy and the European Convention on Human Rights*, in *Contemporary Issues and Trends at the Beginning of the 21st Century* 232–239 (Institute for State-Church Relations 2008), *id.*, *Disciplinary Action and Freedom of Artistic Expression* (2022) 1 The Cambridge Journal of Law, Politics and Art 320 (2022). *See*, however, *X Ltd and Y v. the United Kingdom*, Decision of 7 May 1982; 28 Decisions and Reports 77, *Wingrove v. the United Kingdom*, Judgment of 25 Nov. 1996; Reports 1996-V; *Otto Preminger Institut v. Austria*, Judgment of 20 Sep. 1994; Series A No. 295-A.

it tends to lead to the depravity and corruption of persons who might read, watch or listen to such publication.[183] A person might be considered as publishing obscene publications not only if he publishes, distributes, circulates or sells it but also if he imports it, lends it, shows it, or presents it in any way. Proving that the publication contributes to science, literature, and art or is related to other matters of general interest constitutes a defence to the criminal offence, while the defendant may submit as evidence expert opinions on the quality and value of the publication. A high-profile case occurred during the Presidency of Demetris Christofias when the police pressed criminal charges against the well-known editor of a satirical newspaper, which opposed the Government, for a publication which included a photo-collage of former President Christofias containing certain offensive words. The District Court correctly held that such charges against the press could not be justified in the twenty-first century, and it promptly dismissed the charges.[184]

§2. Civil Law Defamation

I. Constitutionality

113. The tort of defamation is covered under sections 17–24 of the Civil Wrongs Law, Cap. 148, whereas section 25 of Cap. 148 deals with the tort of injurious falsehood.[185] In *Aloneftis* the appellants argued that the provisions of Cap. 148 on libel contravened Article 19 of the Constitution safeguarding freedom of speech and of expression. The Full Bench of the Supreme Court held that the relevant provisions were constitutional, as freedom of speech and of expression could be restricted in order to protect the rights and freedoms of others and their right to personality.[186] The decision of the Supreme Court in *Aloneftis* was affirmed by the ECtHR, which held that there had been no violation of Article 10 of the ECHR.[187] It was held that domestic Cypriot legislation does not in principle restrict freedom of expression to an unreasonable extent and that Article 10 of the ECHR does not preclude a provision which requires a defendant to prove the defence of fair comment or truth on issues of public interest. It was further held that the exercise of freedom of expression implies also duties and responsibilities which apply to the press. Accordingly, freedom of expression is safeguarded to the extent that the press acts in good faith in order to provide accurate and reliable information in accordance with the ethics of journalism.

---

183. *Exporama Trading Ltd v. Police* [2004] 2 CLR 199 (in Greek); *Attorney-General v. Iordanous* [1993] 2 CLR 137; *Polykarpou v. Police* [1967] 2 CLR 164.
184. *Police v. Ftochopoulos*, Case No. 14809/08, District Court Judgment of 29 Apr. 2010. *See also* 23 Apopsi Magazine 50 (2010); A. Emilianides, *The Undermining of Democratic Principles During the Presidency of Demetris Christofias* in *Demetris Christofias: Path of Devastation* 13–20 (Aigaion 2013, in Greek).
185. *See* in detail P. Polyviou, *Modern Law of Defamation* (Chrysafinis and Polyviou, 2013, in Greek).
186. *Alithia Publishing Company Ltd v. Aloneftis* [2002] 1 CLR 1863 (in Greek).
187. *Alithia Publishing Company Ltd and Constantinides v. Cyprus*, Judgment of 22 May 2008; hudoc.

II. Defamatory Publications

114. Section 17 of Cap. 148 provides that defamation consists of the publication by any person, by means of print, writing, painting, effigy, gestures, spoken works or other sounds or by any other means whatsoever, including broadcasting by wireless telegraphy, of any matter which:

(a) imputes to any other person a criminal offence, or misconduct in any public office;[188]
(b) naturally tends to injure or prejudice the reputation of the other person in the way of his profession, trade, business, calling or office; or
(c) is likely to expose him to general hatred, contempt or ridicule or to cause him to be shunned or avoided by others.

A person is no less liable for defamation by reason only that he/she:

(i) makes it by way of repetition or hearsay; or
(ii) refers at the time or afterwards to the authority on which he/she makes the statement;
(iii) believes the statement to be true, subject to the application of specific defences or privileges in accordance with sections 19–21 of Cap. 148;
(iv) did not, in fact, intend to publish the publication concerning the plaintiff;
(v) was unaware of the existence of the plaintiff, subject to the provisions about unintentional defamation in section 22 of Cap. 148.

However, circumstances under (i)–(v) above may be taken into account by the court in the assessment of damages.

115. Cypriot law distinguishes between libel and slander. Libel refers to defamation by written publications, and it does not require any proof of special damage to be actionable. On the contrary, slander refers to defamation by gestures, spoken words or other sounds, other than broadcasting by wireless telegraphy, and it requires proof of special damage to be actionable, except when the gestures, spoken words or other sounds:

(a) impute a crime for which the plaintiff may be made to suffer imprisonment;
(b) are calculated to injure or prejudice the reputation of the plaintiff in the way of his profession, trade, business, calling or office;
(c) impute to the plaintiff a contagious or infectious disease or impute to a woman or girl adultery or unchastity.

188. In *Arktinos Publications Ltd v. Georgiades* [2011] 1 CLR 407 (in Greek), the Supreme Court noted that there are three levels of imputation which might be defamatory, with differing levels of gravity: Accusation that the plaintiff is guilty (level 1), imputation that there are reasonable grounds to suspect that the plaintiff is involved in the criminal offence (level 2) or that there are grounds to investigate what the plaintiff has done (level 3).

Defamation by the press by definition refers to libel actions, although some actions against journalists might also refer to slander actions.

116. Section 25 of Cap. 148 further provides for the tort of injurious falsehood. This consists of the malicious publication of a false statement by another person, whether oral or written, concerning the profession, trade, business, calling, office, goods or title to the property of that other person. In any action for injurious falsehood, the aggrieved person will only receive compensation if he/she proves that he/she has suffered special damage. However, there is no need to prove special damage if the words upon which the action is founded were calculated to cause pecuniary loss to the plaintiff and if they are published in writing or in another permanent form or if the words are calculated to cause pecuniary loss to the plaintiff in respect of any office, profession, calling, trade or business.

117. Regarding the publication of defamatory matter, section 18 of Cap. 148 states that a person may be considered to have published such matter on condition that he/she causes the print, writing, painting, effigy, gestures, spoken words, or the other sounds or other means by which the defamatory matter is conveyed, to be dealt with, either by exhibition, reading, recitation, description, delivery, communication, distribution, demonstration, expression or utterance or otherwise, so that the defamatory meaning thereof becomes known or is likely to become known to any person other than the person defamed thereby; or the husband or wife of the person publishing the defamatory statement. Communication by open letter or postcard, whether sent to the person defamed or to any other person, constitutes defamation. It is further noted that, by virtue of section 17, paragraph 4 of Cap. 148, it is not necessary for defamation that a defamatory meaning should be directly or completely expressed. It suffices that such meaning, and its application to the person alleged to be defamed, can be collected either from the alleged defamatory statement itself or from any extrinsic circumstances, or partly from the one and partly from the other means. Thus, defamation by innuendo shall also constitute defamation for the purposes of Cap. 148.

118. Whether a publication is defamatory should be considered by the court, which is presumed to express the opinion of the hypothetical reasonable person.[189] Accordingly, evidence or testimony which purports to prove how the publication was understood by the plaintiff or by his/her witnesses is immaterial.[190] The intention of the publisher is further considered to be irrelevant. The text of the publication should be viewed in context and as a whole, with reference to the place and time of the publication and to the dominant public perception of the subject. The

189. *See Constantinou and Another v. Karamesini* [2011] 1 CLR 715 (in Greek); *Koutsou v. Alithia Publishing Company Ltd* [2003] 1 CLR 1198 (in Greek); *Attalides v. Rodoulis* [2002] 1 CLR 854 (in Greek); *Constantinides and Others v. Papassavas* [2004] 1 CLR 981 (in Greek). *See also* A. Emilianides, *The Interpretation of a Defamatory Publication from the View of a Theory of Semiotics* in *Versions of Liberty in our Media Reality. The New Journalism and its Challenges* 177 (S. Iordanidou & C. Stratilatis eds, Metamesonykties Publications 2018, in Greek).

190. *See Papadopoulos v. Kyrix Publications Ltd* [1963] 2 CLR 290; *Arktinos Publications Ltd v. Georgiades* [2011] 1 CLR 407 (in Greek).

words or phrases used should be read reasonably, without over-elaborate analysis or undue suspicion. The publication will not be considered defamatory if it may be reasonably interpreted in a non-defamatory manner.[191] If special knowledge is needed, then the judge will consider how ordinary sensible persons, having the special knowledge proved, could understand the allegedly libellous words.[192]

119. Thus, the governing principle is reasonableness. The hypothetical reasonable reader of the publication must be treated as a person who is not avid for scandal, but who however may indulge in loose thinking and readily appreciate an implication. It is thus not enough to claim that some person might understand the words in a defamatory sense, but that the hypothetical reasonable reader would understand them as such, as he/she is considered to be the representative of those who would read the publication in question. In delimiting the range of permissible defamatory meanings, the court should rule out any meaning which can only emerge as the produce of some strained or forced or utterly unreasonable interpretation.[193]

III. Defences

120. Section 19(a) of the Civil Wrongs Law, Cap. 148 provides that in an action for defamation, it shall be a defence that the matter of which the complaint was made was true; provided that where the defamatory matter contains two or more distinct charges against the plaintiff, the defence of truth shall not fail by reason only that the truth of every charge is not proved, if the defamatory matter not proved to be true does not materially injure the plaintiff's reputation having regard to the truth of the remaining charges. Truth is a complete defence to defamation; accordingly, if the defendant proves that his allegations are true, then this will be deemed sufficient.[194] For the purposes of justification, it is sufficient for the defendant to prove that the substance of the publication is true; if the substance is true, then there is no need to also justify statements which are not actionable by themselves and which are not substantial. When considering substantial truth the court should isolate the essential core of the libel, and should not be distracted by inaccuracies around the edge, as journalists need to be allowed a degree of exaggeration in the context of actual statements.[195] In support of the defence of truth, the defendant may rely not only on facts known to him at the time of the publication but also on facts which he was not aware of.[196]

---

191. *See Constantinou and Another v. Karamesini* [2011] 1 CLR 715 (in Greek), *Mesaritis v. Lazarides*, Civil App. 470/2011, Judgment of 14 May 2018 (in Greek).
192. *See Agathangelou v. S. Mousoulides & Sons* [1979] 1 CLR 272.
193. *See Arktinos Publications Ltd v. Georgiades* [2011] 1 CLR 407 (in Greek); *CyBC and Another v. Georgiades* [2013] 1 CLR 1189 (in Greek).
194. *Waterworld Holdings Ltd v. Republic*, Civil App. 17/2011, Judgment of 22 Feb. 2018 (in Greek).
195. *See Arktinos Publications Ltd v. Georgiades* [2011] 1 CLR 407 (in Greek); *CyBC v. Kapsou* [2009] 1 CLR 1175 (in Greek).
196. *See Eteria Ellinike Ekdosis Glafx Ltd v. Loizia* [1984] 3 CLR 729.

121. Section 19(b) of the Civil Wrongs Law, Cap. 148 further provides that in an action for defamation, it shall be a defence that the matter of which the complaint was made was a fair comment on some matter of public interest; provided that, where the defamatory matter consists partly of allegations of fact and partly of expression of opinion, a defence of fair comment shall not fail by reason only that the truth of every allegation of fact is not proved if the expression of opinion is a fair comment having regard to such of the facts alleged or referred to in the defamatory matter complained of as are proved. It is further provided that the defence of fair comment shall not succeed if the plaintiff proves that the publication was not made in good faith.

122. The publication of defamatory matter shall not be deemed to have been made in good faith by a person if it is made to appear either:

- that the matter was untrue, and that he did not believe it to be true, or that he published it without having taken reasonable care to ascertain whether it was true or false; or
- that, in publishing the matter, he acted with intent to injure the person defamed in a substantially greater degree or substantially otherwise than was reasonably necessary for the interest of the public or for the protection of the private right or interest in respect of which he claims to be privileged.

Comment has been defined as: 'something which is or can be reasonably be inferred to be deduction, inference, conclusion, criticism, remark, observation etc.'[197] The defence of fair comment is founded on the principle that the public interest requires that a person's public conduct be open to the most searching criticism. Not only public conduct but also the private character and conduct of a person who fills a public office or who takes part in public affairs may be the subject for fair comment insofar as it has reference to, or tends to throw light on, his/her fitness to occupy the office or to perform the duties thereof.[198]

123. With respect to the defence of fair comment it is important to distinguish between statements of facts, which may not be protected under the defence, and comments, which may be so protected. It is often difficult to draw such a distinction. Accordingly, the courts should be careful in assessing the words within their context. A comment may sometimes consist in the statement of a fact. This would occur if the statement of fact is, in reality, a reasonable inference arising from other facts, and accordingly, it functions as a comment on the facts that preceded or accompanied it.[199] Such a comment should be a fair and honest one on a matter of public interest. Accordingly, there should be no malice by the author, but simply an

197. *See Arktinos Publications Ltd v. Georgiades* [2011] 1 CLR 407 (in Greek).
198. *See Papastratis v. Hadjiefthymiou and Others* [1983] 1 CLR 905.
199. *See Stephanou v. Hjiefhtymiou and Others* [1976] 1 CLR 225.

honest expression of a person's genuine opinion on the subject, even if such opinion was misguided, exaggerated or prejudiced.[200] Whether a matter is of public interest, of which everyone is entitled to make a fair comment, depends on whether it is such as to affect people at large, so that they may be legitimately interested in what may happen.[201] In this respect, public acts and decisions, speeches by public speakers, terms of employment and conduct of public employees or of public contracts, court proceedings and the administration of justice, medical conduct, books, art and public performances or exhibitions, are all examples of matters of public interest.[202]

124. The press may also rely on the defence of qualified privilege by virtue of section 21 of Cap. 148, which provides that the publication of defamatory matter is privileged if it is published in good faith and if the relation between the parties by and to whom the publication is made is such that the person publishing the matter is under a legal, moral or social duty to publish it to the person to whom the publication is made and who has a corresponding interest in receiving it; provided that the publication does not exceed either in extent or matter what is reasonably sufficient for the occasion. The press is generally regarded as being able to rely on the qualified privilege defence, as they have a moral and social duty to publish material appropriate for informing the public at large, which on its part has a corresponding right to receive the information if in its substance the latter refers to a matter of public interest.[203]

125. Other forms of qualified privilege consist of the following:

(a) the matter is a censure passed by a person on the conduct or on the character of another person in any matter in respect of which he/she has authority, contractual or otherwise, or a complaint or accusation made by a person against another person in respect of his/her conduct or of his/her character to a person having authority by law, contractual or otherwise to inquire into or receive complaints respecting such conduct;
(b) the matter is published for the protection of the rights or interests of the person who publishes it or of the person to whom it is published or of a third party in whom the person to whom it is published is interested;
(c) the matter is a fair and accurate report of anything said, done or published in the House of Representatives.

---

200. *See Stephanou v. Hjiefhtymiou and Others* [1976] 1 CLR 225, *Phileleptheros v. Georgiades and Others* [2014] 1 CLR 1621 (in Greek), *Christodoulou v. Afxentiou* [2016] 1 CLR 705 (in Greek), *Drousiotis and another v. Papasavvas* [2015] 1 CLR 482 (in Greek).
201. *See Stephanou v. Hjiefhtymiou and Others* [1976] 1 CLR 225; *Petrides v. Dias Publishing House Ltd and Others* [2013] 1 CLR 1464 (in Greek).
202. *See Synomospondia Ergaton Kyprou and Others v. Cyprus Asbestos Mines Ltd and Another* [1965] 1 CLR 222.
203. *See* P. Artemis, *Freedom of Speech and Expression, Freedom of the Press, Defamation Law and Qualified Privilege,* 9 Cyprus and European Law Review 425 (2009) (in Greek).

Qualified privilege applies only so long as the publication was done in good faith; the onus of proving that the publication was not made in good faith shall be upon the plaintiff.

126. Defamatory publications are absolutely privileged, by virtue of section 20 of Cap. 148, if:

(a) the matter is published by the President of the Republic, or by the Council of Ministers, or by a Minister, or by the House of Representatives, in any official document or in the course of proceedings or in the Council of Ministers or in the House of Representatives, or by a piece of secondary legislation;
(b) the matter concerns a person subject to military, naval or police discipline, it relates to his/her conduct, and it is published by a person having authority over him/her in respect of such conduct to some other person having similar authority;
(c) the matter is published in the course of judicial proceedings by a Judge, or by an advocate, or by a witness, or by a party to such proceedings;
(d) the matter is a fair report of anything said, done or published in the Council of Ministers or in the House of Representatives, published by order or with the authority of the Council of Ministers or of the House of Representatives;
(e) the matter is a fair, accurate and contemporaneous report of anything said, done or shown in any judicial proceedings, so long as the Court has not prohibited such publication;
(f) the matter is a copy or reproduction or a fair abstract of any matter which has been previously published if this previous publication was privileged;
(g) the person publishing the matter is legally bound to publish it;
(h) the publication is made in any military, naval or police report made for the purposes of the defence or of the security of the Republic.

If a publication is absolutely privileged, it is immaterial whether the publication was true or false, or whether it was published in good faith.

127. Moreover, section 22 of Cap. 148 provides that, if a person claims that the defamatory publication was unintentional, he/she may make an offer for amends. An 'offer for amends' means an offer to publish a suitable correction of the matter complained of; a sufficient apology to the party aggrieved; and taking such steps as are reasonably practicable to notify persons to whom copies of the publication have been distributed that the matter is defamatory of the party aggrieved. If the offer is accepted by the aggrieved person and if it is duly performed, then no proceedings for defamation shall be taken against the person making the offer in respect of the publication in question. If the offer is not accepted by the aggrieved person, then it shall be a defence if the defendant proves that the matter was published innocently and that the offer was made as soon as practicable after the defendant received notice that it might be defamatory for the plaintiff. The matter shall be treated as having been published innocently only if:

- the publisher did not intend to publish it concerning the aggrieved person and did not know of circumstances by virtue of which it might be understood to refer to him; or
- the matter was not defamatory on the face of it, and the publisher did not know of circumstances by virtue of which it might be understood to be defamatory of the aggrieved person.

128. Section 24 of Cap. 148 further provides for a special defence in actions brought against the owner of any newspaper in respect of defamatory matter contained in such newspaper. The owner of the newspaper may pay the court a sum of money which is sufficient amends in the opinion of the court and further prove:

- that the defamatory matter was inserted without actual malice;
- that there was no gross lack of reasonable care for which he was liable; and
- that before the commencement of the action or soon afterwards he/she inserted a full apology in the newspaper.

IV. Case-Law

129. Some leading cases help to clarify the attempt of the Supreme Court to achieve a balance between the need to safeguard freedom of the press, on the one hand, and the need to protect the reputation of innocents, on the other hand. In *Papaefstathiou* the plaintiff was an advocate for thirty years and the Chairman of the Cyprus Bar Association.[204] In his capacity as Chairman of the Cyprus Bar Association, he issued an announcement expressing reservations about amending the legislation governing defamation which he considered as satisfactory. He further criticized statements which were made on the issue by other persons without sufficient scientific knowledge. *Politis* newspaper published a series of articles and satirical sketches which heavily criticized and satirized the plaintiff, implying that he had personal interests in the issue as a lawyer specializing in libel cases and that he inappropriately dismissed the scientific credentials of other lawyers who had expressed the view that the libel legislation ought to be amended.

130. The view that a person should have scientific credentials in order to express an opinion about the issue was also criticized. A sketch portrayed the plaintiff as a man dressed in a military uniform who jailed the Press in a modern Auschwitz. The first instance court held that there was libel. The newspaper appealed. The Supreme Court reversed the first instance judgment, holding that the publications were not defamatory. Whereas the publications heavily criticized the plaintiff, they related to an issue of general interest and they referred to the statements made by the plaintiff. According to the Court, this kind of expression should be tolerated within a democratic society. After these considerations, the sketch was held to be humorous and not defamatory. On the basis of the facts of the case, freedom of expression superseded the right to personality.

204. *Ekdoseis Arktinos Ltd v. Papaefstathiou* [2007] 1 CLR 856 (in Greek).

131. In the case of *Karamesini* the plaintiff was a musician and had composed a musical composition for an event organized by the Bishop of Kykkos within the context of the International Forum of Religions and Cultures.[205] *Politis* newspaper published a series of articles which referred to the plaintiff. The first instance court held that two of the publications were defamatory. It was held that the defamatory publications ridiculed both the plaintiff and the work of the plaintiff. The newspaper appealed. The Supreme Court affirmed the lower court decision. It was held that the intention of the newspaper was to criticize the Bishop of Kykkos and the administration of the property of the monastery of Kykkos. This could not justify an attack, against the plaintiff, of such magnitude, which characterized her work as unimportant and as lacking quality and as which was simply made in order to flatter the Bishop. It was held that the comments were not fair, as the journalist had never heard the musical composition of the plaintiff, while there was no factual basis for the expression of such value judgments, destructive to the plaintiff's reputation. The overall behaviour of the newspaper and their insistence that the defamatory publication was true, in conjunction with the words used, with the fact that the views of the plaintiff were never pursued and with the newspaper's complete disregard for the truth or for the facts of the case, further proved that the publication was made in bad faith.[206]

132. In *Loucaides* the former Cypriot judge of the ECtHR alleged that a publication in a Greek newspaper had defamed him.[207] The publication mentioned that the plaintiff, in his capacity as a judge of the ECtHR, had supported opinions which held that Greece was in violation of the ECHR with regard to the rights of the 'Turkish' and 'Skopje' minorities. The plaintiff was characterized as an anti-Greek traitor and as the best helper of Turkey. The Supreme Court noted that a judge of the ECtHR has a duty to decide in accordance with human rights principles, irrespective of whether the judgment might be contrary to the interests of his country or his motherland. However, the fact that the newspaper disapproved of the judgments issued by the plaintiff and even called him a traitor did not amount to defamation, as the newspaper had not questioned the motives of the plaintiff. Since, however, the very notion of a traitor (an *Ephialtes*, according to the publication) implies that there has been some extraneous motive (i.e., receiving monetary compensation), it is rather questionable whether the facts of the case did not constitute defamation in the opinion of the Supreme Court.

133. In *Georgiades* it was held that publications which referred that the plaintiff was under the investigation of the police and that the police had reasonable suspicions that the plaintiff was involved in the criminal offences were not defamatory.[208] The content of the publications was true, and the newspaper had expressed no opinion or innuendos regarding the guilt of the plaintiff. Besides, the comments

205. *Constantinou and another v. Karamesini* [2011] 1 CLR 715 (in Greek).
206. *Ibid. See also Phileletheros Public Company Ltd and another v. Kantounas*, Civil App. 320/2014, Judgment of 24 Jun. 2022 (in Greek).
207. *Loucaides v. Proto Thema and Others* [2013] 1 CLR 313 (in Greek).
208. *Arktinos Publications Ltd v. Georgiades* [2011] 1 CLR 407 (in Greek).

made by the newspaper had been fair and they were covered by qualified privilege. Even harsh comments could be justified under the circumstances.[209] Furthermore, in *Yennaris* the Supreme Court held that a newspaper article which stated that a television talk show promoted Turkish-Cypriot propaganda was not defamatory. The Court noted that the relevant article did not claim that the plaintiff himself promoted Turkish-Cypriot propaganda, but rather that his show promoted such propaganda through its guests. Whereas the plaintiff had properly presented Turkish-Cypriot views in his show, it was also the right of the newspaper to consider such views as propaganda and criticize them. The mere fact that the journalist who wrote the offending publication did not share the view that all opinions should be presented is not by itself defamatory.[210]

134. In *Koulias* the defendant, a member of the House of Representatives, had criticized the action of Greek-Cypriot politicians to visit the occupied areas. In this respect he referred to the plaintiff, another politician, mentioning that he had received money from a Turkish company and that the next day he made comments benefiting the Turkish regime. The Supreme Court, reversing the first instance judgment, held that there was an innuendo that the plaintiff had received money in order to act favourably to the Turkish regime; therefore, the publication was deemed defamatory.[211] Moreover, in *Mavros* the Supreme Court held that an article by a journalist against the political views of a well-known politician was not defamatory; the statement that the politician was acting against the struggle of the people of Cyprus for freedom was critical of the politician's political views and accordingly did not amount to a defamation of his person but to political criticism.[212]

V. Remedies

135. The case-law has traditionally held that the prior restraint of publication of a newspaper, normally through an interim order, may occur only in exceptionally serious cases. As it forms a drastic interference with freedom of speech, this should be ordered only when there is a substantial risk of grave injustice and where the libel is wholly unjustified, inflicting the most serious injury to the plaintiff. The court should never grant an injunction in respect of libel when the defendant claims that

209. *Dias Publishing House Ltd v. Georgiades*, Civil App. 339/2008, Judgment of 24 Mar. 2020 (in Greek).

210. *Dias Publishing House Public Ltd and Another v. Yennari* [2011] 1 CLR 1952 (in Greek).

211. *Themistokleous v. Koulias* [2012] 1 CLR 76 (in Greek). In *Koulias v. Cyprus*, Judgment of 25 May 2020; hudoc, the ECtHR held that there was a violation of Art. 6 of the ECHR because the presiding judge's son had been working in the firm which had taken over the appellant's representation before the hearing of the appeal, and the judge had not disclosed the connection during the proceedings. A petition by the defendant to invalidate any further proceedings was dismissed, and the Court awarded damages in favour of the plaintiff. *See Koulias v. Themistocleous*, Civil App. 79/2013, Judgment of 16 Nov. 2021 (in Greek); *Koulias v. Themistocleous*, Civil App. 79/2013, Judgment of 16 Feb. 2022 (in Greek).

212. *Mavros v. Papapetrou,* Civil App. 59/2012, Judgment of 29 May 2018 (in Greek). *See also Kyriacou and another v. Loucaides*, Civil App. 103/2014, Judgment of 18 Dec. 2020 (in Greek); *Arktinos and another v. Angelides*, Civil App. 315/2013, Judgment of 3 Dec. 2020 (in Greek).

the words are true or that they were fair comments or that they were covered by privilege. It is only in cases where it is shown that the defendant knows the libel to be untrue and where it is clearly malicious that an interim injunction might be considered a remedy.[213] The usual remedy in defamation cases will thus be the award of damages.

136. The objective of an award of damages is to monetarily restore the plaintiff to the position he would have been in if the tort had not been committed. The principle of *restitutio in integrum* is well embedded in the assessment of damages. In cases of defamation, *restitutio in integrum* has a high subjective element, as it is not possible to ascertain how far other people's minds have been affected. Thus, a person defamed should be compensated because he was injured in his reputation, both as a vindication of the plaintiff to the public and as a consolation for a wrong done. The extent of damages in cases of defamation depends on the nature of the libel, the conduct of the plaintiff, his position and standing, the mode and extent of the publication, the absence or refusal of any retraction or apology and the whole conduct of the defendant from the time when the libel was published until the issue of judgment.[214] The extent of the attack on the person's reputation and the hardship that the plaintiff suffers due to the publications should also be taken into account.[215] The extent of damages should further be reasonable.[216]

137. Section 23 of Cap. 148 provides that the defendant in any action for defamation may, after reasonable notice to the plaintiff of his/her intention so to do, prove, in mitigation of any compensation that may be awarded, that he/she made or offered an apology to the plaintiff before the commencement of the action or as soon afterwards as he had an opportunity, if the action was commenced before he/she had an opportunity of so doing. For an apology to be a mitigating factor, it should be practically sufficient; it should thus amount to a full, honest and unreserved withdrawal of the charges or suggestions conveyed, and it should contain an expression of regret that they were ever made. Failure to apologize might in some cases even be considered by the court as a factor aggravating the amount of damages to be ordered.[217] Other factors which may be taken into account for mitigation are:

(a) if the defamatory matter was contained in a newspaper and the plaintiff has already recovered, or brought an action for, or received compensation in respect of the defamatory matter to the same purpose or effect;

---

213. *See C.T. Tobacco Ltd v. Arktinos Publishing Company Ltd* [2003] 1 CLR 853 (in Greek); *Panayiotou v. Moulazimi* [2007] 1 CLR 78 (in Greek).
214. *See Saveriades and another v. Georghiades and others* [1983] 1 CLR 574.
215. *See Alithia Publishing Company Ltd v. Nicolaou* [1993] 1 CLR 285 (in Greek); *Dias v. Nathanael* [1993] 1 CLR 893 (in Greek); *Constantinou and another v. Karamesini* [2011] 1 CLR 715 (in Greek); *O' Dwyer and another v. Christophoros Karayiannas & Sons Ltd*, Civil App. 435/2012, Judgment of 21 Feb. 2020 (in Greek); *Ahtar and another v. Iacovides and another*, Civil App. 363/2014, Judgment of 4 Jul. 2023 (in Greek).
216. *See Saveriades and another v. Georghiades and others* [1983] 1 CLR 574.
217. *Ibid.*

(b) if, prior to the publication, the plaintiff was of a general bad reputation in connection with that particular trait of his character which is assailed by the defamation; or
(c) if the defendant received provocation from the plaintiff.

VI. Private International Law Aspects

138. The Rome II Regulation[218] excludes from its scope obligations arising out of violations of privacy and of rights relating to personality, including defamation. This effectively means that defamation continues to be governed by the pre-existing common law rules of private international law and by the rules contained in Cap. 148.[219] Section 3 of the Civil Wrongs Law, Cap. 148 provided that any person who shall suffer any injury or damage by reason of any tort committed in the Republic, or within three miles of the coast thereof, measured from low water mark, shall be entitled to recover from the person committing or liable for such tort the remedies which the court has power to grant. In *Georghiades*[220] the Supreme Court confirmed that the scope of section 3 of Cap. 148 had been enlarged; as a result, not only the torts specified in Cap. 148 but also those recognized by common law were actionable in Cyprus unless clearly excluded by some legislation.[221]

139. In the leading case of *Jupiter* the appellants were being sued by the respondent for damages for personal injuries suffered while being employed by them in Libya.[222] The Supreme Court considered the question of whether the Cypriot courts had jurisdiction in the matter, and if so, what was the law to be applied to the dispute, i.e., that of Cyprus or Libya. The underlying question was whether section 3 of Cap. 148 excluded the application of private international law in relation to torts committed outside of Cyprus. The Supreme Court held that this was not the case and that the common law rules of private international law apply under section 29, paragraph 1(c) of the Courts of Justice Law 14/60. The Supreme Court held that Cypriot courts had jurisdiction to consider an action in respect of a tort committed abroad insofar as the event which caused the injuries is actionable as a tort according to both Cypriot law and the law of the country where the damage occurred. Consequently, both the law of Cyprus and the law of Libya had to be considered in order to decide whether the claim of the respondent based on a tort was actionable.[223]

---

218. Regulation (EC) No. 864/2007 of the European Parliament and of the Council of 11 Jul. 2007 on the law applicable to non-contractual obligations.
219. *See* A. Emilianides et al., *Private International Law in Cyprus* (Kluwer 2015), A. Emilianides and C. Markou, *Tort Law in Cyprus* (Kluwer 2021).
220. *Georghiades & Son v. Kaminaras* [1958] 23 CLR 276.
221. *See also Vassiliou v. Vassiliou* [1939] 16 CLR 69; *The Universal Advertising and Publishing Agency and Others v. Vouros* [1952] 19 CLR 87.
222. *Jupiter Ltd v. Christides* [1975] 1 CLR 144.
223. Also *Satu v. Welsen Shipping Co Ltd* [1998] 1 CLR 1115 (in Greek). *See*, however, the criticism of P. Artemis & G. Erotocritou, *Cap. 148: Torts* 26 (2003, in Greek).

140. Thus, the principal common law rule prevailing in Cyprus was that the tort should be actionable on the basis of both the *lex fori* and the *lex loci delicti*, i.e., the law of the place where the tort was committed (double action ability rule). Once liability is established, it is the *lex fori* which shall govern the case, but only insofar as it is consistent with the rights available under the *lex loci delicti*. The application of both the *lex fori* and the *lex loci delicti* implies that the claimant must show that he/she has the right to sue the particular defendant for the tort under both laws. This is an inflexible rule, which is, however, complemented by an exception, in accordance to which a particular issue may be governed by the law of the country which is most closely connected to the wrong committed, to the issue or to the parties involved, irrespective of whether such law is the *lex loci delicti*, the *lex fori*, or the law of a third country.

141. Section 3 of the Civil Wrongs Law, Cap. 148 was amended by Law 129(I)/2006. It is now provided that, without prejudice to the application of any rule of private international law, Cap. 148 applies to any tort committed within the territory of the Republic,[224] as well as to any tort committed against a person or immovable property which was situated in the territory of the Republic at the time that the tort was committed. In the above cases, the tort is applicable in accordance with the *lex fori*, irrespective of whether the act or omission is actionable also in accordance with the law of the country where the tort was committed. Thus, if the person against whom the tort was committed was situated in Cyprus, Cypriot law would be applicable irrespective of whether the tort is also applicable in accordance with the *lex loci delicti*. This is an express and important limitation to the common law double actionability rule.[225]

§3. Protection of Privacy

142. Article 15 of the Constitution stipulates that every person has the right to respect his private and family life.[226] There shall be no interference with the exercise of this right except such as is in accordance with the law and as is necessary only in the interests of the security of the Republic; or the constitutional order; or the public safety; or the public order; or the public health; or the public morals; or for the protection of the rights and liberties guaranteed by this Constitution to any person. Article 15 corresponds to Article 8 of the ECHR. Therefore, each individual has a right to privacy, including, *inter alia*, religious, philosophical, or moral beliefs, family and emotional life, friendship, or personal health, activities of professional and business nature, as well as the right to establish and develop relationships with other human beings.[227] The notion of 'private life' or 'family life' should not be

224. This would include territorial waters and airspace. It further includes ships and airplanes registered in the Republic, irrespective of where they are situated, unless such are exclusively governed by foreign law in accordance with the rules of private international law and because of their location at a given time.
225. *See also* P. Polyviou, *The Current Law of Defamation* (Chryssafinis & Polyviou, 2013), 506.
226. A. Emilianides, *Constitutional Law in Cyprus* (2nd ed., Kluwer, 2019), 160ff.
227. *See inter alia Niemietz v. Germany*, Judgment of 16 Dec. 1992; Series A 251-B.

interpreted narrowly, since their aim is to safeguard fundamental rights. Such rights may be restricted only in accordance with the law, so far as it is necessary for one of the reasons specified in Article 15 and, in addition, insofar as the restriction is justified in a European democracy. The Supreme Court has held that a law obliging high state officials to reveal and submit information about their property and about the property of their family members is inconsistent with Article 15 of the Constitution.[228]

143. The Supreme Court has repeatedly held that a person's reputation has to be protected, as reputation is an integral part of the dignity of the individual, forming the basis for his/her well-being in a democratic society; damaging one's reputation with unfounded accusations is contrary to the public interest.[229] In defamation cases, there are two conflicting human rights which need to be balanced: the right of freedom of speech and of expression, on the one hand, and the right to safeguard one's personality, fame and integrity, on the other hand. In Cyprus, this second right is safeguarded under Article 15 of the Constitution and under Article 8 of the ECHR. Both rights are equally important. The courts should express care and sensitivity so as to safeguard that any restrictions to either right are absolutely necessary.[230]

144. It has accordingly been held by the Supreme Court that the right to personality is recognized as one of the grounds on the basis of which the right to freedom of expression may be restricted. There is thus no general right to defame another person.[231] When examining cases of defamation, the courts should strive to balance the two rights on the basis of the principle of proportionality, in order to assess whether in each given case the protection of the personality of an individual should be considered more worthy of protection than the freedom of expression or the freedom of the public to receive information on issues of general interest.[232]

145. It should further be noted that in the leading judgment of *Yiallouros v. Nicolaou,*[233] the Supreme Court indirectly adopted the legal concept of *Drittwirkung*, in accordance to which an individual plaintiff can rely directly on the constitutional provisions safeguarding fundamental rights in order to sue another individual or the

228. *President of the Republic v. House of Representatives* [2000] 3 CLR 238.

229. *See Alithia Publishing Company Ltd v. Aloneftis* [2002] 1 CLR 1863 (in Greek).

230. *See Ekdoseis Arktinos Ltd v. Papaefstathiou* [2007] 1 CLR 856 (in Greek); *Constantinou and Another v. Karamesini* [2011] 1 CLR 715 (in Greek); *Alithia Publishing Company Ltd v. Leonida* [1997] 1 CLR 550 (in Greek); *Dias Publishing House Public Ltd and another v. Yennari* [2011] 1 CLR 1952 (in Greek).

231. *Ekdoseis Arktinos Ltd v. Papaefstathiou* [2007] 1 CLR 856 (in Greek); *Steel and Morris v. UK*, Judgment of 1993.

232. *See* C. Markou, *Journalism and Freedom of Speech under the Limitation of the Protection of the Right to Reputation. The Cypriot Reality in Versions of Liberty in our Media Reality. The New Journalism and Its Challenges* (S. Iordanidou & C. Stratilatis eds, Metamesonykties Publications 2018, in Greek). 133.

233. [2001] 1 CLR 558 (in Greek). *See* P. Konstantinidis, *The Drittwirkung of Fundamental Rights in the Cypriot Legal Order* (Hippasus 2016, in Greek). S. Papasavvas, *There Is Drittwirkung of Human Rights in the Cypriot Legal Order: Comments and Thoughts on the Judgment of the Supreme Court in Civil Appeal 9931 Yiallouros v. Nicolaou* 15 Dikaiomata tou Anthropou 837 (2002): 837 (in Greek). *See also Police v. Georghiades* [1983] 2 CLR 33.

government for the violation of those rights. Yiallouros, the Director of the Sewerage Board of Nicosia had, during a whole year, taped and monitored the telephone conversations of Nicolaou, an employee of the Sewerage Board. In addition, Nicolaou was put on probation in light of the content of his telephone conversations. Nicolaou sued Yiallouros before the District Court, requesting compensation for the violation of his constitutional rights, namely of his right to privacy safeguarded by Article 15 of the Constitution, and of his right to secrecy of communications safeguarded by Article 17 of the Constitution (both protected under Article 8 ECHR). The District Court held that Yiallouros was liable to pay compensation to his employee. Yiallouros appealed arguing that there is no direct right to sue for violation of constitutional rights, when such violations do not also constitute torts in accordance with the Civil Wrongs Law, Cap. 148. The Supreme Court affirmed the first instance judgment and held that the violation of the constitutional rights of an individual by another individual vests to the victim the right to invoke legal remedies for the vindication of his/her rights. According to the Court, the effective application of fundamental rights presupposes the right of a person whose constitutional rights have been violated to receive compensation for any damage suffered because of the violation. Consequently, the violation of constitutional rights is directly actionable before the District Courts.

Chapter 4. Right of Reply and to Rectification

146. Section 39 of Law 145/89 provides for the (French-oriented) right of reply, which is an important mechanism for protecting the reputation and personality of persons who are affected by publications in the press.[234] It is thereby provided that the owner, or the person legally responsible or the director of a newspaper or a periodical, where a publication was published in which a person is named or implied, has the obligation to publish the reply to such publication sent by the person concerned. The obligation applies irrespectively of whether the publication was made by the editorial team of the newspaper or by a third party. The reply should be published within three days from its receipt, or in the immediate next issue of the newspaper if it had not been published within three days from receipt of the reply. Besides, the reply should be published in the same position as the original publication which motivated it, without any omissions or additions. However, the reply should not exceed the length of the original publication which motivated it, unless it is up to fifty lines, in which case it must be published as it has, even if the original publication was shorter. The Chairperson of the defunct Press Council (*see* in Chapter 6 of this Part below) was supposed to have the power to increase or limit the extent of the reply.

147. According to other provisions of section 39 of Law 145/89, the right of reply applies irrespective of any civil or criminal liability of the newspaper, irrespective of the right of the affected person to seek compensation under civil law proceedings. Besides, the reply should be published for free, on condition that the original publication was inaccurate or prejudicial to the dignity or to the reputation of the person affected, or if the publication is not an advertisement aiming to serve exclusively commercial transactions. The right of reply might be exercised by the spouse, or by any descendant or ascendant or sibling of the affected person if the latter has deceased prior to the expiration of the ten-day period. A reply by any of the relatives of the affected person extinguishes the relevant right of the remaining relatives.

148. The owner, the person who is legally responsible or the director of a newspaper may refuse to publish the reply if:

(a) it contains clearly defamatory expressions or words which constitute the *actus reus* of a criminal act; or
(b) more than ten days have elapsed since the original publication, and, in case the person who was affected resides abroad, more than ten days since he/she has returned to the Republic.[235]

234. L. Loucaides, *The Right of Reply to the Press*, in *id.*, *Topics of Cypriot Law II* 157–169 (1988, in Greek).
235. This is an odd provision, as an affected person might permanently reside abroad might without ever having the intention to return in Cyprus. Since in this case the period in which to exercise right of reply is associated with his return, it is not clear when the right elapses.

In case of refusal to publish the reply, the owner, the person who is legally responsible or the director of the newspaper was supposed to deposit the text of the reply, and the grounds for the refusal, to the Chairperson of the Press Council, who would decide within twenty-four hours whether the refusal was justified or not. Since a Chairperson of the Press Council has not been appointed since 1993, this provision cannot be implemented in practice. The only remaining remedy is of a criminal law nature: Any unjustified refusal to publish the rectification, or its improper publication, is a criminal offence and is publishable with imprisonment of up to six months and/or a fine of up to approximately EUR 1,700 (paragraph 8 of section 39 of Law 145/89).

149. Section 38 of Law 145/89 further provides for a right to rectification. It is provided that, if an incorrect publication was published which refers to acts relevant to the duties of a public servant, then the owner or the person who is legally responsible or the director of a newspaper has the obligation to publish for free any rectification of the publication sent either by the public servant or by the relevant public authority. The right to rectification applies irrespective of whether the original publication which motivated the rectification was made by the editorial team of the newspaper or by any third party. If the original publication affects the public servant also personally, he/she may additionally exercise his/her right of reply. The rectification should be published in the next or subsequent issue of the newspaper from the day of its receipt, in the same position as the original publication which motivated the reply and without any omissions or additions. The right to rectification applies irrespective of any civil or criminal liability of the newspaper, or to the right of the affected person to seek compensation under civil law proceedings.

150. The rectification should not exceed the length of the original publication and should restrict itself to refuting the inaccuracies of the original publication and stating the true facts. The Chairperson of the defunct Press Council was supposed to have the power to increase or limit the extent of the rectification. The owner, the person who is legally responsible or the director of a newspaper may refuse to publish the reply if:

(a) it contains clearly defamatory expressions or words which constitute the actus reus of a criminal act; or
(b) if more than a month has elapsed since the original publication, and in case the person who is affected resides abroad, more than three months since he has returned to the Republic.

In case of refusal to publish the rectification, the owner, the person who is legally responsible or the director of the newspaper was supposed to deposit the text of the rectification and the grounds for the refusal to the, currently non-existent, Chairperson of the Press Council who would decide within twenty-four hours whether the refusal was justified or not. Any unjustified refusal to publish the rectification, or its improper publication, is a criminal offence and is publishable with imprisonment of up to six months and/or a fine of up to approximately EUR 1,700.

151. An important case which considered the right to rectification, on the basis of the pre-existing Press Law, Cap. 79, is *Hadjidemetriou.*[236] Cap. 79 did not provide for a right of reply, but only for a right to rectification in favour of the public service. However, the findings of the Supreme Court in *Hadjidemetriou* are applicable also to the right of reply. In *Hadjidemetriou*, the *Haravgi* newspaper, which is owned by AKEL, the communist party of Cyprus, published a first-page article stating that several prominent politicians, including the appellant who was the Secretary General of EDEK, the socialist party of Cyprus, participated in a meeting in the Archbishopric which intended to nominate a common candidate by the participants in the forthcoming presidential elections. The Supreme Court held that the right to rectification is necessary to protect the rights of others, and as such it is a constitutionally valid restriction of the freedom of the press. According to the Court, the aim of the right is the immediate restoration of the truth in the mind of the readers of a publication affecting a person.

152. However, the Court noted that any penal statute has to be construed narrowly in favour of the press. The newspapers had a statutory duty, as they do now, to publish a correction without additions or omissions, whereas the request should be in writing by the person referred to in the statement. The correction should be further limited to a denial of a statement of fact which is alleged to be incorrect, and it should set the correct facts. However, the appellant had requested the newspaper to publish a part of the letter which included an apology emanating from the newspaper. This was held to be outside the ambit of the right to rectification, as the aim of the right is to give the reader the opportunity to read the true version as stated by the person affected. The Court further added certain obiter comments, calling for the expansion of the right of reply both with respect to statements of facts and with respect to comments. The Court noted that the right of reply is more necessary where the press is controlled by strong financial or political interests. It could be argued that the right of reply as introduced in Law 145/89 has been expanded in accordance with the Supreme Court's obiter comments in *Hadjidemetriou.*

153. However, the UCJ vehemently opposed the relevant provisions of Law 145/89. It stated that the latter provides for a reply of such length that ends up being an abuse of the right and a danger to freedom of the press. Whereas the UCJ stated that in principle it favours a right of reply and a right to rectification, it also noted that the newspaper should not have to publish the reply or the rectification in the same position as the original publication and in the same length, on the grounds that this was unreasonable and that would endanger the nature and mission of newspapers.[237] The UCJ effectively considered that the right of reply should be allowed in specific parts of the newspaper, and not necessarily in the same position as the original publication, and to the extent deemed fit by the newspapers themselves. The failure to establish a Press Council in order to oversee the provisions of Law 145/89

236. *Hadjidemetriou v. Telegraphos Publishing Company Ltd and Another* [1983] 2 CLR 268.
237. Union of Cyprus Journalists, *Journalistic Ethics* 60 (Union of Cyprus Journalists Publications).

with regards to the right of reply and to rectification eventually meant that overseeing the proper application of such right would be with the Media Complaints Commission (*see* in Chapter 6 of this Part below), which partly echoes the understanding of the UCJ on how the right of reply and the right to rectification ought to be implemented in practice.[238]

154. The JEC provides that the media (hence, not only the printed press but also the AVMS providers) should give a fair opportunity to reply, in the appropriate case, to those affected by a publication, particularly when they have been attacked. This opportunity should not be given so long after the time of publication that the right of reply shall have no meaning. The media have the right to edit long letters in a way which will not affect the substance of the reply, and they may also refuse publication of letters which may have legal repercussions on them or on third parties. A comparison between the provisions of Law 145/89 and the relevant provisions of the JEC indicates serious differences. It is submitted that the provisions of the legislation should prevail and that, accordingly, the adoption of ethical rules which are inconsistent with the legislation is highly problematic. If the media edits a reply, then they will have acted in accordance with the JEC, but at the same time, they will have committed a criminal offence.

238. *See* on this, K. Kouros, *The Mass Media Law in the Republic of Cyprus,* fn. 51 above.

Chapter 5. Access to Public Information

§1. Public Documents and Meetings

155. Section 7 of Law 145/89 provides that any journalist, irrespective of nationality, has the right to freely seek and receive information from private sources, without any interference on behalf of state organs and irrespective of boundaries. He/she may also freely transmit such information in any way unless this is restricted due to grounds relating to state security, public or constitutional order, public safety or the protection of reputation and the rights of others. Such right is consistent with the constitutional right to freedom of expression, as safeguarded by Article 19 of the Constitution and by Article 10 of the ECHR. Section 7 of Law 145/89 further provides that any journalist has the right to free access to state sources of information, as well as the right to seek and receive information from any competent authority of the Republic, and the right to freely transmit such information in any way. State authorities have the obligation to provide any information requested as soon as possible unless this is restricted due to grounds relating to state security; public or constitutional order; public safety; or the protection of reputation and of the rights of others.

156. Whereas the scope of section 7 of Law 145/89 might seem sufficiently wide, its application is heavily restricted by section 67 of the Public Service Law 1/1990, providing that any written or oral information which becomes known to a public servant during the exercise of his/her duties is confidential and may not be communicated to any other person other than for the proper execution of an official duty or subsequent to an express authorization by the competent authority. Furthermore, no public servant may provide any technical or scientific advice to any person without the permission of the competent authority, unless this is done in order to carry out an official duty. It has been properly argued that section 67 of Law 1/90 expresses a rather outdated perception of the role of the administration in a modern democratic state, imposing such a general prohibition of communication of information that it ends up granting an extremely wide discretion to the administration on whether to communicate information or not.[239]

157. Following a lengthy debate, the Republic of Cyprus eventually enacted the Right of Access to Information of the Public Sector Law 184(I)/2017, which is a specialized piece of legislation safeguarding the right of natural or legal persons to request access to information which are in the possession of public authorities. Prior to the enactment of this specific legislation the only piece of special legislation regulating access to information related to environmental issues.[240] Law 184(I)/17 restricts, however, the right of access when the request refers to personal data; or

239. N. Charalambous, *The Freedom to Access the Files of the Administration*, 1 Cyprus Law Tribune 36 (1992) (in Greek). *See* E. Nicolaou, *The Obligation of the Administration to Provide Information to the Citizens*, 1 Cyprus and European Law Review 99 (2006) (in Greek).

240. Law 119/2004 on the access of the public to information relevant to the environment, transposing Directive 2003/4/EC of the European Parliament and of the Council of 28/1/2003 on public access

when the request is incompatible with obligations imposed by the EU; or when it would amount to contempt of court. Furthermore, the public authority may refuse to disclose the information in a significant number of cases. These include cases where the information refers to security organs; or it might prejudice the security, defence, economic policy, or international relations of the Republic; or it is included in judicial records; or refers to the exercise of police powers to investigate, or certain executive powers or the exercise of governmental policy; or when the information had been given on the condition of confidentiality; or when it refers to parliamentary information; or if it might hinder the health or safety of any person; or when the applicant has access through other prescribed methods.

158. The Commissioner for Information shall oversee the application of Law 184(I)/17, having the right to determine that public authorities have violated their obligations under the legislation and to impose a fine in case of non-compliance. The enactment of Law 184(I)/17 is a significant development since without access to documents, transparency, one of the main pillars of accountability and, accordingly, of the legitimacy of the actions of the administration, cannot be properly achieved.[241] However, it should be noted that the exceptions to the right of access to information remain very wide and thus in practice access to information may well remain very limited. Administrative authorities regularly refuse to provide access to journalists, alleging that the information is confidential on grounds relating to public security or public safety, or in order to safeguard the rights of others.[242] The right of privacy of third parties is also often invoked as a ground for restricting the right of journalists to have access even to public documents.

§2. Court Hearings and Documents

159. By virtue of Article 30 of the Constitution (corresponding with Article 6, paragraph 1 of the ECHR), every person is entitled, in the determination of his/her civil rights and obligations or of any criminal charge against him/her, to a fair and public hearing within a reasonable time by an independent, impartial and competent court established by law. Court judgments shall be reasoned and shall be pronounced in a public session. However, the press and the public may be excluded from all or from any part of the trial upon a decision of the court, where such exclusion is in the interest of the security of the Republic; or the constitutional order; or the public order; or the public safety; or the public morals; or where the interests of

to environmental information. *See* C. Fryda, *Legislation on the Right of Access of the Public to Information Relevant to Environmental Issues*, 2 Cyprus and European Law Review 311 (2006) (in Greek).

241. *See* Nicolaou, *The Obligation of the Administration,* fn. 239 above. *See* further, e.g., P. Dyrberg, *Accountability and Legitimacy: What Is the Contribution of Transparency?* in *Accountability and Legitimacy in the European Union* 86 (A. Arnull & D. Wincott eds, Oxford University Press 2002); *Transparency: The Key to Better Governance* (C. Hood & D. Heald eds, Oxford University Press 2008).

242. For a general study *see* Open Cyprus Alliance, *The Right of Access to Information in Cyprus* (2011, in Greek).

juveniles or the protection of the private life of the parties so require; or, in special circumstances, where, in the opinion of the court, publicity would prejudice the interests of justice.[243] The general practice is that, whereas journalists have free access to courtrooms, unless there are grounds justifying for the trial to be held in a close session, television cameras have always been excluded from the courtroom. Journalists generally enjoy free access to court documents to the extent that they are not confidential. The Supreme Court and District Courts promptly deliver their judgments to journalists who deal with judicial reporting as well as to other journalists who might occasionally have an interest in specific cases. It should be noted, however, that on 19 July 2018, the Supreme Court reached a decision to partly anonymize court judgments, in order to safeguard that certain personal information is not disclosed through publication.[244]

243. *See* C. Clerides, *The Access of Mass Media Communication to Court Proceedings*, 49–50 Cyprus Law Review 7157 (1995) (in Greek).

244. *See also* C. Middleton, *The Directive for the Anonymization of Judicial Decisions*, *psychonomika* 21.7.2021.

Chapter 6. Press Council, Press Authority and Self-Regulation

§1. The Press Council

160. The Press Law 145/89 envisages the establishment of a Press Council. However, the relevant provisions of the Law have not been implemented. Section 3 of Law 145/89 provides that the Press Council shall be responsible for safeguarding the freedom and independence of the Cypriot press, as well as its proper function in accordance with the Law and with the journalist code of conduct to be issued by the Press Council. In this respect, the Press Council has jurisdiction to, *inter alia*, take all necessary action vis-à-vis the competent authorities of the Republic of Cyprus and foreign countries; regulate the code of conduct of the press and of the journalistic; take action *ex proprio motu* or examine complaints against newspapers and journalists for conduct or actions which are contrary to the professional rules; issue journalist identities to Cypriot journalists who fulfil the legal criteria; and revoke such journalist identities to those who no longer fulfil the legal criteria.

161. Section 4 of Law 145/89 provides that the Press Council is appointed by the Council of Ministers. It is chaired by a Chairperson, who is a lawyer of supreme professional and moral standards and who is not related to the press. It is further composed of three members who are appointed following a recommendation by the ANPP and the other three members who are appointed following a recommendation by the UCJ. Additional members were to be appointed by the Council of Ministers, following a recommendation by the parliamentary political parties, so far as each political party is represented by one member. Each political party should submit a list of three members and the Council of Ministers should choose one member out of the list as a representative of the political party in question.

162. It is further provided that the term of the Council is for three years and it is renewable. The Council of Ministers may further appoint alternative members who shall substitute the regular members if they are absent for whatever reason. If, however, the Chairperson is absent, the eldest of the members shall exercise all the competences of the Chair. If there is a vacancy due to death or resignation of the Chairperson or of a member of the Press Council, the Council of Ministers may appoint a new Chairperson or member for the remainder of the Council's term. The Press Council is convened by the Chairperson, in accordance with section 5 of Law 145/89, whenever he considers this to be necessary, or whenever at least three members request so and simultaneously propose an agenda. Six members present constitute a quorum. Decisions are taken by majority, and if there is a tie, the Chairperson has the casting vote.

163. It is noted that the provision in accordance to which members are to be appointed by the Council of Ministers, following a recommendation by the parliamentary political parties, so far as each political party is represented by one member, is clearly unconstitutional. In *Karayiorges* the Supreme Court considered the constitutionality of a law providing for the presence of observers nominated by parliamentary political parties on the boards of public corporations (the CyBC being included in them), also providing that the Council of Ministers should consult with the parliamentary political parties before appointing members of public corporations.[245] The Supreme Court held by a 5:4 majority that the said law was unconstitutional, *inter alia*, because it ran contrary to Article 54 of the Constitution which entrusts to the Council of Ministers (and not to the House of Representatives or to the parties which are represented in it) the exercise of the executive power. Therefore, the said legislative provisions were found to be inconsistent with the principle of separation of powers between the executive and the legislative insofar as they were enabling parliamentary political parties, and indirectly the House of Representatives, to interfere with the process of appointment of members of the board of administrative organs.

164. In the same judgment it was further held that the principle of equality was violated since the law discriminated between members of parliamentary political parties and citizens who are not members of such parties or who are members of political parties which do not have parliamentary representation. It was held that every individual should have the opportunity to be appointed to a public post irrespective of political convictions or other preferences. It is considered that the same considerations apply also in this case and accordingly, section 4 of Law 145/89 would run contrary to the principle of separation of powers and the principle of equality insofar as it provides that the Council of Ministers shall follow recommendations for appointments submitted by the political parties and that each political party shall be represented in the Press Council.

165. Whereas a Press Council was appointed after the enactment of Law 145/89, the three members representing the UCJ almost immediately quit, asserting that the powers, function and composition of the said organ undermined the freedom of the press and of the journalists. Their reaction was further precipitated due to their opposition to the appointment of George Christofides, a personal friend and close associate of the then President of the Republic George Vassiliou as the first, and so far only, Chairperson of the Press Council. The three members representing the ANPP also quit at a later stage. The Attorney General opined that, due to the refusal of the UCJ to recommend other members in order to fill the vacant positions, the Press Council could not be properly constituted and function. The Chairperson of the Press Council could, however, continue to represent the organ until a solution to the problem was reached. This awkward situation continued until the election of a new President of the Republic in 1993, who decided not to appoint a new Chairperson of the Press Council. The Press Council has not since functioned.[246]

245. *CyBC and another v. Karayiorges and another* [1991] 3 CLR 159 (in Greek). *See* a criticism in A. Emilianides, *The Separation between Political Power and Public Administration in Cypriot Law*, 1 Efimerida Dioikitikou Dikaiou 2-9 (2019) (in Greek); *id., Public Servants and Separation of Powers in the Cypriot Legal Order*, in *Public Administration after the* Crisis 139–154 (X. Kontiades, A. Emilianides & C. Anthopoulos eds, Sakkoulas 2019, in Greek).

246. *See* in detail K. Kouros, *The Mass Media Law in the Republic of Cyprus*, fn. 51 above.

§2. THE PRESS AUTHORITY

166. Section 24 of Law 145/89 further provides for the establishment of an independent Press Authority, which would have the competence to provide opinions to the Minister of Interior on whether to grant or revoke the licence of a press agency or of a related sub-agency. Similarly to the Press Council, however, the Press Authority never properly functioned in practice due to the withdrawal of members representing the UCJ and the ANPP.[247] Nevertheless, the Supreme Court has held that the fact that the Press Authority has not functioned does not affect the validity of the legal provision establishing it; what is missing is the implementation of the legal provisions and not their validity.[248] The Press Authority would further have the competence to determine a maximum price for the sale of newspapers and for the commission given to the press agencies and to sub-agencies, kiosk owners and newspaper sellers. Such maximum prices for the sale of newspapers and for the said commission should not be so low as to deter or restrict the publication of newspapers, or so high as to unreasonably burden the public.[249] In case the Press Authority fails to act and to determine a maximum price, this shall be determined by the Minister of Interior.

167. The Supreme Court has held that the ANPP may determine any price for the sale of newspapers it considers appropriate, so far as it does not exceed the maximum price for the sale of newspapers set by the Press Authority or the Minister of Interior, while the Cypriot Commission for the Protection of Competition (CPC) may not interfere with such decision of the ANPP.[250] The nine members of the Press Authority would be appointed by the Council of Ministers, in accordance with section 25 of Law 145/89. Three of the members would be appointed following a recommendation by the ANPP, one member following a recommendation by the UCJ, one member would be a superior officer of the PIO, two members would be officers of the Ministry of Commerce and Industry, one member would be a representative of the owners of the press agencies and another member would be a representative of the owners of printing shops. One of the three members appointed following the recommendation by the ANPP would act as the Chairperson of the Press Authority, to be substituted in case of absence by another of the members appointed by the ANPP.

168. As in the case of the Press Council, the term of the Press Authority is for three years and it is renewable. The Council of Ministers may further appoint alternative members who shall substitute the regular members if they are absent for whatever reason. If there is a vacancy due to death or resignation of the Chairperson or of a member of the Press Authority, the Council of Ministers may appoint a new Chairperson or member for the remainder of the Authority's term. The Press

247. *Ibid.*, 306ff.
248. *Republic v. Kalamari Publications Ltd and Others* [1997] 3 CLR 531 (in Greek).
249. L. Loucaides, *Can Prices for the Sale of Newspapers Be Determined?* 18 Cyprus Law Review 2659 (1987) (in Greek).
250. *Republic v. Kalamari Publications Ltd and others* [1997] 3 CLR 531 (in Greek).

Authority is convened by the Chairperson, in accordance with section 26 of Law 145/89, whenever he/she considers this to be necessary, or whenever the Minister or at least two members request so and simultaneously propose an agenda. Five members present constitute a quorum. Decisions are taken by majority, and if there is a tie, the Chairperson has the casting vote. A representative of the newspaper sellers or of the kiosk owners may, depending on the case, be present and express an opinion in meetings where issues related to their rights or interests are being discussed.

§3. THE MEDIA COMPLAINTS COMMISSION

169. Following the failure of the Press Council to function, the UCJ promoted self-regulation of the journalistic profession. As already indicated in the General Introduction (§3 VII), the UCJ, the ANPP and the OEMM approved in 1997 the JEC and established the CMCC which was entrusted with the task of overseeing the implementation of the JEC and of dealing with complaints alleging that the JEC has been violated. The CMCC is independent from government interference or control and is entirely self-regulated and self-sustained. Expenses are being equally borne by its three founding organizations. Donations or contributions may be accepted, but only to the extent that they do not hinder or undermine the impartiality of the CMCC. In general, the mission of the latter is to regulate news media, newspapers, periodicals, internet media and television or radio stations. Its motto is: 'for the truth, correct information and for the rights of the citizen and the journalist.'

170. The CMCC consists of seventeen members who should be of high moral standards. The Chairperson of the CMCC should preferably have a legal background. The Chairperson and four of the members of the CMCC are representatives of the civil society and are appointed by the outgoing CMCC. The UCJ and the ANPP each appoint three of the remaining members, whereas OEMM and private TV stations each appoint two members, and the CyBC and private radio stations each appoint one of the members. The tenure of office of the CMCC is for three years. In the case of temporary absence of the Chairperson, his/her duties are carried out by the Vice Chairperson. If a post becomes vacant due to death, resignation, or conviction for an offence involving fraud or on grounds of physical or mental incapacity, he/she is substituted by another member. A quorum is formed only if at least nine members, including the President or the Vice President, are present.

171. The person or the media named in a complaint for violation of the JEC are entitled to be present or to be represented in the procedure before the CMCC, and they should be given every opportunity to be heard, to give explanations and to present their views. The CMCC may deal with a case on its own initiative only if the case concerns a sufficiently serious violation of the JEC. The CMCC may further issue general guidelines for the interpretation of the JEC. The CMCC has the discretion to decide whether to deal with a complaint which is the subject matter of a judicial or administrative procedure. The CMCC will strive to reach a settlement of the dispute, as soon as possible; if no such settlement is achieved, then the CMCC examines the complaint and decides whether the JEC has been breached. The decisions of the CMCC are published, and the journalist or the media which are found in breach of the JEC have the obligation to publish the relevant decision.[251] However, the CMCC is not entitled to impose a fine or to adjudicate compensation, a fact which seriously undermines its ability to deter similar violations in the future.

§4. The Journalistic Ethics Code

172. According to the general provisions of the current JEC which was enacted in 2022, in carrying out their functions, journalists should respect and promote democracy, human rights and fundamental freedoms, and they should act in good faith. They should further show the necessary sensitivity for matters that concern national security, and they should be particularly careful when presenting issues such as violence, crime, sexual offences, human grief and death, as well as information or pictures that are hurtful or might cause panic, horror or revulsion, especially to children. It is further stated that the media and journalists have an obligation to respect the truth and the public's right to receive objective, full and reliable information, as well as the obligation to maintain conduct, dignity, honesty and professionalism of the highest standards. Journalists should refrain from publishing vulgar or obscene stories or language, and they should comment upon the work of their colleagues with due respect, refraining from personal attacks.

173. The Media obligations under the JEC include:[252]

(a) *Accuracy and avoidance of misinformation*: Ensuring that no inaccurate, misleading, imaginary, or distorted news, information or comments are published; if they are, immediate correction should be made, and where appropriate, an apology should be published. Whereas journalists have a right to criticism and satire, as well as to express their opinion, this should not undermine their obligation to corroborate their sources and facts and to not manipulate the news. Trust towards journalists is a cardinal value of journalism and accordingly, journalists should strive to refrain from the transmission of fake news and misinformation, as the latter are dangerous for democracy and freedom of the press.
(b) *Obtaining of information, private life and personal data*: The reputation and private life of every individual should be respected; intrusions and investigations into the private life of individuals without their consent, including the taking of pictures of people, unless they are involved in events which constitute news of general interest, as well as the gathering of information through bugging devices or long lens photography, are generally unacceptable, and their publication could only be justified in exceptional cases in the public interests. Personal data

251. All published decisions of the CMCC since 2003 are available in Greek only in the official site of the CMCC at, https://cmec.com.cy/el/rulings/.
252. Confidentiality, independence and the right of reply are dealt with in the relevant sections.

should be respected pursuant to the legislation in force, and there should be special care for sensitive personal data. As a general rule, journalists should not try to secure information or photographs through false representation or in any other fraudulent manner, or through intimidation or blackmail or bribery of witnesses. The Media and journalists should further refrain from personal attacks.

(c) *Grief and health*: Taking and publishing pictures of persons in hospitals or in other similar institutions should be carried out discreetly and after permission has been obtained and after the identity of the journalist has been duly stated. Any reference to health issues should be accurate, respect human dignity and avoid stereotypes. In cases involving mourning, grief or shock, journalists and media should be discreet and avoid any acts which may increase human pain. The Media should refrain from publishing pictures of people in conditions of mourning, grief or shock. Those cases where the publication of such pictures is justified should be dealt with special care. Furthermore, no news about suicides is published; in those extraordinary cases where circumstances justify publication, sensitivity and special care should be shown so as to avoid details about the method of suicide. The Media should further not reveal the identity of victims of rape or of other sexual offences, and they should not publish or reproduce details which are likely to cause or increase human pain.

(d) *Copyright*: The Media should respect the legislation governing intellectual property rights. Where permitted, reproduction should be done with due respect to the author and source.

(e) *Economic benefits*: Journalists should not accept gifts in connection with their function. Save in exceptional cases, they should not pay out or bribe witnesses or persons involved in criminal cases with the aim of obtaining information or photographs. Furthermore, journalists should not make use of their position for their personal benefit, and before being made available to the general public, any information of an economic nature obtained by them.

(f) *Presumption of innocence*: Presumption of innocence should be fully respected by the Media. Consequently, they should avoid publishing anything which may lead to conclusions regarding the guilt of suspects or of accused persons, or of something which would tend to publicly humiliate them.

(g) *Children*: In sexual offences involving children, the identity of children should in principle not be revealed. Moreover, as a general rule, journalists should not interview or take pictures of children without their consent and without informing an adult being responsible for them. The Media should further comply with the provisions of the United Nations Convention on the Rights of the Child.

(h) *Discrimination*: The Media should avoid any reference or action against a person which contains elements of prejudice or discrimination on any basis. Scorn, ridicule or abuse of individuals and groups is not permissible. They should further avoid the reproduction of stereotypes or anachronistic perceptions or terminology regarding gender, sexual orientation or gender identity. Hate speech, violence or discrimination against any person or specific groups of people, or denial of crimes should not be published or reproduced.

(j) Cases which justify deviation from one of the aforementioned rules by invoking public interest should be mainly cases which help to detect or expose criminal offences; protect public safety and health; safeguard human rights; or prevent deception of the public as a result of acts or statements by individuals or organizations.

174. In addition to the above, the Code of Ethics of the UCJ contains the following principles, which apply to its members, in a manner complementary to the JEC and the IFJC:

- Any form of censorship regardless of its origin and manifestation is prohibited.
- Freedom of the Press, speech, expression, opinion and criticism.
- The journalist shall remain independent of any intervention, influence or pressure, either from within or without the mass information media, seeking to compromise his/her mission of presenting the news correctly, fully and timely.
- The journalist shall always be guided by the truth in reporting unhindered, objective and unbiased information.
- The journalist's access to information sources, state or private, shall be unimpeded; information is not the property of any authority but belongs to the citizen as a fundamental human right.
- There must be true diversity and full transparency in the media; the journalist shall oppose the concentration, oligopoly or monopoly of the media.
- The journalist shall respect the rights and the dignity of the citizen and the private lives of people; a journalist or a press medium may write about the individual lives of people only when this is deemed imperative for the public interest, which in such a case supersedes the obligation to respect private life.
- The right of reply shall be respected.
- The citizens and their agencies shall have access to the media.
- False and damaging reports or broadcasts shall be speedily and satisfactorily rectified.
- Defamatory reports or broadcasts shall be avoided.
- Any form of bribery shall be rejected; the journalist should not accept any consideration or concessions of any kind, which aims at influencing him in the exercise of his professional duties.
- Indiscreet intervention in personal mourning and any reports or broadcasts, which may aggravate human suffering, shall be avoided; where the intervention is deemed necessary, it should be made with understanding and discretion.
- Extra care must be taken in the publication of photographs or the transmission of images, especially in the case of accident and crime victims.
- The identity of rape victims shall not be disclosed and restraint must be shown in publishing details, which might lead to the establishment of their identities.
- The journalist's right to secrecy and confidentiality and non-disclosure of a source of information entrusted to a journalist shall be respected.
- The identity of minor offenders shall not be disclosed and interviewing minors without the presence or the consent of their parents or guardians shall be avoided.

- Restraint shall be shown in referring to prosecuted persons or suspects as being guilty.
- Using images and mentioning the identity of innocent relatives shall not be permitted unless it is absolutely necessary for presenting the facts.
- Direct and honest means should be used in gathering information, taking pictures and making films, tapes and images; unusual methods should be used only when there is no other way of securing information, images and other material, which is absolutely necessary for the public interest.
- The titles used must always correspond to the texts.
- Advertisements and editorial material must be separated.
- The journalist shall disclose his/her identity, and also that of the medium for which he/she is working when making an interview or taking a statement for an article or broadcast. When taping a conversation with or a statement by somebody, live or by telephone, the journalist shall be required to make this known to the interlocutor.
- In presenting controversial issues, the views of all the parties involved must be given.
- Assumptions or speculations shall not be presented as facts.
- Praising and inciting crime and violence is prohibited.
- The intellectual property and creative work of others must be respected.
- The journalist must adhere to the ideals of freedom, democracy and peace, as well as to human values.
- Any form of discrimination and humiliation on grounds of race, religion, nationality, colour, belief, gender, physical appearance, disease, profession or social class must be detestable.
- The trade union and labour rights of journalists must be safeguarded and entrenched, namely to belong to their professional association and to satisfactorily regulate their pay and other work conditions through collective bargaining and collective agreements. Working journalists should participate in the decision-making organs of the media.
- Journalists should not act and write contrary to the JEC and their conscience and should not permit others to force them to do so. They should maintain professional solidarity and a high standard of professional ethics. They should not seek personal advantage at the expense of their colleagues and should not go against the professional aims, objectives and struggles of the UCJ. They should further protect their colleagues from calumny and slander and not exploit or repress their colleagues. Finally, they should not carry on any work which is demeaning to the journalistic profession.

Part III. Regulation of Audiovisual Media (Broadcasting)

Chapter 1. Public Service Broadcasting

§1. The Cyprus Broadcasting Corporation

175. In Cyprus, Public Service Broadcasting (PSB) has always been delivered by the CyBC (in Greek: 'Ραδιοφωνικό Ίδρυμα Κύπρου', '*PIK*').[253] The CyBC was established by Chapter 300A, a legislative instrument that was enacted by the British administration of Cyprus in 1958, just two years prior to Independence. Before that, in the spring of 1951, the British administration had created the Cyprus Broadcasting Service. The first radio programmes in the island were aired in October 1953, and the first TV programmes in October 1957. At the time, Cypriots perceived the news programmes of the Cyprus Broadcasting Service as an instrument of the British colonial rule. For this reason, the facilities of the radio station were one of the first targets of bomb attacks at the beginning of the national liberation struggle of 1955–1959.[254]

176. The establishment of the CyBC was a major step in the development of mass media in Cyprus. The Basic Law for CyBC, that is, Chapter 300A (CyBCL), remained in force after the Independence, under Article 188 of the Constitution, which provides that all laws that were in force on the date of the coming into operation of the Constitution shall continue to be in force until their amendment, being construed and applied with such modifications as may be necessary to bring them into conformity with the Constitution.

177. Article 122 of the Constitution makes specific reference to the CyBC as part of the public service of the Republic and as one of the legal entities under public law (public corporations). Article 171 of the Constitution incorporates the fundamental principle of bi-communality[255] through a series of provisions whose aim

253. *See* Art. 16 A, §1 of CYBCL. For the history of the CyBC in relation to its legislative status, *see* K. Kouros, *The Mass Media Law in the Republic of Cyprus*, fn. 51 above, 365–413 (Vivlioekdotiki 2008, in Greek).
254. *Ibid.*, fn. 77.
255. *See* for this A. Emilianides, *Constitutional Law in Cyprus* (2nd ed., Kluwer 2019).

is to safeguard the interests of the Greek-Cypriot and of the Turkish-Cypriot audience of the CyBC respectively. Despite the fact that Article 171 does not specifically mention the CyBC, it is clear that it applies to the latter's programmes since, at the time of the drafting of the Constitution, private broadcasting did not exist. More specifically, Article 171 stipulates that there must be R/T programmes for both communities, under a general proportion of 70% of R/T time for Greek-Cypriot audience and 30% for Turkish-Cypriot audience (to be noted that the same proportion is constitutionally provided for the allocation of seats in the House of Representatives under Article 62 of the Constitution; for the allocation of Ministries under Article 46 of the Constitution; and for the staffing of public services under Article 123 of the Constitution).[256] As regards radio programmes, Article 171 provides that no less than seventy-five hours per week shall address to Turkish-Cypriot audience, an amount of time that may decrease if the programmes for the Greek-Cypriot audience fall below the same level, and may increase if Greek-Cypriot programmes reach a level of more than 140 hours per week. As regards TV, Article 171 provides that the programmes that address the Turkish-Cypriot community shall cover three days for every ten days of TV time. Besides, it is provided that all official R/T transmissions shall take place both in Greek and in the Turkish language.

178. After the constitutional breakdown of 1964, the Turkish invasion of 1974 and the creation of the so-called Turkish Republic of Cyprus in 1983, the provisions of Article 171 of the Constitution cannot be applied in their entirety. The CyBC TV station still continues to provide a daily news bulletin in the Turkish language and also a daily bi-communal programme with the title 'BIZ/ΕΜΕΙΣ', that is, 'We', focusing on issues of interest for both communities. The second radio channel of the CyBC transmits daily programmes in Turkish from 06.00 to 17.00, in Armenian from 17.00 to 18.00, and in English from 18.00 to 24.00. Besides, the CyBCL still contains its original provisions for the separate Greek Programme and Turkish Programme Advisory Committees (section 20); for the basic news services in Greek, Turkish and English languages (section 21); and for the obligation of the CyBC to provide its broadcasting services with impartial attention to the interests and susceptibilities of the different communities, keeping a fair balance in the allocation of broadcasting hours (section 19).

179. The particular historical and political circumstances of the Republic of Cyprus, and the always present possibility of an armed conflict (as materialized during the events of 1963–1964 and, of course, during the Turkish invasion of 1974) are reflected in certain provisions of the CyBCL, such as the ones of section 44, which authorize the Council of Ministers to declare an emergency situation 'in which it is expedient in the public interest that the Council of Ministers should have control over the transmission of messages or any other matter whatsoever by means of the transmitting stations owned or operated' by CyBC. Under such conditions, the Council of Ministers, or any person properly authorized by the Council, may take possession of any R/T station or any apparatus and: use the latter for official

256. After the withdrawal of Turkish-Cypriots from the organs of the Republic, gradually after the events of December 1963, such constitutional provisions remain inactive.

purposes; place any person in control of any such station or apparatus; direct CyBC to submit any communication tendered for transmission; or direct CyBC to comply with all directions that may be considered as fit with reference to the transmission of communications. In such a case, CyBC shall be compensated for any damage directly attributable to the exercise of the aforementioned emergency powers.

180. The constitutional status of the CyBC is also determined by Article 19 of the Constitution, which safeguards freedom of speech, of information and of the press. Of course, the exercise of such freedoms in the context of the CyBC depends upon the specific organizational rules and procedures, not least those which are relevant to the appointment of the BoD of the CyBC, and those which are related to the supervision of the CyBC by various organs of the Republic.

181. Being the public service broadcaster, the CyBC retained the monopoly of R/T programmes for three decades after Independence, until the emergence of private broadcasting. During this period, and despite the legislative provisions that were safeguarding the independence of CyBC (*see* §3 below), it seems that there have been various political interventions in the fulfilment of CyBC's informative tasks.[257] The political pressure on CyBC decreased, but it was not eliminated, during the 1990s.[258] The issue of political propaganda is still an open one in Cyprus today,[259] not only with regard to the CyBC but also with regard to the private media agents. Besides, a major concern about CyBC has always been its financial sustainability.[260] It was questioned whether the CyBC would manage to survive following the financial crisis that intensified after 2012.[261]

182. In any case, the CyBC has diachronically been an important pillar of freedom of information and of democratic deliberation in the Republic of Cyprus. Despite the hardships of the Republic, the CyBC managed to develop both its material resources and the quality of its programmes. Today the CyBC includes two TV channels (*PIK 1* and *PIK2*) and four radio channels, each with its own special identity; a satellite channel (*PIKSAT*); and regular transmission of its programmes through a new Internet portal.[262] Through the latter, citizens may also receive video- and audio-on-demand services, and RSS feeds services, and they may have access to the rich digitalized archives of the CyBC. Another very important service is the digital platform 'We Report Cyprus', which is also hosted by the Internet portal of the CyBC. This platform gives citizens the opportunity to propose issues for the agenda of news bulletins and of journalistic research within the CyBC; to analyse

257. *See* Kouros, *The Mass Media*, fn. 51 above, 369–370, 396–397, 401–402.
258. *Ibid.*, 370.
259. *See* the special issue 2/2013 of the journal Dimosiografia (The Hellenic edition of Columbia Journalism Review), with articles by A. Emilianides, M. Dimitriou, S. Iordanidou, M. Ignatiou, G. Kentas, M. Kontos and A. Samaras.
260. *See* Kouros, *The Mass Media*, fn. 51 above, 374–382; C. Chrysanthou, *Requiem for the State Radio and Television*, 2 Dimosiografia 28 (The Hellenic edition of Columbia Journalism Review) (2013). *See* further the Annual Reports of the Auditor General of the Republic on CyBC.
261. *See* Chrysanthou, *Requiem*.
262. At: http://www.riknews.com.cy/.

and evaluate the news programmes of the CyBC; to participate in journalistic research and uploading of audiovisual material; and to have a view on the issues that are proposed by other members of the platform community, so that an interactive agenda-setting process takes place.

183. Furthermore, the digital platform of the CyBC hosts *Euronews*, providing twenty-four-hour European and world news services in the Greek language. CyBC is a member of the European Broadcasting Union (EBU), the Commonwealth Broadcasting Association (CBA), the Permanent Conference of the Mediterranean Audiovisual Operators (COPEAM), and the European Association of Regional Television (CIRCOM).

§2. The Concept and Mission of Public Service Broadcasting

I. The Legislative Definition of Public Service Broadcasting

184. The first and most important duty of the CyBC is to operate by sound and/or images public broadcasting service (PSB) for reception by the public (section 17, paragraph 1(a), section 16A, paragraph 1 CyBCL). According to section 16A, paragraph 2 CyBCL, such duty may be fulfilled through all types of Audiovisual Media Services (AVMS), as the latter are defined by the AVMS Directive; that is, both through 'linear' AVMS (regular broadcasting) and 'non-linear' AVMS (including on-demand AVMS).[263] It is stressed that, although the AVMS Directive no longer applies to radio broadcasting, section 2, paragraph 1 CyBCL defines AVMS so that many provisions of the AVMS Directive, as transposed into the CyBCL, apply to radio broadcasting as well.

185. The CyBCL defines and regulates PSB so that the latter complies with the state aid rules of the Treaty on the Functioning of the European Union (TFEU); the Treaty of Amsterdam Protocol on the system of public broadcasting in the Member States;[264] the Communication from the Commission on the application of State aid rules to PSB (henceforth: the '2009 Commission Communication');[265] and all the other guidelines which are relevant with the rules under which the provision of PSB services may take place.[266]

---

263. *See* the definitions of Art. 1, para. 1(a), (e) and (g) of the AVMS Directive.
264. Which provides that: 'The provisions of the TEC shall be without prejudice to the competence of Member States to provide for the funding of public service broadcasting insofar as such funding is granted to broadcasting organizations for the fulfilment of the public service remit as conferred, defined and organized by each Member State, and insofar as such funding does not affect trading conditions and competition in the EU to an extent which would be contrary to the common interest, while the realization of the remit of that public service shall be taken into account.'
265. Communication from the Commission on the application of State aid rules to public service broadcasting, OJ C 257, 27 Oct 2009, p. 1.
266. *See* among others, Commission Decision of 28 Nov. 2005 on the application of Art. 86(2) of the EC Treaty to State aid in the form of public service compensation granted to certain undertakings entrusted with the operation of services of general economic interest, OJ L 312, 29 Nov. 2005, p. 67; Community framework for State aid in the form of public service compensation, OJ C 297, 29

186. Following the call for a clear definition of the public service mandate in Chapter 6.1 of the 2009 Commission Communication, section 2 CyBCL defines PSB as follows:

> [S]ervice of general economic interest which directly corresponds to the democratic, social and cultural needs of Cypriot society, and to the need to ensure pluralism, *inter alia*, of the cultural and linguistic differences in mass media, and which includes the provision of a balanced package of services, consisting of informative, cultural and entertainment programmes, social contribution programmes, programmes which address to expatriates,[267] as well as programmes relevant with emergency situations and civil defence, as such package is defined by Regulations which are issued by authorization of this Law, and as such package may be broadened or otherwise diversified, under such Regulations, in view of the technological developments in the audiovisual sector or in view of new conditions and data.

II. The Specification of the Public Service Mandate

187. By virtue of the aforementioned authorization (*see also* section 22A, paragraph 2 CyBCL), and following the demand for a precise definition of the public service mandate by the earlier 2001 Communication from the Commission on the application of State aid rules to PSB (henceforth 'the 2001 Communication'),[268] the CyBC has issued, and the Council of Minister has approved, the Cyprus Broadcasting Corporation (PSB) Regulation 616/2003 for the harmonization of the Cypriot legislation with the said Communication. Rule 3, paragraph 1(a) of Regulation 616/

Nov. 2005, p. 4; and the European Parliament Resolution of 25 Sep. 2008 on concentration and pluralism in the media in the EU, 2007/2253(INI), stating that: 'regulations governing State aid are devised and implemented in a way which allow the public service and community media to fulfil their function in a dynamic environment, while ensuring that public service media carry out the function entrusted to them by Member States in a transparent and accountable manner, avoiding the abuse of public funding for reasons of political or economic expediency.'

267. The Greek word 'απόδημοι' which is used here, indicates Cypriots who live abroad, and not immigrants from other countries who live in Cyprus.

268. Communication from the Commission on the application of State aid rules to public service broadcasting, OJ C 320, 15 Nov. 2001, p. 5, at §45: 'The definition of the public service mandate by the Member States should be as precise as possible. It should leave no doubt as to whether a certain activity performed by the entrusted operator is intended by the Member State to be included in the public service remit or not … ' and at §47: 'At the same time, given the specific nature of the broadcasting sector, and the need to safeguard the editorial independence of the public service broadcasters, a qualitative definition entrusting a given broadcaster with the obligation to provide a wide range of programming and a balanced and varied broadcasting offer is generally considered, in view of the interpretative provisions of the Amsterdam Protocol, legitimate under Article 86(2). Such a definition is generally considered consistent with the objective of fulfilling the democratic, social and cultural needs of a particular society and guaranteeing pluralism, including cultural and linguistic diversity. As expressed by the Court of First Instance, the legitimacy of such a widely defined public service remit rests upon the qualitative requirements for the services offered by a public service broadcaster.'

2003 stipulates that, as regards TV programmes, and in order to fulfil its PSB duties, the CyBC shall dedicate no less than 40% of its annual screen time to news and current affairs programmes; no less than 10% of its annual screen time to cultural programmes; and no less than 50% of its annual screen time to entertainment programmes. The relevant thresholds for radio transmissions are as follows: 25% for information programmes; 5% for cultural programmes; and 70% for entertainment programmes.

188. For the purposes of the aforementioned provisions, Rule 4 of Regulation 616/2003 defines 'information programmes' so as to include the following:

- news bulletins in Greek, Turkish, English, and sign languages;
- current affairs programmes;
- documentaries and discussions on political, economic, social, and scientific issues;
- information programmes which address to the Turkish-Cypriot community and to the minority religious groups;
- programmes which are relevant to emergency situations or civil defence.

189. Rule 5 of Regulation 616/2003 defines cultural programmes under the concept of PSB so as to include the following:

- programmes focusing on the natural environment, art and the traditional cultural activities of the Cypriot communities, such as music, dance, poetry, pantomime, painting, and sculpture;
- European and international cultural products, including classical music, opera, ballet, traditional music, traditional dancing and theatrical performances;
- cultural magazines covering cultural activities in Cyprus and abroad, including cinema festivals, concerts, dancing, theatre, cinematography, opera, and ballet;
- Cypriot comedy sketches and Cypriot theatrical performances;
- documentaries and discussions on cultural affairs;
- performances of ballet, opera, and symphonic orchestras, etc.

190. Rule 6 of Regulation 616/2003 defines entertainment programmes for the purposes of PSB so as to include the following:

- entertainment programmes which are included in the catalogue of events of major importance for the Cypriot TV audience (*see* for them Chapter 6 of this Part), including, *inter alia*, the Olympic Games, the World Football Championship, the European Football Championship, the games of European Champions League, and the Eurovision song contests;
- athletic tele-magazines, and studio discussions on athletic issues;
- programmes covering athletic events;
- children's programmes, including, *inter alia*, tele-magazines addressed to children, cartoons of good quality, theatrical performances for children, TV series for children and quizzes;

- lifestyle programmes, including, *inter alia*, programmes dedicated to fashion, to cooking, to the household, and to decoration;
- general entertainment programmes, such as cinematographic films, TV series, and high-quality quizzes.

III. The Economic Aspects of Public Service Broadcasting

191. The supervision of CyBC and its funding will occupy the next parts of this chapter. For the moment, it is observed that the CyBC may be both funded by the state budget (section 24A CyBCL) and acquire financial resources through its own commercial or other activities insofar as the latter does not affect its PSB mission, as defined above (section 16A, paragraph 3 CyBCL). The CyBC shall carry out its commercial or any other activities in a manner which ensures more choice for the audience, without disturbing the good overall quality of its programmes (section 16B, paragraph (a) CyBCL). Furthermore, when conducting its commercial or any other activities, the CyBC shall secure resources for re-investment in the PSB programmes that have already been transmitted (section 16B, paragraph (c) CyBCL). Of course, the activities of the CyBC, and therefore its PSB functions, must be consistent with the legislative provisions and with the administrative regulations of the Republic (section 16B, paragraph (b) CyBCL).

192. State funding shall be used for the purposes of PSB, as defined above, on condition that the activities of CyBC do not distort competition to an extent which is contrary to the public interest (section 24A, section 16B, paragraph (d) CyBCL). Furthermore, section 24A CyBCL provides that any new public funding shall recover, but shall not exceed, the net additional costs which are connected with the provision of PSB. The relevant assessment shall be carried out on the basis of the principle of proportionality, taking into account past state funding contributions. Besides, the commercial transactions of the CyBC shall be based on fair pricing, reflecting the principles of cost orientation and transparency (section 16 B, paragraph (d) CyBCL). The decision of the Council of Ministers in 2013 to prohibit commercial advertisements in CyBC so as to deter it from competing with private TV stations, has led to it becoming fully dependent on the state contribution; considering the financial problems that the Cypriot economy has been facing during the past decade, this has proved very problematic for CyBC.

IV. Emphasis on Cultural, Linguistic and Religious Diversity

193. A more specific requirement, which determines the PSB mission of the CyBC, and which at the same time reflects the historical, political and constitutional conditions of the Republic of Cyprus, is the obligation to ensure 'impartial attention and respect for the interests and sensitivities both of the Greek-Cypriot and of the Turkish-Cypriot communities, as well as of the [other] religious groups and the various minorities on the island' (section 19, paragraph 1 CyBCL). Besides, PSB shall be provided in Greek, Turkish, English, and in any other language. Section 19, paragraph 2 CyBCL leaves the relevant decision 'at the discretion' of CyBC. However, the latter 'shall at all times keep a fair balance in the allocation of the overall radio and TV hours to programmes, transmissions and issues which are transmitted in these languages' (section 19, paragraph 2 CyBCL).

194. In accordance with Article 6 of the AVMS Directive, the CyBC shall ensure that the provision of PSB will not incite violence or hatred towards any person or group in a way that would violate rights protected by the Constitution or the EU Charter of Fundamental Rights, or that would publicly provoke the commission of terrorist offences. The CyBC should take all necessary and proportional measures, respecting the principle of human dignity (section 19, paragraph 3, section 18B CyBCL). In conducting its supervisory role, the CRTA is particularly severe when enforcing this latter obligation. In a 2013 decision, the CRTA imposed on the CyBC an unusually high administrative fine for a comment, made by a guest of the daily current affairs tele-magazine of the station, which related to the behaviour of immigrants.[269] The decision of the CRTA was based, among else, on the fact that the journalist – coordinator of the tele-magazine did not properly react to what was said by her guest.

195. PSB, as delivered by the CyBC, is further specified by the provisions of the CyBCL and by the provisions of the CyBCR about the principles and standards of journalistic ethics, political independence and fairness, respect for private life, protection of minors, etc. Such provisions are largely similar to the ones that apply to private broadcasters and will be jointly presented in the relevant chapters of this Part.

V. The Supreme Court on the Role of the Cyprus Broadcasting Corporation

196. The Supreme Court has had the opportunity to express its views on the role and mission of the CyBC in the context of disputes about the constitutionality of the (now abolished) system of funding the CyBC through a special contribution ('εισφορά'), which was charged on the electricity bills of citizens, depending on the amount of electricity which each household consumed.[270]

---

269. CRTA, Case No. 53/2013(68), Decision of 16 Oct. 2013 (in Greek). The comment of the guest had as follows: 'Too much democracy is an illness for a place [...] I like this thing that Golden Dawn [i.e. the ultra right-wing party in Greece] is doing in Athens now [...]When I walk down the street and I am being watched by 800 foreigners who have done I don't know what in their country, I am not racist, but I can't watch that. I can't watch you commit a crime, be my guest, let me feed you and give you water, and give you the cheques while you just do not respect me, because I am respectful when I go to your country Mr Pakistani and Mr Indian and whatever, I am respectful because I am in your country.' The Decision of the CRTA was preceded by a Decision of the CMCC finding a violation of the Journalistic Ethics Code.

270. *See* the Cyprus Broadcasting Corporation (Imposition of Contribution) Law 14/1979, abolished by Law 64(I)/2000.

197. In *Constantinides*[271] the Supreme Court held that this contribution was a tax under Article 24 of the Constitution, and that, being a tax, it was reasonably scheduled, in view of the 'essential public service' for which it was constituted. The Court also concluded that the contribution was scheduled so as to be compatible with the principle of equality under Article 28 of the Constitution. For this conclusion, the Court appealed to an empirical survey establishing a correlation between the consumption of electricity and the income of households. As regards the nature and the means of PSB, the Court was content to confirm that radio and TV broadcasting renders to people an 'essential social service', as the Preamble of the Law imposing the special contribution stated. In this context, the Court also ascertained that the legislative intention was to provide CyBC with adequate resources since the mechanisms for the imposition and collection of funds used in past had proved to be ineffective.[272]

198. Such succinctness about the nature and means of PSB was reasonable at the time (1982) since the CyBC was the only broadcasting operator, and private broadcasting was just a remote possibility. Interestingly enough, the Supreme Court affirmed the ruling of *Constantinides* twenty years later, in the *Antenna* case, when private broadcasting stations had already been a reality with a history of more than ten years.[273] This time the Court devoted extensive extracts to the role and mission of PSB. This was so not least because one of the arguments of the applicants (among them, the largest private TV station in Cyprus at the time, Antenna TV) was precisely that the ruling of *Constantinides* should be overruled as being obsolete after the introduction of private broadcasting. According to the applicants, such an introduction meant that CyBC was no longer the exclusive provider of public services in the field of broadcasting because citizens were now in a position to receive similar and free-of-charge services from private broadcasters as well.

199. Referring to this argument, the Supreme Court first affirmed the ruling of the first instance Court, to the effect that the introduction of private broadcasting did not rescind the duty of the CyBC to deliver its public utility services; therefore, since the imposition and the collection of the special contribution is connected with the sustainability of CyBC, preservation of such contribution is still a matter of public interest.[274] Then the Court engaged in a lengthy discussion of its views on the role and mission of PSB in the context of the broadcasting system as a whole:

---

271. *Constantinides v. The Electricity Authority of Cyprus* [1982] 3 CLR 798.

272. *Ibid.*, 804.

273. *See Antenna T.V. Ltd et al. v. The Electricity Authority of Cyprus and the CyBC* [2002] 3 CLR 793 (in Greek). *See also* the judgment of the first instance Court, *Antenna T.V. Ltd et al. v. The Electricity Authority of Cyprus and the CyBC* [2000] 4 CLR 657 (in Greek); *Ekdotikos Oikos Dias Ltd v. CRTA* [2001] 4 CLR 1113 (in Greek), both affirming the ruling of *Constantinides*. Another interesting case, in which a private station argued that the CyBC was unduly privileged, since it had the exclusive right to organize a TV lottery, is *Sigma Radio T.V. Ltd. v. CTRA*, Judgment of 19 Jan. 2007, Case No. 272/2005 (in Greek). The Court rejected the claim of the private station that the principle of equality was violated.

274. *See Antenna T.V. Ltd et al. v. The Electricity Authority of Cyprus and the CyBC* [2000] 4 CLR 657, 662 (in Greek).

> The creation of private radio and television stations may contribute to polyphony in the sector of information, and, under appropriate circumstances, may ensure real competition and improvement as regards the quality of radio and television programmes. Nevertheless, we must be mindful of the fact that private radio and television stations are managed by private undertakings, which, as it is natural, set profit as their target. In Greece, radio and television broadcasting fall under direct state control (*see* Article 15.2 of the Greek Constitution). P.D. Dagtoglou … notices that 'direct state control is not incompatible with the organization of radio and television in a manner which guarantees their objectivity, but on the contrary it should constitute an important factor and guarantee of such objectivity' … [P.D. Dagtoglou] notices that radio and television, which objectively is called upon to serve free competition of ideas and of interests, on the one hand, and the publicity of political life, on the other hand, threatens, due to its monopolistic structure, to restrict or even to falsify these constituent element of democracy. He then proceeds into suggesting that the answer to the danger of the common real monopoly is state intervention.
>
> Therefore, we consider that the existence and the functioning of public radio and television in our country, which does not aim at profit, constitutes a form of indirect state control whose aim is also to guarantee the objectivity of private radio and television. Such a guarantee serves the public interest. Therefore, the existence and functioning of the CyBC, which is a Public Utility Organism, serves the public interest. Besides, as the Preamble of Law 14/79 mentions, the functioning of CyBC constitutes in a modern state an essential social service. As a consequence, we consider that the need for safeguarding [financial] resources, which will ensure its sustainability, continues to exist ….[275]

200. By way of a critical remark, it is noticed that the Supreme Court's reference to the Greek Constitution, and to the writings of a scholar whose views are directed towards the clauses of this Constitution, may not be the most appropriate choice insofar as the relevant clauses of the Cypriot Constitution are very different at a crucial point. In particular, Article 19 of the Cypriot Constitution first provides for the protection of freedom of expression and information by any means (media included); then, in the classical liberal fashion, provides for general limiting clauses in the interests of public security, prevention of crime, protection of the reputation, etc.; and in the last paragraph stipulates that 'nothing hinders the Republic' to establish a licensing regime. However, the Greek Constitution also safeguards freedom of expression by any means (Article 14, paragraph 1) and freedom of the printed press (Article 14, paragraph 2), but then it exempts radio, television and all other audiovisual media from such protection (Article 15, paragraph 1), while it also

275. *Antenna T.V. Ltd et al. v. The Electricity Authority of Cyprus and the CyBC* [2002] 3 CLR 793, 812–813 (in Greek). The references of the Court are made to P.D. Dagtoglou, *Constitutional Law: Civil Rights* vol. A' §§790, 799 (Ant. N. Sakkoulas 1991, in Greek).

stipulates that R/T fall under 'direct state control', which takes, among else, the form of a licensing regime (Article 15, paragraph 2). An analysis of the Greek Constitution with regard to the status of R/T does not belong to the present context.[276] It is suggested that the Supreme Court of Cyprus should perhaps be more hesitant to draw from analyses deriving from the clauses of a Constitution, which, as regards the constitutional status of media, are very different from the respective clauses of the Cypriot Constitution.

201. Apart from the above comment, the judgment of the Supreme Court is commendable for its clarity and soundness, not least because of its emphasis on the need to safeguard the democratic values of pluralism and objectivity of information under the oligopolistic circumstances of private broadcasting. Besides, we notice a remarkable similarity of the quoted considerations to the traditional jurisprudence of the German Constitutional Court (the *Bundesverfassungsgericht*) on the dual broadcasting system (i.e., on the co-existence of public and private broadcasters) and on the counter-balancing role of PSB in stimulating pluralism of opinion as against the monopolistic tendencies of the private audiovisual sector.[277] In a subsequent case, the *Sigma* case, which we shall present in detail in Part V, Chapter 3 with regard to another issue (namely, the sanctioning powers of the CRTA), the Supreme Court affirmed the ruling of the *Antenna* case making reference to a judgment of the *Bundesverfassungsgericht*, in order to argue that the co-existence of the CyBC with private stations serves better the public interest.[278] Challenging this ruling before the EctHR, the applicant, another large private TV and radio station, Sigma, supported its complaint about the differential treatment of the CyBC by appealing to the fact that, at the material time, the CRTA did not have the competence to impose administrative fines on the CyBC for violation of the provisions of the CyBCL. The EctHR rejected this claim, which was raised under Article 14 ECHR, noticing that: 'Given... the differences in the legal status and the applicable legal frameworks and the different objectives of private stations and the CyBC in the Cypriot broadcasting system, it cannot be said that they are in a comparable position for the purposes of Article 14 of the Convention.'[279]

276. For an attempt to proceed into a liberal-democratic reading of Art. 15 in conjunction with Arts 14 and 5A of the Greek Constitution, *see* C. Stratilatis, *Constituting the Right to Public Electronic Communication* (Sakkoulas 2006, in Greek).

277. *See* among else 73 BVerfGE 118 (1986); 74 BVerfGE 238 (1987); and 119 BVerfGE 196 (2007). For a brief overview *see* D.P. Kommers and R.A. Miller, *The Constitutional Jurisprudence of the Federal Republic of Germany* 517–518 (3rd ed., Duke University Press 2012); and for a comparative overview of the German broadcasting system *see* W. Hoffmann-Riem, *Regulating Media: The Licencing and Supervision of Broadcasting in Six Countries* 130–139, 281–286 (The Guilford Press 1996).

278. *Sigma Radio T.V. Ltd v. CRTA* [2004] 3 CLR 134, 178 (in Greek).

279. *Sigma Radio Television Ltd v. Cyprus*, Judgment of 21 Jul. 2011, Applications Nos 32181/04 and 35122/05, hudoc, §§211–225 (223).

§3. The Organization of Public Service Broadcasting

I. The Organizational Aspects of the Cyprus Broadcasting Corporation

A. Legal Nature

202. Section 4 CyBCL establishes the CyBC as a 'body corporate with perpetual succession and a common seal and with the power to acquire, hold and dispose of property, to enter into contracts, to sue and to be sued in its said name and to do all things necessary for the purposes of this Law'. The CyBC is a legal entity under public law, belonging to the category of public corporations of the Republic of Cyprus. Such corporations are commonly called 'semi-state organizations' (in Greek: 'ημικρατικοί οργανισμοί'), and, according to Article 122 of the Constitution, they are established by law in the public interest.[280] Their capital is either funded or guaranteed by the Republic, while their management and administration (in Greek: 'διοίκησις') is controlled ('τελεί υπό τον έλεγχον') by the Republic (with the term 'control' meaning here the supervisory competences of the organs of the Republic on the functioning of public corporations).

203. Besides, as the Supreme Court noticed in its landmark judgment *Karayiorges*, which specifically referred to the CyBC, such organizations:

> Function in the sphere of public law, and their mission is to achieve one or more of the aims of the public. The most important feature of the organizations under this category is that they are endowed with decisive competence (*imperium*) in one or more fields of public law ... Even primary functions of the state in the field of the governance of the country may be attributed to organizations of public law ... The appointment of the members of their Boards of Directors constitutes an act of the executive which lies outside the sphere of competences of the legislature.[281]

B. Appointment and Term of Office of the Board of Directors

204. Accordingly, section 5 CyBCL assigns the appointment of the Chairman and of the other eight members of the CyBC to the Council of Ministers. Originally section 5 referred to seven members, a provision which was inconsistent with the subsequent provisions of the Certain Legal Entities Under Public Law (Appointment of BoD) Law of 1988, Law 149/1988, as amended and currently in force, which provides that the BoD of all legal entities falling under the provisions of this Law (CyBC included) is composed of nine members, one of which is the President

280. *See* V. Georghiou, *Public Administration in Cyprus* 309–320, 347–356 (En typois 2012, in Greek); A. Aggelides, *Legal Persons under Public Law*, 3 Lysias 31 (1994) (in Greek). For the legal nature of the CyBC *see also* C. Tornaritis, *The Legal Nature of the Cyprus Broadcasting Corporation*, 1–2 Cyprus Law Tribune 10 (1972) (in Greek).

281. *CyBC and another v. Karayiorges and another* [1991] 3 CLR 159, 174 (in Greek).

and another the Vice President. Law 52(I)/2019 amended section 5 CyBCL so as to provide explicitly that the BoD of CyBC comprises nine members. Therefore, the CyBC is now managed by a BoD consisting of nine members, one of which is its President and another is its Vice President. The *Karayiorges* judgment of the Supreme Court precludes any decisive intervention of the House of Representatives in this respect. In section III the reasoning of the Court, which determines the overall political independence of the CyBC, despite the fact that the members of its administrative body are appointed by the Government, shall be assessed.

205. Section 3 of Law 149/1988 further provides a particular procedure for the appointment of the President, of the Vice President and of the other members of the BoD of a number of public corporations, the CyBC included in them. The competent Minister (in the case of CyBC, the Minister of the Presidency) submits his/her suggestions to the Council of Ministers, which, after a mere briefing (not a consultation) with the House of Representatives, proceeds into the appointment, taking into account the integrity, the prestige, the academic qualifications, the experience, and the social activities and contribution of the persons under consideration. Any citizen may submit his/her *curriculum vitae*, expressing his wish to be considered as a candidate in this procedure. However, on 19 July 2023, the Council of Ministers appointed an Advisory Council, chaired by a former Judge of the Supreme Court and comprising nine members in total, which shall have the responsibility to advertise the positions of members of the BoD of a number of public corporations (CybC included), and propose to the Council of Ministers a list of three candidates for each position, with the Council of Ministers then selecting one appointee out of the three nominees. The Council of Ministers may still deviate from the suggestions of the Advisory Council, but it must provide reasons for the grounds for such a decision. The Advisory Council was advertised as a way to disassociate the selection of members of the BoD of public corporations from political party involvement.

206. Other sections of Law 149/1988 provide certain incompatibilities and impediments for the appointment of a person as a member of the BoD of public corporations, CyBC being one of them. Such incompatibilities and impediments have to do with the criminal record and the debts of the persons under consideration, with conflicts of interest in their or their relatives' persons, with bankruptcy, etc. (sections 3A and 3B Law 149/88). It is also stipulated that the members of the BoD of a public corporation shall not have served the same corporation from the position of the General Director or the Division Director (section 3A, paragraph (c) of Law 149/88). Besides, section 4, paragraph (a) of Law 149/1988 provides that no person may be appointed in the BoD of a public corporation if he/she has been previously appointed twice in the same position unless his/her overall term of office does not exceed a period of sixty months.

207. Section 5, paragraph 2 CyBCL provides that the term of office of the members of the CyBC shall be three years. However, this provision has also been implicitly amended by section 4 of Law 149/1988, providing that the term of office of the BoD of all public corporations (CyBC included) will be thirty months. In the same section, as amended by Laws 115(I)/2013 and 165(I)/2013, it is stipulated that, after each presidential election, and until 31 December of the year in which the election was held, the Council of Ministers has the power to terminate the term of office of the members of the BoD of all public corporations, the CyBC included in them (section 4, paragraph (d) of Law 149/88). In all other cases, the Council of Ministers may remove the President, the Vice President or any of the members of the BoD of public corporations, providing a clear and detailed reasoning for its decision (section 4, paragraph (b) of Law 149/88; *see also* section III below). Section 5, paragraph 2 CyBCL, providing that the Council of Ministers may remove the members of the CyBC without reasoning, should be considered as implicitly rescinded by the aforementioned provision of Law 149/1988. Of course, any member of the BoD of public corporations, the CyBC included, may at any time submit his/her resignation to the Council of Ministers (section 4, paragraph (c) of Law 149/88).

208. Despite the fact that the appointment of the members of the BoD of the CyBC belongs to the exclusive authority of the Government, the provisions about their term of office, in combination with the case-law of the Supreme Court on the requirement of detailed reasoning of any decision which discharges a member of the BoD of public corporations (*see* section III below), provide some, if not adequate at least existing, safeguards with regard to the independence of the CyBC.[282] However, the recent amendment of Law 149/88, to the effect that after each presidential election the new Government may replace the members of the BoD of all public corporations, the CyBC included in them (*see* above), signifies a retreat in this respect. This is so insofar as the new provisions imply that the appointment of someone as a member of the BoD in a public corporation may have political character (if this is not so, then what is the need to provide such a power after an election?) It is noted that the aforementioned amendment took place after the election of a new President of the Republic, and hence of a new Government, at the presidential elections of 2013.

C. Competences of the Board of Directors and of the President

209. The CyBCL does not contain a list of the competences of the BoD of the CyBC. Such a list is provided by the Code of Governance of CyBC, which was adopted by the BoD on 18 January 2011, stating a series of basic principles and rules for the effective functioning of the CyBC.[283] In particular, the BoD has exclusive competence to decide, among else, on the following issues:

- the vision, the aims, and the strategic policy;
- the annual budget and the business plan;
- all official reports that must be submitted to the supervisory organs and agencies;
- the important capital expenditures, the non-ordinary transactions and the disposal of important assets;

282. Compare Kouros, *The Law of Mass Media*, fn. 51 above, 384.
283. *See* Cyprus Broadcasting Corporation, *Code of Governance of the Cyprus Broadcasting Corporation* (in Greek).

- the appointment of the General Director and the termination of his term of office, as well as the appointment of the other Directors of CyBC;
- the approval and inspection of the system of internal control and of the procedures of risk management;
- the monitoring of conflicts of interest in the persons of Directors and of the members of the BoD;
- the appointment of advisory committees and of the members of the Committee of Control, competent for accountancy, auditing, and other issues of an economic nature;
- the assignment of particular competences to the Executive Management Body or to individual members of the BoD.

210. The members of the BoD are not occupied on a full-time basis. Their remuneration is determined by the Council of Ministers. The absence of a member from the meeting of the BoD must be properly justified. The meetings of the BoD must be no less than ten for every year. The President of the BoD has the responsibility for the proper functioning of the BoD. He/she ensures that all issues on the agenda will be discussed on the basis of all necessary information and support by the relevant departments of the CyBC. The President or the Vice President must chair all meetings of the BoD. The quorum for the meetings of the BoD is five members, the President or the Vice President included. The President cannot exercise the duties of an executive director (section 3, paragraph 1 of Law 149/1988, after its amendment by Law 165(I)/2013).

D. The General Director

211. The chief executive officer of the CyBC is its General Director. The General Director is occupied on a full-time basis. He/she is responsible for the implementation of the policy of the CyBC, as suggested by the BoD, and for the administration of its day-to-day business (section 9, paragraph 1 CyBCL). More specifically, in accordance with the CyBC Service Plan for the Position of the General Director (Regulation 284/1992), the General Director is responsible for:

- the efficient organization, direction and supervision of the activities of CyBC;
- the scheduling and the direction of the developmental course of the CyBC;
- the deployment of the CyBC's cooperation with the agents of the cultural, social, economic, artistic, etc. life of the country;
- observance of the objectivity and of the editorial independence by all the programmes of CyBC, the avoidance of any privileged promotion of the views of any political party or of the government or of the governmental work, and the preservation of equality in the presentation of the views and the works of all parliamentary parties, of the President of the Republic and of the Government;
- rigorous observance of any deontological provisions as regards the terms of electoral competition.

The General Director advises the BoD on all policy issues of the organization. He/she takes all necessary actions for the cooperation of the CyBC with foreign public broadcasters. And he/she executes any other task that may be assigned to him/her by the BoD of the CyBC.

212. The appointment of the General Director (on a contractual basis, with a duration of no more than five years, but subject to the possibility for renewal for an additional five years, to the extent that any such renewal shall not exceed the age of mandatory retirement) takes place after a public call and belongs to the competences of the BoD (section 3, paragraph 1 of the Certain Legal Entities Under Public Law (Appointment of General Directors) Law of 1990, Law 115/1990, as amended and currently in force; cf. section 9, paragraph 3 CyBCL). The relevant decision shall be approved by the Council of Ministers, which, in case of disapproval, shall provide due reasoning for its decision (section 3, paragraphs 3 and 5 of Law 115/90, section 9, paragraphs 4 and 5 CyBCL). The Supreme Court held that, in applying the aforementioned provisions, the Council of Ministers should only examine the observance by the BoD of the formal legal requirements for exercising their authority, and it should not enter into examination of more detailed issues, such as the evaluation of the qualifications and of the experience of the candidates. Such evaluation belongs to the exclusive competence of the relevant BoD.[284] Clearly, such case-law provides another guarantee in favour of the independence of the CyBC.

E. Functions of the Cyprus Broadcasting Corporation

213. As all legal entities under public law, the CyBC has administrative and financial independence (in Greek: 'αυτοτέλεια').[285] Such independence is by definition limited insofar as various state organs have the duty to supervise the relevant activities of the CyBC (*see* section II below). Under this proviso, the CyBC has the duty to offer its PSB services; to control and operate its installations, plant and equipment, and its property in general, in such manner as it may seem expedient; to promote the development of broadcasting services in Cyprus or abroad, as far as the latter is practicable; and to advise the competent Minister on all matters relating to the broadcasting service (section 17, paragraph 1 CyBCL).

214. In this respect, the CyBC may, either in its own name or through any agent:

- erect, maintain and operate transmitting and receiving stations;
- instal and operate wired R/T distribution services for the public;
- enter into arrangements with the Government for the purpose of obtaining licences, rights, privileges, and concessions;

284. *See Christoforou v. The Council of Ministers and another*, Judgment of 10 Jun. 2008, Case No. 2285/2006 (in Greek).
285. *See* V. Georghiou, *Public Administration in Cyprus* 316 (En Typois 2012, in Greek).

- produce, manufacture, purchase or otherwise acquire, and sell or otherwise dispose of, any mechanical records and material and apparatus for use in connection with films and records;
- provide and receive from other persons matters to be broadcast;
- organize, provide and subsidize public entertainment for the purpose of broadcasting;
- collect news and information in any part of the world and in any manner that may think fit, and establish and subscribe to news agencies;
- establish offices or agencies in any part of Cyprus;
- acquire or sell copyright;
- publish and circulate printed matter that may be conducive to the performance of any of its duties;
- do anything which it may deem expedient for the purpose of advancing the skill of persons employed, or the efficiency of its equipment, including the provision, by others, of facilities for training, education and research;
- accept advertisements for broadcasting with or without charge, provided that they do not conflict with the general policy of the CyBC;
- with the approval of the Council Ministers, enter into arrangements with commercial broadcasting interests and lease the use of its transmitters and studios for certain specified times;
- do all such other things as the CyBC may consider necessary in the furtherance of its duties (section 17, section 2 CyBCL).

215. Section 10 CyBCL provides CyBC with the authority to 'appoint such employees as it may deem necessary for the discharge of its functions … upon such terms and conditions of service as it may determine.' It is noted that, under Article 125 of the Constitution, in conjunction with Article 122 which renders the CyBC one of the legal persons under public law of the Republic, the appointment, promotion, transfer, etc. of the CyBC's employees should be effected by the Public Service Commission. According to the letter of the Constitution, the Public Service Commission should be composed of representatives of both communities (the Greek-Cypriot and the Turkish-Cypriot). However, after the events of 1963–1964, and after the withdrawal of Turkish-Cypriot officers from the organs of the Republic, the functioning of this Commission in accordance with constitutional provisions became impossible.

216. As a result, another Public Service Commission was created, according to the doctrine of necessity.[286] Besides, again by invoking the doctrine of necessity, Law 61/70 assigned the competence for the appointment, promotion, transfer, etc. of the employees of certain public corporations, CyBC being one of them, to their administrative bodies. In early January 2014, however, the Government submitted a legislative proposal which purports to remove such competences from the BoD of such public corporations and re-assign such competences to the Public Service

286. For extended analysis of the legislative and jurisprudential developments as regards the implementation of the doctrine of necessity on this particular subject *see* Emilianides, *Constitutional Law in Cyprus* (2nd ed., Kluwer 2019).

Commission. The bill is still pending before the House of Representatives. It would seem that there is no political will to enact such a bill into legislation and it should be considered as abandoned. In any case, with the approval of the Council of Ministers, the CyBC may issue Regulations relating to the aforementioned matters and, in general, to all matters which have to do with the conditions of service of its employees (section 12 of CyBCL).[287]

II. Supervision of the Cyprus Broadcasting Corporation

A. *Supervision by the Cyprus Radio and Television Authority*

217. After 2004, the bulk of the supervisory authorities of the Republic over the CyBC have been transferred to the CRTA, which is also competent for the supervision of the private broadcasting sector (for the CRTA *see* Part V). The CRTA shall first conduct an 'annual qualitative audit' with regard to the fulfilment of the PSB mission of the CyBC (section 22B, paragraph 1(a) CyBCL). In this respect, the CRTA inspects whether the CyBC offers a balanced pack of services and programmes, in accordance with Regulation 616/2003 (*see* above, §2 II in this chapter); whether the CyBC really transmits the programmes which fall under the concept of PSB, in accordance with the same Regulation; and whether the contents of such programmes really abide by the qualitative requirements of the PSB under section 19 of the CyBCL (*see* above, §2 IV in this chapter). In the same context, the CRTA has the duty to submit an Annual Report to the Minister of the Presidency, while the CyBC has the obligation to provide CRTA with all necessary information and facilities for the drafting of such Report (section 22B, paragraphs 2 and 3 CyBCL).

218. Second, the CRTA examines, either in its own motion or after a complaint, issues which are relevant to the implementation of all the provisions of the AVMS Directive, as such provisions have been transposed by sections 17A–17E, 18A–18G and 19A–19C of the CyBCL. In this respect, the CRTA, after hearing the interested parties, may impose on the CyBC administrative sanctions for violation of the same sections (section 22B, paragraph 1(c) CyBCL). Depending on the nature, the gravity and the duration of the violation, the CRTA may address to the CyBC a recommendation or a warning or may impose an administrative fine, which, in the case of the TV stations of the CyBC, cannot exceed the amount of EUR 8,500, and in the case of the CyBC radio stations the amount of EUR 3,400 (section 22C CyBCL). Besides, if confronting such violations requires judicial action, the CRTA may request from the Court to issue any prohibitive or imperative order, preliminary injunction included (section 22B, paragraph 1(d), and section 22E CyBCL).

287. *See* for example Regulation 317/1987, providing, among else, that the appointment of public servants to the CyBC will be conducted by its BoD after a reasoned suggestion of an internal Advisory Committee.

219. Third, the CRTA is responsible on a bi-annual basis for the drafting of a Report on the implementation of the provisions of the AVMS Directive for the promotion of European works and independent productions (section 22B, paragraph 4 CyBCL). Such a Report should be notified to the Council of Ministers and to the House of Representatives. Lastly, the CRTA monitors the international developments in the field of PSB, and it is responsible for submitting to the Council of Ministers suggestions for the amelioration of the relevant legislative provisions.

B. Supervision and Possible Interventions by Governmental Authorities

220. Despite the transference of the bulk of supervisory duties to the CRTA, the central governmental authorities still retain some powers of control over the CyBC. In particular, the Minister of Interior may address to the CyBC directions of a general nature which are considered necessary for the interests of the Republic. Such directions should be drafted after consultation with the Board of the CyBC, but once finalized, the CyBC is bound to follow them (section 9A, paragraph 1 CyBCL), provided, of course, that they are compatible with the legislation and with the Constitution. Besides, when asked to do so, the CyBC is required to provide the Minister of Interior with any report, account or information that is relevant to its property and its activities (section 9A, paragraph 2 CyBCL). The Minister of Education, Sport and Youth, however, may address to the CyBC directions which are specifically relevant to the linguistic policy of the Republic (section 9A, paragraph 3 CyBCL).

221. Each year the CyBC shall present to the Council of Ministers its budget for the next year (section 29 CyBCL). In general, after being approved by the Council of Ministers, the budget of all public corporations is finally submitted in the form of a law to the House of Representatives. Adopting or rejecting such budgets, the latter may exercise a form of indirect control over the activities of public corporations.[288] Control of the CyBC's budget is an important power in the hands of the Government.

222. The accounts of the CyBC shall be audited by auditors who are appointed on an annual basis after the approval of the Minister of Interior (section 30, paragraph 2 CyBCL). As soon as the accounts have been audited, the CyBC is required to furnish a copy of the accounts together with the auditors' statement to the same Minister for his/her approval (section 30, paragraph 3 CyBCL). Furthermore, the CyBC is required to submit to the same Minister its Annual Report on its activities, containing not only the relevant financial information but also information on the policy, the aims and the achievements of the CyBC during last year (section 31, paragraph 1 CyBCL). Such Annual Reports are notified to the House of Representatives (section 31, paragraph 3 CyBCL), and they are regularly published in the internet portal of the CyBC.[289]

---

288. *See* Georghiou, *Public Administration*, 318.
289. *See* https://corporate.rik.cy/ετήσιες-εκθέσεις.

223. The provisions of section 22 CyBCL are of particular importance for the determination of the scope of potential governmental interventions in the editorial policy of the CyBC. According to paragraph 1 of the said section, the CyBC 'shall, whenever so requested by an authorized officer in the public service or an authorized police officer, broadcast … any announcement or other matter (with a visual image of any picture or object mentioned in the announcement …) which the officer may request the CyBC to broadcast'. However, such power is efficiently counter-balanced by the provision of the next paragraph: When broadcasting or sending such announcement or other matter, the CyBC may at its discretion announce, or refrain from announcing, that the announcement was broadcast at the request of a public official. The same discretion applies when the Council of Ministers exercises its (very dangerous) power under paragraph 3 of section 22, to 'require the Corporation to refrain at any specified time or at all times from broadcasting or sending any matter … '.[290]

224. The above provisions seem to have played a role on the eve of the presidential elections of 1977, when the Minister of Interior allegedly asked the CyBC to broadcast a plea for the liberation of the kidnapped son of the then President of the Republic by the then imprisoned Nicos Sampson, the appointed 'President' of the eight-day coup d'état government of July 1974.[291] The head of the News Department of the CyBC allegedly appealed to his discretion to make on-air reference to the request of the Minister, and this was apparently the reason why the statement of Sampson was not broadcasted after all.[292] Of course, this was not the only instance of an attempt by governmental agents to intervene in the editorial policy of the CyBC. It seems that such interventions have been the rule at least until the 1990s.[293]

C. *Supervision by the Auditor General of the Republic*

225. The CyBC is required to perform its PSB mission using state funding only for the purposes of the relevant activities, without distorting competition, at least not to an extent which is contrary to the public interest (sections 24A and 16B, paragraph (d) CyBCL). Section 24B CyBCL provides that the fulfilment of such obligation shall be annually audited by the Auditor General of the Republic. The latter is expected to prepare an Annual Report, checking, among else, whether the CyBC has observed its obligation to keep separate accounts for its public service and non-public service activities respectively (following the provisions of section 24B, paragraph 2 CyBCL, which implements the 2001 Commission Communication in this respect). *Sigma*, a private TV station, filed a lawsuit against the CyBC, alleging that

290. In addition to the aforementioned powers of central governmental authorities, the Council of Ministers has the emergency powers (§44 CyBCL) referred above at §1 of this chapter.
291. *See* Kouros, *The Mass Media Law*, fn. 51 above, 368–369, referring to a personal interview with one of the Directors of the CyBC at the relevant time.
292. *Ibid.*
293. *Ibid.*, 369–370.

they were entitled to receive damages, as competitors, for the failure of the CyBC to prepare separate accounts for activities pursuant to its PSB mission and its commercial activities, showing that it had not used state funding in order to distort competition. The Supreme Court held that this did not give rise to an actionable right or to damages and that any failure to prepare separate accounts was merely an issue to be considered by the Auditor-General in his/her report, in order for the issue to be rectified. *Sigma* had also questioned the compatibility of the CyBC's state funding with EU law but eventually withdrew this allegation on appeal, and the Supreme Court anyway observed that the state aid towards CyBC had been approved by the EU Commission and was not subject to judicial review.[294]

III. The Supreme Court on the Independence of the Cyprus Broadcasting Corporation

226. In its landmark *Karayiorges* judgment, the Supreme Court declared the unconstitutionality of certain provisions of Law 149/1988, which introduced the involvement of political parties in the functioning of certain public corporations, the CyBC being one among them.[295] In particular, the said Law provided that the political parties that were represented in the House of Representatives could appoint persons who would attend the meetings of the BoD of public corporations as observers, not having a vote, but having the power to ask for information on every subject. It was also provided that, upon the appointment of the members of the BoD of public corporations by the Council of Ministers, the latter should enter into consultations with the House of Representatives and with the political parties, and that the latter could make suggestions as regards the President, the Vice President and the other members of the BoD of public corporations. Last, it was provided that the Council of Ministers should take seriously into account such suggestions, providing for the equal representation of the political parties in the BoD of the relevant public corporations, CyBC being one of them.

227. The Supreme Court held that these provisions violated the constitutional principle of separation of powers, since the appointment of the members of the BoD of public corporations is by its nature an executive act, falling outside the competences of the legislature.[296] Furthermore, the Supreme Court held that, although political parties are important factors in social and political life, they do not directly participate in the exercise of state power, and they should not be given authorities other than the ones that derive from their participation in the ordinary functioning of the House of Representatives.[297] Besides, the legislative attempt to transfer to the BoD of public corporations the political balances, as expressed in the power of the

294. *Sigma Radio TV Public Ltd and another v. Attorney-General and CyBC*, Civil App. 272/2013, Judgment of 8 Jun. 2021 (in Greek).
295. *CyBC and another v. Karayiorges and another* [1991] 3 CLR 159 (in Greek). *See also* the judgment of the first instance Court, *Karayiorges and another v. CyBC and another* [1990] 3 CLR 2595 (in Greek).
296. *See CyBC and another v. Karayiorges and another* [1991] 3 CLR 159, 174–176 (in Greek).
297. *Ibid.*, 176–179.

political parties in the House of Representatives, violated the principle of separation of the administrative functions of the state from the exercise of political power by state organs; a principle that had long been established through the jurisprudence of the Supreme Court.[298] A crucial aspect of this principle is the requirement 'that organs entrusted with matters such as appointments and promotions of public officers should enjoy the greatest possible, in the circumstances, independence from political organs of Government.'[299]

228. The principle of separation of the administrative functions of the state from the exercise of political power by state organs is closely connected with the principle of equality and with the constitutional requirement that, under conditions of meritocracy, equal opportunities shall be offered to all citizens as regards their service in the public sector.[300] According to the Court, the protection of human rights is feasible only under conditions of meritocracy; that is, only if each individual is evaluated in accordance with his/her individual merits, and not in accordance with his/her political affiliations or sympathies, as regards his/her appointment and career in a public office or position. The principle of equality 'requires that equal opportunities be safeguarded not for the sake of political parties but for each citizen … '.[301]

229. By way of a critical remark, it should be noted that the aforementioned liberal-individualistic approach of the Supreme Court underestimates the structural role of political parties in the functioning of modern democratic states.[302] Such role, and the principle of political parties' pluralism that accompanies it, are especially important in the sphere of R/T broadcasting insofar as a basic principle of Media Law is pluralism of political views that may be expressed in this sphere (the Greek term for pluralism of political views in the Media is 'πολιτική πολυφωνία', political polyphony). Therefore, at least as regards the CyBC, the (non-decisive) powers of the political parties within the process of appointing the members of public corporations should not be understood only as a danger against meritocracy or, in the case of the CyBC, against its political independence (as it certainly might be the case). At the same time, such powers provided an opportunity for the strengthening of pluralism of political views, of 'political polyphony'.

230. In any case, the underlying thoughts of the *Karayiorges* judgment constitute an important jurisprudential safeguard for the independence of the CyBC as against improper exercise of political influence on its editorial policy.[303] Such independence is strengthened even more, if the *Karayiorges* judgment is read in conjunction with another landmark judgment of the Supreme Court, its judgment on the

298. *Ibid.*, 179–180.
299. *C.T.O. v. HadjiDemetriou* [1987] 3 CLR 780, 785, cited with approval in *CyBC and another v. Karayiorges and another* [1991] 3 CLR 159, 180 (in Greek).
300. *CyBC and another v. Karayiorges and another* [1991] 3 CLR 159, 181–182 (in Greek).
301. *Ibid.*
302. *See* the dissenting judgment of Judges Loizou, Stylianides, Poyiadjis, and Chrisostomis, in *CyBC and another v. Karayiorges and another* [1991] 3 CLR 159, 191.
303. Compare Kouros, *The Law of Mass Media*, fn. 51 above, 384.

case of *Stefanides*, which had to do with the power of the Council of Ministers to discharge the members of the BoD of certain public corporations, the CyBC being again one among them.[304]

231. In *Stefanides*, the Supreme Court referred again to the independence of public corporations as a fundamental principle which should direct all relevant state action. The Court interpreted the legislative requirement for a reasoned decision on discharging the members of the BoD of public corporations as a limit upon the discretionary power of the Council of Ministers in this respect.[305] In general, according to the established jurisprudence of the Supreme Court, the mere invocation of the public interest does not suffice for the fulfilment of the requirement for a reasoned decision on the part of the Council of Ministers or of any other administrative organ. If such invocation is to offer adequate support to an administrative act, there must be reference to particular events and circumstances, so that the reasoning can be cast under judicial control.[306] In the *Stefanides* case, the Council of Ministers had referred only vaguely to the public interest and to the well-functioning of public corporations (in particular, the Council of Ministers invoked the need to safeguard such well-functioning with reference to the fact that some members of the BoD of some public corporations, the CyBC being one among them, had resigned, without any explanation as to why such resignation should necessarily lead to a governmental call for the resignation of all members of the BoD).[307] Having failed to substantiate the invocation of the public interest, the relevant acts of the Council of Ministers should be annulled.

232. Of course, the authority of the Council of Ministers to discharge the members of the BoD of CyBC constitutes a danger to the latter's political and editorial independence. The legislative requirement that such decisions be reasoned (section 4, paragraph (b) of Law 149/1988), in combination with the jurisprudence of the Supreme Court, requiring that such reasoning be adequately substantiated, provide some safeguards in this respect. The same can be said with reference to the jurisprudential limitations upon the power of the Council of Ministers to approve the appointment of the CyBC's General Director by its BoD (*see* above, at §2 I D). The Supreme Court plays an indirect but significant role in protecting the CyBC's editorial independence.

§4. The Financing of Public Service Broadcasting

233. The financing of the CyBC is based on the 'dual-funding' scheme, as prescribed in §57 of the 2009 Commission Communication.[308] Thus, on the one hand,

304. *Stefanides et al. v. The Republic of Cyprus* [1993] 3 CLR 367 (in Greek).
305. *Ibid.*, 383–384.
306. *Ibid.*, 388.
307. *Ibid.*, 386–387.
308. Communication from the Commission on the application of State aid rules to public service broadcasting, OJ C 257, 27 Oct. 2009, p. 1, §57: ' … "Dual-funding" systems comprise a wide range of schemes, where public service broadcasting is financed by different combinations of State funds

the CyBC may receive, and actually receives, public funding, which may be used only for the purposes of PSB, and which should not lead to a distortion of competition to an extent that contravenes the public interest (section 24A CyBCL). In this respect, the state has assumed the duty to cover any deficit in the annual budgets of the CyBC, in the form of a state contribution (section 3 of Law 14/1979, as amended by section 3 of Law 64(I)/2000).

234. On the other hand, the CyBC is authorized to develop commercial activities (e.g., transmit advertising upon payment, enter into 'barter agreements', produce its own programmes and sell them) and collect the relevant revenues (section 16A, paragraphs 3 and 4(b) CyBCL), on condition that such activities will meet the five conditions of section 16B CyBCL, namely:

- to safeguard added choice for the viewers/listeners, without degrading the qualitative level of the programmes of the CyBC as a whole;
- to abide by all legislative and regulatory provisions;
- to secure resources for re-investment in the programmes which have been already transmitted;
- to avoid distorting the competition to a degree which is contrary to the public interest, and to apply a transparent pricing policy, which is cost-oriented;
- to respect the requirements of transparency in keeping the financial accounts, and to keep separate accounts for its public and non-public service activities, in accordance with the provisions regarding implementation of the EU state aid rules.[309]

235. Apart from the revenues that may be produced through the commercial activities of the CyBC, the latter may receive funding through sponsorship and through political advertising (section 16A, paragraph 4(c) in conjunction with section 17B CyBCL). Furthermore, after the approval of the Council of Ministers, the CyBC may borrow either from private entities (most importantly, banks) or from the state itself (section 16A, paragraph 4(d), section 23 CyBCL). The Government may guarantee such loans, on conditions that this will not be incompatible with the EU state aid rules (section 25 CyBCL). The CyBC may also raise money through the issuance of stocks or other securities, in accordance with Regulations which are approved by the Council of Ministers (section 24 CyBCL). Of course, the CyBC may also raise money through the management of its property (cf. section 17, paragraphs 1(c) and 2(m) CyBCL). The revenues of the CyBC shall be applied to pay all remunerations, allowances, salaries, pension contributions, gratuities, working expenses and all other outgoings, including the sums that the CyBC may think proper to set aside for reserve fund, extensions, renewals, depreciation, loans and other like purposes (section 28 CyBCL).

---

and revenues from commercial or public service activities, such as the sale of advertising space or programmes and the offering of services against payment.'

309. As mentioned above (under §3 II C) this last obligation has been met only in 2012.

Chapter 2. Private Broadcasting

§1. Different Categories of Private Broadcasters

236. The RTSL provides for four different types of licences for private TV broadcasting (or, in other words, for linear AVMS providers, according to the definition of Article 1, paragraph 1(e) of the AVMS Directive. Three different types of licences are provided for radio broadcasting, and one type of licence for Video on Demand (VoD) services (i.e., non-linear AVMS, as per the definition of Article 1, paragraph 1(g) of the AVMS Directive, which has been transposed by section 2 RTSL).

237. More specifically, the RTSL provides that:

(a) *Licences for TV stations* shall be granted to TV providers whose aim is to transmit objective and impartial information, and other products of speech, of art, and of entertainment. Such programmes should be of a quality as high as it is adequate for the fulfilment of the provider's social mission and for the promotion of the cultural development of the country. There used to be two different categories of licences for nationwide and local TV stations, but Law 197(I)/2021 has amended section 14 § 2 of the RTSL so as to provide for a single licence.
(b) *Licences for thematic TV stations* shall be granted to TV providers whose aim is to transmit programmes of a specific kind (e.g., music, athletics or teleshopping[310] TV stations) on an exclusive basis.
(c) *Licences for encoded programmes TV stations* shall be granted to TV organizations whose aim is to transmit at least 75% of their programmes through a codified signal on a subscription basis. The programmes of such stations can be either of general or of thematic interest.
(d) *Licences for satellite TV stations* shall be granted to providers using satellite up-link capacities that are situated in the Republic. The programmes of such providers shall not be addressed exclusively to the public of the country but may be accessed by the public of other EU Member States as well.[311]
(e) *Licences for nationwide radio stations* shall be granted to providers of radio programmes whose aim is to transmit objective and impartial information and news, products of speech, of art, and of entertainment. Such programmes should be of a quality as high as it is adequate for the fulfilment of the provider's social mission and for the promotion of the cultural development of the country.

---

310. As regards teleshopping stations *see* the judgment of the Supreme Court in *Pediko Kanali To Ena Limited et al. v. CRTA*, Judgment of 27 Apr. 2005, Case No. 341/2004 (in Greek), allowing the granting of a licence to such stations in view of the provisions of the Directive on teleshopping (as such provisions had been transposed by ss 34A and 34B RTSL).

311. It is noted that the RTSL (§3A) has fully transposed the provisions of Art. 2 of the Directive as regards the delimitation of its jurisdiction. *See* Part V, Ch. 2, §2 below.

(f) *Licences for local radio stations* shall be granted to providers of radio programmes of mostly local interest, with the aim here being to promote the cultural development of the region which is covered by the station. The signal of such stations must be of limited power so as not to exceed their local boundaries.
(g) *Licences for small local radio stations* shall be granted to radio organizations which are scheduled so as to cover the needs of a local community or of a relatively small region.
(h) *Licences for video-on-demand services* shall be granted to providers of non-linear AVMS, that is, services for the viewing of programmes at the moment chosen by the user and at his/her individual request on the basis of a catalogue of programmes selected by the AVMS provider.

§2. Licensing Requirements and Procedure

I. Licensing Requirements

238. Article 19, paragraph 5 of the Constitution provides for the power of the Republic to establish a licensing regime. Exercising this power, the Republic may enact such terms and requirements as are deemed to be objectively necessary for the promotion of the public interest,[312] for the protection of society, and for the elevation of culture in the country, taking into account the general limitations upon freedom of speech which are provided by Article 19, paragraph 3 of the Constitution.[313] Such terms and requirements are contained in the RTSL, and are as follows:

A. Absolute Requirements

239. The first set of licensing requirements are of an absolute nature; that is, the licence shall not be granted unless such requirements are fully met. According to section 16 RTSL, the licences for the establishment and functioning of TV broadcasting stations (*see* categories (a) to (d) above under §1), and of nationwide and local radio stations (*see* categories (e) and (f) above under §1), may be granted only to companies, not to individuals. Such companies should have acquired their legal capacity in accordance with the relevant legislation of the Republic of Cyprus, or of another EU Member State. A company which has acquired its legal capacity in

312. *See* on this, with reference to the legislative provisions at the time of its publication, A. Madellas, *The Concept of 'Public Interest' in the Cypriot Legislation for the Establishment of Private Radio and Television Broadcasting*, 49–50 Cyprus Law Review 7205 (1995) (in Greek).
313. *See Sigma Radio T.V. Ltd. v. CRTA (No. 1)* [2001] 4 CLR 1020, 1024; *Pliroforiaki kai Politistiki Eteria 'O Logos' v. CRTA* [2001] 4 CLR 590, 626; *Sigma Radio T.V. Ltd et al. v. CRTA* [2003] 4 CLR 1, 20–26; *Sigma Radio T.V. Ltd et al. v. CRTA* [2004] 3 CLR 134, 173–176 (all cases in Greek); with lengthy references to the case-law of the ECtHR under Art. 10 of the ECHR, as well as to the case-law of the CJEU.

another EU Member State shall prove that it keeps a permanent and stable connection with the economy of this Member State and that it is registered with the Registrar of Companies of the Republic. Licences may also be granted to public corporations which have been instituted in the Republic, or in another EU Member State. Licences for small local radio stations (*see* category (g) under §1 above) may be granted either to companies, under the conditions described in the previous paragraph, or to individuals who are citizens of the Republic, or of another EU Member State.

240. The shareholders of a licensed company may be other companies, and the shareholders of the latter may also be other companies. However, according to section 19, paragraph 1 RTSL, the shareholders of the latter shall be individuals (natural persons), unless the company which is a shareholder in the licensed company is listed on the Cyprus Stock Exchange, or on the Stock Exchange of another EU Member State, provided in this latter case that non-natural persons do not possess or control more than 25% individually or 74% cumulatively of the shares of the listed company. It used to be that no more than 25% of the shares of the licensed company might be controlled by a specific citizen of, or by a company enlisted in, another EU Member State. However, Law 87(I)/2023 has removed such restriction from the RTSL and now provides for the possibility to either acquire or control the totality of the shares of the licensed company, either directly or indirectly. Non-EU Member States individuals may each acquire up to 10% of the shares of the licensed company, but only after the approval of the Council of Ministers. The overall percentage of shares in the licensed company which are possessed by such individuals shall not exceed 25%.

241. Section 19, paragraph 2 RTSL used to provide for additional requirements, in case the shareholders of the licensed company are other companies. Indicatively, a company which is a shareholder in another company might not possess or control, either directly or indirectly, more than 25% of the shares of the licensed company. In case more companies are shareholders in the licensed company, these companies might not possess or control, either directly or indirectly, more than 74% of the shares of the licensed company. Two additional requirements served as safeguards against the possibility of circumventing the above prohibitions. First, relatives up to the level of cousins or spouses may be shareholders in the companies which are shareholders in the licensed company, but in this case, such companies may not possess more than 25% of the shares of the licensed company. Second, for the purposes of RTSL, every company which is a shareholder in the licensed company will be considered a subsidiary company, if its shares are possessed or controlled by another company, or if its shareholders possess or control more than 51% of the shares of another company which is also a shareholder in the licensed company. Law 87(I)/23 has now abolished all such restrictions from the RTSL and has effectively fully liberated the market so as to enable individuals and/or companies to be the ultimate owners or controllers of 100% of the shares of the licensed company.

242. The removal of any impediments to the ownership and/or control of the totality of the shares of the licensed company has been justified on the basis of an alleged failure to safeguard transparency under the previous legal regime; it was argued that owners of the R/T stations were 'forced' to circumvent the prohibitions by having third parties appear as the owners of such stations, despite such persons being merely strawmen. It was therefore suggested that transparency would be increased because the owners would no longer have a reason to conceal themselves since they could now own 100% of the shares without any restrictions. The argument is paradoxical, to say the least. Effectively, the Government and the House of Representatives admit that they had failed to properly enforce that the requirements and prohibitions had been abided with, and thus the solution is to abolish any requirements so as to enable a single person to own the totality of the shares. This, however, does not increase transparency as suggested but rather increases the concentration of media power to a single individual.

243. All the above requirements and prohibitions did not apply to small local radio stations, in case they were operated by a company and not by an individual. According to section 19, paragraph 1(f) RTSL, a company may be granted a licence for a small local radio station irrespective of its shareholding composition. Following the amendments introduced by Law 87(I)/23, the exception of small local radio stations has also been abolished as unnecessary. Besides, although the RTSL provides for licences to be granted to providers of VoD services (non-linear AVMS, *see* above under §1), the aforementioned requirements apply only to companies that operate R/T stations, and not to such providers.

244. Furthermore, it is noted that at least some of the aforementioned requirements are indirectly connected with the cross-ownership rules, which also fall under the category of absolute licensing requirements, and which will be presented separately in Part IV. In particular, the above requirements and prohibitions provide support to monitoring the implementation of the cross-ownership rules, since the latter could be circumvented through appropriate arrangements in the shareholding composition of the companies that are shareholders in the licensed company. Section 19, paragraph 3 RTSL further stipulates that no licence for AVMS (including non-linear or VoD services) may be granted to individuals (natural persons) who have been convicted for an offence involving dishonesty or moral depravity or for corruption or failure to pay tax or social insurance obligations or for sexual harassment or who suffer from mental illness. The same prohibition applies to persons who possess or control more than 5% of the shares of a licensed company.

B. Criteria of Evaluation

245. The second set of licensing requirements are of a relative nature; that is, they serve as criteria for the evaluation of the applicants, in the competitive stage of the licensing procedure (*see* below under II). Such criteria are stipulated by section 22 RTSL and are further specified by the RTSR. The criteria are as follows:

– *Completeness and quality of the programme*: In order to comply with this criterion, the applicants are called to present in detail the contents, the types and the overall philosophy of their programmes. Each applicant should particularly describe its weekly programme; argue why its programme is different from the programme of other stations; determine the sources of external productions; describe the arrangements for acquiring news items and reports, etc. The granting authority, on its part, shall evaluate the quality and the range of the programmes, giving particular emphasis on diversity, so that the applicant covers a wide range of interests, and on the extent of programmes which are relevant to the culture of the country, with issues of special interests, and with the development of Cypriot and of European productions (Rule 4, paragraphs (1)(d) and (f) RTSR). The criterion of completeness does not apply to applicants for licences of thematic and encoded programme stations (section 22, paragraph 1(a) RTSL).

- Experience, knowledge, capacities, and sufficient number of the regular personnel, especially of the persons who shall be occupied in news and current affairs programmes, in educative programmes, and in entertainment programmes: Here the applicants are called to submit the organizational chart of their station, coupled with the CVs of all the basic agents (counsellors, directors, journalists, etc.) of their programmes.
- Commitment to developing the sector of news and information, of education and of entertainment, with particular emphasis on the applicant's contribution to all forms of speech and of art, as well as on its ability to observe its relevant commitments: This criterion is closely connected with the first criterion above. The granting authority takes into account the aims of the programmes and the means for their execution, giving particular emphasis on citizens' information and education as well as on the extent to which the applicant may offer opportunities to young Cypriots in all forms of artistic creation and expression (Rule 4, paragraphs (c) and (e) RTSR).
- Ability and commitment of the applicant to safeguard polyphony in their programmes; access of citizens to them; journalistic and creative independence for all the agents of the station; and regulation of working conditions through collective agreements.
- *Technical and technological capacities of the station*: In this respect, applicants are called to provide detailed description of the transmission technical means and points, of their studios and their technological equipment, and of their technical support (*see* Annex V to the RSTR). As regards the transmission network, technical capacity may be substantiated only through a relevant certificate granted by the Deputy Ministry of Research, Innovation and Digital Policy (Rule 4, paragraph 1(g) RTSR).
- *Financial sustainability of the applicant*: In this respect, applicants are called to submit detailed and well-substantiated accounts about their financial means and predictions, their shareholders, loan agreements, expected revenues from advertising, etc. (*see* Annex V of RTSR).

C. *Terms of Licence*

246. In case the licence is granted, the granting authority may impose any terms as are necessary for ensuring the compliance of the licensed company (or of the licensed individual, in the case of small local radio stations) with all relevant legislation (most importantly, with the absolute licensing requirements), as well as with all the commitments of the station which derive from the aforementioned items of its application (programme, personnel, technical means and equipment, certificates by other authorities, etc.) Particular emphasis is given to the commitment of the licensee to abide by the provisions for fair representation of political parties and of candidates in all kinds of elections (*see* Rule 7, paragraph 1(d) RTSR; for the provisions on fair representation *see* Chapter 4 of this Part).

247. For TV stations, the duration of the licence may be five years,[314] and for radio stations seven years (section 21, paragraph 2 RTSL). After this period, the granting authority may proceed to a renewal of the licence, after an application by the licensee. The RTSL does not provide any specific criteria on which such renewal shall be based, other than stipulating that all the requirements set out in the RTSL should be followed. In general, the RTSL is absent any arrangements, to make such renewal compatible with the possibility of granting new licences in the future. Law 197(I)/2021 has further introduced a new section 21 § 2A of the RTSL, the proviso of which stipulates that if the TV station or its programme is connected with a legal person of public law, then the CRTA may renew the licence even if not all of the requirements set out in the RTSL are fulfilled. Such differentiation between the renewal of licences of public and private operators might potentially raise issues of fair treatment in accordance with Article 28 of the Constitution.

D. Prohibition of Unauthorized Changes: The Logos Case

248. According to section 23 RTSL, the licence is granted in the personal capacity of the licensee. Therefore, the licence may not be transferred to another entity. According to the same section, if the licence has been granted to a company, every amendment of its incorporation documents may take place only after the consent of the CRTA. Such consent is also required in the case of a transfer of the shares of the licensed company, or in the case of any other transaction to the same effect. By way of an exception, in the case of licensed companies which are listed on the Cyprus Stock Exchange, the CRTA's consent is required only if the transfer is conducted by a holder of more than 5% of the shares of the licensed company, and only if such transaction refers to more than 40% of the shares of the licensed company. Consent by the CRTA is also required in case a legal or natural person acquires more than 5% of the shares of a licensed company that is listed on the Cyprus Stock Exchange.

249. The aforementioned provisions acquired prominence in 1999 when the owner of the *Logos TV* station transferred the management of the station to the

314. This time limit begins at the time of the granting of the licence, and not at the time of the actual coming into operation of the station. *See* on this *NBS Enterprises Ltd. v. CRTA* [2009] 3 CLR 225 (in Greek), with the Judges of the Supreme Court proposing an amendment of the legislation at this point (235).

Greek TV station *Mega Channel*.[315] Reviewing the management agreement, the CRTA found that there was a violation of section 23 RTSL. Instead of revoking the licence, the CRTA imposed on the licensee an administrative fine, providing it with the opportunity to make the necessary arrangements so as to comply with the legislation. Before the Supreme Court, the representatives of the station alleged that the decision of the CRTA infringed upon their freedoms under Article 19 of the Constitution and Article 10 of the ECHR. Answering this allegation, the Supreme Court held that neither the Constitution nor the ECHR provides for freedom of broadcasting, in the sense that TV stations may be established and function without being audited by the competent public authorities, in accordance with the relevant legislative provisions.[316] In order to support its ruling, the Court emphasized the fundamental role of polyphony in a democratic society and appealed to the fact that television frequencies are public property, therefore they should be allocated in accordance with the public interest, as the latter may be safeguarded by the legislative restrictions of the licensing regime.[317] Following such considerations, the Supreme Court confirmed the decision of the CRTA.

250. Applying its *Logos* reasoning in another case, the Supreme Court ruled that an agreement of a licensed radio station with another company to share the management of the station should not be accepted, and the relevant application of the station before the CRTA should be rejected insofar as such an agreement was actually circumventing the legislative requirement that licences be granted in the personal capacity of the licensee.[318]

E. Licence Fees

251. According to section 24 RTSL, holders of a licence for TV stations shall pay, by way of a licence fee, each year an amount of EUR 51,400: for nationwide radio stations at EUR 5,100; and for local and small local radio stations at EUR 850. Furthermore, all the aforementioned licensees are required to pay, again by way of a licence fee, 0.5% of their revenues from advertising and other Audiovisual Commercial Communications (AVCCs). This latter fee also applies to AVMS providers, and to managers of advertising and of AVCCs which are addressed to the Cypriot public and which are contained in the programmes of TV organizations having their seat in another country, on condition that such organizations transmit their programmes through an electronic communications network after a relevant authorization by the CRTA.

---

315. *See* Kouros, *The Mass Media Law,* fn. 51 above, 440–442 (with full references to press publications at that time); and *Pliroforiaki kai Politistiki Eteria 'O Logos' v. CRTA* [2001] 4 CLR 590 (in Greek).
316. *See Pliroforiaki kai Politistiki Eteria 'O Logos' v. CRTA* [2001] 4 CLR 590, 622–627 (in Greek).
317. *Ibid.*, 626.
318. *Paizanos and Another v. CRTA*, Judgment of 14 Jan. 2008, Case No. 1222/2006 (in Greek).

F. Revocation of Licence

252. According to section 25 RTSL, the CRTA may, after hearing the interested parties and with a fully reasoned decision of the majority of its members, revoke the licence of an AVMS provider (therefore, all types of licences), if the evaluation criteria, on which the granting of the licence was based, are no longer being fulfilled; or if the licence had been acquired through submission of false information; or if there has been a serious and repeated violation of the terms of the licence; or if a serious violation of the relevant legislative and regulative provisions has taken place; or if the licensee delays for more than two months the payment of the licence fees or of any administrative fines; or if the Director of the Department of Electronic Communications of the Deputy Ministry of Research, Innovation and Digital Policy requests the CRTA to do so, on the basis of the radio-communication legislation; or if the licensee delays more than six months the transmission of its programs, in accordance with the initial timetable after the granting of the licence.

II. Licensing Procedure

253. After the enactment of the RTSL in 1998, the granting of licences has been assigned to the new Independent Authority, the CRTA (*see* Part V).[319] The Supreme Court held that such assignment is compatible with Article 19, paragraph 5 of the Constitution insofar as the meaning of the term 'Republic' (to which the granting of licences is generally assigned) in this article includes not only central governmental authorities but also Independent Authorities,[320] with the latter being in a better position to effectively correspond with the relevant responsibilities.[321]

A. The Plan of Radio Coverage

254. The first stage of the licensing procedure is the drafting and publication in the Government Gazette of the Plan of Radio Coverage (henceforth: 'the Plan'), according to the provisions of section 13 RTSL. The Plan determines the frequencies, the geographical areas to be covered, and the locations from which the licensed stations may transmit their programmes. It is drafted by the Director of the Department of Electronic Communications of the Deputy Ministry of Research, Innovation and Digital Policy. After its first publication, any interested party may raise objections pursuant to the procedure provided in the Radiocommunications Law 146(I)/2002.

---

319. For a detailed historical presentation of the relevant circumstances *see* Kouros, *The Mass Media Law*, fn. 51 above, 420–432.
320. *See Antenna T.V. Limited v. The Republic* [2001] 3 CLR 711 (in Greek).
321. *See Sigma Radio T.V. Ltd et al. v. The Cyprus Radiotelevision Authority* [2004] 3 CLR 134, 177 (in Greek).

255. The amendment of the Plan is, and should be, always possible insofar as if this was not so, the R/T landscape would remain the same to the detriment of pluralism and healthy competition.[322] The technical changes in the Plan may be necessary for the public interest and, therefore, considerations about the economic sustainability of the stations that have already been licensed should be set aside.[323] Besides, although the Plan is a prerequisite for the initiation of the licensing procedure, it should be distinguished from the decision of the CRTA granting the licences (the former cannot be considered as incorporated into the latter, so that an application for the annulment of the latter may invoke defects of the former).[324]

B. Determining the Number and the Type of Licences

256. At the second stage of the licensing procedure, the CRTA first determines the number, the type and the range of coverage of the stations which are to be licensed, in accordance with the Plan (section 13, paragraph 1 RTSL). The CRTA should liaise with the Director of the Department of Electronic Communications of the Deputy Ministry of Research, Innovation and Digital Policy prior to granting licences, so as to ensure that there are available stations for which a licence may be granted. The RTSL does not contain any provision about the criteria on which such a decision should be based. The Supreme Court, on its part, has refused to examine the policies of the CRTA in this respect.[325] It is suggested, however, that the discretion of the CRTA is not unlimited. Its decision should be based on considerations of public interest, as the latter is specified by the fundamental principles of Media Law (freedom of information, pluralism, impartiality, respect for privacy and for reputation, etc.), as well as by the various requirements and criteria of the licensing regime.

257. Such public interest considerations are rather implicit in the public announcement of the CRTA of 20 March 2003, in which the Independent Authority explained its policy as regards the granting of licences after each amendment of the Plan.[326] In this general policy announcement, the CRTA explained that the granting of licences will be based on a public call, addressed to all interested parties, so that they submit their applications within a certain time limit, after which no application will be accepted. In the same announcement, the CRTA also stipulated that the allocation of frequencies, and the consequent granting of licences, shall be based on

---

322. *See Gorna Systems Ltd v. The Republic et al.* [2005] 4 CLR 300 (in Greek).
323. *Ibid.*
324. *See Radiofonikos Stathmos Zenith v. The Republic et al.* [2003] 4 CLR 954, appeal rejected by *Radiofonikos Stathmos Zenith v. The Republic et al.* [2007] 3 CLR 206 (both in Greek).
325. *See Pediko Kanali To Ena Limited et al. v. CRTA* [2007] 3 CLR 609, 614 (in Greek).
326. The contents of this announcement are fully quoted in *K.K. New Extra Ltd. v. CRTA* [2007] 3 CLR 437 (in Greek). In this case, the Supreme Court held that the general policy announcement is not an enforceable administrative act; therefore, it cannot be the object of recourse under Art. 146 of the Constitution. In our view, the rather formalistic approach of the Supreme Court underestimates the (normative) significance of such policy documents for the materialization of the fundamental principles of Media Law during the licensing procedure.

equal treatment of all applicants, and shall be conducted in such a way as to avoid privileging any of the existing stations or confirming any kind of agreements between the existing stations to this effect. In the same announcement, it is also stipulated that the CRTA shall not allocate anew the frequencies which have already been allocated during previous licensing procedures.

258. In 2016 the House of Representatives passed a bill introducing major amendments to the RTSL. As part of these amendments, the bill added a new provision to section 12 of the RTSL stipulating that the CRTA shall not grant a new licence for a TV station if, on the basis of a study of an approved Auditing House, this licence will endanger the financial sustainability of the already established TV stations. Exercising his powers under Article 140 of the Constitution, the President of the Republic referred the bill to the Supreme Court on the grounds that it was incompatible with the TFEU and with the Charter of Fundamental Rights of the EU.[327] As regards the new provision of section 12 RTSL, the allegation was that it infringed upon freedom of establishment under Article 49 of the TFEU insofar as it introduced a discrimination in favour of already established providers of TV services (i.e., Cypriot companies which had already been granted with a license) to the detriment of companies, either Cypriot or EU ones, which would wish to enter into this market.[328] The House of Representatives argued that the new provision was not discriminative and that it served a pressing public interest: the uncontrollable increase of the number of TV stations would diminish advertising revenues and would thus lead to the shutting down of existing stations, something that would entail turbulences in the Cypriot market and unfavourable consequences for public revenues. The Supreme Court dismissed this argument by holding that legitimate restrictions upon freedom of establishment, under Article 49 TFEU and in accordance with the jurisprudence of the CJEU, could not be justified by appealing to economic interests.[329] Thus, the attempt of the House of Representatives to introduce a financial sustainability condition to the procedure of allocation of TV licences failed.

C. Public Call by the Cyprus Radio and Television Authority

259. In any case, after the determination of the number and the types of licences to be granted, the CRTA publishes an announcement, calling all interested persons and companies to submit their applications, with all relevant forms and supporting documents, within a certain time limit. Notwithstanding the prohibition of a TV station holding more than one licence (section 18 RTSL), a company which already

327. *See President of the Republic v. The House of Representatives* [2017] 3 CLR 635 (in Greek).
328. *See ibid.*
329. *Ibid.* To be noticed that at a previous stage the Supreme Court had rejected the request of the House of Representatives to submit a reference for a preliminary ruling of the CJEU. *See President of the Republic v. The House of Representatives* [2017] 3 CLR 327 (in Greek).

has a licence for a local TV station may submit an application for a licence for a nationwide TV station in the new licensing procedure.[330]

D. Evaluation of Applications

260. The sequence in the examination of applications may be determined on the basis of criteria, which are enacted through a decision of the CRTA (Rule 3, paragraph 2 RTSR). However, this does not mean that the CRTA may grant a licence to an applicant, without having previously examined the application of another applicant, which had in general complied with the directions of the CRTA.[331] In any case, the examination of the application cannot but have a competitive character.

261. In the process of evaluation (*see* Rule 4, paragraph 4 RTSR), the CRTA may characterize an application as unsatisfying, in which case the applicant is informed that his/her application was rejected. If the CRTA evaluates an application as incomplete, then the applicant is called to submit supplementary evidence within a month (in case of failure, the application is rejected). The CRTA cross-examines and compares all applications which have been characterized as complete, in order to decide which applicants will be granted a licence. In assessing the validity of the technical study, which supports an application, the relevant time is the one in which the submission of the application takes place and not the one in which the technical study had originally been conducted.[332]

262. The discretion of the CRTA in evaluating the applications is not absolute. The general principles and rules of the Administrative Procedure (Law 158(I)/1999),[333] as supplemented by the procedural Regulations for the functioning of the CRTA (*see* Part V), are fully applicable in the licensing procedure. The Supreme Court, on its part, did not hesitate to annul some of the relevant decisions of the CRTA, not only on purely procedural grounds;[334] but also on the grounds that CRTA did not conduct due inquiry with regard to an allegation that the technical part of an application was copying the schedules of another licensed station;[335] on the grounds

330. *See Fred T.V. Limited v. CRTA* [2007] 3 CLR 335, 340, reversing in this respect the judgment of the first instance Court in *Pediko Kanali To Ena Limited et al. v. CRTA*, Judgment of 27 Apr. 2005, Cases No. 341/2004 et al.
331. *See Tileoptikos Stathmos Nimonia Ltd. v. CRTA*, Judgment of 2 Mar. 2005, Case No. 98/02 (in Greek).
332. *CRTA v. Sisel Holdings Ltd* [2013] 3 CLR 326 (in Greek), reversing *Sisel Holdings v. CRTA*, Judgment of 22 Aug. 2008, Case No. 1998/2006 (in Greek).
333. *See* A. Emilianides, *Constitutional Law in Cyprus* (2nd ed., Kluwer 2019), 227ff, A. Angelides, *The General Principles of Administrative Law Act and the Subsequent Case-Law of the Supreme Court of Cyprus* (House of Representatives 2008, in Greek).
334. *See*, e.g., *N.P.F. Radio Epistrofi Limited v. CRTA*, Judgment of 4 Feb. 2004, Case No. 306/2002 (in Greek).
335. *See Pediko Kanali To Ena Limited et al. v. CRTA* [2007] 3 CLR 609 (in Greek). A new application against the decision of the CRTA on the same grounds was rejected by the Court in *Pediko Kanali*

that CRTA did not provide an adequate specification of the public interest;[336] on the grounds that the CRTA did not provide adequate reasoning for its decision to deviate from an expert's opinion;[337] on the grounds that the differences in the points that a station gained from the points of another station for the same criteria were largely unjustified, in view of the reasoning given by the CRTA;[338] on the grounds that the points given for a specific criterion were not justified, and that the CRTA erred in fact, since it took into account a circumstance (that an applicant's General Director had worked as an electrician in the past), which should have been considered as irrelevant.[339] Of course, in many other instances, the Supreme Court rejected arguments about bad reasoning or lack of objectivity on the part of the CRTA, invoking the latter's discretion as to the content of technical judgments and evaluations,[340] as to whether it should conduct further research on a certain fact (e.g., whether the Director of an applicant station would be available to work for this station at the relevant time),[341] etc.

263. In general, the discretion of CRTA as to the evaluation of applications for being granted a licence, as well as to the determination of the number and types of stations that are to be licensed, remains a central feature of the broadcasting system. This is so not least because of the limited anyway scope of judicial review of administrative acts in the Cypriot legal order (the Supreme Court may assess only the legality of CRTA's administrative acts; *see* the analysis of the *Sigma* case before the ECtHR in Part V, Chapter 3, §3 below).

§3. The Transition to DTT

264. The Republic of Cyprus has since long transposed the Electronic Communication Directives of the EU, and all the other relevant Directives and Regulations (*see* the Regulation of Electronic Communications and Postal Services Law of 2004, Law 112(I)/2004, transposing, among else, the Directives 2002/19-22/EC and

---

To Ena Limited et al. v. CRTA, Judgment of 20 Apr. 2010, Cases No. 915 and 916/2008 (in Greek), since the CRTA proceeded this time into proper investigation, giving adequate justification for its decision.

336. *See Pera Agencies Limited v. CRTA*, Judgment of 21 Feb. 2006, Case No. 314/2002; *Geophorae (Publishing) Ltd. v. CRTA*, Judgment of 30 Jan. 2004, Case No. 309/2002 (both in Greek).

337. *See Geophorae (Publishing) Ltd. et al. v. CRTA*, Judgment of 19 Jan. 2012, Cases No. 30 and 37/2009 (in Greek).

338. *Ibid.*

339. *See Geophorae (Publishing) Ltd. v. CRTA*, Judgment of 21 Nov. 2007, Cases No. 518 and 588/2004. In this respect *see also Geophorae (Publishing) Ltd. v. CRTA*, Judgment of 30 Jan. 2004, Case No. 309/2002, ascertaining error in facts because the CRTA wrongly examined whether the personnel proposed by an applicant was famous or not (both in Greek).

340. *See*, e.g., *Geophorae (Publishing) Ltd. et al. v. CRTA*, Judgment of 19 Jan. 2012, Cases No. 30 and 37/2009 (in Greek).

341. *See CRTA v. Sisel Holdings Ltd. et al.* [2013] 3 CLR 326 (in Greek). *See also* the rejection of a bulk of allegations in most of the judgments which are referred to in the previous notes.

Directive 2002/58/EC),[342] in order to prepare the ground for the transition of R/T broadcasting to the Digital Era. The ECC Directive has since substituted Directives 2002/19-22/EC and has been incorporated in the Cypriot legal order with the RECL. Furthermore, the authorities of the Republic, and among them, the Communications Commissioner have issued and enacted all necessary Regulations and Orders for the concession of rights and for the imposition of obligations on the network providers of DTT.

265. Such rights and obligations occupy Chapter 7 of this Part. For the moment, it is noted that, as regards the provider of the DTT network for private broadcasting, an auction has been conducted, and the relevant licence has been granted to Velister Ltd on 9 November 2010, for a price of EUR 10 million.[343] As regards the CyBC, the relevant licence has been granted to it through negotiations, free of charge, but imposing important limitations and obligations, so that free competition and the principle of universal service can be safeguarded. As a result, all nationwide TV stations, and two local TV stations, are now offering their AVMS in a digital format. The CyBC also offers its radio services in a digital format.

266. The transition to the Digital Era did not take place through a new licensing procedure, which was actually required, since the old licences had expired, and which might be better adapted to the new needs and requirements of DTT. Instead, the legislature and the Government followed the road of transitional legislative provisions, granting already licensed R/T stations the right to renew their licences until the date of the final transition to a fully digitalized environment (*see* section 56 RTSL incorporating the subsequent transitional provisions of Laws 73(I)/2011, 88(I)/2012, 46(I) 2013, 86(I)/2014, 94(I)/2015, 77(I)/2016 and 81(I)/2017). Since May 2020, analogue transmission is no longer in effect.

342. After 2004 and until today, the Law 112(I)/2004 has been repeatedly amended so as to transpose the amendments of the aforementioned as well as of all other Directives and Regulations which were transposed by it.

343. *See Velister Ltd v. Republic and others*, Judgment of 28 Feb. 2014, Case No. 933/2010 (in Greek). The first-instance judgment was set aside in *LRG Enterprises Ltd and the Republic v. Velister*, Adm. Appeals 43/2014 and 48/2014, Judgment of 3 Jun. 2020 (in Greek).

Chapter 3. Programme Standards

§1. Introduction

267. The programme standards for private broadcasting are provided by various sections of the RTSL; by the RTSR; and by the provisions of the Code of Journalistic Ethics for Electronic Media (Annex VIII to the RTSR) (CJE), which were enacted as Annex VIII to the RTSR. The CRTA may impose administrative sanctions for the violation of the above provisions (section 41A and 41B RTSL). Especially with regard to violations of the CJE, a petition by the CMCC is required before the imposition of any administrative sanction by the CRTA (section 41A, paragraph 1(a) RTSL).

268. The programme standards for the CyBC are provided by various sections of the CyBCL; by the CyBC Regulation 93/2001, which, in Annex II, contains a series of important provisions for the CyBC programmes (CyBCR); and by the provisions of the CyBC Code of Journalistic Ethics (Annex VIII to the CyBCR) (CyBC-CJE), which was enacted as Annex I to the CyBCR. The CRTA may impose administrative sanctions only for violations of certain provisions of the CyBCL, and not for violations of the provisions of the CyBCR and of the CyBC-CJE (section 22B CyBCL).[344] Moreover, we notice that, in practice, the contents of the provisions which refer to private broadcasting are similar to (most times, identical to) the provisions which refer to the CyBC. Therefore, the programme standards for private broadcasting stations and for the CyBC respectively shall be jointly presented. Differences, if any, shall be mentioned in the text.

269. Besides, both the RTSL and the CyBCL have incorporated all the relevant provisions of the AVMS Directive. Of course, there are many other provisions regarding programme standards, since the AVMS Directive is restricted to certain issues (prohibition of incitement to hatred, protection of minors, right of reply, etc.), some of which anyway occupy other chapters of this part (AVCCs, access to major events, etc.). In practice, the provisions of the AVMS Directive have been transposed in the text of the primary regulative instruments (i.e., the RTSL and the CyBCL), while the secondary regulative instruments (the RTSR and the CJE as well as the CyBCR and the CyBC-CJE, also the two Codes of Advertising, to which reference will be made in Chapter 5) contain other, more detailed, and thereby more restrictive, provisions.[345] It is observed that, in some rare cases, having mostly to do with advertising, the Supreme Court has ruled that a provision of a secondary instrument should be considered as inapplicable being *ultra vires* the relevant provision of the main instrument (i.e., they exceed the limits of the relevant authorization). All such cases will be mentioned in the text of this and of the next chapter.

344. This restriction of the sanctioning powers of the CRTA over the CYBC is a weakness of the Cypriot Media Law.

345. To be noted here that, even as regards issues belonging to the AVMS Directive's field of application, the Cypriot legal order may adopt more detailed or even stricter rules, provided that the conditions of Art. 4 of the AVMS Directive are met.

270. Another general issue has to do with the field of application of the programme standards from the point of view of different media types. First, it is observed that the provisions of the AVMS Directive, as transposed by the primary regulatory instruments (the RTSL and the CyBCL), are applicable either to all AVMS or only to TV programmes, depending on the regulative choice of the AVMS Directive. But, in contrast to the AVMS Directive, the definition of AVMS by the Cypriot legislative instruments includes radio programmes (section 2 RTSL; section 2, paragraph 1 CyBCL), so that such programmes are also included in the field of application of all provisions making reference to AVMS. However, the secondary regulatory instruments (i.e., the RTSR and the CJE, the CyBCR and the CyBC-CJE, and the two Codes of Advertising, to which we shall refer in Chapter 5) apply only to linear AVMS, radio programmes being included in them, and not to non-linear, that is, VoD, services. Specific rules governing Video Sharing Platforms (VSPs) have been introduced in the RTSL with amending Law 197(I)/2021, which implemented the relevant provisions of the amendments introduced to the AVMS Directive by Directive 2018/1808;[346] however, no secondary legislation has yet been enacted regarding VSPs.

§2. Human Dignity

271. Transposing Article 6 of the AVMS Directive, section 30 RTSL and section 18B CyBCL (applying to all AVMS, radio included) prohibit the transmission of programmes which contain incitement to violence or hatred directed against any person or group of persons or a member of a group in a manner that would violate human rights which are either constitutionally protected or safeguarded by the EU Charter of Fundamental Rights, or which contain any public provocation to commit a terrorist offence. Taking into account the bi-communal character of the Republic, and the existence of important religious or other minorities on the island, such prohibition becomes very important, not only for Media Law but also for the Cypriot constitutional order and for the Cypriot society. Besides, it is not only *violence or incitement to hatred* that is prohibited but also the transmission of programmes that *insult the dignity as such* of the two sexes, of racial, national or religious groups, or of people with disabilities (Rule 26, paragraph (l) RTSR; Rule 3, paragraph 5(n) CyBCR; the latter speaks of 'irreparable' insult).

272. Furthermore, in all programmes language should not be used in a way that could insult the sensitivities of any religious, racial, political or other social groups (Rule 25, paragraph 3(a) RTSR; Rule 3, paragraph 4(3)(a) CyBCR). By way of another provision, TV and radio stations should avoid any direct or other reference against a person, which contains elements of *prejudice* on the basis of race, colour,

346. Directive (EU) 2018/1808 of the European Parliament and of the Council of 14 Nov. 2018 amending Directive 2010/13/EU on the coordination of certain provisions laid down by law, regulation or administrative action in Member States concerning the provision of audiovisual media services (Audiovisual Media Services Directive) in view of changing market realities.

language, religion, political or other beliefs, national or social background, property, age, or of any other characteristic, including physical or mental disability (Article II.13 CJE; Article II.13 of CyBC-CJE).

273. Especially as regards people with disabilities, it is prohibited to use language or specific expressions in a way that might insult such people (Rule 25, paragraph 3(b) RTSR; Rule 3, paragraph 4(3)(b) CyBCR). It is also prohibited to transmit programmes with scenes containing humour to the detriment of such people (Rule 26, paragraph (i) RTSR; Rule 3, paragraph 5(i) CyBCR). Let us also note here that Article 7 of the AVMS Directive, encouraging EU Member States to ensure that AVMS are gradually made accessible to people with a visual or hearing disability, has been transposed into the Cypriot legal order not in an abstract way, but specified into particular must-carry rules (*see* Chapter 6, §4 below in this Part).

274. The CRTA is particularly strict when enforcing the aforementioned prohibitions.[347] Besides, when examining such cases, the CRTA does not take into account whether the insult came from an agent of the station or from a guest in one of its programmes. Thus, a rather humoristic comment of an actor who was a guest in a current affairs programme, suggesting that Cypriot women should never deny sex to their husbands because there are Russian and Romanian girls who might seduce them, led to the imposition of an administrative sanction on the station by the CRTA, since the latter found that such a comment insulted the dignity of the relevant national groups.[348] The same strictness applies to the programmes of the CyBC. Therefore, the CRTA imposed on CyBC a rather high administrative fine of EUR 3,000 for the opinion of a guest in one of its current affairs programmes, claiming that it is wrong to provide illegal immigrants with certain rights and economic assistance when at the same time such immigrants are involved in criminal activities.[349]

§3. Objectivity, Timeliness, and Precision of Information

275. TV and radio stations shall respect the principles of objectivity, of timeliness, and of precision of the information that they broadcast (section 26, paragraph 1 RTSL; Rule 24, paragraph 1(a) RTSR; Article I.4 CJE; Article I.1 CyBC-CJE; Rule 3, paragraph 1(a) CyBCR). More specifically, TV and radio stations should pay adequate attention so that imprecise, false, misleading, distorting the truth, or imaginary information is not transmitted through their journalistic programmes. In case

347. *See*, e.g., CRTA, Decision of 11 Sep. 2013, Case No. 29/2013(3); Decision of 19 Sep. 2005, Case No. 109/2004(1); Decision of 5 Oct. 2011, Case No. 9/2011(14); Decision of 29 Feb. 2012, Case No. 36/2011(14); Decision of 23 Nov. 2016, Case No. 94/2016(3) (all in Greek). *See also* the Decisions which are referred to below. All CRTA's Decisions may be retrieved from its Internet portal, at: http://www.crta.org.cy/.

348. *See* CRTA, Decision of 17 Apr. 2013, Case No. 19/2013(2) (in Greek).

349. *See* CRTA, Decision of 16 Oct. 2013, Case No. 53/2013(68) (in Greek). *See also*, on the same topic, CRTA, Decision of 20 Jul. 2009, Case No. 75/2008(6); Decision of 23 May 2017, Case No. 73/2016(57) (all in Greek).

this happens, they should immediately proceed with a correction and/or an apology (Article II.1 CJE, Article II.1 CyBC-CJE). Substantial mistakes when transmitting facts in a news bulletin must be corrected immediately, during the same news bulletin, if someone indicates them; in any case, they should promptly be corrected in the next news bulletin (Rule 24, paragraph 1(b) RTSR; Rule 3, paragraph 3(1)(b) CyBCR only provides that such mistakes may promptly be corrected in the next news bulletin). Besides, whereas TV and radio stations have the right to support a particular view or opinion, at the same time they are required to distinguish between facts and such opinions, comments, or speculations.

276. Clearly, the aforementioned rules and principles constitute restrictions of journalistic freedom in favour of the right of citizens to information. In general, such restrictions are compatible with the case-law of the EctHR, which construes the media freedoms and rights under Article 10 of the ECHR giving particular emphasis on the citizens' right to information.[350] Furthermore, when treating cases of defamation, the ECHR distinguishes between publications containing statements of fact (whose existence may be demonstrated) from publications containing value judgments (whose truth is not susceptible to proof).[351] The Media Law requirement to make distinct facts from comments, opinions or speculations when transmitting information through electronic media may be considered as supported by such case-law.

277. The requirements that derive from the principle of objectivity are a basic concern of the CRTA. A good example of CRTA finding a violation of this principle was the case of a news bulletin which covered a demonstration outside the House of Representatives, introducing its coverage with the indication that the protesters attempted to 'lynch' the Minister of Health.[352] In fact, neither the images that were transmitted during the news coverage nor the journalist of the TV station who was present at the place suggested that there was really such an attempt. The CRTA proceeded into a lengthy analysis of the meaning of the term 'lynch', contrasting it with the images that were transmitted, emphasizing at the same time the responsibility of the station to avoid misleading descriptions, which distort the truth. The representatives of the station claimed that what was important was not the literal meaning of the word 'lynch', but what could be perceived by the average spectator, who should get the message that the protesters were really angry. Therefore, what should be taken into account was the attempt of the station to inform the public, and not a possible misinterpretation of the wording that was used. The CRTA rejected this argument, emphasizing that the editors of news bulletins should not expect the spectators

350. *See*, e.g., *Bladet Tromsø and Stensaas v. Norway* [GC], Judgment of 20 May 1999, §§58–59; ECHR 1999-III; *Radio Twist A.S. v. Slovakia*, Judgment of 19 Dec. 2006, §51; Reports of Judgments and Decisions 2006-XV.
351. *See*, e.g., *Pedersen and Baadsgaard v. Denmark* [GC], Judgment of 17 Dec. 2004, §76; ECHR 2004-XI; *Petrenco v. Moldova*, Judgment of 30 Mar. 2010, §56; hudoc.
352. *See* CRTA, Decision of 3 May 2006, Case No. 120/2004(1) (in Greek).

to be vigilant enough so as to discern any exaggerations. On the contrary, the information should be transmitted in a way that leaves the space necessary for the spectator to evaluate what he/she watches, without being prejudiced towards a certain direction.

§4. Pluralism and Diversity of Viewpoints

278. The principle of objectivity is closely connected with pluralism in information and access of citizens to a diversity of viewpoints. In fact, pluralistic information, as coupled with the right of reply (*see* below in this chapter), is usually a sufficient condition for safeguarding objectivity. In any case, pluralism and access of citizens to a diversity of viewpoints are also fundamental principles of the Cypriot Media Law (section 26, paragraph 1(c) RTSL), especially with reference to news bulletins (Rule 24, paragraph 1(a) RTSR; Rule 3, paragraph 3(1)(a) CyBCR).

279. Of course, pluralism is a vital condition for a democratic political system. The specification of the principle of pluralism in the field of political broadcasting shall occupy the next chapter. At this point, it is important to notice that, according to section 26, paragraph 2 RTSL, pluralism and objectivity do not concern only political issues but also any other social issue that might be of interest to public opinion. The CRTA does not hesitate to find that the principle of pluralism has been violated in cases of programmes that deal with important social issues, such as the conditions of immigrants or the protection of citizens by the Republic's social services, in which a particular viewpoint has not been represented.[353] The Supreme Court, in its part, has appealed to pluralism in a more general fashion, in order to justify the constitutionality of the licensing regime and its requirements,[354] and the constitutionality of the regulation of advertising.[355]

§5. Other Rules and Standards for News and Current Affairs Programmes

280. Both the RTSR and the CyBCR provide a series of other rules, principles and standards for news and current affairs programmes, reflecting a wide range of values and legislative concerns. Thus, according to Rule 24, paragraphs 2 and 3 RTSR, and Rule 3, paragraph 2 CyBCR, reference to persons who have died should be avoided, unless there is an important reason. Close-ups of dead or seriously injured people are prohibited, and close-ups of persons in situations of extreme grief

353. *See* CRTA, Decision of 20 Jul. 2009, Case No. 75/2008(6) (conditions of immigrants) (in Greek); Decision of 18 Jul. 2012, Case No. 61/2010(3) (protection by social services) (in Greek).

354. *See Pliroforiaki kai Politistiki Eteria 'O Logos' v. CRTA* [2001] 4 CLR 590, 626 (in Greek).

355. *See Sigma Radio T.V. Ltd. v. CRTA* [2003] 4 CLR 1, 21–24; *Pliroforiaki kai Politistiki Eteria 'O Logos' v. CRTA*, Judgment of 18 Jan. 2008, Case No. 1336/2006 (both in Greek).

or anger should be generally avoided.[356] The transmission of obscene scenes or of scenes that might insult the sensitivities of the spectators shall be short and shall take place only after a warning. Special attention should be paid to covering incidents of violence against children, women or old people, which might provoke fear. Any reference to the names of dead, seriously injured or missing people is prohibited before it is ascertained that their relatives have been informed.

281. Furthermore, according to Rule 34 RTSR and Rule 3, paragraph 13 CyBCR, live transmission of terrorist acts, which might provide terrorists with the opportunity to address the public and promote their views, is prohibited. In general, it is prohibited to transmit the views of persons or organizations promoting the use of violence and their criminal activities.[357] Only simple statements by criminals are permitted, and not an interview. In any case, it is prohibited to pay a convict in order to ensure his/her participation in a programme. No details about criminal methods, or about the techniques of police authorities in combating crime, should be transmitted. In general, it is prohibited to commend positively on criminal activities, terrorism, use of violence, or any other degrading or inhuman practices.

282. When transmitting demonstrations (Rule 35 RTSR; Rule 3, paragraph 15 CyBCR), it is prohibited to use director techniques which mislead the spectators. Of course, it is prohibited to encourage spectators to participate in riots or other illegal activities. In general, TV and radio stations should avoid provoking panic in the public (Rule 36 RTSR; Rule 3, paragraph 15 CyBCR), especially when issues of national security are raised (Article II.17 CJE; Article II.17 CyBC-CJE). Unlicensed (video-) recording of military or police facilities is prohibited unless it promotes the public interest in an obvious manner (Rule 37, paragraph (a) RTSR; Rule 3, paragraph 16(a) CyBCR). Journalists should not disclose information which might affect public order, state defence, public interest or the rights of a third person, unless the public interest is promoted by such disclosure, through, *inter alia*, the protection of public safety, or the avoidance of misinformation (Article II.16 CJE; Article II.16 CyBC-CJE). As regards director techniques, it is prohibited to transmit content with a duration of less than three frames (each of them being equal to 1/24 of a second) or to use effects, which might transmit messages to the subconscious or close to the limits of consciousness.

283. Special rules apply to the participation of guests in current affairs or other programmes (Rule 28 RTSR; Rule 3, paragraph 7 CyBCR). In particular, all participants in programmes (including persons participating through telephone,[358] and even persons to whom a simple reference is made)[359] should be treated in a fair, proper and decent manner. It is prohibited to affect the opinions of participants through a change of the regular order of questions and answers, or through the use

356. *See also* Art. II.6 CJE and Art. 6 CyBC-CJE, calling journalists to adopt an approach displaying discreetness, sympathy, and avoidance of anything which might exacerbate human pain in such cases.
357. For an example *see* CRTA, Decision of 19 Oct. 2011, Case No. 21/2011(2) (in Greek).
358. For an example, *see* CRTA, Decision of 31 Jan. 2007, Case No. 141/2005(14) (in Greek).
359. For an example, *see* CRTA, Decision of 22 Mar. 2017, Case No. 5/2017(6) (in Greek).

of audio or visual tricks, or in any other way. Before the commencement of the programme, the guests should have been informed about the agenda; the reason why they are invited; the type of questions; the identity of the other guests, and any subsequent changes that might lead to a different decision upon the participation in the programme; and any opportunities to review the programme before its transmission, in case such a review is possible. Especially as regards participation through telephone (Rule 30 RTSR; Rule 3, paragraph 9 CyBCR), it is prohibited to call somebody without his/her permission, unless the public interest is promoted in an obvious manner. In any case, participants through telephone should be properly informed about the programme and its contents before they come on air.

284. An interesting provision is that which calls the TV and radio stations to avoid the transmission of old events which might confound the feelings of the persons who had been involved in them or the feelings of their families or of other spectators who might have been involved in a similar situation (Rule 39 RTSR; Rule 3, paragraph 17 CyBCR). In case such transmission is going to take place, the editors of the stations are required to inform the persons who are involved. Besides, another Regulation prohibits the transmission of archive material which might have been rendered inaccurate, or which might insult the feelings of the public because of facts that have intervened (death or conviction of a person, etc.) (Rule 37, paragraph (e) RTSR; Rule 3, paragraph 16(e) CyBCR).

§6. Protection of Minors

I. The Provisions of AVMS Directive

285. The Cypriot Media Law legislation has transposed the provisions of the AVMS Directive for the protection of minors, both in the field of television broadcasting (Article 6a) and in the field of non-linear, i.e., VSPs (Article 28b). In particular, as regards VSPs, section 32FA RTSL obliges all providers to take appropriate measures to protect minors from programmes, user-generated videos and AVCCs which may impair their physical, mental or moral development. Measures may include, depending on the case, applying similar terms and conditions in the VSPs as those applied in section 29 RTSL regarding television broadcasting, introducing functionalities for AVCCs, operating transparent mechanisms for users to report or flag content to the VSPs, or rate the content, or introduce age verification content, or parental control systems, or effective procedures for handling user complaints. On-demand service providers should further use, and inform the CRTA about the use of, technical means (especially, user-friendly filtering systems and access passwords), which might be supplied to parents, when they receive such services, in order to ensure that minors will be inhibited from having access to contents that might seriously impair their physical, mental or moral development (section 29, paragraph 9 RTSL).

286. As regards television broadcasting, private TV stations and the CyBC are required to ensure that any programmes which might seriously impair the physical, mental or moral development of minors, are only made available in such a way as to ensure that minors will not normally hear or see them (section 29, paragraph 1 RTSL; section 19, paragraph 5(a) CyBCL). Pursuant to section 29 RTSL and section 19, paragraph 5 CyCBL, such measures may include selecting the time of the broadcast, age verification tools or other technical measures. They shall be proportionate to the potential harm of the programme. Programmes that involve pornography or gratuitous violence are subject to the strictest measures. Besides, as regards programmes which are broadcast in unencoded form, all private TV stations and the CyBC are required to ensure that they are preceded by an acoustic warning, or that they are identified by the presence of a visual symbol throughout their duration (section 29, paragraph 8 RTSL; section 19, paragraph 5(g) CyBCL). The specification and implementation of the aforementioned provisions in the realm of linear AVMS are largely based on a ranking system, which is supplemented by the relevant requirements, warnings and prohibitions.

II. The Ranking System

A. *Private TV and Radio Stations*

287. According to Rule 21 RTSR, all private TV and radio stations shall take the measures which are necessary for ensuring that their programmes are of a quality prescribed by the 'social mission' of R/T and by the 'cultural development' of the country (paragraph 1 of Rule 21 RTSR). In this respect the stations are required to constitute internal committees of deontology, composed of persons with the appropriate capacities, so that they preserve the aforementioned qualitative level, submitting to the CRTA a report every four months (paragraph 2). The stations shall observe the 'generally admitted rules of decency and of good taste in language and in behaviour, taking into account the kind and context of each programme' (paragraph 3). Particular concern for the programmes which are transmitted when minors may watch should be displayed, while the stations shall ensure that the programmes within the 'family zone' are appropriate for the general audience, including children under 15 (paragraph 6). The 'family zone' starts at 5:30 and expires at 21:00 on working days which are followed by a working day, and at 22:00 on non-working days and on days which are followed by Saturday and Sunday, or by a public holiday, under the Regulations on the Functioning of Public Schools (Rule 2, paragraph 1 RTSR).[360] In general, the stations have the responsibility to ensure that the spectators or the audience are always aware of the contents of the programme that they hear or watch (Rule 21, paragraph 5 RTSR).

288. Accordingly, all programmes shall be ranked into five categories, each being indicated by a particular symbol and colour (Rule 22, paragraph 1 RTSR):

360. The exact meaning of the concept of public holidays under these Regulations, in connection with the provisions of the ranking system, has occupied the Supreme Court in *Antenna Limited v. CRTA*, Judgment of 29 Nov. 2002, Case No. 232/2002; reversed by *CRTA v. Antenna Limited* [2006] 3 CLR 151 (both in Greek).

- (K) in green for programmes which are appropriate for the general audience;
- (12) in yellow for programmes which are inappropriate for children under 12;
- (15) in blue for programmes which are inappropriate for children under 15;
- (18) in red for programmes which are inappropriate for children under 18;
- (A) for programmes with 'intense erotic' content.

289. According to Rule 22 RTSR, only encoded transmission stations may transmit programmes of the last category, and this is only from 24:00 to 5:30 each day. Programmes under the categories (15) and (18) may be transmitted by all stations only outside the family zone. The visual indications (15), (18) and (A) should be present not only during the transmission of the programmes but also in trailers. The transmission of any non-news bulletin programme shall be decided though balancing the possible negative effects that such a programme might have on minors if it is transmitted outside the family zone (Rule 32, paragraph 1 RTSR). An appropriate audio warning before the beginning of the relevant programme is applicable to radio transmissions (Rule 22 RTSR). Special programmes which are specifically destined for adults may be transmitted only outside the family zone. Violation of the aforementioned provisions, in combination with violation of the provisions of the AVMS Directive (*see* above under I) and/or with violation of the substantial provisions regarding violence and/or decency (*see* below, under III), is one of the most frequent findings of the CRTA in exercising its supervisory role.[361]

B. Cyprus Broadcasting Corporation

290. According to Rule 3, paragraph 1 CyBCR, the CyBC shall ensure that its programmes respect the qualitative level which is prescribed by its social mission as the public service broadcaster. The CyBC shall take all measures which are necessary in order to observe the 'generally admitted rules of decency and of good taste in language and in behaviour, taking into account the kind and context of each programme.' It shall be ensured that the spectators or the audience are always informed about the contents of the programme that they watch or hear. The programmes which are transmitted within the family zone shall be appropriate for the general audience, including children under 15. The definition of the 'family zone' under the CyBCR is identical to the definition of the RTSR.

291. The TV and radio channels of the CyBC are prohibited from transmitting programmes with 'intensely erotic' content (Rule 3, paragraph 2(a) CyBCR). All relevant warnings should be given, irrespective of whether a programme is broadcast within or outside the family zone. The transmission of any non-news bulleting

361. *See*, e.g., CRTA, Decision of 27 Nov. 2013, Case No. 48/2013(6); Decision of 27 Nov. 2013, Case No. 49/2013(1); Decision of 15 May 2013, Case No. 3/2013(3); Decision of 3 Oct. 2012, Case No. 41/2010(2) (all in Greek). *See also*, in the context of judicial review of CRTA's decisions, *Antenna Ltd v. CRTA* [2005] 4 CLR 260 (in Greek).

programme shall be decided by balancing the possible negative effects of such a programme on minors, in case it is transmitted outside the family zone (Rule 3, paragraph 11(1) CyBCR).

C. The Supreme Court on the Ranking System

292. A major deficiency of the ranking system, as it is provided by the aforementioned Regulations, has been tracked by a judgment of the Supreme Court, exercising its first instance jurisdiction.[362] The Court noticed that the Rules of RTSR vaguely refer to some 'criteria', according to which the ranking is supposed to take place. However, nowhere in the RTSR, nor in the RSTL, one can find such criteria.[363] The Judge of the Supreme Court proceeded one step further, and cast into doubt the possibility itself of providing such criteria, especially with regard to the definition of the concept of 'intensely erotic programmes' (a characterization which, as discussed, leads to the definite exclusion of certain contents from the programme of all unencoded transmission stations): 'Which are the degrees of eroticism, and of intense eroticism? Besides, many would say that quite a lot of admittedly classical works of art have precisely intense erotic content. Should they never be transmitted through television broadcasting?'[364] The reference to another Regulation to pornographic scenes (*see* below under III) does not provide a solution to this problem. 'Certainly, it is not possible to equate pornographic scenes (even if it was possible to define them) with intense eroticism.'[365] Nor the problem may be solved with reference to Rule 21, paragraph 1 RTSR, imposing on stations the obligation to take measures, so that their programmes are of a quality such as is prescribed by the 'social mission' of R/T and by the 'cultural development' of the country. 'Who is going to opine on which is the appropriate qualitative level? And how such a level may be determined?'[366]

293. Another deficiency of the ranking system, as tracked by the same Judgment, is the lack of an answer to the question of who is going to be responsible for the ranking.[367] Nowhere in the RTSR or in the RTSL may one find an authorization to the CRTA, to the effect that it is designated as the competent body for conducting the ranking. The CRTA is only competent for reviewing whether the programmes of a station followed the relevant provisions. But such an *a posteriori* review is not sufficient insofar as the stations should know in advance the CRTA's opinion, so as to transmit the programme in the appropriate zone, providing it with the appropriate sign. However, should we suppose that the stations themselves are competent for the ranking? All these problems and open questions led the Judge of the Supreme

362. *Antenna T.V. Ltd. v. CRTA et al. (No. 1)*[2001] 4 CLR 344, J. Hadjihampis (in Greek).
363. *Ibid.*, 352.
364. *Ibid.*
365. *Ibid.*, 352–353.
366. *Ibid.*, 352.
367. *See ibid.*, 353.

Court to the conclusion that the relevant Rule is imperfect, since it just provides the categories of films and the corresponding signs and indications, without providing for the ranking itself.[368]

294. However, the aforementioned Judgment was reversed by the Plenary of the Supreme Court.[369] Relying on the general provisions of Rule 21 RTSR (*see* above under A), the Supreme Court concluded that the responsibility for the ranking of programmes falls on the stations, while the CRTA is responsible for reviewing whether the stations complied with the relevant provisions and for imposing administrative sanctions, if necessary.[370] By way of a critical remark, let us notice that such an answer on the part of the Supreme Court is not satisfactory insofar as the problem, which was tracked by the first instance Court, was precisely the vagueness of the relevant provisions and the absence of criteria which would safeguard predictability and, hence, fairness in the exercise of the supervisory authorities of the CRTA. In any case, a chance for prompting the legislature into amending the relevant provisions, so that the ranking system is improved, was lost here.

III. Violence, Indecency, and Other Provisions

295. Some (but not adequate) answers to the question of which contents should be considered inappropriate for minors are given by the Regulations on violence and indecency.

A. Violence

296. According to Rule 26 RTSR and Rule 3, paragraph 5 CyBCR, entertainment programmes shall not contain scenes of violence[371] when such scenes are 'mainly' intended to provoke the 'excitement' (in Greek: 'έξαψη') of the spectators (one may wonder here whether there are entertainment programmes with scenes of violence which serve other purposes). Besides, violent scenes are permitted only on condition that they are an integral part of the programme to which they belong (one may wonder again whether this could not be the case). In any case, the transmission of scenes of violence against minors is absolutely prohibited.[372] It is also prohibited to transmit programmes with scenes of family violence during the family

368. *See ibid.*
369. *CRTA et al. v. Antenna Limited* [2004] 3 CLR 287 (in Greek).
370. *Ibid.*, 295–296. *See also Antenna Ltd. v. CRTA*, Judgment of 6 Oct. 2004, Case No. 777/2003 (in Greek), concluding that the Court is responsible for reviewing whether the CRTA observed the limits of its discretionary power in conducting the relevant evaluations; and *Antenna Limited v. CRTA (No. 2)* [2011] 3 CLR 691, 705 (in Greek), with the Court endorsing the CRTA's evaluation of a programme as inappropriate for minors, because it included narration of a rape.
371. For the actual conditions as regards the presence of violence in TV programmes *see* the survey of the CRTA in cooperation with the Centre for the Advancement of Research and Development in Educational Technology (CARDET), *Violence and Crime in the Cypriot Television Landscape and the Role of the Cyprus Radio-Television Authority*, 13 Apr. 2014.
372. For an example *see* CRTA, Decision of 20 Jun. 2012, Case No. 46/2011(3) (in Greek).

zone. Furthermore, it is absolutely prohibited to transmit scenes of extreme violence (the relevant provision of the CyBCR mentions rape as an example of such violence).

297. A very strict and rather unenforceable provision is that which prohibits violence in cartoons or in other children's programmes (Rule 26, paragraph (h) RTSR; Rule 3, paragraph 5(h) CyBCR). According to the literal meaning of this provision, most of the classical Disney or Warner Bros cartoons would be inappropriate for Cypriot TV insofar as their heroes (e.g., the cat Silvestre) employ 'violent' means in order to 'attack' their 'enemies' (e.g., Tweety). It is noted that the same prohibition, but only as regards transmission within the family zone, is contained in Rule 32, paragraph 3(b) RTSR, and in Rule 3, paragraph 11(3)(b) CyBCR, with the latter referring to 'intense' violence. Such contradictions and/or exaggerations are not rare in the Cypriot Media Law. The one referred to here should be resolved in conformity with freedom of (artistic) expression under Article 19 of the Cypriot Constitution and under Article 10 of the ECHR. Therefore, violence scenes in cartoons should be prohibited on condition that they promote violence in reality, by rendering violence the primary topic of the programme, especially when such violence takes place in the context of a realistic scenario.

298. Furthermore, according to the same Rules, and outside the context of children's programmes, TV stations should not transmit contents which exhibit uncommon tools or methods for provoking pain, especially when it is easy to imitate their use.[373] Programmes which may result in encouraging or provoking criminal behaviour are absolutely prohibited. Also, it is prohibited to transmit programmes which present smoking, or the use of drugs, or the consumption of alcohol, as a normal and exciting behaviour, in a way that such activities become part of a socially accepted lifestyle, especially that of younger people.[374] It is absolutely prohibited to transmit scenes which describe in a detailed manner the process of committing suicide.[375] A more problematic provision is that which prohibits the exhibition of dangerous behaviour, which may be imitated (in any case, it is prohibited to transmit programmes exhibiting such behaviour within the family zone).[376] The CRTA found a violation of that provision in the case of a TV series, in which a young girl was encouraged to use contraceptives.[377] The arguments of the representatives of the station, to the effect that the aim of the particular episode in the series was to touch in a dramatic (and hence, appealing) but sensitive manner a serious social problem was rejected by the CRTA.

---

373. For an example *see* CRTA, Decision of 29 Feb. 2012, Case No. 45/2011(2) (in Greek).
374. *See also* Rule 37, para. (b) RTSR, and Rule 3, para. 16(b) CyBCR, prohibiting the transmission of music with verses, of video-clips or of films which 'prettify' crime, drugs or anti-social behaviour (which is the latter, and who might define it?).
375. For an example *see* CRTA, Decision of 18 Jul. 2012, Case No. 37/2011(2) (in Greek).
376. For example *see* CRTA, Decision of 20 Jun. 2012, Case No. 46/2011(3); Decision of 29 Feb. 2012, Case No. 45/2011(2) (both in Greek).
377. CRTA, Decision of 13 Jun. 2012, Case No. 10/2009(1) (in Greek).

B. Indecency

299. Rule 33 RTSR and Rule 3, paragraph 12 CyBCR have to do with the transmission of programmes containing sexual activities. Therefore, programmes in which children are involved in any kind of action which is related to sexual activities are absolutely prohibited. Also, it is absolutely prohibited to transmit programmes containing sadomasochistic or pervert activities, or 'unnatural' activities (in Greek: 'ανωμαλίες') of any other kind. The combination of sex with violence is permitted only to the extent that this is necessary for dramatic (i.e., relevant to the scenario) or educative reasons.

300. A more problematic provision is that which prohibits the exhibition of activities 'with a content that might offend the sensitivities of spectators or of the audience' (Rule 33, paragraph (c) RTSR; Rule 3, paragraph 12(c) CyBCR). Not without dissenting opinions, the Supreme Court has ruled that the CRTA's discretion in concretizing the contents of these concepts is wide, since the Court's judgment may not substitute the (interpretative) judgment of CRTA in this respect.[378] Apparently, the Court's stance leaves open the possibility of discrimination in enforcing this provision (as well as in enforcing many other provisions which also contain abstract evaluative concepts).

301. In any case, the aforementioned provisions should be construed in conjunction with the general provisions of the AVMS Directive for the protection of minors (*see* under I above) and with the provisions on the ranking system (*see* under II above). This means that the primary ratio of these provisions is the protection of minors and not the protection of the prevailing moral attitudes and beliefs in Cypriot society. It also means that the primary tool for enforcing these provisions is a well-functioning ranking system, and not absolute prohibitions to the detriment of freedom of (artistic) expression, especially when such expression can be a means for triggering the sensitivities of the public with regards to issues of great concern for modern societies.

C. Participation and/or Presentation of Minors in/by Audiovisual Programmes

302. According to the new section 29A RTSL (adopted by Law 201(I)/2015), the participation of minors in commercial programmes and transmissions as well as in AVCCs and advertising is permitted only after the written consent of the parents,

378. *See Antenna Ltd v. CRTA*, Judgment of 24 Nov. 2009, Case No. 170/07 (in Greek), applying *Antenna Limited v. CRTA*, Judgment of 20 Oct. 2009, Case No. 1625/2006 (in Greek), which reaches the same conclusion with regard to the concretization of the concepts of 'personality', 'reputation', and 'private life'; cf. *Antenna Limited v. CRTA*, Judgment of 14 May 2009, Case No. 1310/2007 (in Greek), adopting a different stance, but reversed by *CRTA v. Antenna Limited*, Judgment of 30 Nov. 2012, Appeal No. 92/2009 (in Greek); cf. also the two judgments of the Supreme Court to which we referred under II.C in this paragraph above.

while the minor's best interests should be taken into account (paragraph 1). A minor may participate in cultural or artistic programmes, transmissions or AVCCs on condition that his/her freedom to participate or not is guaranteed and that the relevant provisions of labour law are applied (paragraph 2). In any case, minors above the age of 15 shall give their written consent (paragraph 3). For minors below the age of 15, their maturity should be taken into account, and if the minor expresses in any way his refusal to continue participating in the relevant activity, then such participation shall be discontinued (paragraph 4).

303. Another, very important regulative concern has to do with the presence of minors in news bulletins and in other current affairs programmes. Such programmes should not present minors as witnesses or as victims of criminal activities or of accidents, unless, by way of an exception, and only after the written consent of the parents, this is necessary for the information of the public, provided that such presentation does not provoke pain or harm to the personality of the minor (Rule 32, paragraph 3(c) RTSR; Rule 3, paragraph 11(3)(c) CyBCR). However, irrespective of the parents' consent, it is prohibited to publish the names of minors who are involved in police or judicial procedures, and it is also prohibited to provide any other information which could lead to the disclosure of their identity (Rule 32, paragraph 3(d) RTSR; Rule 3, paragraph 11(3)(d) CyBCR). Obviously, in a very 'small' society like the Cypriot one, any information about a certain crime might lead to the identification of the minor who is involved in the relevant police or judicial procedure. This fact should be taken seriously by the CRTA when applying this provision.

304. Article II.11 CJE and Article II.11 CyBC-CJE prohibits the direct or indirect disclosure of the identity of victims of rape and of other sexual offences. As regards minors who might be the victims of, the witnesses of, or the accused of such offences, it is provided that their identity should never be disclosed.[379] Besides, no reference to the relationship of an accused adult with a minor should be made. Rule 31 RTSR and Rule 10, paragraph 10 CyBCR prohibit interviews which are taken from children under 16 without their parents' consent if such interviews have to do with 'substantial issues' (obviously meaning thorny issues of their family life). In any case, irrespective of the parents' consent, it is prohibited to question children under 16 on family issues or on issues about which the child cannot give deliberate answers.[380] The contradiction between these two rules is apparent, and it should be resolved in a manner that achieves a balance between the need to protect minors and their family life, on the one hand, and the right to information about issues of general interest, on the other hand.

---

379. For an interesting case in this context *see* CRTA, Decision of 9 Nov. 2009, Case No. 145/2006 (3) (in Greek).

380. For an example of implementation of most of the aforementioned provisions *see* CRTA, Decision of 16 Oct. 2013, Case No. 36/2013(2) (in Greek).

§7. RESPECT FOR PRIVACY

305. Respect for privacy is another fundamental principle of the Cypriot Media Law (*see* section 26, paragraph 1(e) RTSL; Rule 21, paragraph 1(3) RSTR; Article II.4 CJE; Rule 3, paragraph 1(2) CyBCR; Article II.4 CyBC-CJE), reflecting a basic concern of the Cypriot Constitution (Article 15) as well as of the ECHR (Article 8). Besides the general legislative, jurisprudential or other rules and principles which protect our privacy and our personal data from the serious dangers that derive from our 'information societies', the Regulations for TV and radio broadcasting contain a series of special provisions, which cast particular emphasis on the techniques of secret recording, so common in our days. However, contradictions between the relevant provisions make again their appearance, and they should be resolved through an attempt at a systematic interpretation, which takes seriously the relevant constitutional values and rights, especially as such values and rights have been interpreted and applied by the ECtHR.[381]

306. The provisions of Rule 27 RTSR and of Rule 3, paragraph 6 CyBCR render consent of the interested person a basic requirement for the acceptance of video and sound recording as a legitimate means of journalistic activities. Therefore, such recording, as well as taking photographs from a private place, and the transmission of the relevant material, are prohibited unless the 'involved parties' give their consent (Rule 27, paragraph 1(d) RTSR; Rule 3 paragraph 1(d) CyBCR refers to the consent of the owner of the place).[382] However, this rule partially contradicts the provision of Rule 27, paragraph 1(a) RTSR, and of Rule 3, paragraph 1(a) CyBCR, which permit the *transmission* (not the recording or the taking of photographs) of material from private places without the consent of the interested parties, in case that such transmission is justified by the public interest (in Greek: 'δημόσιο συμφέρον').

307. The meaning of public interest here is closely connected with the right of the public to be informed about issues of general interest. Besides, such cases should be examined with appeal to the relevant jurisprudential standards of the ECtHR (not only the 'public figures' and the 'contribution to a debate of general interest' standards but also the need to take into account the particular aspect of the private life that is infringed upon, the circumstances under which the infringement took place, the scope of the publication and the power of the media concerned, the general climate and the possibility of 'continual harassment', etc.), with the overall aim being to achieve a balanced relationship between protection of privacy and the

381. *See* the relevant case-law under Arts 8 and 10 of the ECHR, among else in D.J. Harris et al., *Harris, O'Boyle & Warbrick Law of the European Convention on Human Rights* (5th ed., Oxford University Press 2023); and in S. A. Aktypis et al., *European Convention on Human Rights* (Nomiki Vivliothiki 2013, in Greek).

382. Such difference might be important in cases where the owner of a private place disagrees, e.g., with the speakers of a conference as to whether recording should be permitted. In any case, Rule 27, para. 1(d) refers to the consent of (all) 'involved parties'.

right to information in a democratic society.[383] Unfortunately, neither the CRTA[384] nor the Supreme Court,[385] are used to referring to the standards of the ECtHR in the context of cases of unauthorized recording.

308. The standards of the ECtHR should also serve as guidelines, in order to implement another problematic provision of Rule 27, paragraph 1(a) RTSR, which prohibits the unauthorized recording or taking of photographs *both in private and in public places* (with the transmission being permitted on the basis of public interest, as explained above). Prima facie, such extension of the protection of private life in public places is consistent with the standard jurisprudence of the ECtHR, to the effect that the concept of private life should include 'the sphere of the relations of individuals between themselves'[386] so that private life should be protected in public places as well. However, as noticed above, the circumstances under which an infringement upon private life took place, including the features of the place itself (e.g., whether it is open to all and under which conditions), should be taken into account in order to assess the permissibility of the infringement within the premises of the balancing test. Therefore, the application of the prohibition of Rule 27, paragraph 1(a) of RTSR should be nuanced in accordance with the standards of the case-law of the ECtHR.

309. Such an approach is implicit in a judgment of the Supreme Court, which dealt with the unauthorized publication by a TV station's news bulletin of a tape that secretly recorded a fight between a teacher and a student in a school classroom.[387] Considering the question of whether a school classroom may be considered a private or as a public space, the Court held that it is irrelevant to take into account whether the school is a public one, or whether the building was a public one.[388] What should be of interest is the fact that, during teaching hours, a school classroom is a place which serves a particular educational purpose, excluding all persons who do not belong to the educational community, which is based on a relationship of intimacy between the teacher and the members of the class; a relationship which

383. *See*, e.g., ECtHR, *von Hannover v. Germany*, Judgment of 24 Jun. 2004; Reports of Judgments and Decisions 2004-VI; *Mosley v. The United Kingdom*, Judgment of 10 May 2011, Application No. 48009/08; *von Hannover v. Germany (No. 2)* [GC], Judgment of 7 Feb. 2012; Reports of Judgments and Decisions 2012.

384. *See*, e.g., CRTA, Decision of 18 Apr. 2012, Case No. 2/2009(3) (in Greek). In this case the CRTA imposed an administrative sanction for secret recording of images from a kindergarten. The sanction was imposed despite the fact that the broadcaster had taken measures so that the persons involved could not be recognized. The 'public interest' allegation of the station before the CRTA was summarily rejected as being contradictory with the other arguments.

385. *See*, e.g., *Antenna Limited v. CRTA (No. 2)* [2004] 4 CLR 411. In this case, to which we shall refer below, the Supreme Court proceeded into a rather literal application of the relevant Rules, without considering the jurisprudence of the ECtHR (the Court referred only to the famous case in the House of Lords, *Campbell v. MGN Limited* [2004] UKHL 22, and only for the purpose of stressing that the station is no less responsible than the persons that proceeded into the secret recording).

386. *See*, e.g., *von Hannover v. Germany (No. 2)* [GC], Judgment of 7 Feb. 2012, §98; Reports of Judgments and Decisions 2012; *X. and Y v. the Netherlands*, Judgment of 26 Mar. 1985, §23; Series A No. 91.

387. *See Antenna Limited v. CRTA (No. 2)* [2004] 4 CLR 411.

388. *Ibid.*, 426.

presupposes the privacy of the place.[389] Furthermore, the Court rejected the allegation of the station that the transmission of the material promoted the 'public interest', arguing that primacy should be given here to the educational process, which was disturbed, not least because secret recording indicates a cunning behaviour that is unacceptable on educational standards.[390] It should be noted that the Court did not fail to mention that a legislative amendment might be useful here.[391]

310. It is noted here that, in contrast with Rule 27, paragraph 1(a) RTSR (which as we have seen prohibits unauthorized recording in public places for all purposes), the relevant Rule for the CyBC (Rule 3, paragraph 6(1)(a) CyBCR) makes a crucial distinction: Video or audio recording in, as well as taking of photographs from, public places are prohibited only when the camera or the microphone continuously focuses on a particular person who moves in roads, in public squares, or in other public spaces.

311. Another provision (Rule 27, paragraph 1(c) RTSR; Rule 3, paragraph 6(1)(c) CyBCR) prohibits the use of hidden or covered video cameras or tape recorders or other machines for the purpose of 'spying on persons' (in Greek: 'κατασκοπί΄α προσώπων'). One may wonder here whether a certain 'spying' intention is required or the mere use of hidden cameras suffices for the implementation of this provision. In any case, the latter prohibits not only the taking of material through such methods but also its transmission, without providing for a 'public interest' exception in this respect. Taking into account the aforementioned jurisprudential standards of the ECtHR and the importance of the right to information, also taking into account that the Journalistic Ethics Codes provide for a 'public interest' exception for the transmission (not for the taking) of material even when hidden cameras are used (Article II.4 CJE, Article II.4 CyBC-CJE), we conclude that such an exception should be also applied here, even if the use of hidden cameras constitutes an aggravating factor for the person who took (and for the station that transmitted?) the relevant material.

312. Could the same considerations apply to the case of Media transmitting telephone conversations which were secretly recorded without the consent of the affected parties? The transmission of such material by the Media is expressly prohibited, with the 'public interest' exception being also absent here (Rule 27, paragraph 1(e) RTSR; Rule 3, paragraph 6(1)(e) CyBCR). The absence of the 'public interest' exception may be explained by the fact that the prohibition of interception by Article 17 of the Cypriot Constitution is very strict, providing for exceptions only in limited cases, mainly concerned with the prevention, investigation or prosecution of serious criminal offences, and only pursuant to a judicial order.[392] Of course, the

389. *Ibid.*
390. *Ibid.*
391. *Ibid.*
392. The text of Art. 17, after its amendment with the Sixth Amendment of the Constitution Law 51(I)/2010, has as follows: '1. Every person has the right to respect for, and to the secrecy of, his correspondence and other communication, if such other communication is made through means not

exceptions of Article 17 may not cover the transmission of secretly recorder material by the Media. Besides, the strict provisions of Article 17 provide protection and are enforceable not only against the State but also in the relationships between individuals, in accordance with the doctrine of *Drittwirkung*, which was adopted by the Supreme Court in its landmark judgment *Yiallouros v. Nicolaou*,[393] referring precisely to Article 17 (*see* for this case above in Part I, Chapter 3, §3). Therefore, in case they transmit secretly recorder material, TV or radio stations may face not only administrative sanctions for violation of the relevant Rules of the Media Law legislation but also the prospect of civil law proceedings in order to compensate the persons whose communication has been intercepted. The jurisprudence of the ECtHR as regards interception is also very strict.[394]

313. However, there is at least one case in which the ECtHR has accepted that the transmission of a telephone conversation between government officials, which was intercepted by an unknown person who delivered the tape to the radio station, served the purposes of Article 10 of the ECHR in a way that finally lets aside the privacy interests of the involved parties.[395] In view of this case-law of the ECtHR, one should not preclude that, appealing to Article 10 of the ECHR, the transmission of an intercepted telephone conversation by a TV or radio station might be permitted, provided that the station had nothing to do with the interception, and also provided that the other standards of the ECtHR (importance of the transmission for a debate of general interest, public figures, etc.) are applicable as well. However, being confronted with such a case, the Supreme Court may choose to prohibit the relevant practice in an absolute way, abiding by the letter of Article 17 of the Cypriot Constitution, which in this case should not necessarily be interpreted in accordance with the ECHR and with the jurisprudence of the ECtHR insofar as the domestic instrument is more protective for the rights of the individuals.

---

prohibited by law. 2. There shall be no interference with the exercise of this right except in accordance with the law in the following cases: A. In cases of convicted and unconvicted prisoners. B. Pursuant to a judicial order which has been issued in accordance with the law, following a petition by the Attorney General of the Republic, and in so far as the interference is a measure necessary in a democratic society only for the interests of the security of the Republic or for the prevention, investigation or prosecution of the following serious criminal offences: (a) premeditated murder or homicide; (b) trafficking of adults or minors, and offences related to child pornography; (c) drug trafficking, supply, cultivation or production of drugs, psychotropic substances or dangerous pharmaceutical drugs, (d) offences related to the currency of the Republic; (e) offences of corruption which provide in case of conviction a sentence of imprisonment of at least five years. C. Pursuant to a judicial order which has been issued in accordance with the law for the investigation or prosecution of a serious criminal offence which provides in case of conviction a sentence of imprisonment of at least five years, while the interference shall concern access to traffic and location data which are relevant with the electronic communication and to other relevant data which are necessary for the identification of the subscriber or the user.'

393. [2001] 1 CLR 558 (in Greek).

394. *See*, e.g., ECtHR, *Malone v. the United Kingdom* (Plenary), Judgment of 2 Aug. 1984; A82; *Copland v. the United Kingdom*, Judgment of 3 Apr. 2007; Reports of Judgments and Decisions 2007-I.

395. *See* ECtHR, *Radio Twist A.S. v. Slovakia*, Judgment of 19 Dec. 2006; Reports of Judgments and Decisions 2006-XV.

314. A more specific provision protecting privacy is that of Article II.5 CJE and of Article II.5 CyBC-CJE, stipulating that the taking of recorded material from hospitals may take place under conditions of discreetness and only after permission has been granted. This provision should be read in conjunction with the prohibition of taking close-ups of persons who are in a situation of deep grief or extreme strain unless all involved parties grant permission to this effect (Regulation 27, paragraph 1(b) RTSR; Regulation 3, paragraph 6(1)(b) CyBCR). Yet another specific provision is that of Rule 27, paragraph 2 RTSR, and of Rule 3, paragraph 6(2) CyBCR, calling all stations, when transmitting material from a place where a crime has been conducted, to take all necessary measures for the protection of passengers who have nothing to do with the incident. However, when conducting an interview from the place of an event, the reporters should not employ offensive, pressing or misleading questions, while the interviewed should have the opportunity to give a complete answer (Rule 27, paragraph 3 RTSR; Rule 3, paragraph 3 CyBCR). Clearly, this provision serves not only the objectivity of information but also the interests of the persons who are involved in the event.

§8. Respect for Personality and for the Presumption of Innocence

315. If the notion of private life under Article 8 of the ECHR includes reputation, honour and other values which are relevant with respect for personality, in Cypriot Media Law the latter has an autonomous value, in spite of its connection with private life under Article 15 of the Cypriot Constitution (whose provisions are identical with those of Article 8 of the ECHR). In any case, a basic principle of Cypriot Media Law is the obligation of all TV and radio stations to safeguard respect for personality, honour and reputation, and for the professional, scientific, social, artistic, political or other activities of any person whose image is transmitted through the programmes of a station, or whose name is referred to, or whose identity may be recognized through the information that is transmitted (Rule 21, paragraph 3 RTSR; Rule 3, paragraph 3 CYBCR, with the latter omitting reference to the possibility of indirect identification of a person). By way of an important addition, Rule 21, paragraph 3 RTSR explains that the aforementioned protection shall be extended to the personality of an individual in his/her quality as a member of a group.

316. Especially as regards persons who are involved in criminal procedures, respect for their personality passes through respect for the presumption of their innocence. In particular, Article II.10 CJE and Article II.10 CyBC-CJE provide that journalists shall respect the principle that the suspect or the accused of any crime is innocent until the opposite is proved in accordance with the law. Therefore, journalists should avoid publishing anything which might lead to conclusions as to the guilt or as to the innocence of the suspect, or of the accused. It is also prohibited to publish anything that tends to traduce or defame such persons. The presumption of innocence is also constitutionally guaranteed (Article 12, paragraph 4 of the Constitution of Cyprus).[396]

317. In an interesting case, the Supreme Court affirmed a decision of the CRTA finding a violation of the aforementioned provisions of Media Law legislation, on the grounds that the news bulletin of a private TV station transmitted a reportage showing clearly the faces of five Pakistanis as they were arrested being suspects for terrorist acts.[397] On the one hand, the representatives of the station argued that the five suspects could not be recognized by the Cypriot public because of their nationality, while, on the other hand, their eventual recognition by their friendly environment could not lead to an infringement upon their personality insofar as their friends would anyway be informed about their arrest. The Court rejected this argument, affirming the evaluation of the facts by the CRTA, to the effect that, both as individuals and as members of an ethnic group, the five suspects were indeed members of the Cypriot society, and their personality should anyway be respected.

318. In this as in other judgments,[398] the Supreme Court expressed its views on CRTA's discretion in specifying the meaning of relatively abstract concepts, such as the concepts of 'personality' and of 'private life'. According to the Court, subsuming the facts to the relevant provisions belongs to the exclusive authority of the CRTA, with the Court being restricted to checking whether, on the basis of CRTA's reasoning, such discretion has been exercised within acceptable limits.[399] In other words, the Court may only check whether the reasoning of CRTA's decision was clear, consistent and sufficient, and not whether the interpretation and the implementation of the relevant Regulations were substantially correct. This means that the interpretive specification of the concepts of personality and private life belongs to the discretion of CRTA, but the Court may check whether the reasoning of CRTA's interpretive judgment was adequate for its purposes. To be noted, however, that in other similar cases, the Court did not hesitate to express its views on the substance of the issue, i.e., on the meaning of such concepts in connection with the facts of the case.[400]

396. A landmark case is *Kyriakides v. Republic* [1997] 3 CLR 485 (in Greek). For the possible effect of Media on the criminal procedure *see Georgiades v. Republic* [2003] 2 CLR 1; *Police v. Fanti and others* [1997] 2 CLR 160 (both in Greek).

397. *See Antenna Ltd v. CRTA*, Judgment of 21 May 2007, Case No. 620/2005 (in Greek); *Antenna Ltd. v. CRTA* [2010] 3 CLR 29 (in Greek).

398. *See*, e.g., *Antenna Limited v. CRTA*, Judgment of 20 Oct. 2009, Case No. 1625/2006 (in Greek); *Antenna Limited v. CRTA*, Judgment of 30 Sep. 2011, Case No. 1829/2008 (in Greek); *CRTA v. Antenna Limited*, Judgment of 30 Nov. 2012, Appeal No. 92/2009 (in Greek); cf. *Politistiki kai Pliroforiaki Eteria 'O Logos' v. CRTA* [2007] 3 CLR 91 (in Greek); *Antenna Ltd. v. CRTA*, Judgment of 23 Jul. 2010, Case No. 1600/2008 (in Greek).

399. *Antenna Ltd v. CRTA* [2010] 3 CLR 29, 43 (in Greek).

400. *See*, e.g., *Antenna Limited v. CRTA (No. 2)* [2004] 4 CLR 411, to which we referred above, under §7 (the case of the secret recording in a classroom, in which the Court expressed its views on the concepts of private life and of private or public spaces).

319. In another interesting judgment, the Court dealt with a CRTA's decision against the current affairs programme of a private TV station, which transmitted the interview of a woman who had been repeatedly raped by Turkish soldiers during the invasion of the Turkish army to the island in 1974, and who described her experience with shocking details.[401] The allegation of the station that the interview, being part of a historical documentary research, had been taken after the informed consent of the victim, so that no harm to her personality could be substantiated, was summarily rejected by the first instance Judge, on the grounds that the CRTA stayed within the limits of its discretionary power.[402] In this respect, the first instance Judge affirmed the view of the CRTA that, despite the woman's consent, she had to live her suffering again, since the interview reinstated her nightmares, something which could not but have resulted in the sharpening of her pain. Taking all these into account, but taking also into account the fact that no complaint by the interviewed woman had been submitted (in fact, it was proved that the interview took place after her insistence, and not after the insistence of the station's journalists), at the second instance the Court proceeded into a lengthy and detailed assessment of the reasoning of CRTA's decision,[403] practically circumventing its own jurisprudence on the CRTA's discretion in specifying the concept of personality in view of the facts of the case.[404] The analysis of the Court aimed to show that the CRTA had underestimated the fact that the interview had been taken from the woman after her informed consent. According to the Court, the reasoning of the CRTA's decision was inadequate in this respect, not least because the transmission of the interview was deferred, so that the woman could have control over her interview even after the latter had ended. The Court concluded that, in view of all these circumstances, no infringement of the provisions protecting the personality of the interviewed woman could be substantiated.

320. The procedure before the CRTA is not the only one that may be followed in case of damage to one's personality. The regular provisions regarding defamation (*see* above, Part II, Chapter 3, §2) are applicable here as well, something which is reminded by section 42 RTSL. Besides, section 43 RTSL provides for the right of whoever considers that his/her personality has been damaged to submit a request for a copy of the relevant material (a video-tape or other) to the station whose programmes provoked such damage. Such right may be exercised within a month from the transmission of the programme. The Attorney General of the Republic may also request such a copy. However, all R/T stations are required to keep the (video) tapes of their programmes for forty-five days after their transmission, so that copies of them may be available for whoever has a legitimate interest in receiving them.[405]

401. *See Antenna Limited v. CRTA (No. 2)* [2011] 3B CLR 691 (in Greek).
402. *See Antenna Limited v. CRTA*, Judgment of 11 Oct. 2007, Case No. 792/2006, J. Artemis (in Greek).
403. *See Antenna Limited v. CRTA (No. 2)* [2011] 3B CLR 691, 700–704 (in Greek).
404. *See ibid.*, 701, where the Court almost openly concedes that it will deviate from its standard jurisprudence on its role when checking the CRTA's decisions.
405. For an interesting case before the Supreme Court on the meaning of such obligation *see CRTA v. Radio Elios Network Ltd* [2005] 3 CLR 215, reversing *Radio Elios Network Ltd v. CRTA*, Judgment of 31 May 2002, Case No. 1597/2000 (both in Greek).

§9. RIGHT OF REPLY

321. Both the RTSL (section 44) and the CyBCL (section 17D) have transposed the provisions of the AVMS Directive (Article 28) on the right of reply. Therefore, it is provided that, without prejudice to other provisions under civil, administrative or criminal law, any natural or legal person, regardless of nationality, or, in the case of a legal person, regardless of the country in which it was incorporated, whose legitimate interests, in particular reputation and good name, have been damaged by an assertion of incorrect or imprecise[406] facts during a programme, has a right of reply, or a right of recourse to equivalent remedies, as against the relevant broadcaster.[407] The CRTA is authorized to ensure that the actual exercise of the right of reply, or of the right to have recourse to equivalent remedies, is not hindered by the imposition of unreasonable and unreasoned[408] terms or conditions.

322. A broadcaster may reject an application for the exercise of the right of reply, or of equivalent remedies, only if the aforementioned requirements do not apply, or if the satisfaction of the relevant claim would involve an act which is punishable under criminal law, or it would render the broadcaster liable to civil law proceedings, or it would transgress standards of public decency (section 44, paragraph 4 RTSL; section 17D, paragraph 3 CYBCL). In case that a broadcaster rejects an application, or in case that an answer is not provided within fifteen days, the applicant may have recourse to the CRTA for a reviewing of its application. If the CRTA finds that the application is well-founded and justified, then it calls the broadcaster to correspond with it and proceed to transmission of the reply (section 44, paragraph 5 RTSL; section 17D, paragraph 4 CyBCL). In case the broadcaster insists on his denial to transmit the reply, the CRTA may impose an administrative sanction for this reason alone (*see* section 41A, paragraph 1(d) RTSL; section 22B, paragraph 1(c) CyBCL), independently from its authority to impose sanctions for the substantial issue (i.e., violation of provisions protecting personality) as well.

323. The reply shall be transmitted within seven days subsequent to the relevant request being received by the broadcaster, or to the day on which the CRTA has

406. This word (in Greek: 'ανακριβών') is an important addition to the original text of the Directive, extending the field of application of the right of reply beyond cases in which an assertion in a R/T programme has been incorrect *sensu stricto*. Such extension is permitted under Art. 4, para. 1 of the Directive.

407. As regards the CyBC, the wording of the relevant provisions renders obligatory the application of the right of reply both to its TV and radio channels. On the contrary, §44 RTSL mentions only TV organizations. However, since the right of reply is also provided by Art. II.3 CJE, applying to TV as well as to radio stations, we conclude that the relevant provisions should be applied in an analogous manner to the private radio stations as well.

408. The Greek word here ('αναιτιολόγητων') is a translation of 'unreasoned', not of 'unreasonable' as per the text of Art. 28, para. 1 of the Directive. However, since the term 'unreasoned' alone would suggest lighter obligations for the stations (the latter would only have to provide *some* reasoning, not necessarily a 'reasonable' one), we suggest that both words render better the meaning of the relevant provision of Art. 28, para. 1 of the Directive. This approach is rather obligatory, in view of the need for uniform application and interpretation of EU Law. For this latter need in the context of another provision of the AVMS Directive, *see* Case C-52/10, *Eleftheri Tileorasi and Giannikos* [2011] ECR I-04973.

called the broadcaster to correspond with its obligations, preferably at the same programme in which the relevant reference had been made (section 44, paragraph 6 RTSL; section 17D, paragraph 5 CyBCL). If the reply is disproportionately long in comparison with the reference which has provoked it, the broadcaster has the right to curtail the reply without affecting its substance (section 44, paragraph 7 RTSL; section 17D, paragraph 6 CyBCL).

324. It is expressly provided that the obligations of the broadcasters as regards the exercise of the right of reply are without prejudice to their eventual responsibility under criminal, civil or administrative law provisions (Article 44, sections 1 and 6 RTSL; Article 17D, sections 1 and 5 CyBCL). Therefore, apart from the eventual initiation of proceedings under the provisions on defamation, and apart from the exercise of the right of reply, the person whose name and reputation have been damaged may also file a complaint before the CRTA, and the latter may initiate the proceedings under the provisions of Media Law which protect the personality and/or the private life of this person. However, a quite different question may also be raised; namely, whether the *actual* exercise of the right of reply should be taken into account when the CRTA or a Court assesses the relevant facts, in order to find whether an infringement upon the relevant rules took place; or, inversely, whether the fact that a person has chosen not to exercise the right of reply should count against the possibility of finding that his/her name and reputation have been damaged.

325. In the case of the school teacher's secret recording (*see* under §7 above), the CRTA rejected the claim of the broadcaster that the non-exercise of the right of reply by the teacher was an indication that his personality had not been harmed, on the grounds that the broadcaster had anyway the obligation to seek for the views of the teacher so that objectivity and diversity of views could be safeguarded.[409] On its part, the Supreme Court reached the same conclusion through a quite different argument; namely, that the infringement upon the provisions protecting the legitimate interests of the teachers was so grave that providing him with the opportunity to express his views would perhaps be a move without any substantial value.[410] In another case, which concerned the allegedly defaming references of a current affairs programme to a functionary of the social services of the Republic, the Supreme Court affirmed the view of the CRTA that the non-exercise of the right of reply by the functionary (with the latter arguing that she could not exercise such right due to her faculty as a functionary of the Republic, as per the relevant instructions) could not function against the finding that her reputation and name had been damaged.[411] These two judgments lead us to the conclusion that, at least (but not exclusively) in cases in which the damaging to one's personality is grave or in cases in which the right of reply cannot for some reason be exercised, it should not play any role in the finding of whether the reputation and name of the interested person was damaged.

409. *See Antenna Limited v. CRTA (No. 2)* [2004] 4 CLR 411, 421 (in Greek).
410. *Ibid.*, 427.
411. *See Antenna Limited v. CRTA*, Judgment of 20 Oct. 2009, Case No. 1625/2006 (in Greek).

Of course, nothing hinders the CRTA from taking into account the actual exercise of the right of reply, and the relevant behaviour of the broadcaster, in order to determine the exact sanction to be imposed.

326. Besides, the opportunity to exercise the right of reply should not have the character of pretence, but it should be provided under conditions of fairness. In another interesting case, the broadcaster had provided the opportunity of a reply, but the latter was distorted so that the impression was that the defamed person confirmed rather than denied the conclusions of the reporters.[412] The Supreme Court summarily affirmed the CRTA's view that the right of reply had, in fact, been attacked so that the right of citizens to objective and impartial information was also infringed.[413]

§10. High Quality, Decency in Language, and the Social Mission of Broadcasters

327. An important standard of the Cypriot Media Law, to which the CRTA frequently appeals,[414] is high quality of programmes (section 26, paragraph 1 RTSL), which is linked with the social mission of broadcasters (Rule 21, paragraph 1 RTSR; Rule 3, paragraph 1(1) CyBCR), and with the cultural development of the country (Rule 21, paragraph 1 RTSR; section 26, paragraph 1(g) RTSL). A relevant concern is observance of the commonly accepted 'rules of decency and of elegance in language, taking into account the kind and the context of each programme' (Rule 21, paragraph 4 RTSR; Rule 3, paragraph 1(3) CyBCR).

328. Doubts have been expressed by at least one Supreme Court Judge as to whether there could ever exist objective and commonly accepted criteria according to which one may determine the content of such abstract concepts as 'high quality', 'social mission', and 'cultural development'.[415] The point of reference of the Judge (quoting among else Oscar Wilde's dictum that there cannot be moral or immoral books, but only books with good or bad taste) was freedom of expression, which should not be restricted on account of the content of expression, much less on account of its 'quality'. In any case, the relevant provisions, on the one hand, make no attempt to provide criteria which might specify what quality consists of; while, on the other hand, the implementation of these provisions leads to administrative, indeed quasi-criminal responsibility of the broadcasters. According to the opinion of the Judge, it should be the latter that should have the responsibility to judge what is qualitative and what is not, while CRTA should not paternalistically impose its views on these issues.

---

412. *See Politistiki kai Pliroforiaki Eteria 'O Logos' v. CRTA* [2004] 4 CLR 710 (in Greek).

413. *Ibid.*, 713, 716.

414. *See*, e.g., CRTA, Decision of 5 Feb. 2014, Case No. 75/2013(2); Decision of 26 Jun. 2013, Case No. 33/2013(3); Decision of 27 Nov. 2013, Case No. 48/2013(6); Decision of 20 Apr. 2016, Case No. 66/2015(2) (all in Greek).

415. *See Antenna Limited v. CRTA*, Judgment of 14 May 2009, Case No. 1310/2007, Judge Hadjihampis (in Greek).

329. However, the Plenary of the Supreme Court, exercising its second instance jurisdiction in the same case, disagreed with the views of the first instance Judge.[416] According to the Court, it is not necessary that the law give definitions or criteria for the definition of abstract evaluative concepts, such as 'high quality' or 'social mission'. In any case, in the view of the Court, such concepts do not suffer from irreparable subjectivity. However, there is no reason to deny the CRTA, and the Court exercising judicial review, the authority to interpret and implement the provisions which contain such concepts. According to the Court, what is at issue here is the adequacy of the reasoning of the CRTA's decision, taking as granted its wide discretion.

330. By way of a critical remark, it is noted that the issue of whether an independent authority, such as the CRTA, should have competence for the interpretive specification and implementation of abstract evaluative concepts is quite different from the issue of whether the adoption of such concepts by the legislature may, at least in some cases, result in the provision of discretion as wide as to render the danger of arbitrariness a legitimate concern. In declaring the unconstitutionality of legislative provisions which contain such concepts the Supreme Court will not infringe upon the principle of separation of powers, nor shall it transgress its standard jurisprudence, which precludes substituting the Administration in exercising its discretion[417] or reviewing the substance of the Administration's technical judgments.[418]

331. It is submitted that the significance of mass media in modern societies is such that concerns about fairness in the process of application of Media Law rules and principles should be minimized. Instead of serving the public interest, the legislative endorsement of concepts, as susceptible to subjective interpretation as 'high quality', 'social mission' and cultural development certainly are, may indeed lead in the opposite direction. It may leave space for the promotion of the private interests of certain broadcasters, as such promotion may take place through (unconscious for the most part) unfairness in the interpretation and implementation of highly abstract legislative provisions. It is concluded that, as concerns the promotion of high quality and the social mission of R/T, the legislature should provide at least some guidelines, according to which such concepts could be specified by the CRTA in exercising its supervisory authorities.

416. *CRTA v. Antenna Limited*, Judgment of 30 Nov. 2012, Appeal No. 92/2009 (in Greek).
417. *See*, e.g., *White Horse Distillers Ltd v. El Greco Distillers Ltd* [1987] 3 CLR 531; *Plough Inc. v. The Republic* [1988] 3 CLR 145.
418. *See*, e.g., *Vryonides v. The Educational Service Commission* [1984] 3 CLR 1567, and in the context of Media Law, *CRTA v. Sisel Holdings Ltd* [2013] 3 CLR 326 (in Greek).

Chapter 4. Political Broadcasting

§1. Fair Representation in Election Periods

I. Introduction

332. Fair representation of political parties and of candidates in R/T programmes, especially during election periods, is another crucial issue for our democratic societies, affecting the function as well as the legitimacy of a modern democratic state. This concern may explain why the relevant provisions of the Cypriot Media Law are very detailed. For the CyBC, such provisions are contained in sections 2–7 CyBCL as well as the CyBCRFT which contains a series of Rules for the Fair Treatment of Political Parties. Annexed to this Regulation is the CyBC Code for Elections (CyBC-CE), containing a series of provisions concerning the coverage of the activities of political parties and candidates during election periods. For private R/T broadcasting stations, the relevant provisions are contained in section 45 RTSL as well as in the RTSRFT, which was enacted by the Normative Administrative Act 193/2006 and was amended by the Normative Administrative Act 207/2009.

II. Cyprus Broadcasting Corporation

A. *Presidential Elections*

333. The six-month period before the presidential elections is divided into two sub-periods, namely the 'first' and the 'second period', covering the first and the last three months of the election period respectively (section 2 CyBCL).

334. During the first period (section 4 CyBCL), the TV and radio channels of the CyBC are required to transmit in a brief and concise manner the electoral activities of all presidential candidates; to transmit through their news bulletins the announcements and statements of all presidential candidates, provided that their duration will be no longer than two minutes; to allot five minutes once a week and fifteen minutes once a month to all presidential candidates, so that they address to the Cypriot people; and to cover one press conference for each candidate up to sixty minutes. During the second period (section 5 CyBCL), the CyBC's stations are required to cover through its news programmes eleven public speeches of the candidates, allotting to each speech ten or five minutes; to announce on a daily basis the events of the electoral campaign of each candidate; to cover one press conference for each candidate; during the last forty-five days, to transmit daily through its radio programmes at 1:45 pm the announcements of the candidates; to invite the candidates to its programme 'Meeting with the press' or in any other similar programme; to transmit one TV interview with each candidate (or its representative), covering their proposals on basic issues of public policy; to transmit through the main news bulletins the statements of the candidates as they have, provided that they do not exceed a period of two minutes; etc.

335. A thorny issue as regards the implementation of the aforementioned provisions is whether they should apply to all persons who have declared their intention to be presidential candidates, irrespective of their influence on the electorate. The CyBCL (section 2) gives a negative answer to this question, adopting a restrictive definition of the concept of 'presidential candidate' for the purposes of fair representation. In particular, each person who has declared his/her intention to be a candidate for the forthcoming presidential election is expected to fulfil one or more of the following requirements:

- to possess the office of the President at the relevant time;
- to be the leader of a political party (for the definition of political parties for the purposes of the CyBCL *see* below in this section);
- to be supported by one or more political parties;
- to be a person who, according to the perception of the average prudent citizen, has played an important role in the political, economic or social life in Cyprus, or is a personality with prestige and/or authority in a part of the electorate.

336. In 1987, when the aforementioned provisions were inserted into the CyBCL, the Supreme Court held that the restrictive definition of the 'presidential candidate' is compatible both with the principle of equality (Article 28 of the Constitution) and with freedom of speech and of information (Article 19 of the Constitution) insofar as it is based on reasonable criteria, which, furthermore, according to the view of Judge Pikis, are closely connected with the functionality of the democratic polity.[419] Besides, in a long series of judgments since then, the Supreme Court has affirmed its position on the constitutionality of the legislative definition of presidential candidates, holding at the same time that the decision on which person fulfils the relevant criteria belongs to the BoD of the CyBC, whose discretion is wide in this respect.[420]

337. In case of a by-election (section 5, paragraph (k) CyBCL), the CyBC is required to cover, both through its radio and its TV stations at least one public speech of each of the two candidates, allotting to each speech twenty minutes. The CyBC is also required to transmit on a daily basis through its main news bulletins the statements of the candidates, provided that they do not exceed a period of five minutes each. Interestingly enough, in its 1987 Judgment, the Supreme Court held that the obligation of the CyBC to invite both candidates to a two-hour special programme, in order to discuss between themselves, was found to be contrary to Article 19 of the Constitution, since (according to the view of the majority) such obligation was indirectly forcing the candidates to be present at the programme (otherwise, the Cypriot public might well suppose that they avoid discussion), to the effect that it contravened the candidates' negative freedom of speech, i.e., their right not to

419. *President of the Republic v. House of Representatives* [1987] 3 CLR 1631, 1636–1637, 1650–1653 (in Greek).

420. *See Georghiades v. CyBC* [1987] 3 CLR 2000; *Mavrogenis v. CyBC* [1993] 4 CLR 186; *Iosifides v. CyBC* [2003] 3 CLR 213; *Iosifides v. CyBC* [2006] 3 CLR 677; *Stylianou v. CyBC*, Adm. App. 126/13, Judgment of 6 Oct. 2020 (all in Greek).

express their views when they do not think it appropriate.[421] Accordingly, the relevant provision of the law was abolished (Law 9/1988).

B. Parliamentary Elections

338. According to the basic principle of section 19, paragraph 6 CyBCL, the CyBC shall at all times keep a fair balance in the overall allocation of broadcasting hours between political parties in its programmes. This principle is specified by the provisions of the CyBCRFT and, as regards the electoral period, by the CyBC Code for Elections (CyBC-CE, Annex B to the CyBCRFT). In particular, according to Rule 6 CyBCRFT, in the electoral period, the CyBC shall ensure fair treatment of all political parties with regard to their announcements and statements, coverage of their activities, invitations to news and current affairs programmes, and allocation of TV and radio time, in order to expose their proposals to the Cypriot public. In this respect, the CyBC is required to cover through its news programmes the public speeches of the leaders of the political parties in the major cities of Cyprus; to announce on a daily basis the agenda of the electoral activities of the parties; to accept announcements of the representatives of the parties themselves up to thirty-five minutes weekly free of charge; to invite the leaders of political parties or their representative to special TV programmes in which journalists selected by the representatives of the press might raise questions; to conduct interviews with the leaders or their representatives on basic issues of public policy; etc.

339. The controversial issue here is again which political party or union should be considered as such for the purposes of fair representation. After an amendment (Law 212/1987), the CyBCL provides a definition, aiming to help the CyBC confront this problem. Under this definition, as now provided by section 2 CyBCL, the political parties which are represented in the House of Representatives are included, as well as any other organization or union which may be considered as a political party in accordance with the perception of the average prudent citizen who is aware of the Cypriot political reality, taking into account the Organization, the structure, the institutions and the aims of the union under consideration.

C. The Supreme Court on Political Parties and Fair Representation

340. The aforementioned legislative definition follows the landmark judgment *Pitsillos* of the Supreme Court,[422] which had been issued in 1982, when the CyBCL contained only the general provision of section 19, calling the CyBC to keep at all times a fair balance in the allocation of broadcasting hours as between political parties. According to the Court, this provision:

421. *See President of the Republic v. The House of Representatives* [1987] 3 CLR 1631, 1636–1637, with the dissenting opinion of Judge Pikis in this respect at 1653–1654 (in Greek).
422. *See Pitsillos v. CyBC* [1982] 3 CLR 208.

read in the context of the law in its entirety, aims to ensure that broadcasting be instrumental to the promotion of democratic rule, requiring that effective opportunity be given to opposing view-points to be put across to the people. The duty of the Corporation is twofold: Firstly to the public who have a right to adequate information on political issues, and secondly to political parties who have a right to a proper platform for the ventilation of their views.[423]

341. Then, given the absence of a definition in the law, the Court proceeded into an analysis of what should be considered as the salient features of a political party. In this respect, the Court noticed that the definition suggested by the applicant, to the effect that a political party is a group of people who have the same inclinations and who share common views and ideas on various issues, was inadequate 'in at least one respect, in that it does not encompass pursuit of political power as a vital element … [which] distinguishes a political party from a pressure group.'[424] After all, the Court continues, the first and foremost consideration in the process of deciding upon the issue of whether a given group may be considered as a political party is 'the regard of the public' itself; while 'a useful test' would be to ask whether 'a reasonable man living in Cyprus and acquainted with the realities of the country' would identify it as such.[425] Such a decision:

in turn would depend on the practical and theoretical aims of the association, its institutions and organization, regional and countrywide, as well as the response of the public to it. Past popularity as such, at any one time, is by no means decisive for in a democracy currents of public opinion change and stock must always be taken of possible swings of the pendulum.[426]

342. On the basis of this last thought, in another important judgment, which was this time issued after the adoption of the legislative definition of political parties for the purposes of fair allocation of broadcasting hours (*see* above), the Supreme Court declared the previous definition of political parties by the CyBCRFT (Rule 2) as null and void, to the extent that this latter definition included only the political parties that had taken at least a 5% of the votes in the past parliamentary elections.[427]Besides, in a series of other judgments, the Supreme Court held that the decision on which union or organization fulfils the legislative criteria belongs to the BoD of the CyBC, whose discretion is large in this respect.[428] In a frequently quoted passage from the judgment *Pakop*, Judge Artemidis rejected the allegation that the adoption of the standard of the average prudent citizen by the legislature was incorrect, expressing the following thoughts:

423. *Ibid.*, 217.
424. *Ibid.*, 218.
425. *Ibid.*
426. *Ibid.*
427. *Liberals Party et al. v. CyBC* [1989] 3 CLR 196 (in Greek).
428. *See Pakop et al. v. CyBC et al.* [1992] 4 CLR 1992; *Popular Socialist Movement v. CyBC* [2005] 4 CLR 675; *Citizens Rights Office Lasok v. CyBC*, Judgment of 31 Oct. 2013, Case No. 572/2011 (all in Greek).

> The duty of the Courts, and of the Corporation [the CyBC], is to implement the Law. The decision upon whether a party is a political party belongs to the exclusive competence of the Corporation, which, of course, is audited in case that the Law or the principles of Administrative Law are violated. In my view, the actual functioning of the idea of 'average prudent citizen' imposes on the one who utters the relevant judgment the abandonment of his own space, in which he keeps accumulated his own ideas, perceptions, beliefs and choices for the issues of life; and [imposes on the one who utters the relevant judgment] the transition to a space where the commonly acceptable view on the same issues prevails. It is reasonable that the Law assigns such functioning and judgment to the Board of Directors of the Corporation. Its capacity as responsible for the functioning of the biggest media corporation renders it the most sufficient [judge]; at the same time, it is expected that it will be the most objective judge as to whether a party, a union or a group falls under the definition of a political party, as such definition is determined by the Law. It is very difficult for such a judgment to be audited by the Supreme Court, which, especially in the field of political issues, does not substitute its own views for those of the Corporation. I say very difficult, in order to reserve for the Court the competence to intervene when an abuse of this power is obviously noticed, or when an obvious to all infringement upon the prevailing view has been proved.[429]

343. This judgment was followed by the Court a decade later in the judgment *Popular Socialist Movement*.[430] In a recent judgment, the Supreme Court affirmed the judgment *Pakop*, adding that the issue of whether a group should be considered as a political party for the purposes of the CyBCL should not be examined *in pari materiae* with Law 20(I)/2011, which provides for the registration, for the financing and for other issues relevant with political parties.[431] According to the Court, both legislative instruments (i.e., the CyBCL and Law 20(I)/2011) are special, in the sense that each one applies to its own field of application. In any case, the decision of the authorities under Law 20(I)/2011 is not legally binding upon the BoD of the CYBC, when the latter decides whether it will consider a given group or union as a political party for the purposes of fair allocation of broadcasting hours under the CyBCL and the relevant Regulations.[432]

344. By way of a critical remark, it is noted that the implicit invocation of the principle of separation of powers by the Supreme Court, in order to grant an almost unlimited discretion to the BoD of the CyBC on the issue at hand, runs contrary both to the democratic principle (insofar as the latter requires that political decisions should be taken by bodies which are politically accountable) and to the rule of

429. *Pakop et al. v. CyBC et al.* [1992] 4 CLR 1992, 1998 (in Greek).
430. *See Popular Socialist Movement v. CyBC* [2005] 4 CLR 675, 679–681 (in Greek).
431. *See Citizens Rights Office Lasok v. CyBC*, Judgment of 31 Oct. 2013, Case No. 572/2011 (in Greek).
432. For Law 20/2011 *see* Emilianides, *Constitutional Law in Cyprus* (2nd ed., Kluwer 2019), 83ff.

law (requiring, among else, that the Courts should control political power, especially if its holders are not accountable to the electorate, and especially if the exercise of such power affects the democratic principle of equal opportunities to participate in the political life of one's country by exposing his/her views to the public).

III. Private Radio and Television Stations

345. According to section 45, paragraph 1 RTSL, during election periods all private radio and TV stations are required to treat in a fair manner, and without distinctions, the members of the legislative and of the executive power; the political parties; the presidential candidates; the members of the European Parliament; and the candidates for the House of Representatives as well as for the European Parliament. Such obligation applies also to the treatment of syndicates and of other social agents; of the municipal and communal authorities; and of the citizens in general. However, by way of an important proviso, it is also provided that such obligation shall not 'affect the right of journalists to assess facts and situations in accordance with their news-casting value and importance.' Besides, section 45, paragraph 2 RTSL prohibits the violation of the aforementioned requirements through the purchase of broadcasting time by any person, natural as well as legal.

346. The requirements of fair treatment are specified by the RTSRFT, which was enacted pursuant to the authorization of section 51, paragraph 2(e) RTSL. The RTSRFT does not contain specific provisions for the presidential elections. Therefore, its provisions apply equally to all elections. Furthermore, the definition of political parties under Rule 2, paragraph 1 RTSRFT is identical to this of the CyBCL (*see* above under II.B). Therefore, the jurisprudential considerations under II.C above apply here as well. Rule 2 defines the election period as the period of forty days before the date of any elections, presidential, parliamentary, municipal, European elections or other. However, this definition contravenes section 45, paragraph 1 paragraph 2 RTSL, defining the election period as the period of three months preceding any election. Insofar as the Regulations must be compatible with the provisions of the Law under which they were issued and enacted, it should be considered that the definition of RTSL also applies here.

347. The first basic principle is pluralism and polyphony without prejudice to freedom of expression and to the journalist's right to evaluate facts and situations according to their value and importance (Rule 3 RTSRFT). The second basic principle is equal treatment (in Greek: ('ισότιμη μεταχείριση') of all political parties and candidates, with the aim being to provide citizens with substantial information (Rule 4, paragraph 1 RTSRFT). Equal treatment is defined on the basis of proportional equality, using as criteria the parliamentary power of political parties *and* the organization of each party at a countrywide scale (Rule 4, paragraph 2 RTSRFT). The principle of fair treatment is applicable to all events, activities and interventions which have, either directly or indirectly, the character of electoral promotion and propaganda (Rule 4, paragraph 3 RTSRFT). For the purposes of observing the principle of equal treatment, the following are taken into account (Rule 4, paragraphs 4–6 RTSRFT):

- the presence of political personalities, such as leaders of political parties, ministers, governmental officers, members of the House of Representatives, holders of offices in municipal or communal bodies, representatives of political parties, and candidates in the programme of a station;
- the radio and/or television coverage of the public speeches of the aforementioned persons;
- that broadcasting hours that are generally dedicated to the activities and to the public interventions of the aforementioned persons;
- the activities and presence in a programme of groups or personalities, irrespective of their capacity as members of a political party, on condition that such activities and presence take place in order to support or promote a particular political party or a particular candidate;
- the statements and activities of persons holding a public office, which, even if they take place within the premises of their competences and jurisdiction, promote or just describe work that has been done, or are exploited so as to transmit messages with electoral content, or so as to exhibit the elements of an electoral programme (however, the statements and activities of holders of public offices which take place in this capacity are not considered as electoral promotion activities).

348. According to Rule 5 RTSRFT, each station shall pay attention so that invitations for participation in its programmes, and provision of access to such programmes, take place in accordance with the principle of equal treatment, without excluding particular parties or candidates. Particular concern for the fair treatment of the two genders is required. The stations shall ensure that the coverage of the public activities of parties and candidates takes into account the number of such activities as well as their importance. However, the stations shall also ensure that, when commenting on or reproducing the activities, the events, the statements or the announcements of parties and candidates, they will not distort their substance and intended meaning.

349. An important provision is that of Rule 6 RTSRFT, calling all stations to ensure that, during election periods, the right of reply will be effectively exercised within forty-eight hours at the latest from the transmission of the relevant programme, which has triggered the reply of a party or a candidate. During election periods, all stations are required to keep a record of their programmes, of the persons who participated in them, and of the daily and weekly broadcasting hours which were dedicated to each party or candidate (Rule 8 RTSRFT). The CRTA, on its part, may request any data or information which might be relevant to its supervisory authorities (Rule 9 RTSRFT).

§2. Political Advertising in Election Periods

350. Until 2006 political advertising was prohibited by Article D.8 of the Code of Advertising, of Tele-Commerce Messages, and of Sponsorship (CA), which is annexed to the RTSR. On the one hand, in 2002 the Supreme Court held that such prohibition is *ultra vires* insofar as there was no provision in the RTSL on which such prohibition could be based; while, on the other hand, political advertising constitutes an expression of opinion, protected by Article 19 of the Constitution.[433] This judgment was affirmed by the Plenary of the Supreme Court at second instance, with the Court stressing the constitutional status of political advertisements.[434] As a result, the prohibition was abolished (Law 192/2006), while new provisions were inserted into the RTSL (section 34D) and the CyBCL (section 17B), containing very detailed requirements and limits on the transmission of political advertising during election periods (including presidential and parliamentary elections as well as Euro-elections). The provisions of both legislative instruments are identical, so they shall be jointly presented.

351. For the purposes of these provisions, the election periods include only the last forty dates before each election (section 34D, paragraph 7 RTSL; section 17B, paragraph 7 CyBCL). In the case of presidential elections, the term 'candidate' indicates the individual presidential candidates, while in the case of parliamentary elections and of Euro-elections the same term may signify either the political parties or independent candidates (i.e., the candidates who are not included in the lists of a political party). Accordingly, in the case of presidential elections political advertising is permitted only for individual candidates, and not, e.g., for the political parties that support a particular candidate, while in parliamentary elections and in European elections political advertising may refer either to political parties or to individual candidates (*see* section 34D, paragraph 1(b)–(c) RTSL, in combination with the definition of the term 'candidate' in paragraph 7 of the same section; *see also* section 17B, paragraph 1(b)–(c) CyBCL in combination with the definition of the term 'candidate' in paragraph 7 of the same section).

352. A set of important requirements is provided by section 34D, paragraph 1 RTSL, and by section 17B, paragraph 1 CyBCL. Political advertising should be separated from other programmes through the use of visual indications and sound warnings, so that one may know in advance that a paid political advertising is forthcoming. Most importantly, political advertising should not constitute 'negative advertising', with the latter being defined as any paid announcement or message which aims to disparage an opponent or a party without adequate substantiation (*see* section 2 RTSL; section 17B, paragraph 7 CyBCL). The issue of negative

---

433. *See Antenna Limited v. CRTA (No. 1)* [2002] 4 CLR 861 (in Greek).

434. *See CRTA v. Antenna Limited* [2005] 3 CLR 383, 390–391 (in Greek). Interestingly enough, the Court rejected the allegation that the prohibition of political advertising is also an infringement upon the principle of equality under Art. 28 of the Constitution, on the grounds that it signifies a differential treatment of R/T broadcasting from printed press (which may freely publish political advertising).

advertising was raised during the campaign for the presidential elections of February 2003, when the CRTA called all stations to abstain from transmitting an advertising which implied that it would be a nightmare to assign to the opponents of the advertised candidate the crucial decisions on the Cyprus issue and on the issues which were related with the financial crisis.[435] However, the CRTA did not react to the advertising of another candidate, the then President of the Republic Nicos Anastasiades, which made negative references to former President Dimitris Christofias. Such discrimination raised serious complaints about the political independence of the CRTA.[436]

353. Another important provision is that of section 34D, paragraph 1(e) RTSL and of section 17B, paragraph 1(e) CyBCL, requiring that all R/T stations transmit political advertising upon the same terms and conditions for all candidates and parties. Equally important is the provision of paragraph 1(f) of the same sections, calling all stations to ensure 'where possible' that an equal proportion of broadcasting hours for political advertising will be allocated between the candidates and parties, taking as point of reference both the 'prime time' zone (for TV this includes the period between 19:00 and 22:00, while for radio it includes the periods from 6:00 to 9:00 and from 12:00 to 14:00; *see* section 34D, paragraph 7 RTSL, and section 17B, paragraph 7 CyBCL) *and* the family zone as a whole (i.e., the period from 5:30 to 21:00 for the days preceding working days, and from 5:30 to 22:00 for the days preceding non-working days; *see* above under Chapter 3, §6 II A).

354. Section 34D, paragraph 2 RTSL, which is also applicable to the CyBC (*see* section 17B, paragraph 2 CyBCL), provides that the overall amount of TV broadcasting hours in all stations (including CyBC), which may be allocated to each presidential candidate, shall not exceed a hundred minutes during the election period (with an additional amount of twenty-five minutes to be allocated to each of the two remaining presidential candidates, in case of a by-election). For radio stations the same limit is set to sixty minutes, providing also for an additional amount of twenty-five minutes, in case of a by-election. For parliamentary elections and for Euro-elections, and as regards TV stations, the limit is again a hundred minutes for each political party and thirty minutes for individual candidates. As regards radio stations, the limit is set to sixty minutes for each political party, and to twelve minutes for each independent candidate.

355. A crucial issue here is how the observance of the aforementioned limits and requirements may be audited. According to section 34D, paragraph 4 RTSL and section 17B, paragraph 4 CyBCL, the candidates in the case of presidential elections, and the political parties or the independent candidates in the case of parliamentary elections and of Euro-elections, are required, five days before the transmission of their first political advertising, to submit to the CRTA their agreements with all R/T

435. *See* G. Kentas, *The Cyprus Radio and Television Authority as an Agent of Political Violence*, 1 Dimosiografia 33 (The Hellenic Edition of Columbia Journalism Review) (2013) (in Greek), where all relevant references.

436. *See ibid.*

stations as regards the programme of their advertising. Furthermore, according to section 34D, paragraph 5 RTSL and section 17B, paragraph 5 CyBCL, all broadcasters are required to submit before the transmission of any political advertising the relevant agreement with all its contents. In case the CRTA notices that the relevant limits are being reached, it may issue directives to the R/T stations, calling them to observe the limits; and, in case of a transgression, the CRTA may initiate proceedings against the station that did not observe the limits (section 34D, paragraph 6 RTSL; section 17B, paragraph 6 CyBCL).

§3. Polls

356. According to section 46, paragraph 1 RTSL and section 7A, paragraph 1 CyBCL, during the last seven days before any election, all R/T stations are prohibited from transmitting or publishing in any other way the results of polls which may be connected with the election.[437] Clearly, the aim of this provision is to safeguard free expression of the political will of the electorate upon exercising the constitutional right to vote (Article 31 of the Constitution). However, taking as granted that no one may practically inhibit the publication of polls on the Internet, such prohibition may have opposite results; that is, it may leave room for the circulation of rumours regarding 'secret polls', which cannot be checked, and which may have distorting effects upon political freedom and rights.

357. Besides, paragraph 2 of the aforementioned sections provides for some procedural safeguards as regards conducting polls during election periods. In particular, all companies conducting polls are required to submit to the CRTA as well as to the BoD of the CyBC a memorandum, explaining the methodology and the sampling that has been used, an analytic review of the population sample, and the questionnaire that has been used. It is expressly provided that all these data shall be kept secret in the hands of the President of the CRTA and of the President of the BoD of the CyBC.

§4. Fair Representation in Non-election Periods

I. Cyprus Broadcasting Corporation

358. The principles of fair representation, of equal treatment and of polyphony do not cease to apply after the elections. As regards the CyBC, the wording of the general provision of section 19, paragraph 6 CyBCL is such that no distinction is

437. For an interesting case, in which the meaning of the term 'polls' was under dispute, *see* CRTA, Decision of 3 Jun. 2009, Case No. 53/3008(19). Proceeding into a teleological interpretation of the relevant provisions, the CRTA decided that even a tele-voting process, which does not provide objective results by any scientific means, may be considered as a poll insofar as it may influence the opinion of the voters before the election.

made between election and non-election periods: The CyBC shall ensure the observance of fair balance in the allocation of the overall radio and TV broadcasting time as between political parties in the transmission of programmes with political content. The same applies to the principles which are provided by Rules 3 and 4 CyB-CRFT (fair treatment of political parties, balanced and objective information of the public as regards the activities of political parties). Besides, the CyBCRFT contains a CyBC Code for the News Coverage of Political Parties (CyBC-CNC), whose aim is precisely the observance of such principles in non-election periods.

359. In particular, the Code requires that the news bulletins of the CyBC TV stations cover the congresses of the political parties, the rallies and the announcements of the political parties, and the public speeches of their leaders; that certain time limits be observed as regards such coverage (five minutes for nationwide congresses and rallies, three minutes for regional congresses and rallies, three minutes for announcements and public speeches); that the duration of the news coverage of other activities of the political parties shall not exceed two minutes for each party; that intra-parties activities shall not be covered; that the criterion for the determination of the sequence to be followed when presenting news about the parties which are represented in the House of Representatives be the votes that such parties have received in the last parliamentary election; that for parties which are not represented in the House of Representative the criterion be the existence of a news item which is connected with them; that the speeches or announcements promoting the views of political parties on current affairs shall be taken as 'opposing views' against the decisions of the Government or of other parties on the same affairs, and they shall not exceed three minutes of broadcasting time.

360. It is also provided that on a yearly basis, the CyBC shall cover up to two press conferences of the leaders or representatives of each political party, dedicating to them a special programme which shall be transmitted immediately after the main news bulletin. Furthermore, the CyBC is required to invite the leaders or the representatives of political parties in current affairs programmes of duration up to sixty minutes. In such programmes, journalists of other media may be invited. Public speeches in religious ceremonies or in other relevant events shall not be covered unless their content is such so as to give them particular importance. Besides, the CyBC is required to provide live transmission of the meetings of the House of Representatives, when a request by the latter is submitted.

II. Private Radio and TV Stations

361. The regulative environment is not so clear as regards the observation of the principle of fair representation of political parties by private radio and TV stations during non-election periods. The general provision of section 45, paragraph 1 RTSL requires that such principle be observed 'especially' during election periods. The same reservation is included in the RTSRFT. In view of such provisions, as well as in view of section 26 RTSL, rendering polyphony and diversity of views basic principles of private broadcasting, we may conclude that, during non-election periods, private R/T stations are required to observe the requirements of fair representation and of equal treatment, making all necessary adjustments. Besides, the general provision of section 45, paragraph 1 RTSL contains a reservation in favour of the journalists' right to assess facts and situations in accordance with their news value and importance. Such reservations should be taken into account when assessing the performances of private broadcasting stations with regard to fairness in political broadcasting.

Chapter 5. Advertising Rules

§1. Introduction

I. Forms of Audiovisual Commercial Communication

362. Both the RTSL and the CyBCL have transposed the provisions and the definitions of the AVMS Directive) for commercial communications. Therefore, AVCC is defined so as to mean:

> images with or without sound which are designed to promote, directly or indirectly, the goods, services or image of a natural or legal entity pursuing an economic activity. Such images accompany or are included in a programme in return for payment or for similar consideration or for self-promotional purposes. Forms of audiovisual commercial communication include, *inter alia*, television advertising, sponsorship, teleshopping and product placement (section 2 RTSL, and section 2, paragraph 1 CyBCL, transposing the definition of Article 1, paragraph 1 (h) of the AVMS Directive).

363. According to the definitions of section 2 RTSL and of section 2, paragraph 1 CyBCL, transposing the relevant definitions of Article 1, paragraph 1 of the AVMS Directive:

- 'television advertising' means any form of announcement broadcast whether in return for payment or for similar consideration or broadcast for self-promotional purposes by a public or private undertaking or natural person in connection with a trade, business, craft or profession in order to promote the supply of goods or services, including immovable property, rights and obligations, in return for payment;[438]
- 'sponsorship' means any contribution made by public or private undertakings or natural persons not engaged in providing AVMS or VSPs or in producing audiovisual works, to the financing of AVMS, VSPs, user-generated videos or programmes with a view to promoting their name, trade mark, image, activities or products;[439]
- 'teleshopping' means direct offers broadcast to the public with a view to the supply of goods or services, including immovable property, rights and obligations, in return for payment;
- 'product placement' means any form of AVCC consisting of the inclusion of or reference to a product, a service or the trade mark thereof so that it is featured within a programme or a user-generated video, in return for payment or for similar consideration.

---

438. For an interesting case on the meaning of advertising under the then applicable provisions of Directive 89/552/EEC before the CJEU *see* C-429/02, *Bacardi France*, Judgment of 13 Jul. 2004, ECR I-6617.

439. By way of an explanation, the relevant definition of §2, para. 1 CyBCL excludes the state contribution for the provision of PSB services (*see* for them Ch. 1 in this Part above).

II. Application of Certain Provisions of AVMS Directive to Radio Broadcasting

364. The provisions of the AVMS Directive apply to providers of linear AVMS which consists of television programmes – this conclusion derives from the definition of AVMS in Article 1, paragraph 1(a)(i) of the AVMS Directive. They also partly apply to VSPs. However, the definition of AVMS by the RTSL (section 2) and by the CyBCL (section 2, paragraph 1) covers not only TV but also radio programmes. On account of this, certain provisions of the AVMS Directive, namely those concerning sponsorship (*see* under §4 in this chapter below), apply to radio stations. The same does not occur as regards the provisions on AVCCs. Both legislative instruments (the RTSL and the CyBCL) have not adapted the definition of AVCC so as to comply with the circumstances of radio broadcasting.

365. Clearly, neither the provisions for television advertising can apply to radio stations. The 'gap' that is produced here is not so wide, since the substance of many of the AVMS Directive's provisions on AVCCs and on TV advertising is included in the provisions of the two Codes of Advertising (CA and CyBC-CA), which expressly provide for their application to radio programmes (Articles A.1 and C CA; Articles A.1 and C CyBC-CA). In any case, let us note that a proposal for a legislative amendment, which is pending before the House of Representatives, contains provisions whose aim is to regulate in a more clear way the transmission of advertising by radio stations.

III. The Two Codes of Advertising

366. Apart from the provisions of the AVMS Directive, the Cypriot Media Law includes the provisions of the CA, annexed to the RTSR; and the provisions of the CyBC Code of Advertising and Tele-Commerce Messages (CyBC-CA), annexed to the CyBC Regulation 93/2001 (CyBCR). As indicated under II above, the provisions of the two Codes apply both to TV and radio stations. In what follows, we shall be presenting, first, the provisions of the AVMS Directive, as they have been transposed by the RTSL and by the CyBCL, including the additional requirements for television advertising, which were enacted by virtue of Article 4, paragraph 1 and Article 26 of the AVMS Directive.[440] Then, we shall be presenting the provisions of the two Codes of Advertising on the same topics.

440. Article 4 of the Directive leaves freedom to Member States to enforce stricter or more detailed rules in the fields coordinated by the Directive, provided that such rules apply to media service providers under their jurisdiction and are further in compliance with EU law (i.e., with the fundamental 'freedoms' enshrined in the TFEU). Article 26 provides that, without prejudice to Art. 4 of the Directive, Member States may, with due regard for EU law, lay down conditions other than those laid down in Art. 20, para. 2 and Art. 23, in respect of television broadcasts intended solely for the national territory, which cannot be received directly or indirectly by the public in one or more other Member States. For the invocation of these provisions in the context of a case before the Supreme Court, *see Sigma Radio T.V. Ltd v. CRTA (No. 2)* [2010] 3 CLR 579, 587–588 (in Greek).

367. As regards the latter, it is noted that they lay down stricter rules for advertising than those that are provided by the AVMS Directive. This is not *by itself* inconsistent with the AVMS Directive insofar as Article 4, paragraph 1 of the latter provides for the ability of EU Member States to apply stricter rules in the fields coordinated by the AVMS Directive, especially in the field of advertising.[441] However, again according to Article 4, paragraph 1 of the AVMS Directive, such rules shall be consistent with the general principles of EU law. In this respect, we should notice that the CJEU gives particular emphasis to the protection of consumers against abuses of advertising, regarding such protection as an overriding reason which may justify restrictions on the freedom to provide services, provided that such restrictions shall be applied so as to ensure the aim pursued and not go beyond what is necessary for that purpose.[442]

368. Besides, the restrictions on advertising which derive from the two Codes of Advertising must be compatible with the Constitution (most importantly with Article 19 of the Constitution, safeguarding freedom of speech and of information) as well as with the provisions of the basic legislative instruments (the RTSL and the CYBCL) by authorization of which such Codes have been issued. In this respect, it is important to consider the jurisprudence of the Supreme Court.

IV. The Supreme Court on Restrictions on Advertising

369. The Supreme Court has had the opportunity to express its views on the constitutionality of various restrictions on TV advertising.[443] In most cases, the Court rejected the allegation that such restrictions are incompatible with freedom of speech and of information under Article 19 of the Constitution. In order to do so, the Court first appealed to the general power of the state, under Article 19, paragraph 5 of the Constitution and under Article 10 of the European Convention of Human Rights, to regulate R/T broadcasting.[444] Then, it proceeded into an analysis of the role of advertising in the modern media landscape, referring to the views of P. Dagtoglou in this respect.[445] In particular, the Court stressed that, although advertising renders TV stations independent from political and state power, at the same time it contains risks for the spectators. Such risks are relevant with the possible

441. *See also* Recital 83 in the Preamble of the Directive: 'In order to ensure that the interests of consumers as television viewers are fully and properly protected, it is essential for television advertising to be subject to a certain number of minimum rules and standards and that the Member States must maintain the right to set more detailed or stricter rules and in certain circumstances to lay down different conditions for television broadcasters under their jurisdiction.'

442. *See* Case C-234/12, *Sky Italia Srl*, Judgment of 18 Jul. 2013, EUR-Lex, para. 24; Case C-6/98, *ARD* [1999] ECRI-07599, para. 50.

443. *See Sigma Radio T.V. Ltd v. CRTA* [2003] 4 CLR 1; *Sigma Radio T.V. Ltd v. CRTA (No. 1)* [2001] 4 CLR 1020; *Sigma Radio T.V. Ltd v. CRTA (No. 2)* [2001] 4 CLR 1086; *Sigma Radio T.V. Ltd v. CRTA*, Judgment of 27 Nov. 2001, Case 810/2000; *Politistiki kai Pliroforiaki Eteria 'O Logos' v. CRTA*, Judgment of 18 Jan. 2008, Case No. 1336/2006; *Politistiki kai Pliroforiaki Eteria 'O Logos' O.E. v. CRTA*, Judgment of 16 Feb. 2007, Case No. 1629/2005 (all in Greek).

444. *See Sigma Radio T.V. Ltd v. CRTA* [2003] 4 CLR 1, 20–21 (in Greek).

445. *Ibid.*, 21–23.

expansion of the advertising time, with surreptitious advertising, and with the possibility of infringements upon the constitutional rights and interests of the citizens. In view of these risks, the imposition of restrictions on advertising, through the provisions of the AVMS Directive and through the more concrete provisions of the national legal order, is compatible with freedom of speech and of information insofar as they stay within the limits of reasonableness, with the aim being to avoid only the abuses of advertising, and not the latter as such. Such jurisprudence is compatible with the provisions and with the spirit of the AVMS Directive as well as with the emphasis given by the CJEU on the protection of consumers from excesses and abuses of advertising.[446]

370. In 2016 the House of Representatives passed a bill that introduced a new section (section 32E) to the RTSL, providing that audiovisual media content transmitted from other EU countries shall not include commercials or other forms of AVCC that are addressed to the Republic. The President of the Republic, exercising his powers under Article 140 of the Constitution, referred this bill to the Supreme Court alleging that the new provision was incompatible with Articles 49 (freedom of establishment) and 56 (freedom to provide services) of the TFEU.[447] The House of Representatives argued that the new provision served proportionately a significant public interest, that is, the avoidance of a reduction of the advertising revenues of the already established providers, something which would lead to the termination of their services (with further negative consequences as regards the Cypriot market and the public revenues). The Supreme Court dismissed this argument by holding that the new provision was incompatible with Article 56 of the TFEU insofar as the latter permits restrictions on the freedom to provide services only for exceptional public interest reasons, which do not include purely economic considerations.[448]

§2. Restrictions on Content and on Form

I. Audiovisual Commercial Communications (Directive)

371. According to section 30E RTSL and to section 18F CyBCL, transposing Article 9 of the AVMS Directive, all AVMS providers and the channels of CyBC shall ensure, first, that AVCCs do not use subliminal techniques; and, second, that

446. *See* in particular Case C-234/12, *Sky Italia Srl*, Judgment of 18 Jul. 2013, EUR-Lex, para. 17; Case C-195/06, *Österreichischer Rundfunk* [2007] ECR I-8817, para. 27; Case C-281/09, *Commission v. Spain* [2011] ECR I-0000, para. 45.

447. *See President of the Republic v. The House of Representatives*, Ref. No. 5/2016, Judgment of 6 Sept. 2017 (in Greek).

448. *See ibid.*, with reference to relevant rulings of the CJEU. To be noticed that at a previous stage the Supreme Court had rejected the application of the House of Representatives for a reference of a preliminary ruling of the CJEU. *See President of the Republic v. The House of Representatives*, Ref. No. 5/2016, Judgment of 5 Apr. 2017 (in Greek).

AVCCs are readily recognizable as such. In particular, surreptitious AVCC is prohibited. It is to be noted that the definition of surreptitious AVCC in the two legislative instruments is identical to that of the AVMS Directive.[449] Pursuant to section 32F RTSL, VSPs should comply with all requirements of section 1 of 30E RTSL regarding AVCCs promoted, sold or arranged by themselves. They should further take appropriate measures to comply with the requirements with respect to AVCCs that are not marketed, sold or arranged by them, taking into account the limited control exercised by the VSPs over those AVCCs. VSPs should further clearly inform users where programmes and user-generated videos contain AVCCs, provided that such AVCCs have been properly declared or the VSPs have knowledge of that fact.

372. Violation of the prohibition on surreptitious AVCC is one of the most common findings of the CRTA.[450] In this context, the CRTA has rejected various arguments of the stations to the effect that they did not have responsibility for the representation that was considered surreptitious advertising; for example, the argument that the station did not have control over the contents of the TV series in which such representation took place insofar as the relevant choices were made by the producer and by the director of the series;[451] or that the representation of the product was closely connected with the scenario.[452] The Supreme Court, in its part, rejected the argument that the prohibition on surreptitious advertising constitutes an infringement upon freedom of speech and of information under Article 19 of the Constitution.[453] Besides, judging the case on its facts, the Court was not convinced that the scenario made necessary the presence of the particular products in the scene under examination.[454]

373. Furthermore, section 30E RTSL and section 18F CyBCL prohibit AVCCs which prejudice respect for human dignity; include or promote any discrimination based on sex, racial or ethnic origin, nationality, religion or belief, disability, age or sexual orientation; encourage behaviour prejudicial to health or safety; encourage behaviour grossly prejudicial to the protection of the environment. All forms of AVCCs for cigarettes and other tobacco products, including electronic cigarettes

449. 'Surreptitious AVCC means the representation in words or pictures of goods, services, the name, the trade mark or the activities of a producer of goods or a provider of services in programmes, when such representation is intended by the media service provider to serve as advertising and might mislead the public as to the character of such representation. A representation of this kind shall be considered as intentional especially if it is done in return for payment or for similar consideration (§2 RTSL and §2, para. 1 CyBCL, transposing Art. 1, para. 1(j) of the Directive). For a case before the CJEU, in which the term 'especially' in the last sentence of the definition acquired significance, *see* Case C-52/10, *Eleftheri Tileorasi and Giannikos* [2011] ECR I-04973.

450. *See*, e.g., CRTA, Decision of 30 Apr. 2014, Case No. 1/2014(2); Decision of 15 Jan. 2014, Case No. 68/2013(6); Decision of 12 Nov. 2013, Case No. 45/2013(68); Decision of 27 Nov. 2013, Case No. 52/2013(6); Decision of 18 Apr. 2012, Case No. 16/2012(57) (all in Greek). *See also* CRTA, 'Study on the Issues of A) Product Placement, B) Programmes Sponsorship, C) Surreptitious Audiovisual Commercial Communication', October 2014, part C (in Greek).

451. *See*, CRTA, Decision of 9 Nov. 2005, Case No. 104/2005(3) (in Greek), applying the older provisions of the Directive regarding surreptitious advertising.

452. *See*, e.g., CRTA, Decision of 23 Jul. 2003, Case No. 12/2003(3) (in Greek).

453. *See Sigma Radio T.V. Ltd v. CRTA (No. 2)* [2001] 4 CLR 1086, 1091–1092 (in Greek).

454. *Ibid.*, 1094.

and refill containers, as well as for medicinal products and medical treatment available only on prescription are also prohibited. AVCCs for alcoholic beverages shall not be aimed specifically at minors and shall not encourage immoderate consumption of such beverages. Section 30E RTSL also prohibits AVCCs which: cause physical or moral detriment to minors; directly exhort minors to buy or hire a product or service by exploiting their inexperience or credulity; directly encourage minors to persuade their parents or others to purchase the goods or services being advertised; exploit the special trust of minors in their parents, teachers or other persons; or unreasonably show minors in dangerous situations.[455]

II. Television Advertising (Directive)

374. Articles 19 and 21–22 of the AVMS Directive on the form and contents of television advertising have been transposed by section 33 RTSL and by section 17A CyBCL. In particular, television advertising shall be readily recognizable and distinguishable from editorial content. Without prejudice to the use of new advertising techniques, private TV organizations, as well as the CyBC, are required to keep television advertising distinct from other parts of the programme, using optical and/or acoustic and/or spatial means to this effect. Isolated television advertising spots are allowed in the transmission of sports events, but are otherwise allowed only by way of exception. It was originally provided that isolated television advertising sports, other than in the transmission of sports events, *shall be exempt from the aforementioned provisions* (section 33, paragraph 1(a) RTSL, and section 17A, paragraph 2(a) CyBCL), which as explained the previous edition of this monograph, constituted a faulty transposition of Article 19, paragraph 2 of the AVMS Directive. The latter provides that isolated advertising and teleshopping spots, other than in transmissions of sports events, *shall remain the exception* (and not that they shall be exempt from the general rule of paragraph 1, which requires in any case that television advertising shall be readily recognizable and distinguishable from editorial content). The relevant provision was amended, as above, pursuant to Laws 53(I)/2019 (amending section 33 RTSL) and 52(I)/2019 (amending section 17A CYBCL), so that the new text is consistent with the AVMS Directive so that isolated advertising spots are treated as an exception, while in any case television advertising shall be readily recognizable and distinguishable from editorial content.

375. Section 33, paragraph 4 RTSL and section 17A, paragraph 4 CYBCL just repeat the provisions of Article 22 of the AVMS Directive on television advertising of alcoholic beverages. Therefore, such advertising shall observe the following requirements: It may not be aimed specifically at minors or, in particular, depict minors consuming these beverages; it shall not link the consumption of alcohol to enhanced physical performance or to driving; it shall not create the impression that the consumption of alcohol contributes towards social or sexual success; it shall not

455. The omission of §18F CyBCL to include this latter prohibition is not so important insofar as the CyBC-CA contains similar provisions on the protection of minors (*see* below under III).

claim that alcohol has therapeutic qualities or that it is a stimulant, a sedative or a means of resolving personal conflicts; it shall not encourage immoderate consumption of alcohol or present abstinence or moderation in a negative light; it shall not place emphasis on high alcoholic content as being a positive quality of the beverages.

376. Transposing Article 21 of the AVMS Directive, section 33, paragraph 3(b) RTSL and section 17A, paragraph 3(b) CyBCL prohibit television advertising of medicines and of medical treatments which are available only on prescription, in accordance with the provisions of the relevant legislation. Section 33 RTSL and section 17A CyBCL contain some other prohibitions, which have been enacted in accordance with Articles 26 and 4, paragraph 1 of the AVMS Directive. More specifically, advertising of betting agencies is prohibited from 6:00 to 23:00.[456] The RTSL (section 33, paragraph 7) also provides that the transmission of TV advertising of teleservices with erotic content is permitted only between 00:00 and 5:00.

377. Last but not least, it is prohibited to transmit television advertising of children's toys from 6:00 to 22:00 on working days which are followed by a working day, and from 6:00 to 23:00 on days which are non-working, or are followed by Saturday and Sunday, or by a school holiday in accordance with the relevant Public School Regulations. Interestingly enough, in two cases in which the CRTA had imposed a fine for the violation of the (then applicable, but similar) prohibition on advertising of children's toys, the applicant stations did not question either the constitutionality of such prohibition or its compatibility with the (then applicable) provisions of the Directive 89/552/EEC.[457] In the first of these cases, the Supreme Court rejected the argument that the characterization of a product as a children's toy should be dependent upon its characterization for customs purposes, and accepted as relevant only the provisions of the (then applicable) Directive 88/378/EEC on toy safety.[458] In the second case, the Court held that the reference of the CRTA's decision to the definition of 'toys' under a well-known dictionary was adequate for the purposes of reasoning, and no further special evidence should have been brought.[459]

456. Section 85 of the Betting Law 106(I)/2012 prohibits and provides criminal sanctions for certain forms of advertising of betting in general (advertising of betting which implies that betting promotes or is relevant with social acceptance, personal or economic success, or solving of financial or personal problems; advertising of betting which includes the support of famous personalities, implying that their success is owed to betting; advertising of betting which may influence in any way minors so that they participate in betting activities; advertising of betting services which are provided by non-licensed agents; advertising of betting which transcends the limits of honesty and decency).

457. *See Politistiki kai Pliroforiaki Eteria 'O Logos' v. CRTA* [2005] 4 CLR 655; *Sigma Radio T.V. Ltd v. CRTA*, Judgment of 1 Mar. 2005, Case No. 1211/2003 (both in Greek).

458. *Politistiki kai Pliroforiaki Eteria 'O Logos' v. CRTA* [2005] 4 CLR 655, 663–664 (in Greek).

459. *Sigma Radio T.V. Ltd v. Cyprus Radiotelevision Authority*, Judgment of 1 Mar. 2005, Case No. 1211/2003 (in Greek).

III. Codes of Advertising

A. Introduction

378. All stations which have been licensed by the CRTA are required to observe the provisions of the CA. The CRTA, which has drafted the CA, interprets its provisions and reviews its implementation by private broadcasters. Thus, the CRTA may request the withdrawal or the modification of a particular advertising, if it sees that this advertising does not comply with the requirements of the CA, or of the RTSL. In case of non-compliance, the CRTA may impose the administrative sanctions which are provided by the RTSL (*see* below, Part V, Chapter 3). The CRTA is not required to provide advice on the appropriateness of any advertising before its transmission. Besides, the CRTA is neither responsible for nor bound by any opinion or advice that some of its members and its personnel may have given.

379. Part A of the CyBC-CA provides that the CyBC (and not the CRTA) shall ensure that all advertisements which are transmitted by its radio and TV channels are compatible with the CyBC-CA or with the relevant provisions of the CyBCL. Neither the latter (section 22B) nor the CyBC-CA authorizes the CRTA to impose administrative sanctions for violations of the CyBC-CA. It is the administrative bodies of the CyBC that may request the withdrawal or the modification of any advertising which is transmitted by the channels of the CyBC and which does not comply with the requirements of the CyBC-CA or of the CyBCL. The CYBC may provide advice on the appropriateness of any advertising before its production, without assuming any responsibility or commitment in this respect. In general, the CyBC is neither responsible for nor bound by any opinion or advice that some of its members and its personnel may have given.

B. General Rules and Principles

380. According to Article B.1 of both Codes, all advertisements shall be honest, truthful, and tasteful, and they shall not contain excessive or false claims. This provision should be read in conjunction with Article D.1 of both Codes, providing that advertisements examined, either as a whole, or in their parts, should not introduce the advertised goods or services in a way that may create false impressions, either directly or by way of the conclusions that one may draw from viewing/listening to them. Following its standard approach on the discretion of the CRTA with regards to the interpretive specification and application of abstract evaluative concepts (*see* under Chapter 3, §§8 and 10 in this Part above), the Supreme Court has rejected allegations about inadequate substantiation of the CRTA's finding that these provisions had been violated.[460] However, in another judgment, the Court did not hesitate to examine the facts of a case which concerned the advertising of the services

460. *See Antenna Limited v. CRTA*, Judgment of 30 Apr. 2010, Case No. 1648/2007 (in Greek).

of an 'intuitionist-psychologist', judging all the same that the decision of the CRTA in interpreting and applying the aforementioned provision was substantially correct.[461]

381. Part B of CA and of CyBC-CA continues by providing that no representation of, or reference to, the private life of particular individuals in advertising shall be permitted unless the involved persons have given their consent. Furthermore, advertisements shall not make unfair references to, or disparage, other products, or advertising, or those who are advertised in them. Exploitation of surreptitious beliefs or feelings of fear on the part of citizens is also prohibited.[462] Besides, advertisements should comply with the provisions of the Trade Descriptions Law. No advertising may contain a description, an allegation, or a representation which, either directly or by way of the conclusions that may be drawn, misleads the viewers/listeners about the good or the service which is advertised, or about the suitability of goods or services for their purposes as advertised. In any case, advertisers are required to present evidence in order to substantiate their descriptions, allegations or representations, if they are requested to do so by the competent public authorities, such as the CRTA or the Courts.

382. The term 'announcement' and its derivatives may be used only in exceptional cases, and only on condition that they follow the name of the advertised. Clearly, this provision aims to preclude the possibility of an advertising misleading the viewers/listeners by imitating the formal tone of an announcement of public authorities. Advertisements which create, or tend to create, friction shall not be accepted. Besides, advertising shall be prepared with a sense of responsibility towards society and shall pay special attention to the moral values which form the basis of every democratic society, and which are common to all Member States of the Council of Europe. Such values include individual freedom, tolerance and respect for the dignity and equality of all people. The use of foreign language words, or of Greek neologisms, which have been created for promotional purposes, shall be examined by the CRTA (CA) or by the CyBC (CyBC-CA) on a case-by-case basis.

C. General Requirements

383. According to Part C of the CA, each station may transmit advertisements only through the frequencies which have been allocated to it, and only during the broadcasting hours which are indicated for this purpose in its licensing documents. Advertising shall be readily recognizable and distinguishable from editorial content. Besides, private radio and TV stations are prohibited from any direct or indirect advertising of goods or services by their journalists during the transmission of

461. *Sigma Radio T.V. Public Ltd v. CRTA*, Judgment of 13 Feb. 2009, Case No. 1327/2007 (in Greek).

462. For an interesting case in this respect *see* CRTA, Decision of 16 May 2008, Case No. 133/2006(2), which concerned the advertising of a security system by appealing to the need for protection of citizens against 'Dracos', i.e., a wanted criminal who had been raping women.

their news bulletins and of other news and current affairs programmes. However, private stations are called to safe keep the copies of the advertisements that they transmitted for a period of six months. Such copies shall immediately be given to the CRTA if the latter requests so. Part C of the CyBC-CA provides that advertising shall be transmitted either in Greek or in any other European language. The CyBC is also expected to keep copies of the advertising material in good condition.

D. Special Categories of Advertising

384. According to Article D.1 of both Codes, advertising, examined either as a whole or in their parts, shall not introduce the advertised goods or services in a way that may create false impressions, either directly or by way of the conclusions that one may draw from viewing/listening to them. More specifically, it is prohibited to use references which may lead the consumers to the conclusion that the advertised item, or its ingredients, are of a special quality; or that it has some special nature which is actually unknown, unrecognized, or non-verifiable. Statistics, scientific terms, quotations from technical publications, and any similar technique shall be used with an absolute sense of responsibility towards the viewers or listeners. It is prohibited to use irrelevant evidence with the aim of showing that a claim is more scientific than it is in reality. Statistics of limited value shall not be presented in a way that renders them generally truthful. The advertisers are required to present evidence, in order to prove the accuracy of any characterization, claim or description if the CRTA requests so. Besides, no imitation shall be used which is likely to mislead the consumers, even if it is not such as to constitute the basis for litigation.

385. Article D.2 of both Codes prohibits the advertising of the following goods or services: tobacco products; medicines and medicinal products which are available only on prescription; firearms and sharpshooting organizations; pornography; provision of loans by banks and by other financial institutions; wedding agencies and correspondence clubs; prediction of fate and the similar;[463] enterprises which are related to death or burial; unlicensed private employment agencies; hypnotism, hypnotherapy, and spiritual services. The absolute prohibition on advertising of betting and of private betting agencies should be considered as non-applicable in view of the provisions of section 33, paragraph 6 RTSL and of section 17A, paragraph 7 CyBCL, which prohibit such advertising only between 6:00 and 23:00 (*see* under II above).

463. In *Sigma Radio T.V. Ltd v. CRTA*, Judgment of 23 Apr. 2007, Case No. 969/2006 (in Greek), the Supreme Court rejected the allegation of the applicant's representatives that this provision is *ultra vires* because Art. 33 RTSL (concerning TV advertising, *see* above under II) does not include such prohibition. According to the Court, the list of prohibited advertisements in §33 RTSL is not exhaustive. In any case, the RTSL prohibits advertisings which prejudice respect for human dignity, on which the prohibition on advertising of fate predictions is based. Furthermore, the wording of §51 RTSL, which authorizes CRTA to draft an Advertising Code, is such that it leaves enough space for prohibitions that are not expressly based on the provisions of the RTSL.

386. Article D.3 of both Codes permits competitive claims in advertising (i.e., claims that are directed against the products of a competitor), on condition that such claims are substantiated and provided that they do not misrepresent or give improper emphasis on certain features of the products of the competitor so that they could mislead the public. In any case, defamatory references are prohibited. Besides, testimonials, certifications, awards, etc. which might be used in advertising shall be genuine and shall not be used in a misleading way. Moreover, there should be evidence supporting the allegations which are contained in such advertising (Article D.4 of both Codes).

387. The use of the term 'guarantee', or of any other similar term, is permitted only on condition that the full terms of the guarantee are available for inspection and they are clearly referred to in the advertising (Article D.5 of both Codes). When permitted by the Cypriot legislation, advertising calling the public to participate in contests shall clearly indicate how one can have access to the printed terms of the contest, including the terms which are relevant to the results and the awards (Article D.6 of both Codes). Advertising concerning the sale of goods on credit or through leasing agreements shall observe the provisions of the relevant legislation (Article D.7 of both Codes).

388. As seen in Chapter 4, political advertising is permitted provided that certain conditions and requirements are met. Article D.8 of both Codes still prohibits advertisements which have to do with labour disputes or make reference to current public policies (in Greek: 'παρούσα δημόσια πολιτική'). It is also prohibited to transmit advertising of organizations whose aims are wholly or mainly of a religious nature. Furthermore, charitable organizations are prohibited from announcing publicly through advertising their needs. As regards charitable organizations, it is only permitted to advertise actions that take place in order to support charitable or artistic events. Although these provisions have not been contested before the Supreme Court, it is considered that they are hardly compatible with freedom of expression under Article 19 of the Constitution and under Article 10 of the ECHR.

389. Article D.9 of both Codes is dedicated to the advertising of services which are relevant to weight loss or control of silhouette. Such advertisements are permitted on condition that the advertised services are based on diet and/or on exercise; that, in the opinion of specialists, such services produce results and do not endanger health; that any claims related to such services are well substantiated; and that any interested may have access to a printed copy of the financial terms before he/she enters into any commitment. Referring to the advertising of educational institutions, Article D.11 of both Codes requires particular attention to be paid by advertisers. Besides, when the CRTA requests so, an opinion by the Ministry of Education, Sport and Youth should be sought.

390. Article D.12 of both Codes refers to the advertising of medicinal products or medical treatments when such advertising is generally permitted (i.e., when such product or treatment may be procured without a doctor's prescription; *see* above under subsection I). In view of the danger of provoking harm to the health of citizens through the use of excessive, misleading and/or irresponsible allegations in the advertising of such products or treatments, the Codes call the CRTA to be as strict as possible, taking into account the progress of medical science. The advertisers, however, are required to discuss such advertising with Medical Services before they transmit them. When the CRTA requests so, the contents of such advertisements shall be approved by the Ministry of Health.

391. In particular, advertising of medicinal products should comply with the requirements of the Law as well as with the terms that are contained in the relevant trade licences or approvals. Most importantly, it is prohibited to have doctors, dentists, pharmacists, or nurses presenting such products, at least when the presentation may give the impression of a professional advice or recommendation. It is also prohibited to appeal to reports which might give the impression of such advice or recommendation. Furthermore, advertising of medicines and medical treatments shall not contain any allegation to the effect that the advertised product may cure an ailment or certain symptoms, or that the use of such product may substitute the appropriate medical treatment. Offers for diagnosis or treatment by correspondence are prohibited. The use of the word 'invigorative', or of other similar assertions, as well as the insinuation that our health may be exposed to risk in case that we do not use diet or vitamin supplements, are also prohibited.

392. Article D.13 of both Codes refers to the advertising of personal hygiene products. The scope here is rather different insofar as the aim of the relevant provisions, as stated in Article D.13, is to display discreetness and to avoid embarrassing the viewers or listeners. In particular, no such advertising may include anything that might provoke embarrassment to somebody or might undermine his/her confidence in his/her personal hygiene attitude. As a rule, detailed descriptions shall be avoided. Visual representations in such advertising shall be tasteful and restrained. It is expressly prohibited to represent unpacked hygiene towels or tampons. However, personal recommendation and praise are acceptable insofar as it does not indicate sexual or social insecurity of those who do not use the advertised product. The use of words such as 'smell', which might insult the viewers, is not permitted. Special attention must be paid in the case of products which are addressed to young women. Such advertising shall not be presented by women who are younger than 16 years old.

E. Protection of Minors

393. The lengthy and detailed provisions of Article D.10 of both Codes aim to protect minors, and they should be read in conjunction with the general programme standards on the same issue (*see* under Chapter 3, §6 in this Part above). In particular, it is prohibited to transmit advertisements which:

- encourage children to enter into unknown places, or to talk to strangers in their effort to collect bulletins, wrappings, etc.;

- imply that, if children do not buy a certain good or service, or if they do not encourage other persons (i.e., their parents) to buy it for them, they will have omitted to execute their duty, or they will be lacking in loyalty towards a certain person (including sacred persons) or a certain Organization;
- undermine the authority of adults or the authority of law and order;
- encourage children to ask their parents or other persons to buy for them the advertised product;
- lead the children to believe that, if they do not possess the product which is advertised, they will be in some way inferior to other children, or they will be subjected to disregard or sarcasm for the reason that they have not acquired such product;
- affect the safety of children;
- give disproportionate emphasis on gifts that might be offered with the advertised product (in any case, it is prohibited to promote products for children using methods such as filling in an album, distributing gifts, or any other method which is based on luck;[464] furthermore, the terms of a children's competition that might be included in advertising shall have the approval of the Director General of the station before their production; in any case, it is prohibited to expand upon the value of the gifts or the chances of success);
- present children using arguments in favour of products or services which they are not generally expected to buy for themselves, or making comments for goods or services for which it is not expected to have the required knowledge (children in advertisements may make comments only for issues which may be of interest for them, but they shall not provide formal testimonials);
- create excessive expectations for toys which are advertised through the use of imaginary scenes and special effects, given that the ability of children to distinguish reality from imagination varies according to their age (in any case, the representation of action games as the child might see them in his/her imagination shall be sparingly used, while it is prohibited to provoke auditory confusion as regards the real noise that is produced by the toy);
- leave margin for misrepresentation, considering the immaturity of children in their judgment and experience;
- undermine the cost of toys with the use of words such as 'only for … ', or other similar words (in any case, advertising of children's toys must provide a general indication of the price).

---

464. In *Politistiki kai Pliroforiaki Eteria 'O Logos' v. CRTA*, Judgment of 18 Jan. 2008, Case No. 1336/2006 (in Greek), the Supreme Court rejected the allegation that these provisions are contradictory between themselves. In the same judgment the Supreme Court found that these provisions are *intra vires*, and also that they are compatible with freedom of expression under Art. 19 of the Constitution (appealing to its case-law on advertising; *see* §1 IV above in this chapter) and with freedom of entering into contracts under Art. 26 of the Constitution (on the grounds that the provisions refer only to advertising, not affecting the right to enter into contracts itself). This judgment has been affirmed and applied in *Antenna Limited v. CRTA*, Judgment of 14 Apr. 2010, Case No. 636/2008 (in Greek). *See also Antenna Limited v. CRTA*, Judgment of 6 Oct. 2010, Case No. 837/2008 (in Greek), applying the standard approach of the Court as regards the CRTA's discretion in specifying abstract evaluative concepts.

394. A more general provision is that of paragraph (1) of Article D.10 of both Codes, prohibiting the transmission of advertisements of any kind (i.e., not only of products that are destined for children) which might harm, upset or scare minors, unless such advertisements are transmitted by the CyBC after 21:00, and by the private stations after 22:00 on working days and after 23:00 on Saturdays and Sundays, on non-working days and on days which are followed by non-working days.[465] The Supreme Court has dealt with this provision in a case which concerned the advertising of a car.[466] The scenario of the advertising was based on 'monsters' which were terrifying two young people in the car that was advertised. In the context of the proceedings before the CRTA, the representatives of the station claimed that the same advertising had been transmitted in many other countries without provoking the reaction of public authorities. Another argument of the station was that the 'monsters' in the advertising were totally fictitious, of a kind which is common in cartoons and in the market of children's toys, so that even kids could not really be scared.

395. The majority of the CRTA's members rejected these arguments, taking nonetheless into account the fact that the station had already stopped transmitting the advertising. In the judicial review proceedings, the representatives of the station argued, first, that the provision of paragraph (1) was *ultra vires* insofar as it violated the general principle that restrictions on constitutional rights (in this case, restriction on freedom of speech) shall not be enacted by secondary legislation, as the CA certainly was, at least not when the primary legislation does not contain a specific provision to this effect. The Court rejected this argument appealing to the authorizing provision of section 51, paragraph 2(g) RTSL in combination with the provisions of RTSL for the protection of minors. Then, the representatives of the station argued that the CRTA had incorrectly interpreted and implemented the relevant provision insofar as, in their opinion, the latter prohibited the advertising of *products* that might scare minors and not scary *advertisements* as such. The Court disagreed, clarifying that the prohibition refers to the advertising and not to the products.

396. In another interesting case, the Supreme Court had to deal with the advertisements of two banks which promoted credit cards that were especially addressed to children.[467] In the first advertisement, a well-dressed child looked at other children adopting the attitude of a businessman. In the second advertisement, two children, after having played tennis, were discussing the privileges that one might get by opening an account in the advertised bank. The Court affirmed the imposition of a fine by the CRTA for violation of the relevant Articles of the RTSL and of the CA. In particular, the Court rejected the allegation of the station's representatives that the CRTA should have provided a detailed definition of the crucial concepts in the provisions that had been violated ('moral or physical detriment to minors', 'exhort

465. The provision of the CA refers to the time limits of §34, para. 3 RTSL, as it had at the time of the enactment of the CA.

466. *See Politistiki kai Pliroforiaki Eteria 'O Logos' O.E. v. CRTA*, Judgment of 16 Feb. 2007, Case No. 1629/2005 (in Greek).

467. *See Antenna Ltd v. CRTA*, Judgment of 23 Jul. 2010, Case No. 1600/2008 (in Greek).

minors to buy a product exploiting their inexperience or credulity'). In the opinion of the Court, such concepts should not be considered abstract or evaluative, needing further specification; such concepts simply reflect the perception of the average prudent citizen. In any case, the Court noted that it cannot substitute the CRTA in analysing concepts which are not susceptible to legal interpretation as the aforementioned ones.

F. Separation of Certain Advertisements from Programmes for Minors

397. Article F.2 of CA contains some additional restrictions, which prohibit the advertising of certain goods or services by way of interruption of programmes which are destined for minors. More specifically, alcoholic beverages containing more than 1.2% alcohol shall not be advertised before, after or in the midst of the transmission of children programmes; before, after or in the midst of programmes which are addressed to persons under 18; and before, after or in the midst of programmes with religious content. Alcoholic beverages containing less than 1.2% alcohol shall not be advertised before, after or in the midst of children's programmes. Gambling games and services shall not be advertised before, after or in the midst of children's programmes and of programmes which are addressed to persons under 18. Trailers for cinematographic works or for videos which have been ranked as inappropriate for persons under 18 or 15 shall not be transmitted before, after, or in the midst of children's programmes.

§3. TIME AND FREQUENCY RESTRICTIONS

I. General Time and Frequency Restrictions (Directive)

398. Both the RTSL and the CyBCL have transposed the provisions of Articles 20 and 23 of the AVMS Directive providing for time and frequency restrictions on TV advertising. Therefore, section 33, paragraph 1(b) RTSL and section 17A, paragraph 2(b) CyBCL provide that, where television advertising is inserted during programmes, all TV stations shall ensure that the integrity of the programmes is not prejudiced, taking into account not only natural break-ins and the duration and the nature of the programme concerned but also taking into account the rights of the right holders. Furthermore, section 33, paragraph 2(a) RTSL and section 17A, paragraph 2(c) CyBCL provide that the transmission of films made for television[468] (excluding series of independent programmes, serials and documentaries), cinematographic works and news programmes may be interrupted by television advertising once for each scheduled period of at least thirty minutes. The transmission of children's programmes may be interrupted by television advertising once for each scheduled period of at least thirty minutes, provided that the scheduled duration of

468. For the meaning of this term *see* CJEU, Case C-245/01, *RTL Television* [2003] ECR I-12505.

the programme is greater than thirty minutes (section 33, paragraph 2(b) RTSL; section 17A, paragraph 2(d) CyBCL). No television advertising shall be inserted during the transmission of religious services (section 33, paragraph 3(a) RTSL; section 17A, paragraph 3(a) CyBCL).

399. Furthermore, according to section 34, paragraph 1 RTSL and section 17A, paragraph 5 CyBCL, the proportion of television advertising spots within the time zones of 06.00–18.00 and 18.00–24.00 shall not exceed 20% for each respective time zone. It was originally provided that the 20% would apply to each given clock time, but this was amended with Law 197(I)/21; the new rule allows the TV stations to have a great number of advertising spots in prime times and a proportionally lesser number of spots in other slots within the respective time zone, so as to not exceed the 20% for the time zone. For the purposes of this last provision, TV advertising does not include announcements made by the broadcaster in connection with its own programmes (i.e., trailers) and ancillary products directly derived from those programmes or to programmes and AVMS of other entities belonging to the same media group; sponsorship announcements; product placements; or neutral framework between programme content and advertising spots (section 34, paragraph 2 RTSL; section 17A, paragraph 1 CyBCL).

400. In a series of judgments which were issued concerning the (similar in this respect) provisions of Directive 89/552/EEC,[469] the Supreme Court initially refused to accept that trailers should be considered as advertising for the purposes of provisions other than the one which contained the 20% per clock hour restriction (as it then was).[470] That is, the inclusion of trailers in the concept of advertising was taken as not applicable to the restrictions which are now contained in Article 20 of the AVMS Directive (then in Article 11 of Directive 89/552/EEC), nor to other national law provisions, as the ones of Article F.3 of the CA, to which we shall refer below. However, at a later stage, the Supreme Court distinguished its earlier findings upon

469. Council Directive 89/552/EEC of 3 Oct. 1989 on the coordination of certain provisions laid down by Law, Regulation or Administrative Action in Member States concerning the pursuit of television broadcasting activities ('Television Without Frontiers Directive'), Official Journal L 298, 17 Oct. 1989, p. 23. Our reference is to the provisions of Directive 89/552/EEC as they stood after their amendment by Directive 97/36/EC of the European Parliament and of the Council of 30 Jun. 1997 amending Council Directive 89/552/EEC on the coordination of certain provisions laid down by law, regulation or administrative action in Member States concerning the pursuit of television broadcasting activities, Official Journal L 202, 30 Jul. 1997, p. 60.

470. *See Sigma Radio T.V. Ltd v. CRTA (No. 2)* [2010] 3 CLR 579, 587–588 (in Greek), with the Court noting that in any case Member States may adopt stricter rules as regards advertising; *Antenna Limited v. CRTA*, Judgment of 16 May 2005, Case No. 555/2004; *Sigma Radio T.V. Ltd v. CRTA*, Judgment of 16 Jan. 2008, Case No. 1996/2006; *Sigma Radio T.V. Public Ltd v. CRTA*, Judgment of 19 Mar. 2010, Case No. 1096/2008; *Sigma Radio T.V. Public Ltd v. CRTA*, Judgment of 10 Jun. 2010, Case No. 1686/2008; *Antenna Limited v. CRTA*, Judgment of 31 Jan. 2011, Case No. 1915/2008 (all in Greek). In the latter case, the Supreme Court also rejected the reference of the applicants to the 'gross principle' of the Judgment of the CJEU in Case C-6/98, *ARD* [1999] ECRI-07599. According to the opinion of the Court, this principle was applicable only for the purposes of Art. 11 para. 3 of the Directive 89/552/EEC, as it had at the material time (non-interruption of certain programmes for forty-five minutes), and not for the purposes of the provision on which the decision of the CRTA was based.

a new reading of the term 'advertising' in the light of the provisions and of the Preamble of the Directive, and it held that trailers should be considered as programmes and not as advertising.[471] In particular, the Court carefully distinguished this ruling from its earlier case-law, noting that the previous cases considered the same issue from another angle. It is to be also noted that the judgment was not unanimous. According to the minority opinion of Judge Christodoulou, there was no sufficient ground to depart from the Court's earlier case-law.[472] This judgment determined the fate of Article F.3 CA, to which we shall immediately refer.

II. The '3.5 Minutes Requirement' of Article F.3 CA

401. According to Article F.3 of the CA, any interruption of programmes for advertising, teleshopping and trailers shall not exceed 3.5 minutes. This means that, apart from the 20% hour restriction of Article 20 of the AVMS Directive, private stations have to also safeguard that any advertising and/or trailer session will be no longer than 3.5 minutes. Naturally, this additional restriction was perceived by stations as being detrimental to their income from advertising. Therefore, they reacted by lodging applications for the annulment of CRTA's decisions which imposed administrative sanctions for violation of this restriction.[473]

402. According to the stations, the provision of Article F.3 of CA was *ultra vires* insofar as compliance with it would leave an amount of time for advertising less than the one that was permitted by the then applicable provisions of section 34 RTSL (20% per clock hour as it then was, and 15% or 20% per daily broadcasting hours restrictions) and of section 33 RTSL (no interruption of certain programmes for forty-five minutes, no interruption of all other programmes for twenty minutes).[474] More specifically, the stations argued that, while the then-applicable provisions of Directive 89/552/EEC, as they were transposed by the RTSL, leaved room for twelve minutes of advertising per hour of broadcasting, the application of the 3.5 minutes requirement of Article F.3, in combination with the application of the other restrictions, left room only for 10.5 minutes of advertising per hour.

471. *See Sigma Radio T.V. Public Ltd v. CRTA*, Judgment of 3 Apr. 2015, Appeal No. 56/2010.

472. The majority ruling on Article F.3 of CA was unanimously followed by *Antenna Ltd. v. CRTA*, Judgment of 15 Feb. 2017, Appeal No. 14/2011.

473. *See Antenna Ltd v. CRTA (No. 2)* [2002] 4 CLR 1077, 1079–1081; *Sigma Radio T. V. Ltd v. CRTA* [2003] 4 CLR 1, 37–38; *Antenna Ltd v. CRTA* [2005] 3 CLR 558, 563–568; *CRTA v. Antenna Limited* [2006] 3 CLR 151, 157–160; *Sigma Radio T.V. Ltd v. CRTA (No. 2)* [2010] 3 CLR 579, 586–591; *Sigma Radio T.V. Ltd v. CRTA*, Judgment of 27 Nov. 2001, Case No. 810/2000; *Antenna Limited v. CRTA*, Judgment of 29 Nov. 2002, Case No. 232/2002; *Antenna Limited v. CRTA*, Judgment of 21 May 2003, Case No. 472/2002; *Antenna Limited v. CRTA*, Judgment of 16 May 2005, Case No. 555/2004; *Antenna Limited v. CRTA*, Judgment of 31 May 2005, Case No. 1261/2003; *Sigma Radio T.V. Public Ltd v. CRTA*, Judgment of 19 Mar. 2010, Case No. 1096/2008 (all in Greek).

474. These provisions corresponded to Arts 11 and 18 of the Directive 89/552/EEC, before the replacement of the latter by the AVMS Directive.

403. In two first instance judgments of the Supreme Court, Judge Gavrielides accepted this argument, annulling the relevant decisions of the CRTA.[475] However, these judgments were reversed by the Plenary of the Supreme Court, exercising its second instance jurisdiction.[476] According to the Plenary, the calculation of the representatives of the stations was mistaken insofar as advertising could be transmitted not only by interrupting programmes but also before and after programmes; therefore, there was enough space for transmitting as much advertising as the provisions of the RTSL, and the corresponding provisions of the Directive 89/552/EEC, permitted.

404. At a later stage, the Supreme Court re-examined its case-law on this issue, and it confirmed that trailers did not fall within the scope of the term 'advertising', as the latter should be read in the light of the provisions and of the Preamble of the Directive.[477] As already noted, the majority of the Court carefully distinguished this ruling from its earlier case-law, holding that the previous cases considered the same issue from another angle. Besides, the relevant legislative authorization to issue Regulations (the CA in this regard) concerned only advertising. Therefore, since the 3.5 minutes requirement of Article F.3 of CA referred not only to advertising but also to trailers, it should be considered *ultra vires*.[478]

III. Other Provisions on Advertising

405. Part F of CA contains some other provisions applying to special categories of advertising. In particular, Article F.4 of CA provides that advertising breaks during the transmission of athletic events should be consistent with the natural breaks of such events (e.g., half-time, time-outs, etc.) The live broadcasting of long-term athletic meetings may be interrupted only when the focus of interest is transferred from one point to another (e.g., from a speed race to pole vault). When foreign athletic programmes are transmitted (e.g., the NBA), the station shall follow the advertising order and timing of the original broadcaster.

406. Article F.5 of CA provides that in the case of advertising spots with duration of more than one minute, it shall be ensured that no risk of confusion with the contents of the programme that is interrupted exists. In any case, the maximum duration of an advertising spot is seven minutes. Advertising spots with duration of more than 3.5 minutes shall not be transmitted during the period from 18:00 to 23:00. If a live programme is interrupted, then the advertising spots shall not use the voice of the broadcaster of this programme.

---

475. *Antenna Limited v. CRTA*, Judgment of 21 May 2003, Case No. 472/2002; *Antenna Limited v. CRTA*, Judgment of 29 Nov. 2002, Case No. 232/2002 (both in Greek).

476. *See CRTA v. Antenna Limited* [2006] 3 CLR 151, 157–160, applying *Antenna Ltd v. CRTA* [2005] 3 CLR 558, 563–568 (both in Greek).

477. *See Sigma Radio T.V. Public Ltd v. CRTA*, Judgment of 3 Apr. 2015, Appeal No. 56/2010.

478. *See ibid*, adopted in *Antenna Ltd. v. CRTA*, Judgment of 15 Feb. 2017, Appeal No. 14/2011.

§4. Sponsorship

I. Basic Requirements (Directive)

407. Both the RTSL (sections 30H–30K) and the CyBCL (section 17C) have transposed the provisions of Article 10 of the AVMS Directive on sponsorship of AVMS or programmes. To be reminded that, on account of the fact that the definition of AVMS by both legislative instruments includes radio programmes, the following provisions are applicable not only to TV but also to radio broadcasting. In particular, sponsored services and programmes shall meet the following requirements (section 30H RTSL; section 17C, paragraph 1 CyBCL):

- their content and, in the case of television broadcasting, their scheduling shall in no circumstances be influenced in such a way as to affect the responsibility and editorial independence of the media service provider;
- they shall not directly encourage the purchase or rental of goods or services, in particular by making special promotional references to those goods or services;
- viewers shall be clearly informed of the existence of a sponsorship agreement. Sponsored programmes shall be clearly identified as such by the name, logo and/or any other symbol of the sponsor such as a reference to its product(s) or service(s) or a distinctive sign thereof in an appropriate way for programmes at the beginning, during and/or at the end of the programmes.

408. Furthermore, it is provided that AVMS or programmes shall not be sponsored by undertakings whose principal activity is the manufacture or sale of cigarettes and other tobacco products, or electronic cigarettes and refill containers (section 30I RTSL; section 17C, paragraph 2 CyBCL). Besides, the sponsorship of AVMS or programmes by undertakings whose activities include the manufacture or sale of medicinal products and medical treatment may promote the name or the image of the undertaking, but shall not promote specific medicinal products or medical treatments available only on prescription in the Member State within whose jurisdiction the media service provider falls (section 30J RTSL; section 17C, paragraph 3 CyBCL).

409. Section 30K, paragraph 1 RTSL and section 17C, paragraph 4 CYBCL prohibit the sponsorship of news and current affairs programmes, exempting from such prohibition weather forecasts, trade bulletins, and sports news, which should, however, be clearly distinct from the general news programmes. Making use of the option which is provided for Member States by Article 10, paragraph 4 of the AVMS Directive, section 30K, paragraph 2 RTSL and section 17C, paragraph 5 CyBCL provide that the showing of a sponsorship logo during children's programmes, documentaries and religious programmes is permitted only for three minutes at the beginning and/or at the end of such programmes.

II. Part E, CA

410. Apart from the aforementioned provisions, private TV and radio stations shall comply with some additional requirements which are provided by Part E of the CA. Article E.1 prohibits sponsorship of news and current affairs programmes as well as of programmes which transmit ecclesiastical ceremonies. Article E.2 aims to prevent circumvention of the aforementioned prohibition. Thus, it prohibits the promotion of logos, emblems or other signs which might be connected with certain organizations, goods or services, before, during and after the programmes which shall not be sponsored.

411. Article E.3 of CA provides that the sponsor's name or logo shall be present only at the beginning and/or at the end of the sponsored programme. The same article prohibits the continuous or at intervals reference to the name, the distinctive sign and the logo of the goods or services of the sponsor during the sponsored programme. Insofar as the new provisions of the basic legislative instruments (section 30H, paragraph (c) RTSL; section 17, paragraph 1(c) of CyBCL), in accordance with Article 10, paragraph 1(c) of the AVMS Directive, permit reference to the sponsorship during the sponsored programme,[479] this provision of Article E.3 should be considered as *ultra vires*.

412. Article E.4 repeats the provision of Article 10, paragraph 1(b) of the AVMS Directive, to the effect that it prohibits any incitement for the purchase or rental of goods or services of the sponsor or of third parties, with reference to the features or to the prices of such products, or to any other information which is related with them. Article E.5 permits reference to the sponsorship in the trailers and in any announcement which is related to the sponsored programme.

413. The very important provision of Article E.6 prohibits sponsorship by sponsors who produce or promote the products which shall not be advertised under Article D.2 of the same Code (*see* under §2 III D in this Chapter above). Insofar as the list of such products is not restricted to tobacco products, to which the provisions of the basic legislative instruments refer (section 30I RTSL, section 17C, paragraph 2 CYBCL), in accordance with Article 10, paragraph 2 of the AVMS Directive, such prohibition should be considered as *ultra vires*. This conclusion is compatible with an older judgment of the Supreme Court holding that Article E.12 (*see* below) is *ultra vires* insofar as it restricts sponsorship beyond the limits which are contained in the provision of the basic legislative instrument.[480] On the contrary, Article E.7 prohibiting sponsorship by political parties should be considered as *intra vires* insofar as it serves the public interest (improper exercise of political influence upon voters) and, at the same time, does not deprive political parties of other means for their advertising (for the advertising of political parties *see* under Chapter 4, §2 above).

---

479. *See* on this also CJEU, Joined Cases C-320/94 et al., *Reti Televisive Italiane SpA* [1996] ECR I-6490.

480. *See Antenna Limited v. CRTA (No. 3)* [2004] 4 CLR 606 (in Greek).

414. Article E.8 prohibits secret sponsorship, in the sense that any sponsorship shall be announced through reference to the sponsor, and shall not remain hidden. Article E.9 prohibits the reference to the sponsor by the presenters or the actors who participate in the sponsored programme. Besides, Article E.10 provides that sponsorship announcements shall not be confused with the contents of the programme. Furthermore, Article E.11 provides that any announcement of sponsorship shall give information only about the relationship of the sponsor with the programme and that any slogans that might be used in the advertising of the sponsor shall be transmitted only by way of a written reference. Besides, Article E.13 provides that any reference to the sponsorship of the transmission of events shall take place in a way that may not give the impression that what is sponsored is the event and not only its transmission. Such provisions remain within the letter and the spirit of the provisions of the basic legislative instruments on sponsorship, and should, therefore, be considered as *intra vires.* As noted above, the Supreme Court found that the provision of Article E.12, prohibiting sponsorship of programmes which contain advice on the use of goods or services by the same persons who produce or sell them, is *ultra vires.*[481]

§5. Product Placement

415. Both the RSTL (section 30G) and the CyBCL (section 18H) had initially transposed the provisions of Article 11 of the AVMS Directive on product placement, making only restricted use of the opt-out clause of paragraph 3 of the said article. In particular, product placement was generally prohibited, and it is admissible by way of derogation only in specific cases. However, section 30G, paragraph 2 RTSL and section 18H, paragraph 2 CyBCL have been amended with Laws 197(I)/2021 and 196(I)/2021 respectively, so as to provide that product placement in AVMS is generally allowed, with the exception of news and current affairs programmes, programmes focusing on consumer issues, religious programmes and children programmes. The amendment applies with regard to programmes created after 19 December 2009.

416. According to section 30G, paragraph 3 RTSL and section 18H, paragraph 3 CyBCL, the programmes that contain product placement shall meet all of the following requirements:

(a) their content and, in the case of television broadcasting their scheduling, or in case of on-demand AVMS their list, shall in no circumstances be influenced in such a way as to affect the responsibility and editorial independence of the AVMS provider;

481. *See ibid.*

(b) they shall not directly encourage the purchase or rental of goods or services, in particular by making special promotional references to those goods or services;[482]
(c) they shall not give undue prominence to the product in question, with the term 'undue prominence' including zooms and/or continuous showing;
(d) viewers shall be clearly informed of the existence of product placement as follows:
  – programmes containing product placement shall be clearly identified, by optical and acoustic means, at the start and the end of the programme, and when a programme resumes after an advertising break or after any other break, in order to avoid any confusion on the part of the viewer;[483]
  – the overall amount of time for the showing and/or reference to goods and services in product placement messages shall be restricted to the less possible duration of the programme that is transmitted; in no case such showing or reference may exceed a period of three minutes for cinematographic works and TV films, and a period of one minute for series, sports programmes and light entertainment programmes.[484]

417. The requirements set out in point (d) (i.e., the requirements under (i) and (ii) above) do not apply when the programme in question has neither been produced nor commissioned by the media service provider itself, or by a company affiliated to the media service provider, on condition that the media service provider does not benefit, financially or in any other way, from the product placement.

418. In any event, product placement of the following products is prohibited:

- tobacco products or cigarettes, as well as electronic cigarettes or refill containers, or products from undertakings whose principal activity is the manufacture or sale of cigarettes and other tobacco products;
- specific medicinal products or medical treatments available only on prescription;
- children's toys, during the time zone in which their advertising is prohibited (*see* under §2 II in this chapter above);
- any other product, good or service whose advertising is prohibited by the RTSL or by the Regulations that are issued by its authorization (including the products which shall not be advertised in accordance with Article D.2 of CA; *see* under §2 III D in this chapter above).

419. Furthermore, it is prohibited to incorporate a product placement message into a programme after its production has been finished (section 30G, paragraph 5 RTSL; section 18H, paragraph 5 CyBCL). Clearly, the aim of this provision is to preclude improper influence upon the contents of a programme by the persons who

482. For cases in which this provision has been violated, *see* CRTA, 'Study on the Issues of A) Product Placement, B) Programmes Sponsorship, C) Surreptitious Audiovisual Commercial Communication', October 2014, part A.2.III (in Greek).
483. For violations of this provision *see ibid.*, part A.2.I.
484. For violations of this provision *see ibid.*, part A.2.IV.

have the editorial responsibility to the detriment of the rights of the persons who have been involved in the creation of the programme.[485] Section 30G, paragraph 6 RTSL and section 18H, paragraph 6 CyBCL further prohibit the free-of-charge provision of goods or services in the cases in which sponsorship is not permitted.

485. For violations of this provision *see ibid.*, part A.2.II.

Chapter 6. Right to Information

§1. Access to Events of Major Importance

I. General Provisions (Article 14 of the Directive)

420. Section 28A of the RTSL transposed the provisions of Article 14 of the AVMS Directive. It provides that TV organizations which fall under the jurisdiction of the Republic of Cyprus shall not broadcast on an exclusive basis the events which are regarded as being of major importance for society, in such a way as to deprive a substantial proportion of the public in the Republic of the possibility of following such events by live coverage or deferred coverage on free television programmes. The list of the events which are considered to be of major importance as well as the measures that will safeguard the availability of programmes covering such events on a free-of-charge basis are specified by the CRTA. The latter notifies the list and the measures to the Commission and then publishes them in the Official Government Gazette.

421. Besides, according to paragraph 3 of section 28A RTSL, TV organizations which fall under the jurisdiction of the Republic shall not exercise exclusive rights in such a way that a substantial proportion of the public in any other EU Member State is deprived of the possibility of following events which are designated by that other Member State, for objective reasons in the public interest and in accordance with its legislation, and have been notified to the Commission, as events of major importance for society, by whole or partial live coverage or, where necessary or appropriate, by whole or partial deferred coverage, on free television. Paragraph 6 of section 28A RTSL (*see also* section 51, paragraph 2 RTSL) authorizes the CRTA to issue, after the approval of the Council of Ministers, Regulations which shall specify the criteria and the procedures for the compilation of the list of events of major importance as well as the restrictions on exclusive rights and the required ways of transmission of such events.

II. Specification of Criteria and Procedures

422. After the approval of the Council of Ministers, the CRTA has issued the EMIR. According to Rule 2 EMIR, 'events of major importance' are defined events of an athletic or non-athletic nature which fulfil at least two of the following criteria:

(a) the event itself, as well as its progress, has special and the broadest (in Greek: 'ευρύτατο') interest for the Republic, and it is of interest for individuals other than the ones who often follow events of this type in television;
(b) the event has the broadest recognition by the general public (in Greek: 'γενικό κοινό'), it has particular cultural significance, and it stresses the cultural identity of the Republic;

(c) the national team participates in the event and more specifically in a particular athletic event of an important international championship;
(d) the event is traditionally transmitted by non-subscription TV channels, and it acquires high rates of viewership in the Republic.

423. 'Free television station' means a TV station under the provisions of RTSL (*see* under Chapter 2, §1 in this Part above), which includes a channel or a group of channels providing free of charge services at least to a 75% of the population, without additional costs on part of the public for technical equipment and facilities. An encoded programmes station may also be considered as a free television station, but only as regards those of its programmes which are transmitted in non-encoded form.

424. According to Rule 3 EMIR, the list of events of major importance (henceforth: 'the list') is drafted, amended or abolished by the CRTA. It consists of Part I, which includes the most important international and national events, and Part II, which includes important national events. Before the drafting or the amendment or the annulment of the list, the CRTA is required to proceed into consultations with all free television stations as well as with other stations. The list is published in the Official Government Gazette through a Notification by the CRTA.

425. Rule 4 EMIR provides that, by way of a rule, the events included in Part I of the list shall be transmitted by live coverage, and only exceptionally by deferred coverage, on condition that such deferral is owed to one of the following objective reasons:

(a) the event takes place at a time between 24:00 and 6:00; or
(b) the event coincides with other most important events which are in progress during the same time; or
(c) the live coverage presupposes rescheduling of the transmission of another event of major importance for society.

The events which are included in Part II may be transmitted by deferred coverage, which shall take place on the same day in which the event takes place.

426. Rule 5 EMIR provides that any exclusive rights on the transmission of events that are included in the list shall not be exercised in such a way as to deprive a substantial proportion of the public of the possibility of following such events on free television stations, by live or by deferred coverage, in the case of the events of Part I of the list, and by at least partial live or deferred coverage for the events of Part II. The transmission of such events by an encoded programmes station shall be considered as deprivation in this sense unless the event is, at the same time, transmitted by a free television station whose programmes may be received by at least 75% of the population without any additional cost for technical equipment and facilities.

427. Encoded programmes stations which have obtained exclusive rights on the transmission of the events that are included in the list, and which cannot transmit by themselves the programmes in a non-encoded form, may exercise their exclusive rights only on condition that they are in a position to ensure, through an agreement with other station(s) or through any other appropriate means, that there will be no deprivation in the aforementioned sense. There can be a derogation of this latter obligation in case the encoded programmes station proves to the CRTA that no free television station was disposed to proceed into an agreement for the concession of the exclusive rights on terms, including prices, which are common in the relevant market under conditions of free competition. In this case, the CRTA has the responsibility to determine the terms and conditions on which such derogation shall be dependent.

428. In particular, free television stations to which an agreement for the concession of exclusive rights has been offered by the encoded programmes station that has obtained such rights, are required to express in writing their interest within fifteen days of receiving the written offer. Such expression of interest should include any specific information on the event and on the required price for the concession agreement. In case of a dispute between the interested stations on the price, the interested parties or the CRTA may request an opinion from the CPC. Such an opinion is issued after hearing the interested parties and shall be based on the conditions of the relevant market. Besides, such opinion shall be binding for the interested parties, in case they decide to proceed to the conclusion of the agreement.

429. Rule 7 EMIR provides for procedures that may be followed in case the aforementioned Regulations are violated. In particular, any television station which alleges that an infringement upon these Regulations by the acts of another station has already taken place, or is about to take place, may submit a complaint to the CRTA. The latter shall initiate an investigation and, if it ascertains that the complaint is substantiated, has all the powers under the relevant provisions of the RTSL (*see* Part V, Chapter 3 below).

III. The List of Events of Major Importance

430. The first list of events of major importance was drafted by the CRTA and was published in the Official Government Gazette on 7 September 2001, through Normative Administrative Act 362/2001, under the then applicable provisions of the Directive 89/552/EEC, as they had been transposed into the RTSL. This list included, among else, international cultural events, such as the Oscar awards and the Eurovision song contest; cultural events of importance for the Cypriot society, such as wine and flower fests; international scientific conferences; international athletic events such as the Olympic Games, the Mediterranean Games, the final phases of the Football World Cup and of the Football European Championship, as well as the games of the national football team in any phase, the European Champions League and the games of the UEFA Cup, the finals of national football, basketball and volleyball Organizations, the final phase of the European Basketball Championship, Formula 1, the Wimbledon final in tennis, etc.

431. The 2001 list has now been abolished by virtue of section 57 paragraph (b) of Law 118(I)/2010. Besides, the compilation of a new list was postponed while the important Judgments of the CJEU on UEFA and FIFA cases were pending. After such Judgments were issued,[486] the CRTA proceeded into consultations with the interested parties, most importantly with Cytavision, which had obtained exclusive rights on the transmission of significant games of the national football championship. The consultations resulted in an agreement on 6 June 2014 between the CRTA and Cytavision, and the CRTA finalized the list, which is now pending before the Commission.

IV. The Special Right of the Cyprus Broadcasting Corporation (Section 17e CyBCL)

432. A further guarantee of the right to information is provided by Article 17E of the CyBCL, which grants to the CyBC, being the national public service broadcaster, the right to cover on a free-of-charge basis 'events of general interest' for which exclusive rights have been obtained. Such right may be exercised without prejudice of the Intellectual Property Rights or of any other rights deriving from the event (section 17E, paragraph 2 CyBCL). Besides, the coverage to which the right refers shall take place only for the purposes of news bulletins and only for a duration which shall not exceed three minutes (paragraph 3).[487] Especially as regards sports events, the three minutes limit shall apply to all the matches or events of each day.

433. Furthermore, it is provided that the right of the CyBC shall be exercised in a way that does not affect the event (paragraph 4). The right shall not be exercised in case that the public interest might be affected, or in case that the safety of the public or of the State might be endangered, or if the transmission or the recording might affect the event. Besides, the organizers of the event may claim compensation for any damages that may be provoked by the exercise of CyBC's right. The CyBC is required to notify the organizers in advance of its intention to cover the event, and the organizers are required to inform the CyBC whether any special technical arrangements for the coverage have taken place. An important provision is that of paragraph 7, providing that, when technical arrangements cannot be satisfactory for all the licensed stations and for the CyBC, preference shall be given to those stations to which the organizers or the sponsors have specific contractual obligations. In any case, the organizers may give preference to any of the interested stations, with their decision being dependent upon their view on the character and content of the event, and on its best possible coverage.

---

486. *See* Case C-201/11 P, *UEFA*, Judgment of 18 Jul. 2013, EUR-Lex; Case C-205/11 P, *FIFA*, Judgment of 18 Jul. 2013, EUR-Lex.

487. This restriction brings the special right of the CyBC very close to the simple right for short news coverage, to which we shall refer below under §2, with the only difference being that the CyBC shall also cover the event (something which entails further costs).

434. If the CyBC has been preferred for the coverage of the event, then it is required to dispose its signal to other stations, which they had not been preferred, upon compensation that shall not exceed a reasonable level (cf. below the relevant provisions as regards the right to have access to short news reporting on events of high interest for the public). Besides, in case the CyBC has been preferred by the organizers or the sponsors, the latter are required to permit one more station to cover the event. This last station may further dispose its signal to any other interested station upon reasonable compensation. If the coverage is based on material that has been acquired by another station, then the logo of this station must always be shown during the transmission of the material.

§2. Short News Reporting

I. The Transposition of Article 15 of the Directive into the Cypriot Media Law

435. Both the RTSL (section 28B) and the CyBCL (section 17F) have transposed the provisions of Article 15 of the AVMS Directive on short news reporting. Therefore, section 28B, paragraph 1 RTSL and section 17F, paragraph 1 CyBCL provide that all TV broadcasters, including the CyBC, which exercise exclusive rights on the transmission of events of major importance for the public shall provide other TV organizations, which have been established in the Republic or in another EU Member State, with short extracts from events of major importance for the public, exclusively for the purposes of general news programmes, that is, news bulletins and news and current affairs programmes. Access to such excerpts shall be provided on fair, reasonable and non-discriminatory terms, financial or other. The TV broadcaster which has obtained exclusive rights shall timely announce such terms before the event so that all interested parties have adequate time to decide whether they shall exercise the right of access.

436. If another broadcaster established in the same Member State as the broadcaster seeking access has acquired exclusive rights to the event of high interest to the public, access shall be sought from that broadcaster (section 28B, paragraph 2 RTSL). The TV organization which has acquired the exclusive rights shall pay attention so that it ensures access by allowing broadcasters to freely choose short extracts from the transmitting broadcaster's signal (section 28B, paragraph 3 RTSL; section 17F, paragraph 2 CyBCL), upon the following terms and conditions (section 28B, paragraph 4 RTSL; section 17F, paragraph 3 CyBCL):

- short extracts shall be used solely for general news programmes, that is, news bulletins and news and current affairs programmes; also they may be used in on-demand AVMS, but only if the same programme is offered on a deferred basis by the same media service provider;
- the transmission of the extracts shall take place after the end of the particular event, during a period which shall not exceed twenty-four hours from the event's end;

- the duration of the transmission of the extracts shall not exceed 180 seconds; the transmission may be repeated up to three times within the twenty-four hours period after the end of the event;
- where compensation is provided for, it shall not exceed the additional costs directly incurred in providing access;
- during the transmission of the extracts the TV organization that transmits them is required to retain on the screen the logo of the TV organization from which access to the extracts has been obtained.

II. The *Sky Österreich* Judgment of the CJEU

437. The importance of the aforementioned provisions for the right to information has been stressed by the Grand Chamber of the CJEU, in the *Sky Österreich* Judgment of 22 January 2013.[488] First, the Court concluded that a holder of exclusive broadcasting rights relating to events of high interest to the public cannot rely on the protection afforded by Article 17, paragraph (1) of the Charter of the Fundamental Rights of EU, safeguarding the right to property.[489] Then, the Court found that, although the rights and obligations under Article 15 of the AVMS Directive constitute a limitation upon freedom to conduct business under Article 16 of the Charter, as long as they oblige the holders of exclusive rights to provide access to extracts upon compensation which shall not exceed the costs incurred by providing access, they nonetheless do not affect the core content of freedom to conduct business. This is so insofar as the relevant provisions do not 'prevent the holder of those rights [i.e., the exclusive rights] from making use of them by broadcasting the event in question itself for consideration or by granting that right to another broadcaster on a contractual basis for consideration or to any other economic operator.'[490]

438. Furthermore, assessing the proportionality of the interference upon the freedom to conduct business by the measures that are indicated by Article 15 of the AVMS Directive, the Court noticed, first, that 'the marketing on an exclusive basis of events of high interest to the public is increasing and liable to restrict considerably the access of the general public to information relating to those event'; but this is exactly the aim of Article 15 of the AVMS Directive: 'to safeguard the fundamental freedom to receive information, guaranteed under Article 11(1) of the Charter, and to promote pluralism of the media in the production and programming of information in the EU, protected under Article 11(2) of the Charter.'[491] The importance of the right to information 'in a democratic and pluralistic society must be stressed in particular', even more in the case of events of high interest to the public.[492]

488. Case C-283/11, *Sky Österreich GmbH*, Judgment of 22 Jan. 2013, EUR-Lex.
489. *Ibid.*, paras 31–40 (40).
490. *Ibid.*, para. 49.
491. *Ibid.*, para. 51.
492. *Ibid.*, para. 52.

439. Besides, the measures of Article 15 of the AVMS Directive were found to be appropriate for the purpose of safeguarding the right to information. In this respect, the Court noticed that 'access is guaranteed to them (i.e., broadcasters) irrespective of their commercial power and financial capacity, on the one hand, and the price paid to acquire the exclusive broadcasting rights, the contractual negotiations with the holders of such rights and the scale of the events at issue, on the other.'[493] As concerns the necessity of the measures of Article 15, the Court noted that, although 'a less restrictive measure could have consisted in providing compensation to holders of exclusive broadcasting rights in excess of the costs directly incurred in providing access to the signal', 'it is apparent that less restrictive legislation would not achieve the objective pursued by Article 15(6) of the AVMS Directive as effectively as the application of that provision,' because any compensation exceeding the costs of providing access would 'deter or even prevent certain broadcasters from requesting access … and thus considerably restrict the access of the general public to the information.'[494]

440. Finally, as regards proportionality *sensu stricto*, the Court noted that the requirements of Article 15 (use of extracts only for general news programmes, duration and time limits, identification of the source), as coupled with the fact that the holder of exclusive rights will certainly take into account the requirements of Article 15, in order to proceed into any contractual negotiations for the price paid for the acquisition of such rights, ensure 'that the extent of the interference with the freedom to conduct a business and the possible economic benefit which broadcasters might draw from making a short news report are confined within precise limits.'[495] 'By contrast, in so far as concerns the rights and interests which Article 15 of the AVMS Directive seeks to protect, it should be noted that the marketing on an exclusive basis of events of high interest to the public is … increasing and may significantly restrict the access of the general public to information relating to those events.'[496] The aforementioned thoughts of the CJEU should be taken seriously into consideration by the CRTA and by the Supreme Court of the Republic of Cyprus, in case of a dispute or litigation on the right of access to short news reports.

§3. Obligation to Transmit News and Current Affairs Programmes

441. Another guarantee of the right to information derives from section 26, paragraph 1(a) RTSL, which renders completeness of programmes a basic principle of the Cypriot Media Law. In order to ensure completeness, private TV and radio stations shall devote to news and current affairs programmes (other than news bulletins) no lower than 7% of their weekly broadcasting hours in the period between 12:00 and 24:00. The same threshold as regards the transmission of cultural programmes is 2% of the broadcasting hours between 12:00 and 24:00, excluding from

493. *Ibid.*, para. 53.
494. *Ibid.*, paras 54–55.
495. *Ibid.*, paras 58–64 (61).
496. *Ibid.*, para. 65.

the basis of calculation the time that is devoted to news bulletins, to sports events, to advertising and to teleshopping services.

442. Section 21 CyBCL is vaguer. According to it, the CyBC 'shall include in its programmes a service of basic news which shall be transmitted daily as frequently as the CyBC may determine in the Greek, Turkish and English languages, and may at its discretion include additional news bulletins in the Greek and Turkish languages devoted to news of particular interest to communities concerned.' Such vagueness is alleviated by the provisions of the CyBC (PSB) Regulation 616/2003, which stipulate that the CyBC shall dedicate no less than 40% of its annual TV broadcasting hours to news and current affairs programmes (for more details *see* above under Chapter 1, §2 II in this Part).

443. Besides, implementing Article 7 of the AVMS Directive, section 18C CyBCL requires that the CyBC ensure that its services are gradually made accessible to people with a visual or hearing disability. In this respect, the CyBC has the obligation to transmit during 18:00 and 22:00 at least a five minutes special news bulletin which can be followed by people with such disability. Furthermore, section 18C, paragraph 3 CyBCL provides that the CyBC shall submit to the CRTA a timetable which shall indicate specific targets as regards the gradual increase of the percentage of its other programmes which will be accessible to people with visual or hearing disability (the legislative target is 5% of the programmes). Section 30B RTSL, applying to private AVMS providers, contains provisions identical to those of section 18C CyBCL. Other than the news bulletin which is expressly provided in section 30B RTSL and section 18C CYBCL, there has not been any accessibility progress since the obligation was first introduced. The issue has been discussed by the Human Rights Committee of the House of Representatives, where it was noted that there has been virtually no progress on further implementing measures for the accessibility of persons with disability to television broadcasts. The media service providers have pointed to the high cost needed, but the House of Representatives argued that this is no excuse for not properly implementing the legislation and called on the CRTA to oversee that there is sufficient progress. The Ombudsman has further concluded, following an investigation of a relevant complaint, that there has been no development of an action plan by any media service provider since 2010 when the obligation was initially introduced, and that there has been no effort to comply with their statutory obligations, and has called upon the CRTA to act accordingly.[497]

497. The Ombudsman's full report (in Greek) is available in, http://www.ombudsman.gov.cy/ombudsman/ombudsman.nsf/All/43E196A2303415C8C225850300343B71/$file/8641263_19.pdf?OpenElement.

Chapter 7. Access to Networks

§1. Must-Carry Rules

I. On Must-Carry and Universal Service Generally

444. According to the traditional conception of must-carry rules in the US,[498] cable TV operators are required to reserve a certain part of their channel capacity in order to carry local broadcast stations. Every three years, all public and private broadcasters may choose whether they wish to qualify for a must-carry status. The alternative is to elect the 'retransmission consent' status, which relieves cable operators from the obligation to carry and leaves space to broadcasters for negotiating the compensation to be received for the transmission of their programmes. Cable TV must-carry rules have been coupled with the 'carry one, carry all' principle for Direct Broadcast Satellite operators (i.e., the obligation of such operators to carry the signals of all other local broadcast stations, in case they decide to carry one of them);[499] and with the much debated 'digital must-carry' rules.[500] The latter required cable operators to safeguard that, during the transition from analogue to digital TV, all signals carried in fulfilment of the must-carry requirements will be provided to every subscriber, either in an analogue or in a digital format.

445. During the 1990s, in its *Turner Broadcasting* judgments, the US Supreme Court held that on the one hand, cable TV must-carry rules are compatible with freedom of speech, since they are 'content neutral' (i.e., they do not directly affect the content of the programmes which are to be transmitted), while, on the other hand, they promote the widespread dissemination of information from a multiplicity of sources and fair competition in the market of television programming.[501]

---

498. *See* R. Frieden, *Analog and Digital Must-Carry Obligations of Cable and Satellite Television Operators in the United States*, 15 Media L. & Pol'y 230 (2005–2006); K. Creech, *Electronic Media Law and Regulation* 85–94 (6th ed., Routledge 2013); N. Van Eijk & B. Van der Sloot, *Must-Carry Regulation: A Must or a Burden?* 19–20.
499. *See* Frieden, *Analog and Digital,* 240–245.
500. *See* T.W. Hazlett, *Digitizing 'Must-Carry' Under Turner Broadcasting v. FCC* (1997), 8 Sup. Ct. Econ. Rev. 141 (2000); A.N. Lung, *Must-Cary Rules in the Transition to Digital Television: A Delicate Constitutional Balance*, 22 Cardozo L. Rev. 151 (2000–2001); J. Timmer, *Broadcast, Cable and Digital Must-Carry: The Other Digital Divide*, 9 Comm. L. & Pol'y 101 (2004); A. D. Cotlar, *The Road Not Yet Traveled: Why the FCC Should Issue Digital Must-Carry Rules for Public Television 'First'*, 57 Fed. Comm. L.J. 49 (2004–2005); J. Brown, *Digital Must-Carry & the Case for Public Television*, 15 Cornell J. L. & Pub. Pol'y 73 (2005–2006); Frieden, *Analog and Digital,* 236–240; N. Laughner & J. Brown, *Cable Operators' Fifth Amendment Claims Applied to Digital Must-Carry*, 58 Fed. Comm. L.J. 281 (2006).
501. *See Turner Broad. Sys. Inc. v. FCC*, 520 U.S. 180 (1997); *Turner Broad. Sys. Inc. v. FCC*, 512 U.S. 622 (1994); and for discussion *see* among much else, M. Peritz, *Turner Broadcasting v. FCC: A First Amendment Challenge to Cable Television Must-Carry Rules*, 3 Wm. & Mary Bill Rts. J. 715 (1994); R. Pilon, *A Modest Proposal on 'Must-Carry', the 1992 Cable Act, and Regulation Generally: Go Back to Basics*, 17 Hastings Comm. & Ent. L.J. 41 (1994–1995); J.-Y. Kim, *Empirical Testing on an Unasked Question in Turner v. FCC: Do Must-Carry-Rules Enhance Diversity?*, 21 Comm. & L. 55 (1999); R. Mathew Warner, *Reassessing* Turner *and Litigating Must-Carry Law Beyond a Facial Challenge*, 60 Fed. Comm. L.J. 359 (2007–2008).

446. In the EU, the prospect of must-carry rules is embedded in a wider principle of universal service,[502] as the latter was expressed by the provisions of the Directive 2002/22/EC[503] and the ECC Directive that replaced it. Article 114 of the ECC Directive allows EU Member States to impose must-carry obligations[504] 'for the transmission of specified R/T broadcast channels and complementary services, particularly accessibility services to enable appropriate access for end-users with disabilities and data supporting connected TV services, on undertakings under their jurisdiction providing electronic communications networks and services used for the distribution of radio or television broadcast channels to the public,' provided that 'a significant number of end-users of such networks use them as their principal means to receive R/T broadcast channels;' that the relevant must-carry obligations 'are necessary to meet general interest objectives as clearly defined by each Member State;' and that such obligations are 'reasonable', 'proportionate and transparent' in the light of the objectives for which they have been scheduled.[505] The relevant provisions of the ECC Directive are further discussed in the EU volume of this series.

II. Must-Carry Rules in Cyprus?

447. Neither the basic legislative instruments of Cypriot Media Law (the RTSL and the CyBCL) nor the Regulations that have been enacted under them (the RTSR and the CyBCR) contain provisions which might resemble must-carry rules. Of course, the Republic of Cyprus has transposed Article 114 of the ECC Directive. Such transposition originally took place through section 72A of the Regulation of Electronic Communications and Postal Services Law of 2004, Law 112(I)/2004. Section 72A was, however, repealed with amending Law 23(I)/2022. The new RECL does not directly harmonize Cypriot law with Article 114 of the ECC Directive, as the pre-existing legal regime. Pursuant to section 25 RECL the Communications Commissioner shall ensure that all consumers in the Republic of Cyprus, including small-medium enterprises and organizations of a non-for-profit character, and taking into account the national circumstances, have the possibility to access adequate internet broadband services in an affordable price. The Commissioner may further safeguard the affordability of services not offered on a regular basis, if this is required in order to ensure the full social and economic participation of consumers in society. The Commissioner may issue a Regulatory Decision in order to determine the broadband; the area for the universal provision of services; the quality of

502. *See* P. Valcke, *The Future of Must-Carry: From Must-Carry to a Concept of Universal Service in the Info-Communications Sector*, 15 Media L. & Pol'y 247 (2005–2006).

503. Directive 2002/22/EC of the European Parliament and of the Council of 7 Mar. 2002 on universal service and users' rights relating to electronic communications networks and services (Universal Service Directive), OJ L 108, 24 Apr. 2002, p. 51; as amended by Directive 2009/136/EC of the European Parliament and of the Council of 25 Nov. 2009, OJ L 337, 18 Dec. 2009, p. 11.

504. *See* for it, and for its history, T. Roukens, *What Are We Carrying Across the EU These Days? Comments on the Interpretation and Practical Implementation of Article 31 of the Universal Service Directive*, 15 Media L. & Pol'y 201 (2005–2006).

505. *See* Art. 31, para. 1, in combination with Recital 43 of the Preamble of the Universal Access Directive and with Recital 48 of the Preamble of the Directive 2009/136/EC.

the provision of services included in the area of universal provision of services; and the obligations of the provider of universal electronic communications services.

448. The relevant Decision of the Commissioner was enacted with Normative Act 297/2022, which provides for the specific conditions and prices under which universal access to broadband services may be safeguarded for end-users with disability, or with low income or special social needs. Prices constituting affordable access may be determined by the Commissioner on the basis of non-discrimination and proportionality, and by determining the quality of access. Whereas the conditions described in Normative Act 297/2022 are sufficiently detailed, there is a lack of a specific provision imposing reasonable must-carry obligation (in Greek: 'εύλογη υποχρέωση μεταφοράς σήματος') for certain radio and TV broadcast channels as well as for complementary services, particularly services for disabled end-users, on electronic communications network providers used for the transmission of radio and TV broadcast channels to the public, in a manner similar to the pre-existing section 72A of Law 112(I)/04 (despite its short-comings as analysed in the previous edition of this monograph). However, this omission has not in any way precluded the Commissioner from exercising his powers.

449. The authority of the Commissioner to determine and impose must-carry obligations on cable or other pay TV providers was exercised with the Regulatory Decision 431/2022 of 11 November 2022, on the Determination of a Relevant Market, the Analysis on the Existence of Effective Competition and the Determination of a Provider Having Significant Market Power in the Relevant Market and the Regulatory Measures Plan regarding the wholesale provision of local access to a fixed position ('the CYTA Significant Market Power Decision'). The Commissioner determined that CYTA had a significant market position in the market of wholesale provision of local access to a fixed position and that the said market was not sufficiently competitive, thus requiring an *ex ante* regulatory intervention. The CYTA Significant Market Power Decision imposed several obligations on CYTA, including an obligation to grant access to, and common use of, specified elements and/or facilities of the network to all interested providers. Such obligation includes access to its copper network, the use of the vectoring technique within a period not exceeding nine months, offering simulative access to the fibre optic supply network and to technical infrastructure works, as well as the obligation to inform providers of any changes.

450. Additional obligations were imposed on CYTA with the CYTA Significant Market Power Decision. These include an obligation to non-discriminate, so as to offer equivalent treatment to persons offering equivalent services and who are in equivalent circumstances, to provide the same quality of services and prices to interest parties as it provides to its own subsidiaries, and to generally cease discriminative treatment against alternative providers. new services and facilities. CYTA is further required to safeguard transparency in the terms and conditions it applies, so as to enable regulatory oversight, and to ensure that there is separation of accounts. Such obligation applies to the activities of CYTA which are relevant to the provision of its services and the determination of its wholesale prices and its internal transfer prices, in order to ensure, *inter alia*, compliance with the obligation of non-discrimination and prevention of unfair cross-subsidies. The accounting methodology which is used for the purposes of the obligation of accounting separation shall be reviewed by the Commissioner and shall be consistent with the accounting methods which Velister applies in providing its other services. CYTA should further adopt a cost-oriented model of pricing policies. Price control and determination of wholesale fees shall be conducted on the basis of the Top Down FDC methodology, taking into account the efficient functioning of the network. However, TV market conditions are such that all communications networks and service providers wish to offer as much content (and hence carry as many channels) as possible. Especially as regards the provider of the DTT network for private TV channels (*see* next section of this chapter). Under such conditions, a discussion on a 'must-offer' regime would perhaps be more appropriate than the prospect of must-carry obligations.[506]

451. The CYTA Significant Market Power Decision is an important one, as CYTA is currently by far the largest pay TV provider, as well as a public corporation. It effectively introduces must-carry rules in order to avoid distortion in the broadband market. It refers, however, primarily to its competitors in the broadband market, rather than the imposition of specific TV channels. The CyBC and major TV channels have always had a strong presence in the media sphere, and their programmes could always be, and were, received by the vast majority of residents in Cyprus, even before the introduction of DTT. Furthermore, their channels have always been included in the basic packages of most cable TV or other pay TV[507] providers (Cablenet, CYTA, Prime Tel). These thoughts do not preclude the possibility of situations in which must-carry rules would be necessary, in order to avoid distortion of the competition in the TV market, e.g., in case a major pay TV provider decides to transmit on an exclusive basis the programmes or the channels of a certain content provider. In the past, similar problems were dealt with in the context of the general rules and principles of competition Law.[508] Furthermore, it is noted that certain must-carry obligations are implicit in the access obligations of the DTT network provider for private broadcasting (Velister Ltd). Such obligations shall be presented in the next section of this chapter.

506. Compare T. Roukens, *What Are We Carrying Across the EU These Days? Comments on the Interpretation and Practical Implementation of Art. 31 of the Universal Service Directive*, 15 Media L. & Pol'y 201, 226–227 (2005–2006).

507. We use the term 'pay TV' as synonymous with the term 'conditional access system', as the latter is defined by Art. 2(12) of the ECC Directive: 'any technical measure and/or arrangement whereby access to a protected radio or television broadcasting service in intelligible form is made conditional upon subscription or other form of prior individual authorisation.'

508. *See*, e.g., the Decision of the CPC of 2 Jun. 2006, File No. 11.17.14/2006 (in Greek), on the agreement between LTV (the main content provider in the market of encoded programmes at that time) and Multichoice (Cyprus) Ltd (a company managing the most widespread pay TV network at the time), to the effect that the latter acquired the exclusive right to distribute the channel of the former. The Commission took into account the conditions of the pay TV market and held that such agreement distorted competition. The decision was annulled by the Supreme Court in Cases No. 1522/ 2006 and 1523/2006 (yet unpublished) on the grounds of bad composition of the administrative organ, without the substance of the Commission's decision having been reviewed.

§2. ACCESS OBLIGATIONS OF THE DTT NETWORK PROVIDERS

I. The Regulatory Status of DTT Network and Services Providers

452. The licensing of the DTT network and services providers in Cyprus is based on the EU common regulatory framework for electronic communications and networks, as this framework had originally been transposed by the Regulation of Electronic Communications and Postal Services Law of 2004, Law 112(I)/2004, and by the Radio-Communications Law of 2002, Law 146(I)/2002, which have both been effectively substituted by the RECL. Such licensing takes place through the granting of individual rights to use radio frequencies by the Communications Commissioner. The first licence for the establishment and operation of a DTT network was granted to the CyBC after negotiations on 19 March 2010, and a second licence was granted after a competition to Velister Ltd on 9 November 2010.[509] The DTT network of the latter supports the transmission of the programmes of private TV broadcasters, including all nationwide TV channels, local stations, and thematic channels.[510]

453. The regulatory status of DTT network providers is determined by the general provisions of the RECL, transposing the provisions of the ECC Directive; and as regards access to Velister's network and services, by the specific provisions of the Decision of the Commissioner on the Results of the Market Survey, and on the Imposition of Obligations on the Organization with Significant Market Power, in the Wholesale Market of Transmission Services for the Distribution of Television Contents to End-Users, as such Decision was enacted by NAA 156/2016 (henceforth: 'the Velister Significant Market Power Decision').[511] A series of other provisions applying to the holder of Significant Market Power, i.e., Velister Ltd, are contained in the Decrees which accept and introduce amendments to the Reference Offer of Velister's services (Decree of 2011, as enacted by NAA 805/2011; Decree of 2013, as enacted by NAA 336/2013; Decree of 2014, as enacted by NAA 194/2014; Decree of 2015, as enacted by NAA 445/2015).

II. Access and Other Relevant Obligations of Velister Ltd

454. The Velister Significant Market Power Decision has been issued after a public consultation and after receiving the comments of the Commission in the context of the notification procedure under Article 7 of the then applicable Framework

509. Registry of Electronic Communications Licences No. 13/2010.

510. *See*, http://www.velister.com.cy/ (last access 4 Jul. 2017).

511. This Decision replaces the Concession of Rights to, and Imposition of Obligations on, the Provider of DTT Network and Services, Concerning Access to DTT Networks, Decree of 2009, as such Decree had been issued by the Commissioner and had been enacted by Normative Administrative Act (NAA) 200/2009.

Directive.[512] In this Decision, the Commissioner first defined the relevant markets in accordance with the relevant Commission Recommendation[513] and identified two relevant markets for the distribution of TV content to end-users: First, the market for DTT services, and second, the market for digital non-terrestrial TV broadcasting.

455. Assessing the competitive conditions on the two relevant markets, the Commissioner concluded that, while the market for digital non-terrestrial TV broadcasting services meets the relevant criteria so as to be susceptible to *ex ante* regulatory intervention, the market for DTT services is not adequately competitive insofar as it is monopolized by Velister Ltd. Therefore, the Commissioner designated Velister Ltd as having Significant Market Power and imposed on it several *ex ante* regulatory obligations.

456. Whereas, the pre-existing legal regime was more detailed, the RECL is more vague, granting the Commissioner wide powers in order to exercise regulatory oversight. Section 15 of Law 23(I)/22 provides that the Communications Commissioner may issue a regulatory decision that shall determine the conditions pursuant to which providers of DTT T are required to carry TV programmes. The issue has been dealt with secondary legislation, enacted by Normative Act 405/2022 and titled the Granting of Access under Conditions to transmission infrastructure of digital R/T. Normative Act 405/2022. The Velister Significant Market Power Decision effectively provides for the imposition of the following obligations:

(a) Obligation to grant access to, and common use of, specified elements and/or facilities of the network to all interested AVMS providers: Such obligation includes access to technical interfaces, protocols or other key technologies that are indispensable for the interoperability of services; co-location or other forms of facility sharing, including duct, building or mast sharing; and specified services needed to ensure interoperability of end-to-end services to users. The negotiations between Velister Ltd and the interested AVMS providers must be conducted in good faith and shall be based on a Reference Offer whose minimum contents are determined by Annex I of the Decision and which may be amended by a Decree of the Commissioner.[514] Such Reference Offer shall contain, among else, the basic costs and the principles of pricing policies, a detailed description of the technical characteristics of the network and of the relevant services, the procedures for the satisfaction of any kind of requests on the part

512. *See* Commission Decision concerning Case CY/2015/1798: Market for broadcasting transmission services, to deliver broadcast content to end users in Cyprus Comments pursuant to Art. 7(3) of Directive 2002/21/EC, Brussels, 4 Dec. 2015, C(2015) 8918.

513. *See* Commission Recommendation 2014/710/EU of 9 Oct. 2014 on relevant product and service markets within the electronic communications sector susceptible to *ex ante* regulation in accordance with Directive 2002/21/EC of the European Parliament and of the Council on a common regulatory framework for electronic communications networks and services, OJ L 295, 11.10.2014.

514. The procedure for the imposition of amendments to the Reference Offer by the Commissioner was provided by another Decree, which has been enacted by NAA 112/2007.

of the AVMS providers, the terms and conditions of technical support, the procedure to be followed in case of non-compliance with the terms of the contract, etc.

(b) *Transparency obligation:* Velister Ltd is required to publish the terms and conditions of access to its services, including the price of the fees and all other information (accounting information, technical specifications, network characteristics, terms and conditions for supply and use, etc.) which shall allow the Commissioner to review whether the provider complies with its other obligations. The Reference Offer shall be publicly available[515] and shall be adequately analytical, describing the relevant offers separated per item, so that interested parties may not pay for facilities which are not necessary for the services requested.

(c) *Obligation of non-discrimination*: Such obligation refers to any kind of unequal treatment of the clients of Velister Ltd. The latter shall ensure that equivalent conditions are applied in equivalent circumstances for all interested parties (including its own subsidiaries) as regards the quality of the services which are to be provided, service times, cost accounting and prices, and the development and provision of new services and facilities.

(d) *Obligation of accounting separation*: Such obligation applies to the activities of Velister Ltd which are relevant to the provision of DTT network services. In particular, the Commissioner may require Velister to make transparent and distinct its wholesale prices and its internal transfer prices, in order to ensure, *inter alia*, compliance with the obligation of non-discrimination and prevention of unfair cross-subsidies. The accounting methodology which is used for the purposes of the obligation of accounting separation shall be reviewed by the Commissioner and shall be consistent with the accounting methods which Velister applies in providing its other services.

(e) *Price control and cost accounting obligations*: According to Article 12 of the Velister Significant Market Power Decision, Velister Ltd shall adopt a cost-oriented model of pricing policies. Price control and determination of wholesale fees shall be conducted on the basis of the Top Down FDC methodology, taking into account the efficient functioning of the network, in accordance with the Determination of the Methodology for the Calculation of Cost, and of the Methodology for the Accounting Separation, Decree of 2008 (NAA 320/2008) as currently in force. The annual fees per service item are publicly available as part of Velister's Reference Offer.

457. The Commissioner has the authority to examine complaints about violations of the Velister Significant Market Power Decision and may impose on Velister Ltd administrative sanctions. The amendment of this Decision shall take place after consultation with all interested parties, including all electronic communications network and services providers as well as representatives of the end-users of such networks and services.

515. The Reference Offer of Velister Ltd, as amended and approved by the Commissioner, is published at the website of the company, http://www.velister.com.cy/.

Chapter 8. Standards and Interoperability

458. The technical standards of the equipment that was needed for the reception of digital TV and radio services were determined in accordance with the relevant provisions of the EU common regulatory framework for electronic communications, as such provisions were originally transposed by sections 63, 64 and 72 of the Regulation of Electronic Communications and Postal Services Law of 2004, Law 112(I)/2004. Section 72, paragraph 2 of Law 112(I)/04 provided that a person who places on the market, for sale or rent, or otherwise makes available consumer equipment intended for the reception of digital television signals that were capable of descrambling digital television signals should ensure that such equipment possesses the capability to:

- allow the descrambling of such signals according to the common European scrambling algorithm as administered by a recognized European standards Organization; and
- display signals that have been transmitted in clear, provided that, in the event that such equipment is rented, the rentee is in compliance with the relevant rental agreement.

459. The Commissioner should ensure that analogue television sets with an integral viewing screen of visible diagonal greater than 42 cm are fitted with at least one open interface socket (as standardized by a recognized European standards organization) permitting simple connection of peripherals, especially additional decoders and digital receivers. Paragraph 5 of the same section calls the Commissioner to ensure that digital television sets with an integral screen of visible diagonal greater than 30 cm are fitted with at least one open interface socket (either standardized by, or conforming to a standard adopted by a recognized European standards organization, or conforming to an industry-wide specification) permitting simple connection of peripherals, and able to transmit all the elements of a digital television signal, including information relating to interactive and conditionally accessed services. This is no longer applicable due to the termination of analogue broadcasting.

460. With regards to digital interactive television services for distribution to the public within the EU that would be made available on digital interactive television platforms, regardless of the transmission mode used, an open Application Programme Interface (API) was to be used. All enhanced digital television equipment deployed for the reception of digital interactive television services on interactive digital television platforms shall comply with an open API in accordance with the minimum requirements of the standards or specifications which are applicable under the relevant EU regulatory framework. The providers of digital television services and equipment shall cooperate in order to offer interoperable TV services to disabled end-users. Proprietors of rights to APIs will make available on fair, reasonable and non-discriminatory terms, and against appropriate remuneration, all such information as is necessary to enable providers of digital interactive television services to provide all services supported by the API in a fully functional form.

461. The Commissioner was authorized to issue a Decree which would determine the technical features of digital television equipment intended for wide consumption so that the interoperability of such equipment is ensured. Furthermore, he was authorized to issue a Decree in order to specify the terms of access to conditional access systems of digital TV and radio services irrespective of the means of transmission. He may further periodically review the conditions applied by undertaking a market analysis. Where, as a result of this market analysis, the Commissioner finds that one or more undertakings do not have Significant Market Power on the relevant market, he/she might amend or withdraw the conditions with respect to those operators, but only to the extent that such amendment or withdrawal would not adversely affect:

(a) accessibility for end-users to R/T broadcast, broadcasting channels and other relevant services;
(b) the prospects for effective competition in the markets for retail digital television and radio broadcasting services and for conditional access systems and other associated facilities.

462. The Commissioner is also authorized to impose obligations in relation to the presentational aspects of Electronic Programme Guides (EPGs) and of similar listing and navigation facilities. Exercising his/her authorities under the aforementioned provisions, the Commissioner has issued the Digital Television (imposition of obligations as regards access to APIs and to EPGs, and as regards the presentational aspects of EPGs and of relevant listing and navigation facilities) Decree 117/2009; and the Digital Television (determination of technical features of digital television equipment for wide consumption) Decree 118/2009, as amended by NAA 397/2009.

463. Decree 118/2009 adopts the IEC 62216-Edition 1.0-2009-05 (DTT Receivers for the DVB-T System) standard for the purposes of determination of the obligatory technical features of the basic digital television equipment which is intended for wide consumption in the Republic of Cyprus. As a minimum requirement, such equipment shall be compatible with the MPEG4 Standard Definition, supporting the scrambling of images up to ISO/IEC 14496-10 Main Profile Level 3.0. If the equipment is compatible with MPEG4 High Definition, it shall additionally support the scrambling of high-definition images up to ISO/IEC 14496-10 High Profile Level 4.0. In any case, the equipment shall comply with the electric safety and electromagnetic compatibility requirements of the EU legislation and shall bear a clear and intelligible CE marking. The basic equipment for the reception of digital television services may not support an API. If it does, then it shall comply with the ETSIES 201 812 V1.1.2 (2006–08) – Digital Video Broadcasting (DVB); Multimedia Home Platform (MHP) Specification 1.0.3 standard, in order to ensure the interoperability of digital interactive television services and enhanced digital television equipment (Rule 6 and Annex I of Decree 117).

464. Rule 7 and Annex II of Decree 117/2009 refer to EPGs, calling their providers to:

(a) ensure that agreements with TV organizations for the provisions of EPG services shall take place under fair, reasonable and impartial terms;
(b) publish and comply in an objective way with the presentational aspects of the information that they provide;
(c) avoid special treatment of a particular TV station, in case that they are somehow connected with it;
(d) ensure that viewers have the option to receive all information which is included in the EPGs on the same basis, taking as granted that they possess the equipment necessary for reception of EPG services;
(e) ensure that access to all television services, which are referred to in the EPGs, is easily available to all viewers who have the relevant equipment;
(f) comply with any other guideline which the Commissioner may address to them in relation to the aforementioned obligations as well as in relation to the provision of additional services to be used by disabled end-users.

465. Rule 8 of Decree 117/2009 stipulates that conditional access systems for the reception of digital TV and radio services, irrespective of the means of transmission, shall comply with the requirements of Part 1 of Annex I to the Access Directive, which have as follows:

> In relation to conditional access to digital television and radio services broadcast to viewers and listeners in the community, irrespective of the means of transmission, Member States must ensure in accordance with Article 6 that the following conditions apply.
>
> a. conditional access systems operated on the market in the community are to have the necessary technical capability for cost-effective trans control allowing the possibility for full control by network operators at the local or regional level of the services using such conditional access systems;
> b. all operators of conditional access services, irrespective of the means of transmission, who provide access services to digital television and radio services and whose access services broadcasters depend on to reach any group of potential viewers or listeners are to:
>   – offer to all broadcasters, on a fair, reasonable and non-discriminatory basis compatible with EU competition law, technical services enabling the broadcasters' digitally-transmitted services to be received by viewers or listeners authorized by means of decoders administered by the service operators, and comply with EU competition law;
>   – keep separate financial accounts regarding their activity as conditional access providers.
> c. when granting licences to manufacturers of consumer equipment, holders of industrial property rights to conditional access products and systems are to ensure that this is done on fair, reasonable and non-discriminatory terms. Taking into account technical and commercial factors, holders of rights are not to subject the granting of licences to conditions prohibiting, deterring or discouraging the inclusion in the same product of:

- a common interface allowing connection with several other access systems; or
- means specific to another access system, provided that the licensee complies with the relevant and reasonable conditions ensuring, as far as he is concerned, the security of transactions of conditional access system operators.

466. The standards of digital television equipment are further analysed by an Explanatory Report of the Commissioner.[516] Some such standards are as follows:

- Screen formatting/aspect ratios: 4:3 and 16:9.
- Wide Screen Signalling compliance: ETSI EN 300 294.
- Subtitles compliance: EN 300 743 DVB; Subtitling systems, including character set ISO/IEC 8859-7.
- Language/character set compliance: ISO/IEC 8859-7.
- EPG compliance: ETSI EN 300 468 – DVB; Specification for Service Information (SI) in DVB systems, supporting character set ISO/IEC 8859-7.

516. Office of the Commissioner for of Electronic Communications and Postal Regulation, Explanatory Document in Relation to the Minimum Technical Features of Digital Television Equipment of Wide Consumption for the Reception of DTT in Cyprus, March 2010.

Part IV. Cross-Ownership Regulation

§1. Introduction

467. Media pluralism is a fundamental aspect of freedom of information and of the press in democratic societies.[517] Cross-ownership regulation is considered to be a necessary, if not sufficient, condition for media pluralism.[518] As the ECtHR has observed:

> A situation whereby a powerful economic or political group in society is permitted to obtain a position of dominance over the audiovisual media and thereby exercise pressure on broadcasters and eventually curtail their editorial freedom undermines the fundamental role of freedom of expression in a democratic society as enshrined in Article 10 of the Convention, in particular where it serves to impart information and ideas of general interest, which the public is moreover entitled to receive [...] The Court observes that in such a sensitive sector as the audiovisual media, in addition to its negative duty of non-interference the State has a positive obligation to put in place an appropriate legislative and administrative framework to guarantee effective pluralism.[519]

468. The RTSL contains some simple and strict rules for the avoidance of concentration both in the market of one particular medium (horizontal/monomedia ownership requirements) and in the media market as a whole (vertical/crossmedia ownership requirements). Such rules are supported by a set of transparency obligations, which must be read in combination with the transparency obligations that are

---

517. *See* Art. 11, para. 2 of the Charter of Fundamental Rights of the EU; European Parliament resolution on the risks of violation, in the EU and especially in Italy, of freedom of expression and information (Art. 11(2) of the Charter of Fundamental Rights) (2003/2237(INI)), OJ C 104E, 30 Apr. 2004, p. 1026; CJEU, Case C-250/06, *United Pan-Europe Communications Belgium SA* [2007] ECR I-11149, para. 41; ECtHR (Grand Chamber), *Centro Europa 7 S.r.l. and Di Stefano v. Italy*, Judgment of 7 Jun. 2012, paras 129–134; hudoc; Art. 10*bis* of the European Convention of Transfrontier Television, as amended and currently in force; Council of Europe, Recommendation CM/Rec (2007) 2 of the Committee of Ministers to Member States on media pluralism and diversity of media content.
518. *See* Commission Staff Working Document, *Media pluralism in the Member States of the European Union*, SEC(2007)32; C. Stratilatis, *Entrepreneurial Pluralism and Information Polyphony in Mass Communication Media*, in *Democracy and Mass Media* 37 (K. Zoras et al. eds, Livanis 2011) (in Greek).
519. ECtHR (Grand Chamber), *Centro Europa 7 S.r.l. and Di Stefano v. Italy*, Judgment of 7 Jun. 2012, paras 133–134; hudoc.

contained in the absolute licensing requirements (*see* Part III, Chapter 2, §2 I A above). Avoidance of circumvention of cross-ownership regulation is also served by the prohibition of unauthorized changes in the shareholding composition of licensed companies through (co-)management agreements (*see* Part III, Chapter 2, §2 I D above). It should be noted, however, that the importance of such rules has been significantly weakened since the abolition of the major restrictions of monomedia ownership requirements by Law 87(I)/2023.

§2. Monomedia Ownership Requirements

469. Section 18 RTSL prohibits the granting of more than one licence for the establishment and operation of a TV station to the same legal entity. The same prohibition applies to the granting of radio station licences to legal entities and to natural persons (to be reminded that small radio stations may be owned by natural persons as well as by companies; *see* Part III, Chapter 2, §2 I A above). Section 19, paragraph 1(b) RTSL further stipulated that no shareholder of a licensed company might own more than 25% of its shares. As indicated, however (Chapter 2, §2 I A above) such restrictions have been abolished with Law 87(I)/23, which now allows ownership to effectively 100% of the shares of the licensed company.

§3. Crossmedia Ownership Requirements

470. Section 19, paragraph 3 RTSL prohibits the ownership of any number of shares or control of a licence to a nationwide, or thematic TV station, an encoded programmes TV station, or a radio station, to any natural or legal person who owns any number of shares to a different media group, or to a natural or legal person that has been granted a licence for a TV or radio organization owned by a different media group. A media group is a group of companies or media acting as a single entity with a common source of control.

471. Section 19, paragraph 4 RTSL used to extend the above requirements also to the shareholders of the licensed companies. It further sought to avoid the circumvention of all the above prohibitions. Thus, for the purposes of such prohibitions, the number of shares which were owned by spouses and/or by relatives up to the second degree were included in the overall percentage of the shares which the shareholders of licensed companies may own or control. However, following the abolition of restrictions on the ownership of shares by a single shareholder, which were introduced with Law 87(I)/2023, the relevant requirements of section 19, paragraph 4 RTSL were also abolished.

§4. Transparency Obligations

472. According to section 20, paragraph 1 RTSL, the names of the holders of more than 5% of the shares in licensed nationwide TV organizations or national or local radio organizations shall be published each January in two daily newspapers. This obligation also pertains to persons who have rights to more than 5% of the shares in a licensed company.[520] Paragraph 2 of the same section provides that any changes in the shareholding composition of a licensed company must be notified in the same way (i.e., through publishing an announcement in two daily newspapers) within one month from the date of the change. Such obligation is also applicable in the case of licensed companies which are listed on the Cyprus Stock Exchange.[521] Paragraph 3 of section 20 RTSL requires the notification of any change in the shareholding compositions of such a company to the effect that a shareholder acquires more than 5% of its shares.

473. Section 20, paragraph 4 RTSL refers specifically to licensed companies which are listed on the Cyprus Stock Exchange. The President, the members of the BoD, the Director General, the secretaries, the auditors, etc. of such companies have the obligation to provide the CRTA with all information or announcements which shall be notified to the Council of the Cyprus Stock Exchange or the Cyprus Securities and Exchange Commission in accordance with the relevant legislation. Irrespective of such obligation, the CRTA may also request from licensed companies which are listed on the Stock Exchange any document or information which might be deemed necessary for exercising its supervisory authorities.

474. It is noted that violation of the cross-ownership rules, which were presented above in this chapter, and of the relevant transparency obligations under section 19 RTSL (most of these obligations have been presented in Part III, Chapter 2, §2 I A above) does not only entail the imposition of administrative sanctions up to revocation of the licence of the radio or TV station (*see* for the revocation Part III, Chapter 2, §2 I F) but also criminal responsibility under section 19, paragraph 5 RTSL, providing for imprisonment up to three years and/or a fine up to EUR 85,400 to be imposed on any individual or legal entity who/which violates any of the provisions of section 19.

520. Section 19, para. 4 RTSL requires that, in the case of possessing shares through proxies, a declaration under oath must be signed as regards possession rights on such shares.

521. According to §19, para. 7 RTSL, cross ownership requirements apply equally to licensed companies which are listed on the Cyprus Stock Exchange.

Part V. Supervision: Media Regulator

Chapter 1. Organization

§1. The Cyprus Radio and Television Authority

475. The CRTA was established by the RTSL.[522] Before that, the licensing of radio and TV stations and the supervision of private broadcasting were part of the competences of the Council of Ministers, in accordance with the provisions of the Radio Stations Law 120/1990 and of the Televisions Stations Law 29(I)/1992.[523]

476. The CRTA is a legal entity under public law,[524] with its own legal standing and legal personality (*see* section 3, paragraphs 1 and 3 RTSL). It is composed of seven members, one of which is its President and another is its Vice President (section 4, paragraph 1 RTSL). The CRTA is represented before any administrative or other public authority by its Director or by any other officer who is properly empowered to this effect (section 8, paragraph 1 RTSL). The contracts into which the CRTA enters must be signed by its President, its Director or any other officer who is duly authorized for this purpose (section 8, paragraph 2 RTSL).

477. Section 3, paragraph 1 RTSL characterizes the CRTA as an 'independent authority'. Indeed, the legislative framework for CRTA contains some provisions which could be taken as guarantees of its independence vis-à-vis the Government and the other organs of the Republic (e.g., the capacity of the CRTA to issue directly enforceable administrative acts, the strict conditions for discharging the members of the CRTA, etc.; *see* below).[525] However, there are no constitutional guarantees for the existence and for the independence of the CRTA,[526] as is the case, e.g., in Greece (*see* Articles 101A and 15, paragraph 2 of the Greek Constitution). Nor does the

522. For an overview of the discussions in the House of Representatives and in the Executive which led to the introduction of CRTA as the Media supervisor in Cyprus *see* K. Kouros, *The Mass Media Law in the Republic of Cyprus,* fn. 51 above, 420–432 (Vivlioekdotiki 2008, in Greek).
523. For an overview of the discussions which accompanied the then applicable legislative framework *see* K. Kouros, *The Mass Media Law in the Republic of Cyprus:* fn. 51 above, 225–259 (Vivlioekdotiki 2008, in Greek).
524. *See*, e.g., *Sigma Radio T.V. Ltd v. CRTA* [2004] 3 CLR 134, 169 (in Greek).
525. *See* in this respect, http://crta.org.cy/ανεξαρτησία.html.
526. Compare *Antenna T.V. Limited v. The Republic* [2001] 3 CLR 711, 720 (in Greek), holding that Art. 19 para. 5 permits (it does not require) the assignment to the CRTA of the task to grant licences; *Sigma Radio T.V. Ltd et al. v. CRTA* [2004] 3 CLR 134, 177 (in Greek), noticing that CRTA is in a better position to effectively correspond with the responsibilities of the media regulator.

Constitution provide for some politically consensual procedure in order to appoint the members of the CRTA (as is again the case of the Greek Constitution, which in Article 101A requires a majority of 4/5 in the relevant parliamentary committee in order to appoint the members of all independent authorities, including the Greek National Radio and Television Council).

478. According to section 4, paragraph 1 RTSL, the President and the Vice President of the CRTA are appointed by the Council of Ministers after a recommendation of the President of the Republic, while the other five members of the CRTA are appointed by the Council of Ministers. The discretionary power of the latter is limited by the criteria which are provided by paragraph 2 of the same section, stipulating that the members of the CRTA shall 'come from the fields of education, of arts, of science or of technology, or shall be persons with expert knowledge and recognized experience in mass media matters, and with high professional and moral esteem.' Besides, paragraph 3 of section 4 prohibits the appointment of any person who has a direct or indirect interest in any AVMS provider. In any case, the fact that the members of the CRTA are appointed by the Council of Ministers could endanger its independence.

479. Such risk is counter-balanced by the legislative determination of the term of office of CRTA's members, in combination with the legislative restriction of the power of the Council of Ministers to remove any of them from his/her position. In particular, the term of office of the CRTA's members is determined to be a fixed period of six years, while the term of the President may be renewed only once (section 4, paragraph 2 RTSL). Vacation of the position of the President, of the Vice President or of any other member before the end of such period may take place only in case of death or of resignation, or in case of a decision of the Council of Ministers to remove the member, which may be based exclusively on one of the following two reasons: taking up by the member of a position in a political party or improper behaviour (in Greek: 'ανάρμοστη συμπεριφορά', section 5, paragraph 1 RTSL).[527] Besides, the President, the Vice President and the other members of the CRTA cannot be criminally persecuted, and are not liable under civil law proceedings for whatever was said or done in exercising their duties in good faith, provided that they remained within the powers assigned to them by the relevant legislation (section 7A RTSL). Clearly, such provisions enhance the functional independence of the CRTA and the personal independence of its Members.

480. However, according to section 10 RTSL, the Minister of Interior has the authority to address to the CRTA 'directions of a general nature in relation to the exercise of its powers, which are necessary in the general interest of the Republic.'

527. The fact that a member of the CRTA takes up a position in a political party does not automatically entail his/her disqualification from being a member of the CRTA. Nor the presence of this member in the meetings of CRTA results in bad composition. A decision of the Council of Ministers removing the member is always required. *See* on this *CRTA v. Antenna Limited*, Judgment of 2 Apr. 2014, Appeal No. 140/2009; *Antenna Limited v. CRTA*, Judgment of 16 Apr. 2008, Case No. 726/2006; *Antenna Limited v. CRTA*, Judgment of 11 Oct. 2007, Case No. 792/2006 (all in Greek).

Given the independence of the CRTA (section 3, paragraph 1 RTSL), such directions can be relevant only to Organizational and procedural issues, and not to the content of the particular decisions on matters which fall under CRTA's supervisory authorities. Also, the Minister of Education, Sport and Youth may address to the CRTA directions on matters which refer to the linguistic policies of the Republic in relation to the programmes of AVMS providers (section 31, paragraph 1 RTSL).

481. Another institutional feature of the CRTA, which could be taken as a safeguard of its independence, is the direct enforceability of its decisions, i.e., the fact that the decisions of the CRTA can be implemented without needing the approval of some other public authority. The decisions of the CRTA can be challenged only before the courts. Before the Eighth Amendment of the Constitution (Law 130(I)/2015, amending Article 146 of the Constitution) and the creation of the new Administrative Court (*see* Law 131(I)/2015 on the Establishment and on the Functioning of an Administrative Court), the decisions of the CRTA were challenged through a recourse before the Supreme Court. However, since then, the competence for first instance examination of such recourses passed to the new Administrative Court (the Supreme Court may still adjudicate appeals against the judgments of the Administrative Court). The Administrative Court has the competence to suspend the implementation of the CRTA's decision until the issuance of its final judgment. However, such powers to suspend a decision are rarely applied as suspension may be only ordered if there is flagrant illegality or irreparable harm.[528] If such suspension does not take place, the decision of the CRTA shall be executed immediately after its notification to the interested party.[529]

482. In case a TV or radio station omits payment of a fine that was imposed by the CRTA, the latter may take judicial action in order to collect it (section 41B, paragraph 3 RTSL; Rule 48 RTSR; section 22C, paragraph 3 CyBCL). In such judicial proceedings, the competent Court may not examine assertions about the legality or the constitutionality of the decision of the CRTA in its substance.[530] In general, apart from its power to impose administrative sanctions (*see* Chapter 3 of this Part), the CRTA may also submit to the competent Courts all kinds of judicial recourses requesting orders or other measures to the effect that an AVMS provider ceases a violation of the Media Law rules and principles (section 41C RTSL; section 22D CyBCL).

483. The functional independence of the CRTA is enhanced by the fact that it has its own separate services with officers who are appointed by the Board of CRTA,

528. *See* A. Emilianides, *Criteria for Interim Orders for Suspension in the Administrative Trial*, 10 Cyprus and European LR 757–772 (2009, in Greek).

529. Rule 47 RTSR provides that licence fees and administrative fines shall be paid independently of any objection or appeal. Obviously this provision does not preclude the power of the Court to suspend the implementation of the CRTA's decision until the issuance of its final judgment. For the immediate enforcement of the decisions of the CRTA with appeal to the presumption of legality of all administrative acts *see Sigma Radio T.V. Ltd v. CRTA* [2005] 1 CLR 408; *Antenna Limited v. CRTA* [2010] 1 CLR 1079 (both in Greek).

530. *See* on this *Antenna Limited v. CRTA* [2010] 1 CLR 1079 (in Greek).

serving the purposes of the CRTA in accordance with the relevant Regulations[531] (section 9, paragraphs 1, 3 and 5 RTSL). The CRTA may also employ, on a contractual basis, experts on matters falling under its competences, including matters relevant to journalistic ethics (section 3, paragraph 4 RTSL). The administrative services of the CRTA are directed by its Director who is appointed on a contractual basis for a period of six years (section 9, paragraph 4 RTSL). The Director is the supreme executive organ of the CRTA, and he/she is responsible for the execution of the decisions of the CRTA as well as for the fulfilment of any other duty that is assigned to him/her by the Board (section 9, paragraph 6 RTSL). The Director may be present in the meetings of the Board, albeit without voting rights (section 9, paragraph 8 RTSL). The Board of CRTA may transfer some of its authority to the Director or to committees composed by some members of the Board and/or by other officers (section 9, paragraph 7 RTSL). The procedural rules for the operation of the CRTA in exercising its supervisory authorities shall occupy Chapter 3 of this Part.

484. Furthermore, the CRTA is financially independent to a certain extent. More specifically, the CRTA has its own property (section 40, paragraph 1 RTSL, providing also for the power of the CRTA to proceed into expropriation in accordance with the relevant legislation), and it may enter into contracts and agreements of any kind in order to acquire or dispose such property (section 3, paragraph 3 RTSL). However, the approval of the Council of Ministers is required before the CRTA disposes of its property (section 40, paragraph 2 RTSL). In any case, the CRTA has its own budget, which is annually approved by the Council of Ministers and by the House of Representatives (section 36 RTSL), and it keeps its own books and accounts, which are audited by the Auditor General of the Republic (section 37 RTSL). An important safeguard of the CRTA's financial independence is the fact that the incomes of its budget, apart from state contributions, include revenues from licence fees (*see* Part III, Chapter II, §2 I E above) and from the administrative fines which are imposed on licence holders (section 38, paragraph 1 RTSL). This last provision was invoked by the applicants in the *Sigma* case, in order to argue that the institutional framework for the operation of the CRTA violates the principles of natural justice and Article 6, paragraph 1 of the European Convention of Human Rights. This argument was rejected both by the Supreme Court of Cyprus and by the ECtHR (*see* Chapter 3, §3 in this Part below).

§2. The Consultation Committee of Radio and Television

485. According to section 11 RTSL, the CRTA institutes a Consultation Committee of Radio and Television. This Committee shall provide its advice on matters relevant to the tasks of the CRTA. The composition of the Consultation Committee shall reflect public opinion and shall include at least one representative of the following bodies and agents (section 11, paragraph 2 RTSL):

---

531. *See* the Cyprus Radio and Television Authority (Terms of Appointment and of Service of Employees) Regulation 35/1999, as amended by Regulation 110/2007. For the current organizational structure of the CRTA *see*, http://crta.org.cy/οργανική-δομή.html.

- Ministry of Interior.
- Ministry of Research, Innovation and Digital Policy.
- Ministry of Education, Sport and Youth.
- Law Office of the Republic of Cyprus.
- Private TV stations.
- Private radio stations.
- UCJ.
- Local administration.
- Trade unions.
- Cyprus Chamber of Commerce and Industry, and Cyprus Employers & Industrialists Federation.
- Scientific and Technical Chamber of Cyprus.
- University of Cyprus.
- Cyprus Consumers Association.
- Cyprus Sociological and Psychological Association (the representative of such Association is nominated by the Cyprus Parents Confederation).
- Cyprus Advertisers Association.
- Church of Cyprus.
- Artists Organizations.
- ANPP.

486. The competences and procedural rules of the Consultation Committee are provided by the Consultation Committee of Radio and Television Regulation 154/99. According to Rule 10 of Regulation 154/99, the Consultation Committee is competent to advise the CRTA on matters relevant to journalistic independence and ethics; proper use of language; protection of minors; protection of consumers; handling of religious, national or other minority issues; and any other matter on which the advice of the Consultation Committee is requested by the CRTA. In any case, the competence of the Consultative Committee is merely advisory, and the RTSL does not require its intervention in the procedure for the imposition of administrative fines on stations which have violated some provision of the RTSL or of the Regulations which were issued under it.[532]

532. *See* on this *Ekdotikos Oikos Dias Ltd v. CRTA* [2008] 3 CLR 445, 450–451; *Sigma Radio T.V. Ltd v. CRTA*, Judgment of 19 Sep. 2005, Case No. 392/2003; *Sigma Radio T.V. Ltd v. CRTA*, Judgment of 13 Jun. 2007, Case No. 391/2006 (all in Greek).

Chapter 2. Mission and Tasks of the CRTA

§1. The Mission of the CRTA

487. The mission of the CRTA is to regulate and exercise control on the media sector, so as to safeguard the fundamental rights and values under Article 19 of the Constitution of Cyprus and Article 10 of the ECHR (freedom of speech, of information and of the press, diversity of views and opinions, pluralism and avoidance of excessive concentration of media in the hands of a few owners, protection of the rights of individuals from illegal exercise of the freedom of speech, etc.) In particular, the CRTA exercises its regulatory and supervisory authorities with the aim of ensuring that the AVMS which are provided by AVMS providers falling under the jurisdiction of the Republic of Cyprus abide by the RTSL and the Regulations which are issued under it (section 3A, paragraph 1 RTSL) as well as certain provisions of the CyBCL (for the supervisory authorities of the CRTA on CyBC, *see* Part III, Chapter 1, §3 II A and Chapter 3, §1 above).

§2. The Jurisdiction of the Republic and of the CRTA

488. The jurisdiction of the Republic, on which the exercise of the supervisory and regulatory authorities of the CRTA depends, is delimited by sections 3A, paragraphs 2–6 RTSL, in accordance with the detailed provisions of Article 2 of the AVMS Directive. An AVMS provider is deemed to be established in the Republic, and, hence, falls under the jurisdiction of the Republic, when:

(a) it has its head office in the Republic, and the editorial decisions about the AVMS are taken in the Republic;
(b) it has its head office in another EU Member State, but editorial decisions on the AVMS are taken in the Republic, and a significant part of the workforce involved in the pursuit of the AVMS activity operates in the Republic;
(c) it has its head office in the Republic, and a significant part of the workforce involved in the pursuit of the AVMS activity operates both in the Republic and in another EU Member State;
(d) it first began to offer its AVMS in accordance with the law of the Republic, and it maintains a stable and effective link with the economy of the Republic, although a significant part of the workforce involved in the pursuit of the audiovisual media service activity operates neither in the Republic nor in another EU Member State;
(e) it has its head office in the Republic, but editorial decisions on the AVMS are taken in a non-EU Member State, or inversely, provided that a significant part of the workforce involved in the pursuit of the AVMS activity operates in the Republic (section 3A, paragraph 3 RTSL).

489. When the aforementioned provisions are not applicable, AVMS providers are deemed to be established in the Republic, and hence to fall under its jurisdiction, when:

(a) they use a satellite up-link which belongs to the Republic;
(b) although they do not use a satellite up-link which belongs to the Republic, they use a satellite capacity which is situated in the Republic (section 3A, paragraph 4 RTSL).

490. In case the question as to which EU Member State has jurisdiction cannot be answered in accordance with the aforementioned provisions, competence belongs to the Member State in which the AVMS provider is established within the meaning of Articles 49–55 of the TFEU (section 3A, paragraph 5 RTSL). The provisions of the RTSL which correspond with the provisions of the AVMS Directive (section 3, paragraph 2(n), sections 3A and 27–34C RTSL) do not apply to AVMS intended exclusively for reception in third countries, and which are not received with standard consumer equipment directly or indirectly by the public in the Republic, or in one or more other EU Member States (section 3A, paragraph 6 RTSL).

491. The provisions of Articles 3 and 4 of the AVMS Directive on freedom of reception and on its restriction have been transposed by the provisions of Part IX (section 32–32D) RTSL. The CRTA is responsible for ensuring freedom of reception, and it is prohibited from restricting retransmissions on the territory of the Republic of AVMS from other EU Member States for reasons which fall within the fields coordinated by the AVMS Directive (section 32, paragraph 1 RTSL). Derogations from freedom of reception may take place under the procedural and substantial conditions which are stipulated in Article 3, paragraphs 2–6 of the AVMS Directive, with the CRTA taking up all relevant powers and responsibilities (section 32, paragraphs 2–6 RTSL).[533] The provisions of Article 4 of the AVMS Directive with regard to the exercise of the power to adopt more detailed or stricter rules in the fields coordinated by the AVMS Directive (provided that such rules are in compliance with EU Law, under the procedural and substantial conditions of paragraphs 2–5 of the said Article) have been transposed by section 32C RTSL, with the CRTA assuming all relevant powers and responsibilities. Section 32D RTSL empowers CRTA, taking duly into account EU Law, to enforce terms and conditions other than the ones which are applicable to TV advertising within the relevant provisions of the AVMS Directive as regards TV programmes which are intended exclusively for reception on the territory of the Republic, and which cannot be received, either directly or indirectly, by the public in other EU Member States.

492. Section 32B RTSL safeguards freedom of reception for the Member States of the Council of Europe which have ratified the European Convention on Transfrontier Television. Temporary suspension of the retransmission of programmes from TV organizations which operate in such Member States may take place only

533. For freedom of reception under the then applicable provisions of Directive 89/552/EEC and/or freedom of providing services under the Treaties, *see* among else CJEU, Cases C-244/10 and 245/10, *Mesopotamia Broadcast and Roj TV A/S*, Judgment of 22 Sep. 2011, ECR I-8797; Case C-11/95, *Commission v. Belgium*, Judgment of 10 Sep. 1996, ECR I-4153; Case C-288/89, *Collectieve Antennevorziening Gouda*, Judgment of 25 Jul. 1991, ECR I-4035.

for the reasons, and under the procedures, which are provided by the relevant provisions of the Convention, as the latter has been ratified (along with its amendments) by the Cypriot House of Representatives.

§3. The Tasks of the CRTA

493. The tasks of the CRTA are enumerated in section 3, paragraph 2 RTSL, which empowers the CRTA to:

(a) grant, revoke, renew and amend the licences of AVMS providers in the public interest;[534]
(b) issue directives, recommendations and circulars for the observance of the rules and principles of the CJE and of the CA;
(c) examine on its own motion or after a complaint matters relevant with the observance of the basic principles of Media Law, as stipulated by section 26 RTSL, as well as violations which are relevant to the protection of minors and with the prohibition of incitement to hatred, under sections 29 and 30 RSTL respectively;
(d) follow international developments in the field of AVMS and submit suggestions to the Council of Ministers for the improvement and modernization of Media Law legislation;
(e) control the actual conditions of media ownership in the field of AVMS, so as to ensure the independence of AVMS providers and preclude tendencies, acts or intentions towards the concentration of media and towards oligopolistic or monopolistic conditions thereof;
(f) ensure the journalistic and creative independence of all persons who are employed by AVMS providers, in order to inhibit improper interventions of such providers in the work of journalists and creators;
(g) impose administrative sanctions on AVMS providers in accordance with the provisions of Part XIA of the RTSL (*see* next chapter of this Part);
(h) draft every three years a Report on the development of pluralism and polyphony in the AVMS sector, which shall be submitted to the Council of Ministers and to the House of Representatives, with a summary of such Report being published at least in two daily newspapers;[535]
(i) exercise all powers and duties which are assigned to it by the RTSL and by the Regulations which are issued under the RTSL;
(j) address matters which refer to the improvement of the implementation of legislative provisions on AVMS providers, and submit suggestions thereof;
(k) control the observance of the legislative, regulative and other provisions, including the circulars, directives and recommendations which are issued by itself, on the part of all AVMS providers which fall under the jurisdiction of the Republic;

534. For this first and most important task of the CRTA, *see* Part III, Ch. 2 above.
535. The CRTA has published such Reports, as part of more comprehensive Reports of its activities, in its Internet portal at http://crta.org.cy/μελέτες-/-εκθέσεις-/-σημειώματα/.

(l) exercise control over the implementation by AVMS providers which do not fall under the jurisdiction of the Republic of the provisions of Part IX RTSL (which transpose the provisions of Articles 3 and 4 of the AVMS Directive; *see* under §2 above);
(m) exercise all powers and duties which are assigned to it by the CyBCL (*see* Chapter 1 of Part III) or by any international convention adopted by the Republic in the field of AVMS;
(n) cooperate with the regulatory authorities of other countries and with the Commission, in order to exchange all information that is necessary for the implementation of the provisions of RTSL.

494. The powers of the CRTA are not exhausted by the tasks of this list. Section 51 RTSL assigns to the CRTA important legislative-regulative powers, delegating to it the authority to issue, after the approval of the Council of Ministers and of the House of Representatives, secondary legislation instruments, i.e., Regulations,[536] for the specification and best implementation of the provisions of the RTSL. Paragraph 2 of section 51 contains a long indicative list of the matters which can be addressed by such Regulations. Apart from the matters which have been covered in various chapters of Part III under the RTSR, the CA and the CJE, the list includes matters such as the minimum organizational and human resources standards of R/T stations, the qualifications and education of journalists who are employed by R/T stations, the determination of the broadcasting hours which shall be devoted to cultural and news programmes, the safeguarding of journalistic independence and freedom, etc. and virtually all organizational and procedural issues which might arise from the implementation of the RTSL.

495. Several other provisions of the RTSL assign to the CRTA specific tasks, as is, e.g., the specification of the criteria and the drafting of the list of events of major importance (*see* under Part III, Chapter 6, §1 above), control of the proper implementation of the provisions on political advertising (*see* Part III, Chapter 4, §2 above), supervision of the observance of European works and independent production quotas (section 27 RTSL), and of course the imposition of administrative sanctions on AVMS providers which have violated the provisions of the Cypriot Media Law (*see* next chapter). The CRTA further has oversight over the VSPs. Whereas the CRTA should in principle encourage VSPs to promote self-regulation or co-regulation, it may require that VSPs adopt stricter or more detailed rules, and it may keep a list of VSPs and evaluate the measures they are applying. It should further set up necessary mechanisms in order to assess the suitability of measures adopted by the VSPs and may require that they adopt additional measures, whenever necessary (section 32F RTSL).

536. For the legal nature of secondary legislation instruments, *see* Introduction, §3 VI.

Chapter 3. Sanctioning Powers and Procedure

§1. Sanctioning Powers of the CRTA

I. On AVMS Providers in the Private Broadcasting Sector

496. The sanctioning powers of the CRTA over the AVMS providers of the private broadcasting sector are provided by sections 41A and 41B of the RTSL. According to section 41A, paragraph 1, and section 41B, paragraph 2 RTSL, the CRTA may impose administrative sanctions on AVMS providers in case the latter violate *any* provision of the RTSL and of the Regulations which are issued under it (i.e., the RTSR; the CJE; and the CA. After the general reference to the imposition of sanctions for violation of any provision, section 41A, paragraph 1 RTSL contains a list of more specific provisions whose violation may lead to the imposition of administrative sanctions by the CRTA. This list includes the two Codes (CJE and CA); sections 29 and 30 RTSL (the first has to do with the protection of minors, *see* Part III, Chapter 3, §6; and the second prohibits the incitement to hatred on the basis of race, sex, nationality, religion, etc., *see* Part III, Chapter 3, §2 above); section 44 RTSL (right of reply; *see* Part III, Chapter 3, §9 above); the terms of the licence of the AVMS provider; the obligation of licence holders to pay the fees under section 24 RTSL; and the circulars, directives or recommendations which the CRTA may issue in accordance with section 3, paragraph 2 RTSL (*see* Chapter 2 of this Part). The wording of sections 41A and 41B leads to the conclusion that the list is indicative, not exhaustive.[537] If this was not so, the CRTA would not have the power to impose sanctions for the violation of all provisions which fall outside the list.[538] Especially in the case of a violation of CJE, a relevant petition by the CMCC is required before the CRTA may initiate any proceedings (section 41A, paragraph 1(a) RTSL).[539]

497. Paragraph 2 of section 41B RTSL determines the types of sanctions that may be imposed by the CRTA:

- recommendation;
- warning;
- temporary suspension of the operation of the TV or radio station, for a period which shall not exceed three months;
- revocation of the licence in accordance with section 25 RTSL (*see* Part III, Chapter 2, §2 I F);
- administrative fine, in accordance with section 41B RTSL.

537. *See* on this the judgment of the Full Bench of the Supreme Court in *Sigma Radio T.V. Ltd v. CRTA* [2004] 3 CLR 154 (in Greek), 166–168 (in Greek).

538. *See Antenna Ltd v. CRTA*, Judgment of 27 Feb. 2006, Case No. 467/2004 (in Greek).

539. *See* on this *Antenna T.V. Limited v. CRTA* [2002] 4 CLR 824 (in Greek); *CRTA v. Antenna T.V. Limited* [2005] 3 CLR 583, 589–590 (in Greek); *Antenna Limited v. CRTA*, Judgment of 8 Sep. 2003, Case No. 774/2002 (in Greek); all holding that Art. II.19 CJE is *ultra vires* insofar as it provides that the CRTA may impose sanctions for violations of the provisions of the CJE on its own motion.

498. Section 41B, paragraph 1 RTSL provides that the CRTA may impose an administrative fine *for each day* of violation of the provisions of RTSL and of the Regulations which were issued in accordance with the authorization provided by section 51 RTSL. Section 41B, paragraph 1 RTSL sets upper limits as to the amount of such fine, depending on the type of station on which the fine is imposed. Such upper limits are as follows:

(a) EUR 8,500 for nationwide TV stations.
(b) EUR 3,400 for nationwide radio stations.
(c) EUR 1,700 for local radio stations.
(d) EUR 850 for small local radio stations.[540]

499. Section 41B, paragraph 2 RTSL stipulates that the specification of the fine to be paid within the aforementioned upper limits shall be in compliance with the principle of proportionality and the CRTA shall take into account the nature, the gravity, the frequency and the duration of each particular violation. Given the nature of its revisionary powers (*see* below under §3), the Supreme Court may not substitute the CRTA in the assessment of the gravity of the violation and in the subsequent specification of the fine which shall be imposed.[541] However, the Court requires that the specification of the sanctions by the CRTA be duly reasoned and sufficiently analytical.[542] It should be noted that the CRTA has analogous powers to impose administrative sanctions on the VSPs, pursuant to section 32G RTSL. The types of sanctions that can be imposed on the VSPs are similar to the sanctions that can be generally imposed on AVMS providers; however, there is an additional possibility to impose the very grave sanction of an administrative fine not exceeding 5% of the overall revenue of the VSP during the previous financial year, to the extent that it does not exceed EUR 500,000. The provision of this type of sanction for the VSPs only, as opposed to the R/T stations, does not seem convincing.

500. The Supreme Court was called upon to resolve an important interpretative problem, which had to do with the meaning of the legislative term 'for each day of violation' (in Greek: 'για κάθε ημέρα παράβασης'), on which the implementation of the aforementioned upper limits as to the amount of the fines depends.[543] In some judgments the Supreme Court, exercising its first instance jurisdiction, held that the defining term here is that of 'violation' and not that of 'each day', to the effect that where more violations take place during the same day, the CRTA may impose separate sanctions for each violation, with the upper limits applying to each

540. Section 41B, para. 1 RTSL does not provide a threshold for the administrative fines that may be imposed on AVMS providers which hold other types of licence, such as licence for encoded programmes stations or for non-linear AVMS (*see* Part III, Ch. 2, §1).

541. *See*, e.g., *Sigma Radio T.V. Ltd v. CRTA* [2003] 4 CLR 1, 36; *Politistiki kai Pliroforiaki Eteria 'O Logos' v. CRTA* [2007] 3 CLR 91, 95; *Antenna Limited v. CRTA*, Judgment of 31 May 2005, Case No. 1261/2003 (all in Greek).

542. *See Antenna Limited v. CRTA (No. 2)* [2004] 4 CLR 411, 427–429; *Politistiki kai Pliroforiaki Eteria 'O Logos' v. CRTA*, Judgment of 23 Nov. 2004, Case No. 598/2003 (both in Greek).

543. These judgments were issued under the then applicable provisions of §3, para. 2 RTSL, which were almost identical with the now applicable provisions of §41B, para. 1 RTSL.

sanction separately, and not to all of them as a whole (however, according to the same judgments, the CRTA should not impose separate sanctions for violation of one and the same provision during the same day).[544] However, these judgments were overruled by the Plenary of the Supreme Court, which held that the upper limits apply to the overall amount of the fines that the CRTA may impose on a station for each day, irrespective of the number of violations which took place during this day.[545]

501. On the one hand, such jurisprudence results in unfairness,[546] insofar as one and the same limit applies irrespective of the frequency, the duration and/or the gravity of the violations of Media Law provisions by an AVMS provider during the same day. On the other hand, adoption of the opposite opinion (i.e., that the upper limits apply to each particular violation) could lead to arbitrariness insofar as the CRTA could circumvent the legislative limitation by imposing unreasonably high fines for each one of repeated violations of the same nature during the same day (e.g., repeated violations of the restrictions on the time and frequency of advertising). Of course, the problem could be easily solved by the legislator itself through an explanatory provision. Given the absence of such provision, it is considered that the first opinion (i.e., one of the first instance judgments, which was overruled by the Grand Chamber of the Supreme Court) would provide a more just solution since the stations would not be free to violate during the same day as many provisions as they wish without the fear of a fine that would surpass the aforementioned limits. However, the CRTA is anyway expected to respect the principle of proportionality, avoiding thus the imposition of more sanctions for violation of one and the same provision, or of similar provisions, during the same day.

II. On Cyprus Broadcasting Corporation

502. The sanctioning powers of the CRTA over the CyBC are delimited by sections 22B and 22C CyBCL. According to section 22B, paragraph 1(c)(i) CyBCL, the CRTA may impose on the CyBC administrative sanctions for the violation of certain provisions (sections 17A–17E, 18A–18I, and 19A–19E CyBCL) which are mainly those corresponding with the provisions of the AVMS Directive, having to do with:

- restrictions on the content and on the time and frequency of TV advertising;
- restrictions on political advertising in election periods;
- restrictions on AVCCs, sponsorship, teleshopping, and product placement;
- right of reply;
- transmission of events of major importance for society;

544. *See Antenna Limited v. CRTA (No. 1)* [2004] 4 CLR 121, 128–131, Judge Constantinides (in Greek); *Antenna Limited v. CRTA (No. 2)* [2004] 4 CLR 411, 428–429, Judge Nikolaou (in Greek).
545. *Antenna Ltd v. CRTA* [2005] 3 CLR 558, 568–574, Judge Nikolaou dissenting (in Greek).
546. Admitted by the opinion which was followed by the Plenary of the Supreme Court in *Antenna Ltd v. CRTA* [2005] 3 CLR 558, 570 (in Greek).

– free-of-charge coverage of events of general interest (the 'special right' of the CyBC, *see* part III, Chapter 6, §1 IV above);
– prohibition of incitement to hatred on the basis of race, sex, nationality, religion, etc.;
– access of people with a hearing and/or visual disability to AVMS, and obligation of the CyBC to transmit special news bulletins for them;
– participation of the CyBC in the action 'Education for the Media' of the CRTA;
– transmission of cinematographic works within the periods agreed upon by the right holders;
– obligations of non-linear AVMS providers;
– European works and independent production quotas.

503. Section 22B, paragraph 1(c)(ii) CyBCL determines the sanctions that the CRTA may impose on the CyBC: recommendation, warning, or administrative fine in accordance with section 22C CyBCL. The latter provides that the CRTA may impose on the CyBC an administrative fine which cannot exceed, for each day of violation,[547] EUR 8,500 for violations by a TV programme of the CyBC and EUR 3,400 for violations by a radio programme of the CyBC. The specification of the fine shall be in compliance with the principle of proportionality, taking into account the nature, the gravity and the duration of the violation (section 22C, paragraph 2 CyBCL). The CRTA may take judicial action, in order to collect fines from the CyBC (section 22C, paragraph 3 CyBCL).

§2. Procedure to Be Followed for the Imposition of Sanctions

504. The procedural rules and principles to be followed by the CRTA when it exercises its sanctioning powers are provided by the RTSL (mainly, by sections 7 and 41F RTSL), by Rules 41 and 42 RTSR, and by the General Principles of Administrative Law Act 158(I)/1999, which is the main legislative instrument for the regulation of the administrative procedure in the Republic of Cyprus.[548]

505. The CRTA may initiate proceedings against an AVMS provider either on its own motion or after a complaint of a viewer/listener (section 41F, paragraph 1 RTSL; Rule 41, paragraph 1 RTSR). In contrast to section 41F, paragraph 1 RTSL, which provides that viewers/listeners may submit a complaint for the violation of *any* provision of the RTSL and of the RTSR, the first paragraph of Rule 41 RTSR provides that the CRTA has the authority to examine complaints of the public for specific violations (unfair treatment of somebody by a news or entertainment programme; insult upon private life; transmission of sexual activities or of excessive and unjustified violence; non-observance of common standards of decency; and distortions in the radio frequencies). However, as the Supreme Court has repeatedly

547. For the meaning of the term, *see* above under subsection I in this section.
548. For a presentation and analysis of the rules and principles contained in this instrument *see* A. Emilianides, *Constitutional Law in Cyprus* (2nd ed., Kluwer 2019); N. Charalambous, *Cypriot Administrative Law Textbook* (2d ed. 2013, in Greek).

held, such restriction does not affect the power of the CRTA to examine any issue and initiate or continue the relevant proceedings on its own motion.[549] Therefore, the listing of violations for which viewers/listeners may submit a complaint has no real significance.

506. The proceedings shall initiate through a decision of the CRTA, which may be taken by a functionary (usually, the Director) after proper authorization by the Board of the CRTA.[550] Such a decision may include the appointment of a functionary who shall investigate the alleged violation (Rule 42, paragraph 3 RTSR).[551] The said functionary has the competence to hear any witness and to collect written submissions by all involved parties (Rule 42, paragraph 4 RTSR). After the end of the investigation, he/she shall submit to the Board his/her suggestions, which must be duly reasoned (Rule 42, paragraph 5 RTSR).[552]

507. In general, the CRTA has the authority to demand the submission of any document or of any other evidence which might be deemed as relevant to the case under examination (Rule 42, paragraph 6(c)(ii) RTSR). The accused AVMS provider has the obligation, if requested so, to provide the CRTA with a copy of the audio or videotape of the relevant programme and/or with a written transcript of the text that was used in such programme; to facilitate the access of the person who submitted a complaint to all relevant material; and, in general, to cooperate with the functionaries of the CRTA for the purposes of the investigation (Rule 42, paragraph 7 RTSR).

508. In any case, a prior hearing of the AVMS provider, either through an oral representation or in written (Rule 42, paragraph 6(b) RTSR), is always required, both for the taking of the CRTA's decision on the merits of the case and for its decision on the sanction to be imposed.[553] The Supreme Court has held that irrespective of whether the AVMS provider has been provided with the opportunity to send written submissions to the CRTA, the CRTA is further obliged to provide them with the

549. *See Antenna Ltd v. CRTA* [2010] 3 CLR 29, 36–38; *Antenna Limited v. CRTA (No. 1)* [2004] 4 CLR 121, 126–127; *Antenna Ltd v. CRTA*, Judgment of 21 May 2007, Case No. 620/2005; *Antenna Ltd v. CRTA*, Judgment of 27 Feb. 2006, Case No. 467/2004 (all in Greek).

550. *See* on this *Antenna Ltd v. CRTA* [2010] 3 CLR 29, 38; *Antenna Limited v. CRTA*, Judgment of 16 Apr. 2008, Case No. 726/2006; *Antenna Limited v. CRTA*, Judgment of 11 Oct. 2007, Case No. 792/2006; *Antenna Ltd v. CRTA*, Judgment of 24 Nov. 2009, Case No. 170/2007; *Antenna Limited v. CRTA*, Judgment of 18 Dec. 2009, Case No. 572/2007; *Antenna Limited v. CRTA*, Judgment of 14 Apr. 2010, Case No. 636/2008; *Antenna Limited v. CRTA*, Judgment of 20 Oct. 2009, Case No. 2295/2006; but *see also Antenna Limited v. CRTA*, Judgment of 21 Jul. 2010, Case No. 234/2007; *Antenna Limited v. CRTA*, Judgment of 31 Jul. 2009, Case No. 67/2007, finding that the relevant authorization to the Director of the CRTA did not include the decision to initiate proceedings (all judgments referred to in this note are in Greek).

551. The CRTA may also assign the investigation and the examination of any issue to a committee comprising of at least four of the members of its Board (Rule 42, para. 1 RTSR). Such assignment is not obligatory, but it may take place at the discretion of the CRTA. *See* on this *Politistiki kai Pliroforiaki Eteria 'O Logos' v. CRTA*, Judgment of 6 Oct. 2004, Case No. 415/2003 (in Greek).

552. *See* on this *Politistiki kai Pliroforiaki Eteria 'O Logos' v. CRTA*, Judgment of 6 Oct. 2004, Case No. 415/2003 (in Greek).

553. *See Antenna T.V. Ltd v. CRTA and another (No. 2)* [2001] 4 CLR 565, 568–569 (in Greek).

opportunity of an oral hearing. Thus, whereas the relevant Rule seems to provide for alternative options, failure to provide the opportunity for both written and oral submissions would lead to the annulment of the decision of the CRTA.[554] The decisions of the CRTA must be duly reasoned (Rule 42, paragraph 8 RTSR; for the requirements of due reasoning *see* sections 28–33 of Act 158(I)/1999).[555] The decisions of the CRTA must be further notified both to the accused AVMS provider and to the person who submitted a complaint (Rule 42, paragraph 8 RTSR). Besides, the CRTA may oblige the accused AVMS provider to announce its decision (Rule 41, paragraph 11 RTSR; cf. section 3B RTSL empowering the CRTA to oblige all AVMS to transmit free of charge any message that is connected with the CRTA's mission at a time between 19:00 and 22:00 for TV stations and between 12:00 and 24:00 for radio stations).

509. Section 7 RTSL provides the procedural rules and principles for the meetings of the Board of the CRTA. The meetings are convoked by the President, or by the Vice President in case of absence or incapacity of the President, by sending a written invitation to all members at least seven days before the date of the meeting, unless there is such urgency that makes necessary the convocation of the Board in a shorter period (section 7, paragraphs 1 and 2 RTSL). A meeting can also be convoked if three or more members submit a written request to this effect, and in any case, the CRTA shall meet at least once a month (section 7, paragraph 3 RTSL). In practice, the CRTA used to determine in advance a day of the week on which its meeting was to take place. However, the Supreme Court found that this practice is problematic in view of the obligation of the President to send a written invitation for each particular meeting.[556] In any case, there must exist evidence proving that the invitations were properly sent.[557]

510. The meetings are chaired by the President, or in case of absence or incapacity of the President, by the Vice President, or in case of absence or incapacity of the latter, by another member chosen for this purpose (section 7, paragraph 4 RTSL). The quorum is four members (out of the seven members of the Board of the CRTA), and decisions are taken by the majority of present members; in case of equality in votes, the vote of the chairing member counts twice (section 7, paragraph 5 RTSL). The same members must be present in all meetings on the same

554. *CRTA v. Antenna Ltd*, Adm. App. 38/2019. Judgment of 30 Nov. 2021 (in Greek).
555. For examples of the Supreme Court annulling decisions of the CRTA which imposed sanctions on account of undue reasoning, *see Radio Elios Network Ltd v. CRTA*, Judgment of 28 Feb. 2002, Case No. 1596/2000; *Sigma Radio T.V. Ltd v. CRTA*, Judgment of 30 Jul. 2004, Case No. 1158/2002 (both in Greek).
556. *See Sigma Radio T.V. Ltd v. CRTA* [2007] 3 CLR 258; and *Sigma Radio T.V. Ltd v. CRTA* [2007] 3 CLR 299, reversing *Sigma Radio T.V. Ltd v. CRTA*, Judgment of 25 Feb. 2005, Case No. 668/2003; *see also Sigma Radio T.V. Ltd v. CRTA*, Judgment of 29 Sep. 2006, Case No. 629/2003; *Sigma Radio T.V. Ltd v. CRTA*, Judgment of 28 Sep. 2004, Case No. 769/2002; cf. *Antenna Limited v. CRTA*, Judgment of 28 Feb. 2011, Case 1647/2007 (all in Greek).
557. *See* on this *Sigma Radio T.V. Ltd v. CRTA* [2009] 3 CLR 30 (in Greek), containing a good analysis of all previous judgments of the Supreme Court on the same issue.

case; if a member was absent from a previous meeting on the same case, he/she must be duly informed about what was discussed at that meeting, before the procedure can continue; however, a member that was present at a previous meeting on the same case cannot be absent from the next meeting on the same case without proper and binding justification (section 22 of Act 158(I)/1999). Violation of this last provision led to the annulment of several decisions of the CRTA.[558] Finally, section 7, paragraph 6 RTSL provides that a member of the Board of the CRTA who has a personal interest in the outcome of a case shall notify such impediment and shall be absent from the discussion and from the voting on this case. The Supreme Court has rejected several excessive claims about the violation of this provision.[559]

§3. The Sigma Case before the European Court of Human Rights

I. The Judgment of the Supreme Court

511. During the first half of the 2000s, one of the largest TV stations of Cyprus, *Sigma*, attempted to challenge the sanctioning powers of the CRTA as a whole, raising the claim that such powers contravene several provisions of the Constitution of Cyprus and Article 6, paragraph 1 of the ECHR. One of the arguments supporting this claim was that the sanctions which are imposed by the CRTA are of a criminal character, something which entails a breach of the principles of natural justice under Articles 12 and 30 of the Constitution as well as an infringement of the principles of fair trial under Article 6, paragraph 1 of the ECHR. It was argued that insofar as in the proceedings for the imposition of sanctions the CRTA acts in many capacities (namely, as prosecutor, as investigator-witness and, at the same time, as judge), while the fines which the CRTA imposes are paid into its own fund (something

558. *See Antenna Limited v. CRTA*, Judgment of 20 Sep. 2013, Case No. 100/2008; *Antenna Limited v. CRTA*, Judgment of 20 Sep. 2013, Case No. 468/2009; *Antenna Limited v. CRTA*, Judgment of 12 Apr. 2013, Case No. 167/2009; *Antenna Limited v. CRTA*, Judgment of 30 Sep. 2011, Case No. 1451/2008; *Antenna Limited v. CRTA*, Judgment of 28 Feb. 2011, Case No. 1647/2007; *Antenna Limited v. CRTA*, Judgment of 13 Dec. 2010, Case No. 112/2007; *Antenna Limited v. CRTA*, Judgment of 4 Oct. 2010, Case No. 437/2008; *Antenna Limited v. CRTA*, Judgment of 14 Jul. 2009, Case No. 649/2007; *Antenna Limited v. CRTA*, Judgment of 29 Apr. 2004, Case No. 671/2003; *Sigma Radio T.V. Ltd v. CRTA*, Judgment of 7 Aug. 2007, Case No. 390/2006. But *see also Antenna Limited v. CRTA*, Judgment of 14 May 2009, Case No. 1310/2007; *Sigma Radio T.V. Ltd v. CRTA*, Judgment of 13 Jun. 2007, Case No. 391/2006; *Antenna Limited v. CRTA*, Judgment of 20 Oct. 2009, Case No. 1625/2006 (all in Greek).

559. *See Antenna Limited v. CRTA*, Judgment of 11 Oct. 2007, Case No. 792/2006; *Antenna Limited v. CRTA*, Judgment of 18 Dec. 2009, Case No. 572/2007; *Antenna Limited v. CRTA*, Judgment of 16 Apr. 2008, Case No. 726/2006; *Antenna Ltd v. CRTA*, Judgment of 24 Nov. 2009, Case No. 170/2007; *Antenna Limited v. CRTA*, Judgment of 23 Mar. 2010, Case No. 573/2007; *Antenna Limited v. CRTA*, Judgment of 14 Apr. 2010, Case No. 636/2008; *Antenna Limited v. CRTA*, Judgment of 6 Oct. 2010, Case No. 837/2008; *Antenna Limited v. CRTA*, Judgment of 14 May 2009, Case No. 1310/2007; *Antenna Limited v. CRTA*, Judgment of 20 Oct. 2009, Case No. 2295/2006 (all in Greek).

which implies a financial interest of the CRTA in imposing sanctions), and in any case the constitutional and the ECHR conditions for the imposition of criminal sanctions are not met.[560]

512. The Full Bench of the Supreme Court considered and rejected this argument with a majority of eleven to two votes in its *Sigma* Judgment of 24 February 2004.[561] The Court first found that the proceedings which were followed by the CRTA abided by the principles of fairness and impartiality, since 'there has been a satisfactory distinction between the various stages, which consisted in the collection of the facts, their preliminary examination, the briefing of the applicants in relation to these, affording them the right to be heard, in writing or orally, and the final adjudication.'[562] The Court also held that the fact that the fines are deposited with the CRTA is not by itself inconsistent with impartiality, because 'no private or personal financial interest is involved,' while the CRTA, being a legal entity under public law, 'functions in an impersonal manner, in order to promote the aims of the Law', with its revenues from various sources (licence fees, examination of applications, etc.) aiming to 'safeguard [its] financial sustainability, so as to execute its particularly important in a modern society work.'[563]

513. As regards compatibility of the proceedings before the CRTA with Article 6, paragraph 1 ECHR (almost identical to Article 30, paragraph 2 of the Constitution of the Republic of Cyprus), the Supreme Court referred to the case-law of the ECtHR, placing particular emphasis on the possibility to challenge the sanctioning decisions of administrative organs before a Court, which in some cases (decisions by professional disciplinary bodies) shall have full jurisdiction in relation to both factual and legal matters, and in other cases (belonging 'to a domain where the need for recognition of the state authority in the determination of policy ought to prevail') may have more limited judicial review competence.[564]

514. The crucial question of whether the limited judicial review powers of the Supreme Courts are sufficient when reviewing the decisions of the CRTA was raised. According to the general standards of judicial control of administrative acts under Article 146 of the Constitution,[565] which follow the continental system standards of the French *Conseil d'État* and of the Greek *Council of State* (*Symvoulio tis*

560. This argument was part of a more comprehensive argumentation against the establishment and the operation of the CRTA itself, including the claim that the competence of the latter to grant licences violates Art. 19 of the Constitution (for the rejection of this argument by the Supreme Court *see* above, under Part III, Ch. 2, §2 II) and the claim that the principle of equality is violated in view of the differential treatment of private stations in comparison with the legal and financial status of the CyBC (for the rejection of this argument by the Supreme Court *see* Part III, Ch. 1, §2 V above).
561. *Sigma Radio T.V. Ltd v. CRTA* [2004] 3 CLR 134 (in Greek).
562. *Ibid.*, 168–169.
563. *Ibid.*, 169.
564. *Ibid.*, 169–170, with the reference being to Harris, O'Boyle and Warbrick's *Law of the European Convention on Human Rights* (1995 edition), citing the judgment of the ECtHR, *Zumtobel v. Austria*, Judgment of 21 Sep. 1993, Series A No. 268-A.
565. *See* on them A. Emilianides, *Constitutional Law of Cyprus* (2nd ed., Kluwer 2019); N. Charalambous, *Cypriot Administrative Law Textbook* (3rd ed., 2016, in Greek), A. Angelides & S. Angelides,

Epikrateias), the Supreme Court has the competence to annul (i.e., to declare null and void), but not to amend, acts or omissions of organs exercising executive or administrative authority which are contrary to a provision of the Constitution, or of any law, or are made in excess or in abuse of powers vested in such organ. Challenges for annulment may include, *inter alia*, lack of competence or jurisdiction; problems in the composition of a collegial organ; errors or misconception of law; lack of due reasoning; failure to comply with the rules of natural justice (especially, the principle of impartiality and the right to prior hearing) and of good administration; lack of proper enquiry (i.e., failure to ascertain the facts properly; *see* section 45 of the General Principles of Administrative Law Act 158(I)/1999); misconception of fact (i.e., omission to take into account material facts, or taking into account of facts which were, by means of an objective judgment, inexistent; *see* section 46 of Act 158(I)/99); and proper exercise of the discretion of the organ (*see* section 44 of Act 158(I)/99), in accordance with the law and with the rules and principles of administrative procedure. However, in no case shall the Supreme Court go into the merits of the administrative organ's decision and substitute it with its own decision. Nor does the Supreme Court have the competence to examine and assess the facts of the case, deciding upon them afresh. If the Supreme Court annuls the act or decision in question, the matter shall be remitted to the appropriate administrative authority or organ for re-examination.

515. Bearing in mind such standards, in the *Sigma* case the Supreme Court held that its judicial review powers are adequate for the purposes of complying with Article 6, paragraph 1 ECHR:

> We are of the view that in the case where the infringement of the regulatory provisions of the law is examined in the particularly sensitive and significant domain of radio and television, the decision in matters which by their nature may be characterized by subtle nuances and many gradations is justifiably left, as a matter of state policy, to a special independent Public Authority. We are of the view that the judicial review provided for in our system is adequate. We do not, therefore, discern a violation of the rules of natural justice which are embodied in Article 6 (1) of the European Convention and Article 30.2 of the Constitution.[566]

516. Another argument of the applicant station was that Article 19, paragraph 3 of the Constitution, providing for limitations upon freedom of speech and of the press, refers to 'penalties'. Such 'penalties' may be only considered as sanctions imposed by a criminal Court, and not as administrative sanctions imposed by an

---

Administrative Procedural Law (2nd ed., Cyprus Bar Assn. 2020, in Greek); C. Paraskeva, *Cypriot Administrative Law* (Nomiki Vivliothiki 2017, in Greek), *id.*, *Cypriot Administrative Procedure Law* (Nomiki Vivliothiki 2020, in Greek), C. Melides, *Administrative Law*, in Andreas Neocleous & Co LLC, *Introduction to Cyprus Law* 87–117 (3rd ed., 2010); Z. Nedjati, *Cyprus Administrative Law* (1970); A. Angelides, *Administrative Law: Article 146 of the Constitution*, 12 Cyprus L. Rev. 1926 (1985); 13 Cyprus L. Rev. 2111–2128 (1986) (in Greek); S. Angelides, *Administrative Law in the Republic of Cyprus*, 8 Cyprus & European L. Rev. 213 (2008) (in Greek).

566. *Sigma Radio T.V. Ltd v. CRTA* [2004] 3 CLR 134, 170–171 (in Greek).

administrative authority, as the CRTA is. Therefore, according to the applicant station, the imposition of the fines by the CRTA was contrary to Article 19, paragraph 3 of the Constitution. The Supreme Court dismissed this argument by appealing to paragraph 5 of Article 19 of the Constitution, which provides for a licensing regime. According to the Court, such a regime necessarily implies a system of control, including the authority to impose administrative sanctions. Such an authority, and the management of the licensing regime as a whole, may legitimately be assigned to the CRTA irrespective of whether the term 'penalties' under paragraph 3 of Article 19 of the Constitution refers only to criminal sanctions or not.[567]

517. Finally, the applicant station raised the claim that the sanctioning powers of the CRTA violated the principle *ne bis in idem* provided by Article 12, paragraph 2 of the Constitution insofar as, in parallel with the administrative sanctions, the RTSL provided also criminal sanctions for the persons who violated any of the provisions of the RTSL.[568] The Supreme Court summarily rejected this claim, observing that, 'while the parallel criminalisation creates disharmony from which problems could arise, the characterisation of the cases as administrative is nevertheless not reversed.'[569] In fact, this argument did not provide a satisfactory reply to the argument about the violation of the *ne bis in idem* principle. The problem was implicitly recognized by the legislature itself, which in 2004 abolished the criminal law provisions of section 48 RTSL, and replaced them with the new section 41D RTSL, which provides for criminal sanctions only for specific actions (transmission without licence, attempt to influence a member of the CRTA, frequency distortions), and not for violation of any provision of the RTSL.

II. The Judgment of the European Court of Human Rights

518. Reacting against the judgment of the Supreme Court, *Sigma* filed an application to the ECtHR alleging violation of Articles 6, paragraphs 1, 10 and 14 ECHR and Article 1 of the First Protocol to the ECHR.[570] The most interesting part of the ECtHR's judgment, and the one which interests us here, has to do with the allegation of *Sigma* about the violation of Article 6, paragraph 1 ECHR.[571] This allegation was finally dismissed as being manifestly ill-founded, but the ECtHR devoted extensive thought to the scope and nature of the judicial review of the CRTA's decisions by the Supreme Court.

---

567. *Ibid.*, 171–177, with lengthy references to the case-law of the ECtHR under Art. 10 ECHR and to the case-law of the ECJ under the provisions of Directive 89/552/EEC, to the effect that a licensing regime including a system of control and of administrative sanctions is perfectly compatible both with the ECHR and with the EU Law.
568. Section 48, para. 6 RTSL, as it had at the material time.
569. *Sigma Radio T.V. Ltd v. CRTA* [2004] 3 CLR 134, 173 (in Greek).
570. *See Sigma Radio Television Ltd v. Cyprus*, Judgment of 21 Jul. 2011, Applications No. 32181/04 and 35122/05; hudoc.
571. The allegation about violation of Art. 10 ECHR concerned the precision and clarity of the provisions for the violation of which the CRTA had imposed sanctions (i.e., with the foreseeability requirement under the term 'prescribed by law'); with the 'legitimate' character of the aims that

519. Examining the claims about lack of 'structural' or objective impartiality of the CRTA in exercising its sanctioning powers, on account of the multiplicity of its functions within the sanctioning process, the ECtHR first took notice of the procedural guarantees which were provided by the law for the proceedings before the CRTA (obligation to inform the station about the details of the probable violation or of the complaint raised against it; opportunity to make written and/or oral submissions during the hearing of the case, not only with regard to the merits of the case but also with regard to the imposition of the fine; obligation of the CRTA to give a reasoned decision).[572] The ECtHR also took notice of the combination of different functions of the CRTA, and casting particular emphasis on the fact that the fines are deposited to the CRTA's own fund, held that concerns about its impartiality were prima facie legitimate.[573] However, according to the established jurisprudence of the ECtHR, taken into account by the Supreme Court as we saw above, an administrative organ which assumes an adjudicative role, determining disputes over 'civil rights and obligations' under Article 6, paragraph 1 ECHR, may not fully comply with the requirements of the said article so long as the proceedings before such administrative body can be subject to the subsequent control by a judicial body which may provide 'sufficient review'.[574]

520. In assessing the sufficiency of judicial review, the ECtHR takes into account the limited scope of such review in several Member States, which have adopted the administrative procedure premises of the French *Conseil d'État*.[575] In particular, the ECtHR has regards to the powers of the judicial body in question, in combination with other factors such as:

---

were pursued by such provisions; and with the proportionality of the fines that were imposed. The ECtHR had no difficulty to dismiss these allegations (most of them were found to be manifestly ill-founded, and one was rejected on its merits), finding, among else, that protection of consumers and children from unethical advertising practices, including surreptitious advertising, and the need for a fair and accurate presentation of facts and events constitute legitimate aims under Art. 10 ECHR (*see* paras 200–201). The allegation about violation of Art. 14 ECHR concerned the claim of *Sigma* that the treatment of private stations was unequal to that of the CyBC insofar as the latter did not have to pay a licence fee and was not monitored (at the material time) by the CRTA. The ECtHR dismissed this claim as manifestly ill-founded, given that, in view of 'the differences in the legal status and the applicable legal frameworks and the different objectives of private stations and the CyBC in the Cypriot broadcasting system, it cannot be said that they are in a comparable position for the purposes of Article 14 of the Convention.' The allegation about violation of Art. 1 of the First Protocol, which concerned the alleged disproportionate nature of the fines, was also summarily dismissed by the ECtHR.

572. *See ibid.*, §149.

573. *See ibid.*, §150.

574. *See ibid.*, §§151–152, citing *Albert and Le Compte v. Belgium*, Judgment of 10 Feb. 1983, §29, Series A No. 58; *Zumtobel*, §§31–32; *Bryan v. the United Kingdom*, Judgment of 22 Nov. 1995, §§43–47, Series A No. 335-A; *Müller and others v. Austria* (Dec.), Judgment of 23 Nov. 1999, Application No. 26507/95; hudoc; and *Crompton v. the United Kingdom*, Judgment of 27 Oct. 2009, Application No. 42509/05, §§71 and 79; hudoc.

575. *See Sigma*, §153.

(a) the subject matter of the decision appealed against, in particular, whether or not it concerned a specialized issue requiring professional knowledge or experience and whether it involved the exercise of administrative discretion and if, so, to what extent;
(b) the manner in which that decision was arrived at, in particular, the procedural guarantees available in the proceedings before the adjudicatory body; and
(c) the content of the dispute, including the desired and actual grounds of appeal.[576]

521. As easily understood, much depends on the circumstances of a given case: 'the Court [i.e., the ECtHR] will confine itself as far as possible to examining the question raised in the case before it and to determining if, in that particular case, the scope of the review was adequate.'[577] This point is very important because it restricts the scope of the relevant jurisprudence of the ECtHR, irrespective of whether the judicial review of the domestic Court is found to be sufficient or not.[578] And it was this point that, in our view, determined the outcome of the *Sigma* case.

522. In particular, the ECtHR first found that the powers of the Supreme Court are in principle adequate for the purposes of the relevant question insofar as the Supreme Court 'could have annulled the decisions on a number of grounds, including if the decision had been reached on the basis of a misconception of fact or law, there had been no proper enquiry or a lack of due reasoning, or on procedural grounds.'[579] Then, the ECtHR noted that the subject matter of the CRTA's decisions was 'a classic exercise of administrative discretion in the specialised area of law concerning broadcasting taken in the context of ensuring standard setting and compliance with the relevant legislation and regulations pursuant to public interest aims;' and that 'a number of uncontested procedural guarantees were available to the applicant in the proceedings before the CRTA,' while 'the applicant's allegations as to shortcomings in the proceedings before the CRTA, including those concerning objective partiality and the breach of the principles of natural justice, were subject to review by the Supreme Court.'[580] Besides, the applicant had the opportunity to raise a number of different claims before the Supreme Court, which concerned, among else, the interpretation and the constitutionality of the relevant legal provisions as well as shortcomings in the proceedings, such as lack of proper enquiry and of due reasoning, and composition problems.[581] In this respect, the ECtHR referred to the extensive reasoning of the Supreme Court, and the fact that the latter 'examined all the above issues, point by point, without refusing to deal with any of them. The Supreme Court gave clear reasons for the dismissal of the applicant's points.'[582]

---

576. *Ibid.*, §154, citing *Bryan*, §§44, 45 and 47; and *Crompton*, §§71–73 and 77.
577. *Sigma*, §155.
578. Compare the numerous, positive as well as negative on this issue, judgments referred to by the Court at §§156–157 of the *Sigma* judgment.
579. *Ibid.*, §159.
580. *Ibid.*, §§161–162.
581. *See ibid.*, §§163–164.
582. *Ibid.*, §165.

523. However, it is submitted that the most crucial points of the judgment of the ECtHR were the ones that followed the above considerations. At §166 the ECtHR noticed that 'the applicant's cases did not centre on a fundamental question of fact which the Supreme Court did not have jurisdiction to revisit,' contrasting the *Sigma* case with the *Tsfayo* case in this respect.[583] Then, answering the argument of the *Sigma* that the crux of its case before the Supreme Court was the necessity and proportionality of the fines imposed by the CRTA, questions which, according to the applicant, the Supreme Court did not have power to examine,[584] the ECtHR pointed out that 'these issues were not raised by the applicant before that court [i.e., the Supreme Court] in the legal points on which its recourses were based,' and that it is not the task of the ECtHR to 'decide *in abstract* that the Supreme Court would not have examined these issues if raised or that it would have declined jurisdiction to deal with them. Such an exercise would, in the circumstances of the present application, be pure surmise.'[585] In view of these considerations, the ECtHR finally found that 'the scope of the review of the Supreme Court in the judicial review proceedings in the present case was sufficient to comply with Article 6 of the Convention.'[586] And rejecting some other arguments of *Sigma* about the fairness of the proceedings before the Supreme Court itself (concerning the impartiality of judges), the ECtHR concluded that the allegations about violation of Article 6, paragraph 1 ECHR were manifestly ill-founded.

524. In view of the thoughts on which the ECtHR based this judgment, one may retain legitimate doubts as to whether the judgment would be different if questions of fact, or questions about the proper interpretation and implementation of the legislative provisions in view of the specific facts of the case, had been raised before the Supreme Court by the CRTA. Such doubts are reinforced by bearing in mind the jurisprudence of the Supreme Court on the interpretative specification and implementation of 'abstract evaluative' concepts, such as 'private life', 'personality', 'high quality of programmes', etc., which are central to the exercise of the monitoring powers of the CRTA under the programme standards of the Cypriot Media Law. As seen in the relevant parts of this monograph (*see* Part III, Chapter 3, §8 and §10 above), the Supreme Court has developed a strict doctrine of separation of powers, to the effect that it is very hesitant to control the discretion of the CRTA in specifying and implementing such legislative concepts. In view of such case-law,

---

583. *See Tsfayo v. the United Kingdom*, Judgment of 14 Nov. 2006, Application No. 60860/00; hudoc. *Tsfayo* was appealed to by *Sigma* (*see Sigma*, §133), while the Cypriot Government provided detailed argumentation in order to convince the ECtHR about the differences of the *Tsfayo* case from the *Sigma* case (*see ibid.*, §§136, 139).

584. *See ibid.*, §132, with the Government replying by citing a series of cases in which the Supreme Court had examined the amount and proportionality of fines that were imposed by some other administrative authority, namely the Cyprus Securities and Exchange Commission (*see ibid.*, §§140–141).

585. *Ibid.*, §§167–168. In order to support this latter argument, the ECtHR noticed that the applicant did not put forward any case-law in support of its claim, while, the Government 'referred the Court to a number of Supreme Court judgments in judicial review proceedings which indicate that the Supreme Court has the competence to examine such issues in its judicial review role' (*ibid.*, §168).

586. *Ibid.*, §169.

one may wonder whether the judgment of the ECtHR would be the same if the question of compatibility with Article 6, paragraph 1 ECHR was raised in the context of a dispute which would involve the implementation of 'abstract evaluative' concepts. In any case, the substantial parts of the ECtHR judgment on the *Sigma* case indicate the need for a relaxation of the jurisprudential doctrine of the Supreme Court and, consequently, the need for a more comprehensive control of the sanctioning powers of the CRTA, when the exercise of such powers depends upon hard interpretative choices and balancing tests.

Selected Bibliography

In Greek

Aktypis S.H., Jougleux P., Synodinou T.E. (eds) *Freedom of Expression of Journalists and Caricaturists. Protection and Restrictions in Greek and Cypriot Law.* Sakkoulas, Athens – Thessaloniki, 2016.

Artemis P. 'Freedom of Speech and Expression, Freedom of the Press, Defamation Law and Qualified Privilege', *Cyprus and European Law Review* 9 (2009): 425.

Charalambous N. 'The Freedom to Access the Files of the Administration', *Cyprus Law Tribune* 1 (1992): 36.

Charalambous N. *Cypriot Administrative Law Textbook.* 3rd edn. 2016.

Clerides C. 'The Access of Mass Media Communication to Court Proceedings', *Cyprus Law Review* 49–50 (1995): 7157.

Dagtoglou P. *Constitutional Law – Civil Rights.* 4th edn. Sakkoulas, Athens – Thessaloniki, 2012.

Iordanidou S. Stratilatis C. (eds), *Versions of Liberty in our Media Reality. The New Journalism and Its Challenges*, Advanced Media Institute & Metamesonykties Publications, Athens, 2018.

Kapardis A. 'Freedom of the Press, Crime Reporting by Newspapers and Criminal Justice', *Cyprus Law Review* 1 (1983): 1204.

Kentas G. 'The Cyprus Radio and Television Authority as an Agent of Political Violence', *Dimosiografia (The Hellenic Edition of Columbia Journalism Review)* 1 (2013): 33.

Kouros K. *The Mass Media Law in the Republic of Cyprus: An Adumbration of the Evolutionary Formation of the Legal Framework of the Press Law from 19th Century Until Today* (Vivlioekdotiki 2008).

Loizou A. *Constitution of the Republic of Cyprus* (2001).

Loucaides L. 'Freedom of the Press and the Administration of Justice' in idem, *Topics on Cypriot Law* (1982): 105–110.

Loucaides L. 'Can Prices for the Sale of Newspapers be Determined?', *Cyprus Law Review* 18 (1987): 2659.

Loucaides L. 'The Right of Reply to the Press' in idem, *Topics of Cypriot Law II* (1988): 157–169.

Loucaides. 'Freedom of Expression and the Right to Respect Private Life', *Cyprus and European Law Review* 6 (2008): 449.

Loucaides L. 'Freedom of Speech in the Republic of Cyprus', *Cyprus and European Law Review* 11 (2010): 7.

Selected Bibliography

Madellas A. 'The Concept of "Public Interest" in the Cypriot Legislation for the Establishment of Private Radio and Television Broadcasting', *Cyprus Law Review* 49–50 (1995): 7205.

Nicolaou E. 'The Obligation of the Administration to Provide Information to the Citizens', *Cyprus and European Law Review* 1 (2006): 99.

Papapetrou M. 'Freedom of Speech in Cypriot Society', *Cyprus and European Law Review* 11 (2010): 16.

Pavlides A. 'Cyprus Broadcasting Corporation'. In *Great Cypriot Encyclopedia* 15, Filokypros, 1996, 247–249.

Polyviou P. *Modern Law of Defamation.* Chrysafinis and Polyviou, 2013.

Polyviou P. *Administration and Justice. The Protection of Competition Authority and the Securities and Exchange Commission in Cypriot Law*. Chrysafinis and Polyviou, 2017.

Polyviou P. *The Right to Personality in Cypriot Law*. Nomiki Vivliothiki, 2018.

Polyviou P. *Defamation in Cypriot and European Law*. Nomiki Vivliothiki, 2019.

Tornaritis C. *The State Law of the Republic of Cyprus.* Cyprus Research Centre, 1982.

Sofokleous A. *Contribution to the History of the Cypriot Press.* Vols. I–IV. Intercollege Press, 1995–2007.

Sofokleous A. *The Cypriot Media of Mass Information.* Nikokles, 2008.

Stratilatis C. *Constituting the Right to Public Electronic Communication.* Sakkoulas, Athens-Thessaloniki 2006.

Vassiliadou M., 'The Cypriot Media Landscape' in G. Terzis (ed.), *European Media Governance: National and Regional Dimensions* 203–204. University of Chicago Press 2007.

In English

Ebeku K. 'Revisiting the Acquittal of 10 Policemen: Issues of Judicial Independence, Trial by Media and Fair Trial in Cyprus', *European Journal of Crime, Criminal Law and Criminal Justice* 18 (2010): 1.

Emilianides A. *Constitutional Law in Cyprus*. 2nd edn. Kluwer, 2019.

Emilianides A. Markou C. *Tort Law in Cyprus*. Kluwer, 2021.

Evangelides P. *The Republic of Cyprus and Its Constitution with Special Regard to the Constitutional Rights*. Difo-Druck GmbH, 1996.

Madella A. 'Le régime juridique de la radio-télévision à Chypre', *Revue de la Recherche Juridique-Droir Prospectif* 44(1) (1991): 122–144.

Tornaritis C. *The Human Rights as Recognised and Protected by Law with Special Reference to the Law of Cyprus,* 1967.

Index

The numbers here refer to paragraph numbers.

Access
- of political parties to programmes, 347-349
- to diversity of viewpoints, 278
- to events of major importance, 420–440
- to information, 55–56, 109, 155, 157-158, 174, 438-440
- to media, 20, 174
- to networks, 444–457

Advertising, 32-33, 49, 58, 234-235, 245, 251, 258, 269-270, 279, 302, 350-353, 355, 362-363, 365-370, 372-406, 413-414, 416, 418, 441, 491, 495, 501-502
- audiovisual commercial communication, forms of, 285, 362
- political advertising, 235, 350-353, 355, 388, 495, 502
- product placement, 362-363, 399, 415-419, 502
- sponsorship, 235, 350, 362-364, 399, 407-414, 419, 502
- teleshopping, 237, 362-363, 374, 401, 441, 502

AVMS Directive, 38, 184, 194, 218, 219, 236, 269–271, 273, 285, 289, 301, 321, 362–367, 369, 371, 374–376, 398, 400-401, 407, 409, 411–413, 415, 420, 435–440, 443, 488, 490-491, 493, 502

Censorship, 55, 76, 100, 174

Communications Commissioner, 264, 447, 456

Conditional access, 461, 465

Confidentiality of sources, 174

Court hearings, 159

CRTA, 51, 194, 201, 217-220, 247-253, 255-263, 267-268, 274, 277, 279, 285, 287, 289, 293-294, 298-300, 303, 307, 317-331, 349, 352, 355, 357, 372, 377-384, 389-390, 394-396, 401, 403, 420-422, 424, 427-431, 440, 443, 473, 475-488, 491, 493-514, 516-519, 522-524

CyBC, 19–20, 23, 27, 30, 33, 35, 46, 52, 83, 87–88, 163, 170, 175–184, 187, 191-199, 201-218, 220-226, 229-235, 265, 268, 271, 274, 286, 290, 291, 310, 332, 334, 336-340, 342-344, 354, 357-358, 360, 366, 371, 374, 379, 382-383, 394, 432–435, 442–443, 451-452, 487, 502–503

Decency, 287, 289-290, 322, 327 505

Defamation, 46, 66, 81, 98, 110, 113–115, 117, 120-121, 127, 129, 132, 134-138, 143-144, 276, 320, 324

Diversity, 174, 245, 278, 325, 361, 487

Erotic content, 288, 291-292, 376

Events of major importance, 49, 190, 421-422, 424, 430, 435, 495, 502

Fair
- advertising, 382
- comment, 68, 113, 121-123, 135
- report, 126
- representation of political parties, 226, 246, 332, 335, 339, 358, 361
- treatment of guests, 283

Good faith, 65, 80, 113, 121–122, 124-126, 172, 456, 479

Hidden camera, 311

Impartiality, 60, 62, 72, 77-78, 169, 256, 512, 514, 519, 523

Index

Interoperability, 456, 461, 463

Language requirements, 86, 97, 172, 177-178, 183, 187, 193, 272-273, 287, 290, 327, 382 383, 442, 466, 486
Libel, 77, 110, 113, 115, 120, 129-130, 135-136
Licensing requirements and procedure, 239, 244-246, 254-257, 259, 262, 266, 468

Management contract, 249, 250, 468
Minors, 46, 174, 195, 269, 285-287, 289, 291, 295-296, 301, 302-304, 373, 375, 393-397, 486, 493, 496
Must-carry, 273, 444–451

Network providers, 264, 448, 451, 453
Non-linear AVMS, 184, 236-237, 243-244, 270, 285, 502

Objectivity, 199, 201, 210, 262, 275, 277-279, 314, 325

Pluralism, 33, 186, 201, 229, 255-256, 278-279, 347, 438, 467, 487, 493
Presumption of innocence, 173, 316
Privacy, 138, 142–145, 158, 256, 305, 307, 309, 313-314
Proportionality, 65-66, 71, 144, 192, 438, 440, 448, 499, 501, 503, 523

Ranking of TV programmes, 286, 292-294, 301
Right of reply, 146-147, 149, 151-154, 174, 269, 278, 321-322, 324-326, 349, 496, 502
Right to information, 276, 304, 307, 311, 432, 437-439, 441

Sanctions, 66, 218, 267-268, 274, 294, 312, 322, 325, 378, -379, 401 457, 474, 482, 493, 495-497, 499-503, 504, 508, 511, 513, 516-517, 519, 524
Sexual
 activities, 299, 505
 insecurity, 392
 offences, 172–173, 304
 success, 375
Short news reporting, 434-435, 440
Standardization (technical), 459
Supreme Court, 7, 10, 50–51, 58, 62, 64-66, 68-69, 71-72, 74-80, 93, 95, 103, 113, 129–134, 138–139, 142–145, 151–152, 159, 163, 166–167, 196-201, 203–205, 208, 212, 225, 226-227, 229-232, 249-250, 253, 256, 258, 262-263, 269, 279, 292-294, 300, 307, 309, 312-313, 317-318, 325-326, 328-330, 336-337, 340, 342-344, 350, 368-370, 372, 377, 380, 388, 394, 396, 400, 403-404, 413-414, 440, 445, 481, 484, 499-501, 505, 508-510, 512-519, 522-524

Transparency, 158, 174, 192, 234, 242, 450, 456, 468, 474

Violence, 3, 65, 172-174, 194, 271, 280-281, 286, 289, 295-297, 299, 505

www.ingramcontent.com/pod-product-compliance
Lightning Source LLC
Chambersburg PA
CBHW071437230926
51846CB00001B/259

* 9 7 8 9 4 0 3 5 1 6 0 8 0 *